Nicaragua is a land born of poetry, fire and brazen revolutionary spirit; few countries can boast such an authentic character. Located at the heart of the Central American isthmus, it is a nation of energy and possibility, a nation forged by episodic upheaval, and in modern times by the burning idealism of the 1979 Sandinista Revolution – as a symbol of collective liberation, the overthrow of the Somoza family continues to inspire great national pride and endless passionate discourse.

The Nicaraguan *campo* or countryside is a vision of rural utopia – a lush, pastoral ramble of organic coffee fincas and cattle ranches, communal cooperatives and family-owned ranchos. The country's urban spaces are vehicles of economic change. They include the rival Spanish colonial cities of Granada and León, both with evolving cultural scenes and centuries of turbulent history. Near the great lakes of Cocibolca and Xolotlán, a mesa of ancient towns specializes in the production of art and *artesanías*. And on the politically autonomous Caribbean coast, indigenous and African traditions include a sultry Creole maypole dance and Garífuna drumming that echoes backwards and forwards through time.

Nicaragua revels in unique forms of art, music and dance, but most of all it breathes poetry, the unrivalled national passion. In fact, Nicaragua has produced some of the most important poets in the history of the Spanish language. The natural landscapes that supplied much of their literary inspiration – and which together guard seven percent of the Earth's biodiversity – include a cloak of primordial rainforests and a spine of 19 volcanoes, many of them prone to violent explosions. Nicaragua is as wild as it is striking, fierce as it is generative. It is a youthful and charismatic country, revered by adventurers and beloved by dreamers.

Richard Arghiris

Best of
Nicaragua

top things to do and see

❶ Laguna de Apoyo

Take a dip in the thermally heated waters of this *laguna*, the most stunning of Nicaragua's 15 crater lakes, which changes colour through azure, turquoise and navy blue. Surrounded by dense tropical forest teeming with wildlife, it has some great hikes around its shores. Page 66.

❷ Isla de Ometepe

Sling a hammock on the magical island of Ometepe, a bastion of peace, tranquillity and numinous volcanic beauty. Set on the largest lake in Central America, Lago Nicaragua, it's also home to twin volcanoes and mysterious pre-Columbian idols. Volcán Concepción is active, while the extinct Volcán Maderas has a mist-shrouded crater lake near its summit. Page 112.

④ León

Propose a toast to revolution in Nicaragua's hip and buzzing party town, home to a mighty cathedral, handsome plazas and a wealth of regal colonial houses, as well as being one of Central America's finest colonial cities. León is surrounded by active volcanoes which are good for climbing, hiking and sandboarding. Page 148.

❸ Río San Juan

Navigate the remote Río San Juan which flows from Lake Nicaragua to the Caribbean. There's excellent wildlife spotting, including howler monkeys, macaws and toucans, in the protected rainforest and wetlands lining the river. Along the way, stay in riverfront fishing communities, their houses perched on stilts over the water. Page 138.

Caribbean Sea
HONDURAS
COSTA RICA
Pacific Ocean
Living Creek
Cabo Viejo
Kampa
Tuskru Sirpe
Laguna de Bismuna
Waspam
Leimus
Río Coco (Segovia)
La Moskitia
Sandy Bay
Pahra
Auastara
Sangni Laya
Reserva Biosfera Bosawás
Yulu Tingne
Manu Watla
Puerto Cabezas/ Bilwi
Musawas
Kukalaya
Sahsa
Susun
El Encanto
Bonanza
La Rosita
Haulover Creek
Banacruz
Siuna
El Empalme
Saslaya
Wani
Alamikamba
Limbaika
Cordillera Isabela
Las Manos
Ocotal
El Garrobo
El Porvenir
Company Creek
Somoto
Condega
El Espino
La Cruz de Río Grande
Siawás
Sandy Bay Sirpi
Esteli
Lago de Apanás
Jinotega
Pauta Dimon
Río Kurinwás
Kara
Gulf of Fonseca
San Juan de Limay
San Isidro
Río Blanco
Tortuguero
Guasaule
Matagalpa
Volcán Cosigüina
Somotillo
Sébaco
Matiguás
Laguna de Perlas
Potosí
Cosigüina Peninsula
Puerto Morazán
Ciudad Darío
Chinandega
Chichigalpa
V Momotombo
Santa Lucía
Lago de Managua
Rama
Sisi
To Islas de Maíz /Corn Islands
Corinto
León
La Libertad
La Gateada
Río Escondido
Poneloya
V Momotombito
Bluefields
Las Peñitas
Juigalpa
MANAGUA
Masaya
Granada
Cara del Moro
Nueva Guinea
Puerto Díaz
Acoyapa
Laguna de Apoyo
San Juan de Oriente
Isla Zapatera
V Mombacho
Altagracia
Isla Ometepe
V Concepción
San Jorge
San Miguelito
Rivas
Lago de Nicaragua
San Juan de Nicaragua
San Juan del Sur
San Carlos
El Castillo
Islas Solentiname
Peñas Blancas
Refugio de Vida Silvestre Los Guatuzos
Río San Juan
N
50 km
50 miles

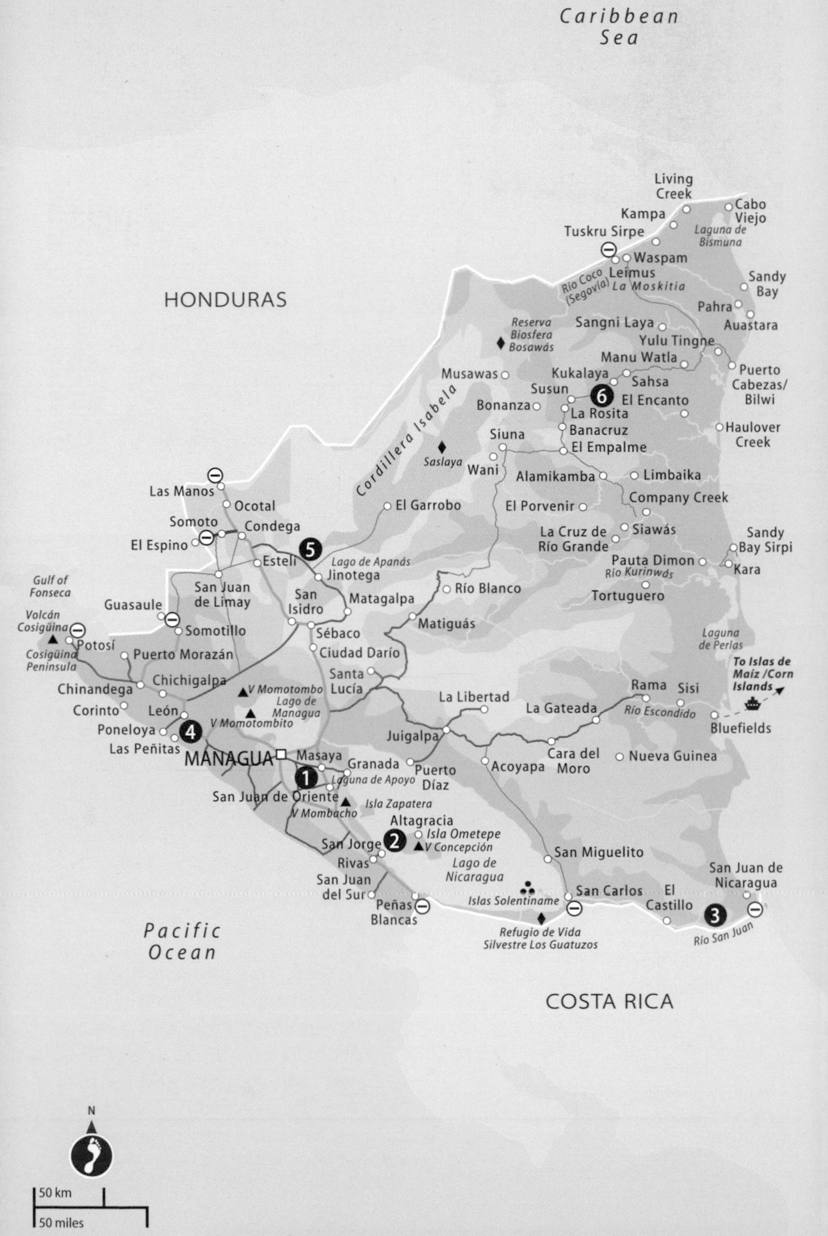

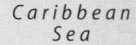

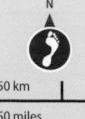

❺ Northern highlands

A chain of volcanoes lie in the rugged northern highlands where *campesino* culture predominates. In the fertile coffee-growing mountains you can sip a cup of coffee, then hike to see where it's grown. You can also explore misty highland villages, precious cloudforest reserves and pine forests, and see interesting crafts being made. Page 170.

❻ Northern Caribbean Coast Autonomous Region (RACCN)

Discover lost-in-time Miskito and Afro-Caribbean communities in this isolated area. Surrounded by dense forests, a sturdy boat and a trustworthy guide will be necessary to navigate the river and remote Miskito settlements around Bilwi and Waspam. Only the truly brave and adventurous will get this far. Page 211.

Volcán Mombacho Natural Reserve

Route planner

putting it all together

For such a tiny country, there's a lot to see and do in Nicaragua. Fortunately, road communication in the Pacific Basin is good and most areas of interest are less than 200 km from the capital. A great deal of ground can be covered in a matter of days using express intercity buses, local tour operators or hired taxis.

The rest of Nicaragua is off the beaten track with large nature reserves and small villages devoid of travellers and commercialization. Travel on the east side of the country can be particularly time-consuming and comparatively expensive. If time is limited, plan carefully and weigh the benefits of your chosen destinations against the hours or days that might be spent in getting there.

Two weeks: León, Pacific coast and northern highlands

coffee, communities and revolution

The areas north and northwest of Managua are rich in coffee plantations, remote farming communities, verdant nature reserves, smoking volcanoes, rolling mountains and gripping tales of the Revolution. Their appeal is often unconventional, but the region is no less rewarding than the more-visited sites in the south of the country.

The vibrant colonial city of León lies under two hours from the capital and is a great place to begin. Be sure to summit a volcano or two from the adjacent Maribios range, perhaps boarding down the slopes of Cerro Negro before finally hitting the Pacific beaches of Las Peñitas and Poneloya. More intrepid travellers can continue to the remote Cosigüina Peninsula before backtracking and cutting east to the coffee capital of Matagalpa, two or three hours away.

Scores of intriguing coffee fincas pepper the hills around Matagalpa, including the German-built Selva Negra and the award-winning Esperanza Verde. An hour north of Matagalpa up a winding mountain road is the refreshing highland city of Jinotega with its access to fine nature reserves and Apanás lake. From Jinotega, you can descend the mountains to the agricultural city of Estelí, where the finest cigars in Central America are rolled.

The massive Reserva Natural Miraflor, just outside the city, is the best community tourism project in the country and offers visitors the rewarding chance to experience rural life up close.

From Estelí it's possible to continue north to the sleepy village of Somoto and, in the dry season, take a lazy trip through its nearby canyon. Beyond, the village of Totogalpa offers glimpses of lost-in-time rural life, as does Ciudad Antigua, which is best accessed from the border town of Ocotal. Now a stone's throw from Honduras, getting back to the capital is simply a matter of jumping on a southbound express bus.

Two to three weeks: Granada, Masaya and San Juan del Sur
the best of southern Nicaragua

After arriving at the international airport, most travellers skip Managua and make a bee-line for the laid-back colonial city of Granada, just one hour away. The city's touristic infrastructure is well developed and it makes a safe base for exploring the region.

In Granada, few visitors can resist a jaunt on Lake Nicaragua, Central America's largest freshwater lake, or a trip to Volcán Mombacho, where you can hike or zip-line through cloud-drenched forests. Alternatively, many head to the mysterious island of Zapatera, or to the rural communities perched on Mombacho's slopes.

A shopping trip to the city of Masaya, just 30 minutes from Granada, is an obligatory venture. Few fail to be refreshed by the tranquil waters of Laguna de Apoyo, whilst side-trips to smoking Volcán Masaya, the pottery town of San Juan de Oriente and the flower-filled village of Catarina are also rewarding.

From Granada, it's just a two-hour bus journey to the city of Rivas. From there, you can hop straight on a bus to the sunny town of San Juan del Sur, 45 minutes away, to enjoy the crashing surf of the Pacific and, if in season, the unforgettable spectacle of thousands of hatching sea turtles at the Refugio de Vida Silvestre La Flor.

If you can tear yourself away, backtrack to Rivas and beat a path to the port of San Jorge on Lake Nicaragua, 15 minutes away. From there, boats regularly depart to the glorious island of Ometepe with its rustic villages and twin volcano complex. You'll need a few days to soak up the ambience and explore everything it has to offer.

If time is not an issue, extend your adventure in Río San Juan department, a far-flung biodiversity hotspot in the southeast corner of Lake Nicaragua. Once you've arrived in the jungle gateway of San Carlos, you'll have the option to explore the teeming wetlands of Guatuzo or the bucolic artists' colony of the Solentiname archipelago.

A trip down the Río San Juan to the old Spanish fortress of El Castillo, however, is the real highlight of the region. From there, you'll be able to organize expeditions into the virgin rainforests of the Indio-Maíz reserve. Of course, getting back to Managua from this remote area is an adventure in itself.

Two to three weeks: Bluefields, Corn Islands and Miskito heartland
Caribbean dreams

Nicaragua's Caribbean coast is a world unto itself, with few roads and almost zero touristic infrastructure. It offers some seriously challenging adventure travel for those bold enough to tackle it, and, beyond the well-visited Corn Islands, careful planning is required to safely navigate this wily frontier land.

Bluefields, the heart and soul of the South Caribbean Coast Autonomous Region, is a sensible place to start. A lightly dilapidated but reasonably populated coastal port, it offers a manageable introduction to the multicultural world of the Caribbean. Just one hour away along jungle-shrouded rivers, the diverse communities of the Pearl Lagoon basin offer the chance to really relax into the local way of life.

If it's beaches you're seeking, the fabled paradise atolls of the Corn Islands lie five to eight hours from Bluefields by ferry. Some serious hammock time is mandatory, but don't forget to check out the scintillating coral reefs just off shore.

Back on the mainland, the adventure really begins as you head north to Bilwi, the Miskito capital of the North Caribbean Coast Autonomous Region. There are no roads from Bluefields so, unless you're prepared to slog up the coast on random fishing boats, a plane is the best way in. From Bilwi, you have the option to visit all kinds of interesting end-of-the-world communities, including the village of Waspam on the Río Coco. This is deep in Miskito territory and the ride only gets wilder the further you go.

South of Waspam, a rugged seasonal road connects with the interior of Nicaragua. Several bumpy hours away the mining triangle towns of Rosita, Bonanza and Siuna promise fascinating encounters with indigenous communities and provide access to the majestic Bosawás Biosphere Reserve. From the mining triangle the road continues its long, arduous route back to Managua, concluding one of the most awesome journeys this side of space travel.

When to go

Climate

Most people prefer to visit western and northern Nicaragua during the rainy season or shortly after the rains have ended. During the dry season the Pacific Basin receives practically no rain at all and from mid-February until the rains arrive in late May the region is very hot and dry. During the rainy season the Pacific Basin is bright green and freshened daily by the rains, which normally last for less than two hours in the afternoon before clearing and then falling again during the night. December is an extraordinarily beautiful time to visit the Nicaraguan Pacific, with all the landscape in bloom, the air still fresh and visibility excellent across the volcanic ranges.

The dry season becomes shorter the further east you travel, and in the Caribbean Basin it can rain at any time of year. For diving and snorkelling, March to mid-May and late September to October offer the best chances of finding calm waters with great visibility. For birdwatching in the rainforest areas of the Río San Juan, the dry season is best as you'll have the chance to see the many migratory species and nesting birds. **Note:** Nicaraguans consider the dry season (December-May) summer and the rainy season winter, which can lead to confusion considering the country lies well north (11-16°) of the equator.

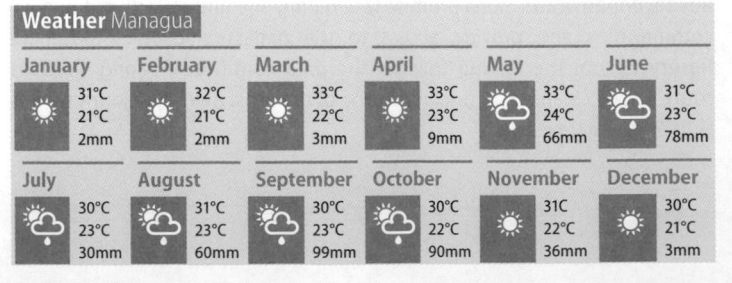

Weather Managua

January	February	March	April	May	June
31°C	32°C	33°C	33°C	33°C	31°C
21°C	21°C	22°C	23°C	24°C	23°C
2mm	2mm	3mm	9mm	66mm	78mm

July	August	September	October	November	December
30°C	31°C	30°C	30°C	31C	30°C
23°C	23°C	23°C	22°C	22°C	21°C
30mm	60mm	99mm	90mm	36mm	3mm

During Easter week and between Christmas and New Year all of Nicaragua rushes to the beach, lake and riverfront areas to swim, drink and dance; avoid these dates if you don't want to encounter massive crowds and fully booked hotels.

Festivals

Local celebrations of each town's patron saint are listed throughout the book.

1 January **New Year's Day**.
March/April The week leading up to Easter Sunday is **Semana Santa** (Holy Week), with massive celebrations countrywide, religious processions starting on Palm Sunday and ending on Easter Sunday. All rivers, lakes and beachfronts are full of holidaymakers, most businesses close at 1200 on Wednesday and don't reopen until the Monday following Easter.
1 May **Labour Day**.
30 May **Mother's Day**, many businesses close after 1200.
19 July **Anniversary of the 1979 Revolution**, most offices close.
14 September **Battle of San Jacinto**, the first victory against William Walker.
15 September Nicaragua's **Independence from Spain**, nationwide celebrations, all businesses close and there are school parades.

2 November **Día de los Difuntos** (Day of the Dead), when families visit grave sites and decorate their tombs with flowers and fresh paint; most businesses close after 1200.
7-8 December **La Purísima**, a celebration of the Immaculate Conception of Virgin Mary and the most Nicaraguan of all celebrations. It's celebrated countrywide with home altars being visited by singers after 1800 on 7 December and massive fireworks. Most businesses close at 1200 on the 7th and don't reopen until the 9th.
24-25 December **Christmas** is celebrated with the family on the evening of 24 December; most businesses close at 1200 on the 24th and reopen on the 26th, although some stay closed from 23 December to 2 January.
31 December **New Year's Eve** is normally spent with family members, or at parties for Managuans, most businesses close at 1200.

What to do

from diving and snorkelling to whitewater rafting

Nicaragua has a number of options for independent and organized special-interest travel. Many activities, such as whitewater rafting, free climbing or windsurfing, provide good opportunities for the experienced adventure traveller who wants to explore without tourist infrastructure or a safety net. Those listed below are ones which have been developed by local tour operators and are accessible to independent travellers. Further details are available in the relevant chapters.

Archaeology

Although the archaeology is not as inspiring as the Mayan temples further north, Nicaragua's pre-Columbian history is fascinating. Around the country, museums display artefacts that have been discovered in each region; the best are at the **Palacio Nacional de la Cultura** in Managua (page 34), the **Museo Antiguo Convento de San Francisco** in Granada (page 77) and **Museo El Ceibo** on Isla Ometepe (page 116). In Lake Nicaragua, there are some remains on the islands of **Zapatera** (page 87) and **Ometepe** (page 112), where you can see some large basalt statues. Petroglyphs are also present on many islands in Lake Nicaragua as well as numerous sites around the mainland. Colonial archaeology can be examined in the UNESCO World Heritage Site of **León Viejo** (page 162). A guide is recommended since English-language books on Nicaragua's archaeological heritage are virtually non-existent.

Birdwatching

According to the latest count Nicaragua is home to over 700 species of bird, including boat-billed flycatcher, collared aracari, black-headed trogon, wood stork, roseate spoonbill, long-tailed manikin and osprey. The national bird is the turquoise-browed mot-mot, beautiful and common in the highlands of Managua. The sheer number of birds in Nicaragua is amazing.

Reserva Biológica Indio Maíz (page 139) in Río San Juan area has primary rainforest with the scarlet macaw still filling the sky with red plumage. The **Refugio de Vida Silvestre Los Guatuzos** (page 131) has gallery forest and ample wetlands teeming with birds. The **Archipiélago Solentiname** (page 132) has two islands that are massive nesting sites. In the northern

Final frontiers

San Juan de Nicaragua

Located at the yawning mouth of the Río San Juan, the Caribbean port of San Juan de Nicaragua, formerly known as San Juan del Norte, marks the end of a long, meandering trip on jungle-shrouded river. No roads connect it with the outside world and the surrounding rainforests – the ancestral home of the indigenous Rama people – are among the most pristine in Central America. Page 142.

Laguna de Perlas

The diverse and hospitable communities of the Pearl Lagoon Basin, an hour outside of Bluefields by high-speed *panga*, are home to an intriguing blend of Afro-descendant and indigenous cultures. Creole, Garífuna and Miskito villages sit side by side and maintain a traditional lifestyle very much grounded in fishing and subsistence agriculture. Page 197.

Waspam

Perched on the banks of the mighty Río Coco, Waspam is the spiritual heart of the ancient Miskito Kingdom. As a trading centre for scores of remote communities up and down the river, it is just the starting point for a rare cultural odyssey that leads deep into a mysterious and extraordinary lost-in-time indigenous world. Page 212.

Las Minas

A trio of old mining outposts – Bonanza, Rosita and Siuna – offer glimpses into a lawless frontier-land that's more than a little reminiscent of the Wild West. Thanks to the rising price of gold, these towns are booming again after years of neglect, but still remain isolated with only rough airstrips and a long, painful dirt road (often washed out in the wet season) to connect them with the capital. Page 212.

Alamikamba

Alamikamba lies at the end of the road on the banks of the winding Prinzapolka river. It has experienced numerous episodes of boom and bust serving as an indigenous trading post, river port, ranching centre and hub for banana production. Today it is the seat of government for the local municipality and offers some of the best sport fishing anywhere. Page 213.

Reserva de la Biósfera Bosawás

Few places are as wild and untamed as the Reserva de la Biósfera Bosawás, the largest protected area in Nicaragua. The reserve can be accessed from the remote highlands of Jinotega or the equally remote environs of the mining triangle, but neither journey is easy. However, few destinations are so rewarding – the wildlife, forests and scenes of rugged natural beauty are nothing short of spectacular. Page 214.

mountains of **Jinotega** (page 181) and **Matagalpa** (page 172) the cloudforests are home to many prize bird species like the quetzal. The **Montibelli Private Nature Reserve** (page 43), **Laguna de Apoyo** (page 66) and the **Reserva Natural El Chocoyero** (page 43), located just outside the capital, also offer a chance to see many interesting species including 1000 or so nesting parakeets. For those with time, patience and rugged constitutions, the hard-to-reach **Bosawás Biosphere Reserve** (pages 15 and 214) promises some of the best birding in Central America with over 400 resident species.

Climbing

Guided climbs are non-technical in nature. There is potential for technical climbing, but routes are undeveloped and you need to have to your own gear as there are no climbing outfitters or stores.

The most popular location is the **Maribios** volcanic range (page 163), set on a broad plain just 30-50 km inland from the Pacific Ocean and made up of more than 20 volcanoes, five of which are active. Another key spot is the island of **Ometepe** (page 112) which has two cones with sparkling lake views. While the Pacific volcanoes are no higher than 1700 m, the climbs are not as easy as they might seem. Most routes start just above sea level and are steep with difficult conditions including sharp rocks, sand and loose terrain, combined with serious heat. See also box, opposite.

Cycling

The options for cycling in Nicaragua are good, with a network of relatively flat, paved roads connecting the traditional villages of the **Pueblos Blancos** (page 67). For those who like their biking rugged, the hills around **Matagalpa** (page 172) have lots of potential.

In the dry season, confident cyclists should consider a foray into the **North Caribbean Coast Autonomous Region** (page 211). The villages from Bilwi to Waspam are joined by an extensive web of flat, easy-to-traverse and relatively empty dirt roads and expansive pine forests, but you will need a good map, equally good Spanish and even some wilderness experience to safely navigate the region. (For more information on cycling, see Getting around, page 261.)

Diving and snorkelling

There are professional dive operators on both of the **Corn Islands** (page 202). To find any depth a boat trip is needed, but the reefs lining both islands are beautiful and the marine life is rich. Snorkelling in the waters that wash the Corn Islands is world class and a real joy. Though scuba gear can be rented for diving, snorkellers would be wise to bring their own gear as most equipment available outside the dive operations is of poor quality. Snorkelling is also good around the **Pearl Cays** (page 197), but access is by expensive charter boat. The Pacific coast, beaten by waves, is usually too rough for diving or snorkelling. **Laguna de Apoyo**

SIX OF THE BEST
Volcano adventures

Volcán Masaya
The Parque Nacional Volcán Masaya is home to one of the world's most accessible volcano complexes – and one of the most active. Perpetually smoking and threatening cataclysm, the yawning chasm of its Santiago crater was long thought to be a gateway to hell. Surrounded by stark black lava fields and swathed in sulphurous vapours, it's not hard to see why. Page 65.

Volcán Mombacho
As the ever-present backdrop to the city of Granada, Volcán Mombacho, 1345 m high, is the one of the easiest volcanoes to experience in the country. Its lower slopes are dotted with tranquil villages that can be visited with the UCA Tierra y Agua community tourism project. Its upper slopes are home to cloudforests, hiking trails and heart-pounding zip-lines. Page 88.

Volcán Maderas
On Isla Ometepe, the slopes of Volcán Maderas are littered with ancient petroglyphs depicting everything from pre-Columbian deities to lizards, crocodiles and frogs. Now extinct and swathed in vegetation, Maderas is home to numerous distinct life zones, including misty cloudforests at its higher altitudes. You'll enjoy views of its tranquil crater lake from the 1394-m summit. Pages 115 and 120.

Volcán Cerro Negro
Reminiscent of a stark lunar landscape, Cerro Negro, 675 m, is one of Latin America's youngest volcanoes, emerging from the earth in just 1850. Vegetation has yet to colonize its slopes, which are instead covered in rolling dunes of black sand and gravel – the perfect environment for the now popular sport of volcano boarding. Don't miss this high-speed thrill. Page 163.

Volcán San Cristóbal
At 1745 m, Volcán San Cristóbal is Nicaragua's highest volcano and, following a decade of frequent eruptions, it remains in a volatile state. It is a challenging ascent through tropical dry forests which finally rewards persistent climbers with awesome views of its 500-m-wide crater. Be sure to use a guide and check on the current safety status before setting out. Page 164.

Volcán Cosigüina
Volcán Cosigüina is renowned for the diverse wildlife inhabiting its tropical dry forests, including a precious population of scarlet macaws – the last remaining in Pacific Nicaragua. The volcano once stood at a height of 3000 m, but following the most violent eruption in Latin American recorded history, it now stands at an altitude of 859 m. Nonetheless, the views from its summit are inspirational, encompassing El Salvador to the north and Honduras to the east. Page 168.

(page 66) offers diving opportunities for those interested in taking part in scientific research.

Fishing

Nicaragua is a fisherman's paradise, with its wide selection of rivers, lakes and seas. Deep-sea fishing can be arranged in **San Juan del Sur** (page 96) or **Marina Puesta del Sol** (page 168) in the Pacific and bonefishing is possible on the **Corn Islands** (page 202). **Lake Nicaragua** is great for bass fishing. The island of **Zapatera** (page 87) and its archipelago are home to Central America's biggest annual freshwater tournament. In **Pearl Lagoon** (page 197) and **Alamikamba** (page 213) on the Caribbean side and on the **Río San Juan** (page 138) tarpon and snook fishing is very good.

Spectator sports

Baseball

Baseball is the national sport in Nicaragua. The first league games were organized over 100 years ago and there is a very hard-fought national championship for the first division and many minor divisions. Nicaraguans follow the major leagues in the United States with more fervour than many Americans. The regular season begins in November and runs until the championships in February. Games are played all over the country during the dry season on Sunday in stadiums that are in themselves a cultural experience.

Bullfighting

Bullfighting in Nicaragua is a strange hybrid of bullfighting and bull rodeo.

The bull is not killed or injured, just intensely annoyed. The beast is brought inside the ring roped by a few mounted cowboys and tied to a bare tree in the centre. Someone mounts its back using a leather strap to hold on and the angry bull is released from the tree. The rider tries to stay on top and a few others show the animal some red capes for as long as they dare, before running off just before (in most cases) being impaled. When the bull gets too tired, a fresh one is brought in, mounted and shown more capes. Every patron saint festival has a bullfight.

Cockfighting

Cock fights (*peleas de gallo*) are legal and take place every Sunday all over the country. Like bullfighting, cockfighting in Nicaragua is non-lethal, but it is bloody and birds do occasionally die. Most of them will live to fight another day, though. The biggest time for the fights is during the patron saint festival of each town. To find the fight rings you will need to ask around (they do not have signs). The fight ring in Estelí is one of the most serious, with bets of over US$3000 being waged.

Surfing

Nicaragua's Pacific coast is home to countless beautiful breaks, many of which are only just starting to become popular. Most surfing is done along the coast of Rivas, using **San Juan del Sur** (page 96) as a jumping-off point to reach breaks to the north and south. The country's biggest and most famous break is at **Popoyo** (page 104) in northern Rivas. It is possible to rent boards in San Juan del Sur, but in most cases you will need to bring everything with you, as even wax can be hard to find at times. Many used to rave at the tube rides and point breaks that lie empty all year round, but recent complaints include surf operators converging on breaks with a boat full of clients.

Trekking

Most of Nicaragua's Pacific Basin is great walking country. You will need to speak some Spanish to get by, but once outside the city a whole world of beautiful landscapes and friendly people awaits you. Fences outside cities in Nicaragua are for animals, not people, and if you respect the privacy and rights of the local residents you need not worry about trespassing. Local guides are helpful and you should ask around each village to see who can accompany you and how far. Accommodation will be in hammocks (see Camping, page 24). Due to wild driving habits, avoid walking along the road wherever possible and use the volcanoes as landmarks.

It is possible to trek the **Maribios** volcano range (page 163) in north-western Nicaragua, starting at the extinct lake-filled crater of **Volcán Cosigüina** (page 168), which is the most westerly point of Nicaragua, and taking in all 21 cones, five of which are active. The route passes through many ranches and farms, where you can ask for directions if you need to. Another great place for trekking is the island of **Ometepe** (page 112) with its breathtaking beauty, friendly people and many dirt trails; it is essential to use local guides here.

Whitewater rafting

Nicaragua's rugged northern highlands are criss-crossed by a network of powerful and lively rivers, but rafting has yet to become an established activity. That may be set to change in the coming years, as tour operators are now beginning to make explorations of local waterways and their challenging rapids. **Matagalpa Tours** (page 179) is the main pioneer and is pleased to offer whitewater trips in the hills outside Matagalpa City.

Improve your travel photography

Taking pictures is a highlight for many travellers, yet too often the results turn out to be disappointing. Steve Davey, author of Footprint's *Travel Photography*, sets out his top rules for coming home with pictures you can be proud of.

Before you go
Don't waste precious travelling time and do your research before you leave. Find out what festivals or events might be happening or which day the weekly market takes place, and search online image sites such as Flickr to see whether places are best shot at the beginning or end of the day, and what vantage points you should consider.

Get up early
The quality of the light will be better in the few hours after sunrise and again before sunset – especially in the tropics when the sun will be harsh and unforgiving in the middle of the day. Sometimes seeing the sunrise is a part of the whole travel experience: sleep in and you will miss more than just photographs.

Stop and think
Don't just click away without any thought. Pause for a few seconds before raising the camera and ask yourself what you are trying to show with your photograph. Think about what things you need to include in the frame to convey this meaning. Be prepared to move around your subject to get the best angle. Knowing the point of your picture is the first step to making sure that the person looking at the picture will know it too.

Compose your picture
Avoid simply dumping your subject in the centre of the frame every time you take a picture. If you compose with it to one side, then your picture can look more balanced. This will also allow you to show a significant background and make the picture more meaningful. A good rule of thumb is to place your subject or any significant detail a third of the way into the frame; facing into the frame not out of it.

This rule also works for landscapes. Compose with the horizon two-thirds of the way up the frame if the fore-ground is the most interesting part of the picture; one-third of the way up if the sky is more striking.

Don't get hung up with this so-called Rule of Thirds, though. Exaggerate it by pushing your subject out to the edge of the frame if it makes a more interesting picture; or if the sky is dull in a landscape, try cropping with the horizon near the very top of the frame.

Fill the frame
If you are going to focus on a detail or even a person's face in a close-up portrait, then be bold and make sure that you fill the frame. This is often a case of physically getting in close. You can use a telephoto setting on a zoom lens but this can lead to pictures looking quite flat; moving in close is a lot more fun!

Interact with people

If you want to shoot evocative portraits then it is vital to approach people and seek permission in some way, even if it is just by smiling at someone. Spend a little time with them and they are likely to relax and look less stiff and formal. Action portraits where people are doing something, or environmental portraits, where they are set against a significant background, are a good way to achieve relaxed portraits. Interacting is a good way to find out more about people and their lives, creating memories as well as photographs.

Focus carefully

Your camera can focus quicker than you, but it doesn't know which part of the picture you want to be in focus. If your camera is using the centre focus sensor then move the camera so it is over the subject and half press the button, then, holding it down, recompose the picture. This will lock the focus. Take the now correctly focused picture when you are ready.

Another technique for accurate focusing is to move the active sensor over your subject. Some cameras with touch-sensitive screens allow you to do this by simply clicking on the subject.

Leave light in the sky

Most good night photography is actually taken at dusk when there is some light and colour left in the sky; any lit portions of the picture will balance with the sky and any ambient lighting. There is only a very small window when this will happen, so get into position early, be prepared and keep shooting and reviewing the results. You can take pictures after this time, but avoid shots of tall towers in an inky black sky; crop in close on lit areas to fill the frame.

Bring it home safely

Digital images are inherently ephemeral: they can be deleted or corrupted in a heartbeat. The good news though is they can be copied just as easily. Wherever you travel, you should have a backup strategy. Cloud backups are popular, but make sure that you will have access to fast enough Wi-Fi. If you use RAW format, then you will need some sort of physical back-up. If you don't travel with a laptop or tablet, then you can buy a backup drive that will copy directly from memory cards.

Available in both digital and print formats, Footprint's Travel Photography by Steve Davey covers everything you need to know about travelling with a camera, including simple post-processing. More information is available at www.footprinttravelguides.com

Where to stay

Nicaragua has a rapidly expanding choice of lodging options, from million-dollar private ecolodges to backpacker hostels. Most quality lodging is limited to the Pacific Basin and other select areas. Note beach hotels raise their rates for Holy Week and almost all hotels charge higher prices for the Christmas holiday season with sell-outs common months in advance. Airbnb (Airbnb.com) is increasingly available in Nicaragua's main tourist destinations. **Note** It is wise to pull the bed away from the wall in the tropics so whatever is crawling on the wall does not see your head as a logical progression.

Hotels and hospedajes

Outside Managua, hotels at the top end of the $ range are adequate and some good deals can be found. Budget travellers have the option to stay in basic *hospedajes* (guesthouses) and they should bring a padlock, toilet paper, soap, insecticide, mosquito net, a sheet sleeper and a decent towel. Do not put toilet paper or any non-organic material in any toilet; you will find a little wastebasket for that purpose. Electric showers are common in highland areas and getting them to work is a matter of finding the right water pressure. Never touch the shower head once the water is running or you'll get a nasty shock. In remote areas, meals are often included in the price and electricity is produced by a diesel generator that runs for only a few hours after sunset.

Price codes

Where to stay	Restaurants
$$$$ over US$150	$$$ over US$12
$$$ US$66-150	$$ US$7-12
$$ US$30-65	$ US$6 and under
$ under US$30	

Price of a double room in high season, including taxes.

Price for a two-course meal for one person, excluding drinks or service charge.

Hostels

New hostels are opening all the time, especially in the cities of León and Granada, where you'll find no shortage of choice. Most of them offer economical dorm beds for US$5-10 along with a range of amenities including free coffee, breakfast, Wi-Fi, lockers, tours and information. Private rooms in hostels are not necessarily good value and couples and groups may get more bang for their buck in small hotels. As ever, hostels are a sociable option and the best place to meet other travellers or get together groups for tours.

Fincas and ecolodges

Private coffee fincas are an increasingly popular option in rural areas, especially in the northern highlands and along the volcanic slopes of Isla Ometepe. Most of them are peaceful retreats steeped in bucolic surroundings. To qualify as an ecolodge, a hotel needs to address the issues of renewable energy, water recycling, fair wages and social responsibility. There are comparatively few places that actually manage this and their facilities are sometimes more rustic than luxury. Wilderness lodges are a different category of accommodation. They vary wildly in cost and philosophy but are generally united by their pristine natural setting and access to protected areas. The decent ones will be able to recommend excursions and hook you up with professional guides.

B&Bs

The extent and popularity of B&Bs has taken off in recent years and most of them offer a level of quality, comfort and personal service above and beyond your bog-standard hotel. Some of the converted townhouses in Granada and León are especially beautiful. On the Pacific coast, 'rustic chic' *cabañas* have become de rigueur. Most good B&Bs cost upwards of US$40 per night and it's worth shopping around as style, comfort, intimacy and overall value vary greatly between establishments. Also check what kind of breakfast is included, as some do not extend to a full cooked spread.

Homestays

Homestays are a great way to learn about local culture and are best arranged through Spanish schools or community tourism projects. Reasonably comfortable options are available in big towns and cities, but expect rustic conditions in rural places, including an outdoor toilet, little or no electricity, and cold running water (or just a bucket and a wash bowl). Simple meals are usually included in rates.

Camping

In the heat of Nicaragua the thought of putting yourself inside a tent – or worse, inside a sleeping bag inside a tent – can be unpleasant. However, relief from the heat can be found in the northern mountains or on the slopes of the volcanoes. In more remote areas you can usually find a roof to hang your hammock under (ask for permission first). A mosquito net, which you should bring from home, will keep off the vampire bats as well as the insects.

Food
& drink

from fritanga to Flor de Caña

Nicaragua has a great selection of traditional dishes that are usually prepared with fresh ingredients and in generous portions. The midday heat dictates that you get out and tour early with a light breakfast, head for shelter and enjoy a long lunch and rest, then finish with an early dinner.

Food

Gallo pinto, the dish that keeps most of Nicaragua alive, is a mixture of fried white rice and kidney beans, which are boiled apart and then fried together. Equally popular *nacatamales* consist of cornmeal, pork or chicken, rice, *achiote* (similar to paprika), peppers, peppermint leaves, potatoes, onions and cooking oil, all wrapped in a big green banana leaf and boiled. Lunch is the biggest meal of the day and normally includes a cabbage and tomato salad, white rice, beans, tortilla, fried or boiled plantain and a meat or fish serving. *Asado* or *a la plancha* are key words for most foreigners. *Asado* is grilled meat or fish, which often comes with a chilli sauce. *Carne asada*, grilled beef, is popular street food. *A la plancha* means the food is cooked on a sizzling plate or flat grill. In the countryside *cuajada* is a must. It is a soft feta-type cheese made daily in people's homes, lightly salted and excellent in a hot tortilla. There are other white cheeses: *queso seco* is a slightly bitter dry cheese and *queso crema* a moist bland cheese that is excellent fried. Regional dishes are described in the relevant chapters.

Drink

Since Nicaragua is the land of a thousand fruits, the best drink is the *refresco* or *fresco*, fruit juices or grains and spices mixed with water and sugar. Options include pineapple, carrot, passion fruit, beetroot, orange, mandarin, lemonade, grenadine, tamarind, mango, star-fruit, papaya and more. Two favourites are *cacao* and *pitaya*. *Cacao*, the raw cocoa bean, is ground and mixed with milk, rice, cinnamon, vanilla, ice and sugar. *Pitaya* (or *pitahaya*) also known as dragon fruit, is a distinctive pink-skinned cactus fruit with white flesh, which is usually blended with lime, sugar and water.

The usual fizzy **soft drinks** are also available and called *gaseosas*. For **beer** lovers there are four national brands (all lagers), the strongest being *Cerveza Victoria*, with *Toña* a softer choice. *Flor de Caña* has been called the finest rum in the world and its factory – more than 100 years old – is a national institution. Nicaraguans often spend a night round the table with a bottle of *Flor de Caña*, served up with a bucket of ice, a plate of limes and a steady flow of mixers. Although Nicaraguan **coffee** is recognized as one of the world's finest, most Nicaraguans are unable to pay for the expensive roasts and prefer to drink instant coffee. In the cities ask for *café percolado*, which is often quite good if it's available.

Bottled water is available throughout the country and is recommended as a precaution, but please help to reduce plastic waste by using refillable flasks wherever possible. Most lodgings and households have a returnable 20-litre *garrafón* containing UV-treated potable water for your daily needs.

Restaurants in Nicaragua

Outside the main tourist hubs, anyone looking for decent international cuisine will be disappointed as choices and quality tend to be poor. The most expensive dish is not always the best, but a crowded mid-range restaurant is a good indication of a successful kitchen. Many restaurants offer *comida corriente* (also called *comida casera*), a set menu that works out far cheaper than ordering à la carte. Generally speaking, *fritanga* (street food), costs about US$2 and is best for the cast-iron stomach crowd, while the US$3-4 *comida corriente* is often tastier, though a bit salty and/or oily. The good eating starts at US$5 and runs up to US$12 a dish in most places. Some travellers complain that Nicaraguan cuisine is excessively bland and the more jaded among them carry bottles of hot sauce wherever they go.

FOOD AND DRINK
Menu reader

A

agua water
agua mineral con gas water, carbonated
agua mineral sin gas water, still mineral
aguacate canelo native avocado
aguardiente firewater
aji/pimiento chilli or green pepper
ajillo garlic butter sauce
ajo garlic
a la plancha food cooked on a sizzling plate or flat grill
arroz blanco boiled rice
asado roasted or grilled meat or fish
azúcar sugar

B

batido fruit milkshake
beber to drink
bebida drink
bistec beef steak or pork fillet
bistec encebollado steak with onions
boa en salsa boa constrictor in tomato sauce
bocadillo sandwich
borracho/a drunk
botella bottled
¡buen provecho! enjoy your meal
burrito flour tortilla stuffed with meat, rice and vegetables

C

cacao raw cocoa bean, ground and mixed with milk, rice, cinnamon, vanilla, ice and sugar
café coffee
café con leche coffee, white
café de palo home-roasted coffee
café percolado percolated coffee
cajetas traditional sweets, candied fruit

cajeta de leche milk sweet
cajeta de zapoyol cooked zapote seeds and sugar
calabaza squash
calamares squid
caldo clear soup, stock
caliente hot
camarones de río freshwater prawns
carne meat
carne asada grilled beef
carne de res beef
cebolla onion
cena supper
cerdo asado grilled pork
cerveza beer
ceviche raw fish marinated in onions and lime juice
chicha corn-based drink, sometimes fermented to alcohol
chimichangas fried burritos
chivo goat
chorizo sausage
churrasco steak grilled steak in garlic and parsley sauce
comidas meals
comida corriente/comida casera set menu
comida económica cheap food/menu
cocktail de pulpo octopus
cuajada lightly salted, soft cheese
curvina sea bass
curvina a la plancha grilled sea bass
cuzuco armadillo
cuzuco en salsa armadillo in tomato sauce

D

desayuno breakfast
dorado a la parilla grilled dorado fish

E

empanadas pastries filled with meat or chicken
enchilada meat or chicken wrapped in flour tortilla
ensalada salad

F

frijoles beans
fritanga street food
frío cold
frito fried

G

gallo pinto fried white rice and kidney beans, with onions and sweet pepper
garbanzos chick peas
garrobo black iguana
garrobo en caldillo black iguana soup
gaseosas fizzy drinks
guardatinaja large nocturnal rodent
guapote local, large-mouthed bass

H

hamburguesa hamburger
helado ice cream
hervido/a boiled
hielo ice
huevo egg
huevo de toro asado grilled bull's testicles
huevos scrambled eggs

I

indio viejo cornmeal and shredded beef porridge with garlic and spices

J

jamón ham
jugo pure fruit juice

L

langosta lobster (*langosta blanca* 'white lobster' is cocaine)
lata canned
leche milk
legumbres vegetables
licuado fruit milkshake
limón lime
limonada lemonade
lomo relleno stuffed beef
longaniza sausage

M

mahi mahi grilled dorado fish
mantequilla butter
manzanilla camomile tea
mar y tierra surf and turf
mariscos seafood
melocotón star fruit/peach
menta mint
mermelada jam
mojarra carp
mole chocolate, chilli sauce

N

nacatamales cornmeal, pork or chicken and rice, achiote (similar to paprika), peppers, peppermint leafs, potatoes, onions and cooking oil, all wrapped in a big green banana leaf and boiled
naranja orange
níspero brown sugar fruit

P

paca large, nocturnal rodent
pan bread
panadería bakery
papa potato
pargo al vapor steamed snapper
pargo rojo/blanco red/white snapper
para llevar to take away

parrillada Argentine-style grill
pastel cake
pavo turkey
pescado fish
pescado a la suyapa fresh snapper in a tomato, sweet pepper and onion sauce
picadillo minced meat
picante hot, spicy
pimiento pepper
piniona thin strips of candied green papaya
Pío V corn cake topped with light cream and bathed in rum sauce
pitaya cactus fruit, blended with lime and sugar
plátano banana/plantain
plato típico typical Nicaraguan food
pollo chicken
pollo asado grilled chicken
pomelo grapefruit
posol grainy indigenous drink served in an original jícaro gourd cup
pupusas tortillas filled with beans, cheese and/or pork

Q

quesadillas fried tortilla with cheese, chilli and peppers
quesillos mozzarella cheese in a hot tortilla with salt and bathed in cream
queso crema moist bland cheese, good fried
queso seco slightly bitter dry cheese

R

refresco/fresco fruit juice or grains and spices mixed with water and sugar
restaurante restaurant
revueltos scrambled eggs
robalo snook
ron rum
rosquillas baked corn and cheese biscuits

S

sábalo/sábalo real tarpon/giant tarpon
sal salt
salsa sauce
sopa soup
sopa de albóndiga soup with meatballs made of chicken, eggs, garlic and cornmeal
sopa de mondongo tripe soup
sopa de tortilla soup of corn tortilla and spices
sopa huevos de toro bull testicle soup
sopa levanta muerto literally 'return from the dead' soup
sorbete ice cream
surtido sampler or mixed dish

T

tacos fried tortilla stuffed with chicken, beef or pork
tacos chinos egg rolls
taza cup
té tea
tres leches very sweet cake made with three kinds of milk (fresh and tinned)
tamales cornmeal bars boiled
tilapia African lake fish introduced to Nicaragua
tiste grainy indigenous drinks served in an original jícaro gourd cup
tipitapa tomato sauce
tomar to drink
toronja grapefruit
tostones con queso flat plantain sections fried with cheese

V

vaso glass
vigorón banana leaf filled with fried pork rind, cabbage salad, yucca, tomato, hot chilli and lemon juice
vino blanco wine, white
vino tinto wine, red

Managua
& around

If, as the local saying goes, Nicaragua is the country where 'lead floats and cork sinks', Managua is its perfect capital. It's certainly hard to make any sense of a lakefront city which ignores its lake and where you can drive around for hours without ever seeing any water. Managua has 20% of the country's population, yet there is little overcrowding; it has no centre and lots of trees (from the air you can see more trees than buildings); it is a place where parks are concrete, not green, spaces – there are too many of those already; and where, when directions are given, they refer to buildings that haven't existed for over 30 years. Managua is the capital without a city, a massive suburb of over a million people (there was a downtown once but it was swept away in the 1972 earthquake). And yet, despite having no centre, no skyline and no logic, Managua is still a good place to start your visit. It is full of energy and is the heartbeat of the Nicaraguan economy and psyche.

Essential Managua

Getting around

Managua has nothing that even remotely resembles a city grid and walking is a challenge and unsafe for those who are not familiar with the city. The best bet is to get to Metrocentro and not travel more than five blocks on foot (see Safety, right). Local buses are confusing, crowded and not recommended due to thieves. Taxi is the preferred method of transport for newcomers. Unfortunately, hiring a Managua taxi is not as safe or straightforward as you might hope, but once mastered it is an efficient way to explore Managua. Negotiate the fare before getting in (see page 54). It is cheaper to ride *colectivo* (shared), but not recommended due to safety concerns (see below).

Best restaurants

Rancho Tiscapa, page 47
El Churrasco, page 48
A La Vista Buffet, page 48
El Muelle, page 48

Safety

Like most capitals, Managua suffers from a healthy criminal population, so be sure to take all the usual precautions. At night, do not walk more than a few blocks anywhere, as the streets are deserted and there are almost no police. The Metrocentro area is relatively safe, but it's still best not to walk alone after dark. Parts of Martha Quezada are now unsafe at all hours, particularly on the roads between the Ticabus terminal and Plaza Inter; ask locally about the situation before setting out. Do not ride in unlicensed taxis, especially with helpful local 'friends' you have just met, as you risk being kidnapped and robbed. Always ask to see the driver's ID and check the license plate number matches the one on the taxi door.

When to go

There are daytime highs of 30-33°C year round; nights tend to be cool from October to early January. Try and avoid the end of the dry season (March to mid-May), when blowing dust and smoke from surrounding farmlands combine with hot temperatures.

Time required

Three to four days.

Weather Managua

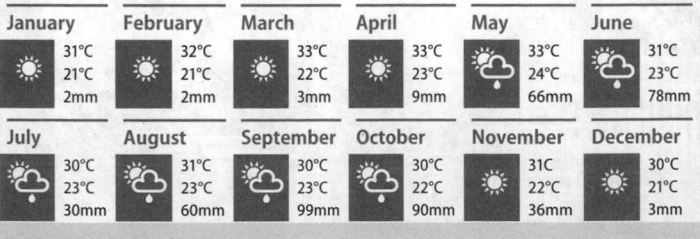

January	February	March	April	May	June
31°C	32°C	33°C	33°C	33°C	31°C
21°C	21°C	22°C	23°C	24°C	23°C
2mm	2mm	3mm	9mm	66mm	78mm

July	August	September	October	November	December
30°C	31°C	30°C	30°C	31C	30°C
23°C	23°C	23°C	22°C	22°C	21°C
30mm	60mm	99mm	90mm	36mm	3mm

From the *malecón* in Managua (altitude 40-200 m), the Península Chiltepe can be seen jutting out into Lake Managua, part of an ancient volcanic complex that includes two crater lakes, Apoyeque and Xiloá.

Malecón

The *malecón* is the site of a popular touristic development with a parade of rancho-style eateries, **Puerto Salvador Allende** ⓘ *www.epn.com.ni, entrance US$0.15*, built by the FSLN and named after the famous Chilean president. Boat tours depart from the pier for nearby **Isla de Amor** ⓘ *Isla de Amor, Tue-Fri 4 daily 1100-1700; Sat-Sun 7 daily 1000-1830, 45 mins, US$2.15, top floor 'VIP' rate US$3.05, children US$1.50; night tours of the lake depart Tue-Sun 1830, US$3.05, children US$1.50*. The stage with the giant acoustic shell right next to the *malecón* is used for concerts, political speeches and rallies. The area in front of the stage, **El Parque Juan Pablo II**, has been turned into a monument and park in honour of Pope John Paul II who preached here in 1996.

Teatro Nacional

T2222-7426, www.tnrubendario.gob.ni, US$1.50-20, depending on show.

Southeast of the malecón stands the Teatro Rubén Darío or Teatro Nacional, a project of the last Somoza's wife, which survived the earthquake of 1972 and provides the only quality stage in Managua for plays, concerts and dance productions. There are occasionally temporary art exhibitions in the theatre so, in the day, ask at the window to view the exhibit and you can probably look inside the auditorium as well.

Parque Rubén Darío

Just south of the theatre is the Parque Rubén Darío, a small park with one of the most famous monuments in Nicaragua. Sculpted from Italian marble in 1933 by Nicaraguan architect Mario Favilli and restored in 1997, it is said to be the aesthetic symbol of modernism, the poetry movement which Darío founded. Passages from some of his most famous poems are reproduced on the monument.

Parque Central and around

In front of the statue is the Parque Central. Now central to almost nothing, it was once surrounded by three- to five-storey buildings and narrow streets that made up the pre-1972 Managua. The **Templo de la Música** erected in 1939 is at the centre of the park and there's a monument above the burial site of the revolutionary Sandinista ideologue, Carlos Fonseca.

Next to the park is a dancing, musical fountain and the garish **Casa Presidencial** that has been described (generously) as 'post-modernist eclectic'.

Palacio Nacional de la Cultura

Directly opposite is the neoclassical Palacio Nacional de la Cultura, finished in 1935 after the original was destroyed in an earthquake in 1931. The elegant interior houses two gardens, the national archive, the national library, and the **Museo Nacional de Nicaragua** ① *T2222-4820, www.museonacional.inc.gob.ni, Tue-Fri 0800-1700, Sat 0900-1600, Sun 1000-1700, entrance US$5, children US$1, bilingual guides available.*

Catedral Vieja

Next to the Palacio de la Cultura is the Old Cathedral. Baptized as La Iglesia Catedral Santiago de Los Caballeros de Managua, it is now known simply as La Catedral Vieja. The church was almost finished when it was shaken by the big earthquake of 1931, and when the earth moved again in 1972 it was partially destroyed. It has been tastefully restored; only the roof of narrow steel girders and side-window support bars were added to keep it standing. There is something romantic about this old and sad cathedral in ruins; a monument to what Managua might have been. Earthquake damage has closed the old church indefinitely, though the Mexican government has promised funds to restore it.

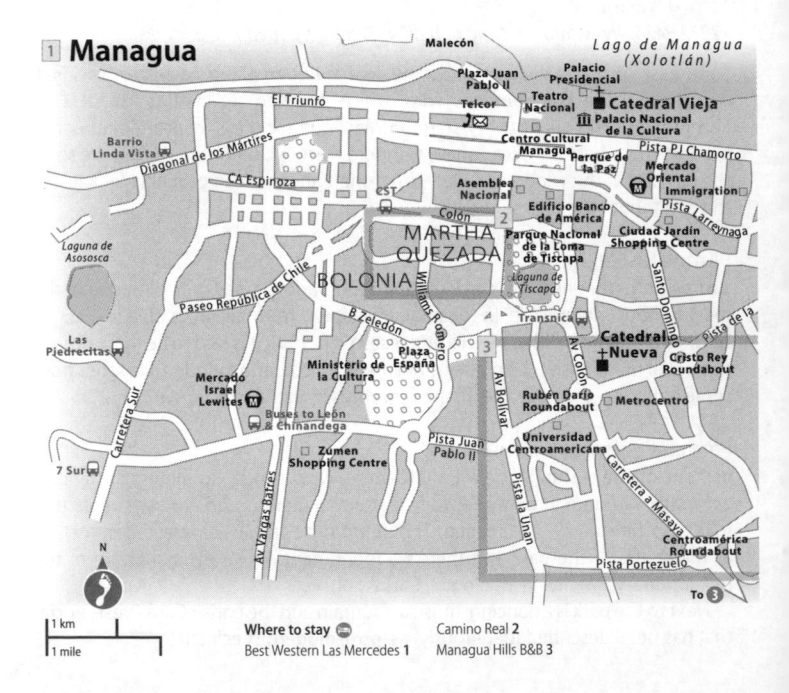

Where to stay 🛏
Best Western Las Mercedes **1**
Camino Real **2**
Managua Hills B&B **3**

Centro Cultural Managua
On the south side of the Palacio de la Cultura, T2222-592.

The Centro Cultural Managua was built out of the ruins of the Gran Hotel de Managua, the best hotel in town from the 1940s to 1960s. Now, as a cultural centre, it has a selection of before-and-after photos of quake-struck Managua in 1972, art exhibits and temporary antique and craft shops. The centre is also home to the national art school and the national music school. There are art exhibits downstairs in the galleries and temporary antique and craft shops. The central area is used for performances (check the Thursday newspapers or ask staff to see what is coming up). On the first Saturday of every month an artisans' fair gives craftsmen from outside Managua a chance to show and sell their wares.

Parque de la Paz
Across the Carretera Norte from the Centro Cultural Managua, the Parque de la Paz (Peace Park) is a graveyard for a few dozen truckloads of AK-47s and other weapons which were buried here as a monument to the end of the Contra War; some can be seen sticking out of the cement. Sadly, the park is now unsafe to visit; check with a taxi driver about the current situation.

Asemblea Nacional
Heading south from the old centre down the Avenida Bolívar is the Asemblea Nacional (parliamentary building) and the **Arboretum Nacional**, which houses 180 species of plant including Nicaragua's national flower, the *sacuanjoche* (*Plumeria rubra*).

➡ **Managua maps**
1 Managua, page 34
2 Martha Quezada and Bolonia, page 37
3 Metrocentro, page 40

Managua

The southern shore of Lake Managua has been inhabited for at least 6000 years and was once an area of major volcanic activity with four cones, all of which are now extinct. Managua means 'place of the big man' or 'chief' in the Mangue language of the Chorotega indigenous people who inhabited Managua at the arrival of the Spanish. At that time it was a large village that extended for many kilometres along the shores of Lake Managua (whose indigenous name is Ayagualpa or Xolotlán). When the Spanish first arrived Managua was reported to have 40,000 inhabitants, but shortly after the conquest, the population dropped to about 1000, partly due to a brutal battle waged by the Chorotegas against Spanish colony founder Francisco Hernández de Córdoba in 1524. Managua remained a stopping-off point on the road between León and Granada, and so avoided some of the intercity wars that plagued the country after Independence. In 1852 it was declared the capital of Nicaragua as a compromise between the forever-bickering parties of León and Granada, even though its population was still only 24,000. Today it remains the centre of all branches of government and it often seems that life outside Managua is little noticed by the media and political leaders.

The land under Managua is very unstable and the city experiences a big earthquake every 40 years or so, with those of 1931 and 1972 generating widespread damage and erasing a city centre populated by 400,000 residents. Managua's crippled infrastructure was further damaged by the looting of international relief aid in 1972 and aerial bombing in 1979 by the last Somoza and his National Guard troops. Following the troubled years of the 1980s and the resulting waves of migrations from the countryside, the capital now has an inflated population of over one million. Since 1990 the city has been rebuilding and trying to catch up with its rapid population growth. Investment has intensified in the early 21st century, solidifying Managua as the economic heart of the country.

Two blocks south of the government offices is the historic pyramid-shaped Intercontinental building, now home to the Hotel Crowne Plaza.

West of here, the streets descend to the district of Martha Quezada, also known as 'Ticabus', where you'll find a concentration of budget accommodation and two of the international bus stations. **Note** It is unsafe to walk from the Intercontinental building to the barrio.

Avenida Bolívar runs up the hill from the Intercontinental and down to a traffic signal which is the road that runs west to Plaza España or east for Carretera a Masaya and Metrocentro. Plaza España, marked by the grass mound and statues of Rotonda El Güegüence, is a series of small shops, banks, airline offices and a big supermarket. Just to the north of Plaza España and west of Martha Quezada is Managua's gallery district, which provides some more comfortable accommodation as well.

South of Martha Quezada is Bolonia. With its quiet tree-lined streets, it is inner Managua's finest residential neighbourhood, and home to all of Nicaragua's major television networks, most of its embassies, some art galleries well worth visiting and several good eating and sleeping options. The area is bordered by Plaza España to the south, Martha Quezada to the north, Laguna Tiscapa to the east and the sprawling barrios that run to Mercado Israel Lewites to the west.

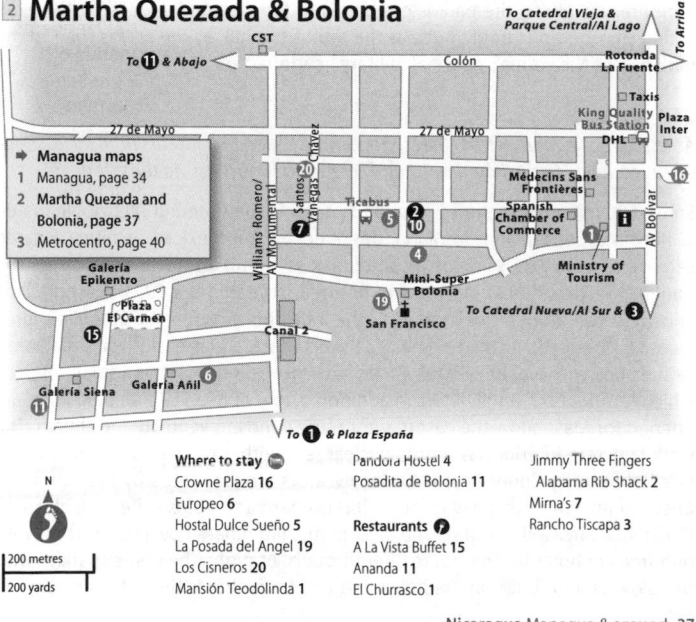

2 Martha Quezada & Bolonia

Managua maps
1 Managua, page 34
2 Martha Quezada and Bolonia, page 37
3 Metrocentro, page 40

Where to stay
Crowne Plaza 16
Europeo 6
Hostal Dulce Sueño 5
La Posada del Angel 19
Los Cisneros 20
Mansión Teodolinda 1
Pandora Hostel 4
Posadita de Bolonia 11

Restaurants
A La Vista Buffet 15
Ananda 11
El Churrasco 1
Jimmy Three Fingers
Alabama Rib Shack 2
Mirna's 7
Rancho Tiscapa 3

Laguna de Tiscapa and around

crater lake set in a protected area

The Parque Nacional de la Loma de Tiscapa (Tuesday-Sunday 0900-1730, US$1 admission for pedestrians, US$2 admission for cars) has a fabulous panoramic view of Managua and is great for photographing the city. It is reached by the small road that runs directly behind the Crowne Plaza Hotel. At the top, a giant black silhouette of Augusto C Sandino looks out over the city and Laguna de Tiscapa on the south side of the hill. The perfectly round lake has been polluted by years of street run-off but is undergoing an intense clean up and is home to many turtles as well as the occasional caiman.

This park is also the site of the **former presidential palace** (ruined by the earthquake in 1972). Sandino signed a peace treaty here in 1933 and, after dining here with the then President Sacasa one year later, was abducted and shot under orders of the first Somoza, who would push Sacasa out of office in 1936 and found a 43-year family dynasty. Both father and son dictators used part of the palace to hold and torture dissidents. The old torture cells can be seen from the eastern part of the park near the drop-off to the crater lake. Next to the statue of Sandino are two tanks, one said to have been a gift to the first Somoza from Mussolini and the other taken from the National Guard during the Sandinista battle for León in 1979. The graffiti on the tank was written by rebels in memory of a fallen female revolutionary named Aracely. The remains of the presidential palace are used for temporary exhibits; the park is popular with families on Sundays. **Note** Avoid taking photographs until you're at the top of the hill, as the access road to the park passes Nicaragua's national military headquarters.

Catedral Nueva
Access for pedestrians is from the Metrocentro junction and for cars from the east side entrance. Avoid flash photography and entering during Mass via the side doors.

Some 500 m south of the Laguna de Tiscapa is the Catedral Metropolitana de la Purísima Concepción de María, designed by the Mexican architect Ricardo Legorreta, who has said his inspiration was found in an ancient temple in Cholula, Mexico. Begun in 1991 and finished in September 1993, it is popularly known as La Catedral Nueva (New Cathedral). This mosque-like Catholic church faces south–north, instead of the usual west–east, and is basically a squat, anti-seismic box with a beehive roof. Each of the roof's 63 domes has a small window, which lets heat out and light in. In addition, a row of massive side doors that are opened for Mass allow the east to west trade winds to ventilate the church. The stark concrete interior has a post-nuclear feel with a modern altar reminiscent of a UN Security Council setting. Many visitors are fascinated by the Sangre de Cristo room, which vaguely recalls a Turkish bath and holds a life-size, bleeding Christ icon encased in a glass and steel dome, illuminated by a domed roof with hundreds of holes for the sun to filter through. At night, the dome sparkles with the glow of light bulbs in the holes. The bell tower holds the old bells from the

What lies beneath

In 1972 the Tiscapa fault ruptured, less than 5 km beneath the lakefront, sending forth a 6.6 earthquake that rocked the city and crumbled (and later burned) all that could be considered downtown. The quake came cruelly just after midnight on Saturday 23 December, a day before Christmas. Most of Managua was inside, enjoying big parties; many were never found. Half the population (then 200,000) was left homeless, and at least 5000 Nicaraguans were killed.

There are plenty of reasons not to rebuild the high-rises that once constituted the city's downtown. In fact, 14 good reasons, and that is counting only the principal seismic fault lines that run underneath greater Managua. As a consequence, today's 21st-century Managua is one of the greenest capitals in the world, wide open spaces stretch in every direction, with sprawling barrios and a couple of new low-rise office and hotel buildings looking very much out of place. Much of what was downtown became a sort of monument valley, home to a confused garden of statues, concrete parks and a few new government buildings. With a proper sense of Nicaraguan irony, the new presidential office was built directly over the epicentre of the 1972 quake.

ruins of the Catedral Vieja. The church has capacity for 1500 worshippers at any one time, but is filled well beyond that every Sunday at 1100, for what is the most popular Mass in the capital.

South of the bizarre New Cathedral stands the big fountains of Rotonda Rubén Darío (Rubén Darío roundabout), right next to the cloistered Metrocentro shopping centre. From here, the Carretera a Masaya runs south to the Rotonda Centroamérica, thereafter passing the Camino de Oriente shopping centre and the upmarket Galerías Santo Domingo mall, finally exiting the city to connect with Nindirí, Masaya and Granada. The web of streets surrounding the northern section of the Carretera are home to middle-class residences, restaurants, bars, and galleries. The Universidad Centroamericana (UCA), where express buses to Granada and León depart, lies some 300 m west of Metrocentro.

3 Metrocentro

→ Managua maps
1 Managua, page 34
2 Martha Quezada and Bolonia, page 37
3 Metrocentro, page 40

N
200 metres
200 yards

Where to stay 🛏
Aloha **6**
Colibrí **8**
El Almendro **1**
Elements Boutique Hotel **11**
Los Robles **2**
Managua Hills B&B **5**
Managua Backpackers' Inn **3**
Real Intercontinental Metrocentro **4**

Restaurants 🍴
Casa del Café **1**
Casa de las Nogueras **2**
Don Cándido **14**
Don Parrillón **15**
El Guapinol **16**
El Muelle **3**
La Cocina de Doña Haydée **6**
Terraza Cevichería **5**

Bars & clubs 🍸
Chamán **35**

Directions in Managua and beyond

How do you find anything in a country without street names or numbers? Sometimes visitors feel as if they are going round in circles, quite literally in the case of Managua with its epidemic of dizzying *rotondas* (roundabouts). The Nicaraguan system is foolproof – as long as you know every landmark that exists, or used to exist, in the city which means that, more often than not, foreigners spend most of their time completely lost.

In Managua, directions are based around the lake, so it is essential to know where the lake is and keep a bird's eye view of the city in your mind. With the location of Lake Managua you have north (*al lago*); away from the lake is south (*al sur*). Then you need to use basic Spanish and the sun. Where the sun comes up (*arriba*) is east and where it goes down (*abajo*) is west. City blocks are *cuadras* (abbreviated in this book as 'c'), and metres are better known here by their old Spanish approximation – *varas* (vrs). The key element once you fix your compass is the landmark from which directions begin, which can be a hotel, park, pharmacy, factory or, in worst-case scenarios, where a factory used to be before the earthquake in 1972! Once you find the landmark, getting to your ultimate destination is simple. For example, take El Caramanchel, Plaza Inter, 2 c sur, 15 varas abajo: to sip Nicaraguan rum here first you need to locate Plaza Inter, then go two blocks south and continue 15 m west.

Outside Managua you may also hear the standard orientation points of *norte*, *sur*, *oeste* and *este*. In Granada, *al lago* refers to the east; on the Pacific coast *al mar* refers to the west, on the Caribbean side it means east. In mountainous areas, *arriba* and *abajo* may also indicate the rise and fall of the land, so it can get confusing. In smaller towns, many directions are given from the Parque Central or Iglesia (central church). It is useful to remember that nearly all the façades of Catholic churches in Nicaragua face west; so when stepping out of the church the north is to your right, south to the left, etc. If the worst comes to worst, hire a taxi, give the driver the coordinates and let him figure it out.

East of Metrocentro, the **Roberto Huembes market** or **Mercado Central** is the best place for shopping in the capital. It is an interesting visit just for the fruit, vegetable and meat sections, which are found inside the structure proper, along with flowers and other goods. At the northwest corner of the market is a very big craft section with goods from all over the country. While the market in Masaya is more famous and more pleasant to shop at, the artisan section of Huembes is in some ways more complete, if more jumbled and difficult to move about.

Museo Las Huellas de Acahualinca

Along the lake, 2 km due west of the Museo Nacional, T2266-5774, Mon-Fri 0830-1500, Sat-Sun by appointment only. **Note** *At the time of research, the museum was temporarily closed due to long-term renovation work; contact in advance before setting out. Taxi recommended as it is hard to find.*

In 1874, during digging for quarry stone near the shores of Lake Managua, one of the oldest known evidences of human presence in Central America was found: footprints of men, women and children left in petrified subsoil. Radiocarbon-dated to 4000 BC, the tracks were imprinted in fresh volcanic mud, the product of a burning cloud eruption. What were these ancient ancestors doing when they made these perfectly preserved footprints? After numerous theories, studies have now determined that they were made by 10 different people walking upright, some weighed down, perhaps with children or supplies. The footprints were undoubtedly covered in volcanic sand shortly afterwards, preserving an ancient passage and a modern enigma. This small but interesting museum was created around the original excavation site of the so-called Huellas de Acahualinca ('footprints in the land of sunflowers').

Las Sierras de Managua

Behind the suburban sprawl of Managua, Las Sierras rise 950 m above sea level into a broad area of forest and mountains. Considering it is less than 30 km from a city of more than a million people, the diversity of wildlife and vegetation that can be found here is remarkable. Accommodation is extremely limited but the area can be visited as a day trip from Managua or Granada.

Along the Carretera Sur

The Carretera Sur is one of the most dramatic roads in Nicaragua, with expansive views and several crater lakes to be seen as it rises up into the mountainous region of Las Sierras de Managua. At Km 6 is the little park **Las Piedrecitas**, which fills up at weekends with children, families and couples and has a cheap café serving bad hamburgers. The park has a great view of **Laguna de Asososca** ('blue waters' in Náhuatl), the principal reservoir of drinking water for Managua. It is a pretty lake and the view extends to Lake Managua and the Chiltepe Peninsula where two more crater lakes are hidden. At Km 9 is another crater lake, **Laguna de Nejapa** ('ash waters'), in the wooded crater of an old volcano that is almost dry during the summer. The highway continues south and turns right at a traffic signal 1 km past the final petrol station. From there the road rises gradually past some of the wealthiest homes in Nicaragua.

The section of road from Km 19 to Km 21 has no development, perhaps a coincidence, but some might tell you otherwise, as there is a **haunted house** at Km 20. Past the haunted house the highway twists and climbs to the summit, with its transmitter towers known as **Las Nubes**. You can turn left at the summit, just beyond the towers, and take a narrow road that runs along the ridge. Close to the end of the paved road, a small turning leads to a spectacular view of the valley of Lake Managua, Península Chiltepe, the Pacific Ocean and the northern volcanic chain, Los Maribios, that runs from the province of León and into Chinandega.

Reserva Privada Silvestre Montibelli
Km 19, Carretera a Ticuantepe, T2220-9801, www.montibelli.com, Tue-Sun, turn right at the sign for the reserve and follow signs for 2.5 km, by reservation 3 days in advance only.

Montibelli Private Nature Reserve is a family-owned nature park in greater Managua and one of the Pacific Basin's best forest reserves for birdwatching. Montibelli protects 162 ha of forest at an altitude of 360-720 m. The combination of its forest and elevation allow a more comfortable climate than Managua, with temperatures ranging from 18-26°C. The sandy Sierras' soil is super-fertile, but also very susceptible to erosion, making projects like Montibelli all the more valuable for their preservation of the mountain wildlife and vegetation. The property once had three separate shade-coffee haciendas; today only 22 ha are dedicated to coffee production and another 8 ha to fruit cultivation, the rest is set aside as forest reserve.

The tropical dry forest has three principal nature walks, 1-3 km in length, which you can combine up to 7 km. The forest is home to 115 species of tree and there are more than 100 species of bird including toucans, parrots, mot-mots, trogons, manikins and hummingbirds. There are also an impressive 40 species of butterfly as well as wild boar, agouti and howler monkeys.

The old coffee hacienda house acts as a small museum and on the back patio meals are served by prior arrangement. Birdwatching or a butterfly tour with a local guide is US$45 per person with breakfast. The reserve also offers guided trekking for US$15 per person (minimum of two). Every Sunday there are group nature walks that finish with a farm-style *parillada* of grilled meats and the Belli family's excellent organic coffee.

Reserva Natural El Chocoyero
Km 21.5, Carretera a Ticuantepe, turn right at the sign for the reserve and then follow signs for 7 km, T2276-7810, US$4, the rangers act as guides.

The park's 184 ha is home to 154 species of flora and 217 species of fauna and there are 2.5 km of trails, the best one being Sendero El Congo for its howler monkeys. It is also easy to see agouti, hummingbirds, butterflies and coral snakes, but the big attraction here are parakeets (the park's name comes from the ubiquitous *chocoyo*, Nicaraguan for parakeet). Pacific parakeets (*Aratinga strenua*) nest here in staggering

Tip...
Arriving in the early afternoon allows time to explore the park and see the parakeets coming home to nest: a glorious racket.

numbers –there are around 700-900 couples – and the best place to see them is at the El Chocoyero waterfall where the cliffs are dotted with tiny holes that they use for nesting.

To get to Montibelli or El Chocoyero on public transport, take a bus from Mercado Israel Lewites (or La UCA, Managua's University bus terminal) to La Concepción or San Marcos and tell the driver you want to get off at the entrance; it is then a long dusty or muddy walk depending on the season. Taxis can be hired for US$40-60 return trip with a wait.

Tourist information

Ministerio de Medio Ambiente y Recursos Naturales (MARENA)
Km 12.5, Carretera Norte, T2233-1112, www.marena.gob.ni. Mon-Fri 0800-1700.
Information on nature reserves and parks.

Nicaraguan Institute of Tourism (INTUR)
1 block south and 1 block west of the Crowne Plaza Hotel (the old Intercontinental), T2254-5191, www. visitnicaragua.us. Mon-Fri 0800-1700.
They have maps, flyers and free brochures in English, but are generally not geared up for public visits.
The airport INTUR is just past the immigration check.

Where to stay

Managua Airport

$$$ Best Western Las Mercedes
Km 11 Carretera Norte, directly across from international terminal of airport, T2255-9900, www.lasmercedes.com.ni.
Conveniently located for flight connections. Rooms are generic and comfortable enough, but poor value.

$$$ Camino Real
Km 9.5 Carretera Norte, T2255-5888, www.caminoreal.com.ni.
A popular option for delayed passengers or those en route to other destinations. Rooms are comfortable, modern and well equipped, but those close to the pool are often noisy (early-risers take note).

Martha Quezada
Commonly known as Ticabus after the international bus terminal, Martha Quezada has plentiful budget lodgings, most of them very basic and grungy. The streets are increasingly unsafe for wandering and you should stay alert at all times.

$$$ Hotel Crowne Plaza
'El viejo Hotel Inter', in front of the Plaza Inter shopping centre, T2228-3530, www.crowneplaza.com.
This is one of the most historic buildings in Managua, home to the foreign press for more than a decade and the new Sandinista government briefly in the early 1980s. Some rooms have lake views but are generally small for the price.

$$$ Mansión Teodolinda
INTUR, 1 c al sur, 1 c abajo, T2228-1050, www.teodolinda.com.ni.
This hotel, popular with business people, has good quality, unpretentious rooms, with Wi-Fi and kitchenettes. There's also a pool, bar, restaurant, gym, vehicle rental agency, transport to/from the airport and laundry service. Recommended.

$$-$ Los Cisneros
Ticabus, 1 c al norte, 1½ c abajo, T2222-3535, www.hotelloscisneros.com.
Comfortable apartments and rooms overlooking a lush garden with hammock space. All have cable TV, a/c and Wi-Fi, but only the apartments have hot water. Rooms and apartments are cheaper with fan. Los Cisneros can organize transit to the airport and tours all over the country.

$$-$ Pandora Hostel
Ticabus, 1 c al sur, 1 c arriba, T8408-4282, www.pandorahostel.com.
Light, airy and relaxed, this is a great place to begin or end a journey. A stone's

throw from the Ticabus terminal, they offer affordable dorm beds and chilled-out communal spaces with hammocks and sofas. Safe and recommended

$ Hostal Dulce Sueño
Ticabus, ½ c arriba, T2228-4125, www.hostaldulcesueno.com.
A stone's throw from the Ticabus terminal, this budget hotel has clean, reasonable rooms with fan and private bath (some have TV), and a relaxing patio with rocking chairs. Simple, family-run and economical. Kitchen and laundry service, cooked breakfast on request.

Bolonia

$$$ Hotel Europeo
Canal 2, 75 vrs abajo, T2268-2130, www.hoteleuropeo.com.ni.
Each room is different and some have interesting furnishings. The rooms out back are best. Restaurant, bar, business centre, secure parking, laundry service, guard and pool. Price includes continental breakfast. Staff are friendly and helpful. A quiet location.

$$$ La Posada del Angel
Opposite Iglesia San Francisco, T2268-7228.
This hotel, filled with interesting art work and antique furniture, has lots of personality. Good, clean rooms have private cable TV, a/c, minibar, Wi-Fi and telephone. There's also a pool, restaurant, office centre and laundry service. Breakfast is included. Book in advance.

$$ Posadita de Bolonia
Canal 2, 3 c abajo, 75 m al sur, casa 12, T2268-6692.
This intimate hotel has 8 rooms with private bath, a/c, cable TV, telephone and Wi-Fi. It's in a quiet area, close to several galleries, and operates as

a **Costeña** agent. The friendly owner speaks English and is helpful. Breakfast included. Recommended.

Metrocentro

$$$$-$$$ Elements Boutique Hotel
Colonial Los Robles, contiguo a Plaza Cuba, T2277-0718, www.elements-hb.com.
Stylish and tasteful, this smart place has slick rooms and suites, bar-lounge, garden, pool, gym and all modern amenities. Breakfast included.

$$$ Hotel Los Robles
Restaurante La Marseillaise, 30 vrs al sur, T2267-3008, www.hotellosrobles.com.
Managua's best B&B offers 14 comfortable rooms with classy furnishings, cable TV, Wi-Fi and luxurious bathtubs. The beautiful colonial interior is complemented by a lush, cool garden, complete with bubbling fountain. Book in advance. Recommended.

$$$ Real Intercontinental Metrocentro
Metrocentro shopping plaza, T2276-8989, www.realhotelsandresorts.com.
Nicaragua's finest international hotel, popular with business travellers. It has 157 well-attired rooms, pool, restaurant, bar and secretary service. Special weekend and multi-day rates with some tour operators.

$$$-$$ Hotel El Almendro
Rotonda Rubén Darío, 1 c sur, 3 c abajo (behind big wall, ring bell), T2270-1260, www.hotelelalmendro.com.
2 blocks from La UCA (the university), this private, secure hotel has good, comfortable rooms, pool, pleasant garden space, private parking and studio apartments (**$$$**) with kitchenettes. It's a decent choice. Breakfast included.

$$ Hotel Aloha
McDonald's Metrocentro,
1 c abajo, 2 c norte, T2277-0251,
www.hotelalohanicaragua.com.
Nestled in a quiet residential cul-de-sac, Aloha has comfortable rooms (some are a bit dark, ask to see before accepting) with good solid wooden furniture, cable TV, safe boxes and Wi-Fi. The lobby is clean and secure. Attentive service. Rates include breakfast buffet.

$$ Colibrí
Monte de los Olivos, 1 c al lago,
1½ c abajo, T2252-4300, www.
colibrihotelmanagua.com.
A clean, well-kept hotel with a pleasant little garden. Rooms are small and simple, comfortable and well attired and include cable TV, a/c, safe and Wi-Fi. Breakfast also included. Tranquil, secure and good access to a few nearby restaurants.

$$-$ Managua Backpackers' Inn
Monte Los Olivos, 1 c al lago, 1 c abajo,
½ c al lago, Casa 55, T2267-0006,
www.managuahostel.com.
The only budget hostel in the Metrocentro area is kitted out with thrifty dorms ($) and simple private rooms ($$-$). There's also a pool, hammocks and shared kitchen. They offer tourist information and are happy to help.

Las Colinas

$$$-$ Managua Hills B&B
Primera Entrada a las Colinas,
2 c arriba y 2 c al sur, T2276-2323,
www.managuahills.com.
With a refreshing swimming pool and beautiful leafy grounds, Managua Hills is a world away from the chaos of the city. Accommodation includes a range of well-appointed rooms ($$$-$$) and a mixed 8-bed dorm ($). Recommended.

Restaurants

The Metrocentro shopping centre has several convenient eateries ($) in its food court on the bottom level, including cheaper versions of good Nicaraguan restaurants. Lunch buffets are not all-you-can-eat: rather, you are charged for what you ask to be put on your plate, but this is still the most economical way to eat a big meal in Managua.

Martha Quezada

$$$-$$ Jimmy Three Fingers Alabama Rib Shack
Los Robles, de Marea Alta, 400 vrs arriba,
T2299-9704.
Authentic, home-cooked Southern food. In fact, you won't find better baby-back ribs in all of Central America. Casual and fun. Highly recommended.

$$ Ananda
Estatua de Montoya 10 vrs arriba,
T2228-4140. Daily 0700-2100.
Nicaragua's original non-meat eatery and still one of the best. They serve wholesome vegetarian food, juices, smoothies, breakfasts and soups.

$$ Rancho Tiscapa
Gate at Military Hospital, 300 vrs sur,
T2268-4290.
Laid-back ranch-style eatery and bar. They serve traditional dishes like *indio viejo, gallo pinto* and *cuajada con tortilla*. Good food and a great, breezy view of new Managua and Las Sierras. Recommended.

$ Mirna's
Near Pensión Norma. Open 0700-1500.
Good-value breakfasts and *comidas*, lunch buffet 1200-1500 popular with

travellers and Nicaraguans, friendly service. Recommended.

Bolonia

$$$ El Churrasco
Rotonda El Güegüence, T2266-6661, www.churrasconi.com.
This is where the Nicaraguan president and parliamentary members decide the country's future over a big steak. Try the restaurant's namesake which is an Argentine-style cut with garlic and parsley sauce. Recommended.

$ A La Vista Buffet
Canal 2, 2 c abajo, ½ c lago (next to Pulpería América). Lunch only 1130-1430.
Nicaragua's best lunch buffet. They do a staggering and inexpensive variety of pork, chicken, beef, rice dishes, salads and vegetable mixers, plantains, potato crêpes and fruit drinks. Popular with local television crews and reporters, as well as local office workers, who are often queueing down the street at midday. Highly recommended.

Metrocentro

$$$ Casa de las Nogueras
Av Principal Los Robles No R 17, T2278-2506.
A popular and often-recommended high-class dining establishment. They serve fine international and Mediterranean cuisine on a pleasant colonial patio. The interior, meanwhile, boasts sumptuous and ornate decoration. A Managua institution.

$$$ Don Cándido
Where El Chamán used to be, 75 vrs sur, T2277-2485, www. restaurantedoncandido.com.
The place to enjoy a good grilled steak. Carnivores will delight at the array of

well-presented options, including cuts of *churrasco*, tenderloin, rib-eye, fillet, New York and many others. All meat is certified 100% Aberdeen Angus.

$$$-$$ Don Parrillón
Zona Hippos, 2 c sur, T2270-0471.
Another meat and grill option conveniently located in the heart of Managua's Zona Rosa. Look for the little chimney chugging away on the street.

$$ El Muelle
Intercontinental Metrocentro, 1½ c arriba, T2278-0056.
Well-established Managua seafood joint. There's excellent *pargo al vapor* (steamed red snapper), *dorado a la parrilla*, *cocktail de pulpo* (octopus) and great ceviche. It's a crowded, informal setting with outdoor seating.

$$ La Cocina de Doña Haydée
Carretera a Masaya Km 4.5, 71 Paseo de la Unión Europea, T2270-6100, www. lacocina.com.ni. Mon-Sun 0730-2230.
Once a popular family kitchen eatery that has gone upscale. They serve traditional Nicaraguan food; try the *surtido* dish for 2, the *nacatamales* and traditional *Pío V* dessert, a sumptuous rum cake. Popular with foreign residents.

$ El Guapinol
Food Court Metrocentro. Daily 0800-2100.
The best of the food court eateries with excellent grilled meat dishes, chicken, fish and a hearty veggie dish (US$5). Try *copinol*, a dish with grilled beef, avocado, fried cheese, salad and tortilla and *gallo pinto*, US$4.

$ Terraza Cevichería
Monte de los Olivos, 1 c al lago, 1 c abajo.
A simple little restaurant serving good-value, tasty, fresh ceviche, seafood and

cold beer. Their shrimp and octopus salad claims to be the best in town. There's an open-air seating area, always packed at lunchtime.

Cafés

Casa del Café
Edificio Pellas, 1 c arriba, ½ c sur, T8775-7453, www.casadelcafe.com.ni.
The mother of all cafés in Managua, with an airy upstairs seating area that makes the average coffee taste much better. Good turkey sandwiches, desserts, pies and *empanadas*. There are numerous branches around the city, but none have the charm and fresh air of the Altamira branch. Popular and recommended.

Around Managua

$$$ Gastronomía El Buzo
Carretera Sur Km 13, 100 vrs al sur, 100 vrs arriba, T2265-8336.
Managed by Chef Alessio Casimirri, El Buzo serves superb Mediterranean cuisine. Specialities include seafood, pastas and pizzas. Great reports and attentive service.

$$$-$$ Zacatelimón
Del Club Terraza 3 c arriba, Pista Jean Paul Genie, Centro Comercial El Tiangue 2, www.zacatelimon.com. Mon-Sat 0700-2100, Sun 0800-1600.
American-style comfort food including sandwiches, burgers, milkshakes and pecan pie. Take a taxi to get there.

$$-$ Quesillos el Pipe
Km 12.8 Carretera a Masaya.
A handy pit-stop on the way to Masaya, this popular joint serves traditional *quesillos* (and little else). One is enough for most appetites.

Bars and clubs

The biggest rage in Nicaragua dancing is *reggaeton*, a Spanish language rap-reggae. Dancing is an integral part of Nicaraguan life, at any age, and the line between *el bar* and *la discoteca* is not very well defined. Generally, people over 30 dance at bars and the discos are for 18-30 years.

Bar Chamán
Universidad Nacional de Ingeniería (UNI), 1½ c norte, T2272-1873, www.chamanbar.com.
US$3 entrance which includes US$1.50 drinks coupon. A young, devout dancing crowd sweats it out to salsa, rock and reggaeton.

Entertainment

Cinema
If possible, see a comedy; the unrestrained laughter of the Nicaraguan audience is sure to make the movie much funnier. You'll find screens at all the city's big shopping malls (see Shopping, below). Alternatively, try: **Alianza Francesa**, *Altamira, Mexican Embassy, ½ c norte, T2267-2811, www. alianzafrancesa.org.ni.* Frequent screenings of French-language films from around the world, free admission, art exhibits during the day.

Dance and theatre
Managua has no regular dance and theatre performances so it will take a bit of research to time your visit to coincide with a live show. To find out what's on the cultural and musical calendar for the weekend in Managua, Granada and León, check the *La Prensa* supplement *Viernes Chiquito* every Thu.

Festivals

19 Jul 19 de Julio is the anniversary of the fall of the last Somoza in 1979, a Sandinista party in front of the stage with the big acoustic shell at the *malecón*. The party attracts around 100,000 plus from all over the country; don't forget to wear the Sandinista colours of black and red.

1-10 Aug On 1 Aug a statue of **Santo Domingo**, Managua's patron saint and Nicaragua's most diminutive saint, is brought from his hilltop church in Santo Domingo in the southern outskirts of Managua, in a crowded and heavily guarded (by riot police) procession to central Managua.

7 Dec La Purísima, celebrating the purity of the Virgin countrywide and particularly in Managua in the more than 600 barrios of the city. Private altars are erected to the Virgin Mary and food gifts are given to those who arrive to sing to the altars, with some families serving up as many as 5000 *nacatamales* in a night.

Shopping

Handicrafts

The best place for handicrafts in Managua is the **Mercado Central Roberto Huembes**, where there's an ample selection from most of the country artisans. **Note** All the markets have some crafts, but avoid the **Mercado Oriental**. Possibly the biggest informal market in Latin America, this is the heart of darkness in Managua and unsafe for casual exploration. The most complete of the non-market artisan shops is **Galería Códice** (Colonial Los Robles, Hotel Colón, 1 c sur, 2½ c arriba, No 15, T2267-2635, www.galeriacodice. com, Mon-Sat 0900-1830), whose selection includes rarely found items like rosewood carvings from the Caribbean coast and ceramic dolls from Somoto.

Shopping malls

The 3 big shopping malls, in order of increasing social exclusivity, are the Plaza Inter, Metrocentro and Galerías Santo Domingo. The cinemas are better in Santo Domingo and Plaza Inter, but the food court is much better in Metrocentro.

Supermarkets

3 big chains are represented in Managua, **Supermercado La Colonia** being the best. It is located in Plaza España and at the roundabout in the Centroamérica neighbourhood. **Supermercado La Unión**, on Carretera a Masaya, is similar to La Colonia. **Supermercados Pali**, branches of which can be found scattered around the city, is the cheapest, with goods still in their shipping boxes.

What to do

Baseball

The national sport and passion is baseball, which has been established in Nicaragua for more than 100 years. Games in Managua are on Sun mornings at the national stadium, **Estadio Denis Martínez**, just north of the Barrio Martha Quezada. Check the local newspapers for the game schedule. Seats cost US$1-5 per person.

Language schools

Academia Europea, *Hotel Princess, 1 c abajo, ½ c sur, T2270-3210, www.academiaeuropea.com*. The best school in Managua, with structured classes of varying lengths and qualified instructors.

Universidad Centroamericana, *better known as La UCA, T2278-3923 and T2267-0352, www.uca.edu.ni*. Runs Spanish courses that are cheaper than some private institutions, but with larger classes.

Libraries and cultural centres
Biblioteca Roberto Incer Barquero, *Semáforos del 7 Sur, 300 m al este, T2265-0500, www.biblioteca.bcn.gob.ni*. This modern library next to the Central Bank has a collection of some 70,000 books. It also features art exhibitions and a numismatic collection.

Centro Cultural de España en Nicaragua (CCEN), *1a entrada a Las Colinas, 7 c al este, T2276-0733, www.ccenicaragua.org*. The Cultural Centre of Spain in Nicaragua hosts arts courses and public events, including regular talks and exhibitions. Facilities include a media library and e-LAB for production work.

Centro Cultural PAC, *Rotonda Rubén Darío, 1 c al oeste, 1 c al sur, hispamer.online.com.ni*. Founded by the poet Pablo Antonio Cuadra, this cultural centre offers a host of activities from yoga to painting. There's also an auditorium, bookshop and museum. Located on the top floor of the Hispamer building.

Tour operators
See also local tour operators throughout the book.

Careli Tours, *Las Cumbres, Casa A-14, opposite the Escala building, T2223-2020, www.carelitours.com*. One of Nicaragua's oldest tour operators with a professional service, very good English speaking guides and traditional tours to all parts of Nicaragua.

Solentiname Tours, *Lomas de Monserrat de Albanisa, 1 c abajo última casa, www.solentinametours.com*. Eco-friendly tours of the lake, Caribbean coast, colonial cities and Río San Juan. Spanish, English, German, French and Russian spoken.

Tours Nicaragua, *Centro Richardson, contiguo al Banco Central de Nicaragua, T2265-3095, www.toursnicaragua.com*. One of the best, offering captivating and personalized tours with a cultural, historical or ecological emphasis. Guides, transfers, accommodation and admission costs are included in the price. English speaking, helpful, professional and highly recommended. All tours are private and pre-booked; no walk-ins please.

Va Pues, *Los Robles, Restaurante Don Parrillon, 1 c arriba, ½ c norte, T2270-1936, www.vapues.com*. A highly reputable and long-running tour operator offering cultural and ecological packages to destinations across the country. Options include kayaking on the Río San Juan, hiking in the Maribios, wildlife observation on Ometepe and cultural tours of the Solentiname islands.

Transport

Air
Managua International Airport is on the eastern outskirts of Managua. Upon landing you must pay US$10 at the immigration counter. Taxis to Metrocentro, Bolonia or Martha Quezada should cost US$5-10, but airport taxis may try to charge double; journey time is 20-30 mins in good traffic. Be sure to have precise directions in Spanish and use licensed vehicles only. A taxi hailed on the highway outside will charge US$5-6, but these are less secure and should be avoided if arriving after dark.

Domestic flights Nicaragua's sole domestic airline is **La Costeña**, T2298-5360, www.lacostena.com.ni, which operates a small fleet of single-prop

Cessna Caravans and 2-prop Short 360s. In the Cessnas there is no room for overhead lockers, so pack light and check in all you can. For checked luggage on all flights there is a 15-kg weight limit per person for one-way flight, 25 kg for round-trip tickets; any excess is payable on check-in. There is a US$2 exit tax on domestic flights.

Tickets can be bought at the domestic terminal, which is located just west of the exit for arriving international passengers, or from travel agents or tour operators.

Fuel and ticket prices are rising and schedules are subject to change at any time.

To **Bilwi** (Puerto Cabezas) 0600, 1030, 1400 (Mon, Wed, Fri), 1½ hrs, US$112 one-way, US$164 return; to **Bluefields**, 0630, 1100 (Tue, Thu, Sat), 1430, 1 hr, US$97 one-way, US$152 return; to **Bonanza**, 0800, 1½ hrs, US$111 one-way, US$174 return; to **Corn Island**, 0630, 1430, 1½ hrs, US$122 one-way, US$180 return; to **Siuna**, 0900, 1½ hrs, US$97 one-way, US$142 return; to **Waspam**, 1200 (Tue and Sat), 1½ hrs, US$111 one-way, US$174 return. For return times, see individual destinations. **Note** At the time of research, flights to Isla Ometepe, Rosita, Tola, San Juan de Nicaragua (also known as San Juan de Norte) and San Carlos had been suspended temporarily; contact **La Costeña** for the latest news.

International flights You should reconfirm your flight out of Nicaragua 48 hrs in advance by calling the local airline office during business hours Mon-Sat. Most good hotels will provide this service. There's a US$35 exit tax on all international flights, sometimes included in the price of your ticket.

Bus
Intercity buses Express buses are dramatically faster than regular routes. Payment is often required in advance and seat reservations are becoming more common.

The microbuses at La UCA (pronounced 'La OO-ka'), close to the Metrocentro and opposite the University, are highly recommended if travelling to Granada, León or Masaya. To **Granada**, every 15 mins or when full, 0530-2100, US$1.25, 1 hr. To **Diriamba**, every 30 mins or when full, 0530-2000, US$1.15, 45 mins. To **Jinotepe**, 0530-2000, every 20 mins or when full, US$1.15, 1 hr. To **León**, every 30 mins, 0730-2100, US$2.75, 1½ hrs. To **Masaya**, every 15 mins or when full, 0530-2000, US$0.75, 40 mins.

Mercado Roberto Huembes, also called Mercado Central, is used for destinations southwest. To **Granada**, every 15 mins, 0520-2200, Sun 0610-2100, US$0.75, 1½ hrs. To **Masaya**, every 20 mins, 0625-1930, Sun until 1600, US$0.50, 50 mins. To **Peñas Blancas**, every 30 mins or when full, US$3.50, 2½ hrs; or go to Rivas for connections. To **Rivas**, every 30 mins, 0600-1900, US$2, 1¾ hrs. To **San Juan del Sur**, 1000 and 1600, US$3.25, 2½ hrs; or go to Rivas for connections. To **San Jorge** (ferry to Ometepe), every 30 mins, 0600-2100, US$2.20, 2 hrs; or go to Rivas for connections.

Mercado Mayoreo, for destinations east and then north or south. To **Boaco**, every 20 mins, 0500-1800, US$2, 3 hrs. To **Camoapa**, every 40 mins, 0630-1700, US$2.20, 3 hrs. To **El Rama**, 5 daily, 0500-2200, US$7.50, 6-7 hrs; express bus 1400, 1800, 2200, US$9, 5-6 hrs. To **Estelí**, express bus, hourly 0545-1730, US$3, 2½ hrs. To **Jinotega**, hourly, 0400-

1730, US$3.50, 4 hrs; or go to Matagalpa for connections. To **Juigalpa**, every 20 mins, 0500-1730, US$2.50, 4 hrs. To **Matagalpa**, express bus, hourly, 0330-1800, US$2.10, 2½ hrs. To **Ocotal**, express buses, 12 daily, 0545-1745, US$4.50, 3½ hrs. To **San Rafael del Norte**, express bus, 1500, US$5, 4 hrs. To **San Carlos**, 0500, 0600, 0700, 1300, US$8, 7-10 hrs. To **Somoto**, 8 daily, US$4, 4 hrs.

Mercado Israel Lewites, also called Mercado Boer, for destinations west and northwest. Some microbuses leave from here too. To **Chinandega**, express buses, every 30 mins, 0600-1915, US$3, 2½ hrs. To **Corinto**, every hour, 0500-1715, US$3.50, 3 hrs. To **Diriamba**, every 20 mins, 0530-1930, US$1.10, 1 hr 15 mins. To **El Sauce**, express buses, 0730, 1430, 1600, US$3.25, 3½ hrs. To **Guasaule**, 0430, 0530, 1530, US$3.25, 4 hrs. To **Jinotepe**, every 20 mins, 0530-1930, US$0.50, 1 hr 30 mins. To **León**, every 30 mins, 0545-1645, US$1.50, 2½ hrs; express buses, every 30 mins, 0500-1645, US$1.85, 2 hrs; microbuses, every 30 mins or when full, 0600-1700, US$2.75, 1½ hrs. To **Pochomil**, every 20 mins, 0600-1920, US$1.10, 2 hrs.

International buses If time isn't a critical issue, international buses are a cheap and efficient way to travel between Nicaragua and other Central American countries. When leaving Managua you will need to check in 1 hr in advance with passport and ticket. Several companies operate the international routes, but **Ticabus** is the most popular. See page 257.

Car
From the south, the Carretera a Masaya leads directly to Managua's new centre,

Metrocentro; try to avoid arriving from this direction from 0700-0900 when the entrance to the city is heavily congested. The Pan-American Highway (Carretera Panamericana) enters Managua at the international airport and skirts the eastern shores of Lake Managua. Stay on this highway until you reach the old centre before attempting to turn south in search of the new one. Av Bolívar runs south from the old centre past the Plaza Inter shopping centre and into the heart of new Managua; turn east onto the Pista de la Resistencia to reach the Metrocentro shopping mall. If arriving from León and the northwest you need to head east from Km 7 of Carretera Sur to find new Managua.

Car hire All agencies have rental desks at the international airport arrivals terminal. It is not a good idea to rent a car for getting around Managua, as it is a confusing city, fender benders are common and an accident could see you end up in jail (even if you are not at fault). Outside the capital, main roads are better marked and a rental car means you can get around more freely.

For good service and 24-hr roadside assistance, the best rental agency is **Budget**, with rental cars at the airport, T2263-1222, and Holiday Inn, T2270-9669. Their main office is just off Carretera Sur, Estatua de Montoya, 1 c sur, 1 c arriba, T2255-0001. Approximate cost of a small Toyota is US$50 per day while a 4WD (a good idea if exploring) is around US$100 per day with insurance and 200 km a day included; 4WD weekly rental rates range from US$600-750.

ON THE ROAD
The art of taxi hire

Despite the Managua taxi driver's liberal interpretation of Nicaraguan driving laws, his knowledge of the city is second to none and taxis are often the best way to get around the city. However, a number of travellers have reported disturbing experiences with unlicensed *piratas*, who scout the bus stations for unsuspecting victims or use well-dressed women to befriend potential targets on intercity buses. The experience usually involves the victim being robbed at knife or gunpoint and forced to make cash withdrawals at several different ATMs. These types of incident have been reported in Managua, Masaya and Rivas.

If you must hire a taxi on the street, follow this basic procedure and under no circumstances get into a vehicle with someone you've just met, no matter how friendly or harmless they may seem:

- Check that the number on the side of the vehicle matches the license plate (and make a mental note of it).
- Lean into the passenger window and state your desired destination (veiling your accent as best possible to try and keep the rates down).

- If the driver nods in acceptance, ask him how much – *¿por cuánto me lleva?*
- Haggle if necessary, and insist upon a private fare, not a *colectivo* (shared taxi) – this will cost double, but it is worth it.
- Ask to see the driver's identification.
- Sit next to the driver at all times.

It is normal for most drivers to quote the going rate plus 5 to 20 córdobas extra for foreigners. When you reach your destination pay the driver with the most exact money possible (they never have change, an effective built-in tip technique). Some drivers have been known to feign communication problems for short fares at night, looking for a healthy profit.

For an early morning or late night journey it is especially wise to call a radio taxi, they are private, safer and in most cases in better condition than the other taxis.

Taxi
Taxis without red licence plates are *piratas* (unregistered); avoid them. Taxis can be flagged down in the street. Find out the fare before you board the vehicle. Fares are always per person, not per car. Taxis hired from the airport or shopping malls are more expensive but secure.

Radio taxis pick you up and do not stop for other passengers; they are much more secure for this reason and cost twice as much: **Cooperativa 25 de Febrero**, T2222-4728; **Cooperativa 2 de Agosto**, T2263-1512; **Cooperativa René Chávez**, T2222-3293; **Cooperativa Mario Lizano**, T2268-7669. Get a quote on the phone and reconfirm agreed cost when the taxi arrives.

Masaya
& around

Overlooked by ancient volcanoes and home to communities still rooted in their distant indigenous past, Masaya and the surrounding Pueblos Blancos (white towns) are distinguished by archaic folklore and vibrant craftwork. Irresistibly sleepy until fiesta time, these ancient settlements play host to bustling workshops, Nicaragua's best *artesanía* market and a famously hospitable population who are directly descended from the Chorotega peoples. Among their attributes is a fierce and indomitable spirit that has been roused time and again during difficult periods. It was here that the legendary chief Dirangén fought against the Spaniards; here that bloody rebellions erupted against Somoza; and here that the nation made a final stand against US invader William Walker. It is no surprise then that the region also spawned Augusto Sandino, Nicaragua's most celebrated revolutionary.

Nearly every barrio in Masaya (altitude 234 m, population 140,000) has its own little church, but two dominate the city. In Masaya's leafy Parque Central is La Parroquia de Nuestra Señora de la Asunción, a late baroque church that dates from 1750. The clean lines and simple elegance of its interior make it one of the most attractive churches in Nicaragua and well worth a visit.

San Jerónimo, though not on Parque Central, is the spiritual heart of Masaya. This attractive domed church, visible from miles around, is home to the city's patron Saint Jerome and a focal point for his more than two-month-long festival. The celebration begins on 30 September and continues until early December, making it by far the longest patron saint festival in Nicaragua and perhaps in Latin America. The downtown area can be explored on foot.

Mercado Nacional de Artesanías
Southeast corner of Parque Central, 1 c arriba, daily 0900-1800; folkloric performances Thu 1900-2200. There is a DHL office open daily 1000-1700 inside the market in case you end up buying more than you can carry.

Most people come to Masaya to shop and the country's best craft market is here in the 19th-century Mercado Nacional de Artesanías. The late Gothic walls of the original market were damaged by shelling and the inside of the market burned during the 1978-1979 Revolution. After two decades of sitting in ruins it is today dedicated exclusively to handmade crafts.

There are 80 exhibition booths and several restaurants inside the market. Leather, ceramics, cigars, hammocks, soapstone sculptures, masks, textiles and primitivista paintings are just some of the goods on offer. Every Thursday night from 1900 to 2200 there is a live performance on the market's stage. These usually include one of Masaya's many folkloric dance groups with beautifully costumed performers and live marimba music accompaniment.

A **folkloric museum** ① *US$2*, located inside the market near the administrative offices, features photographic exhibitions, costumes, musical instruments and crafts from Masaya and around.

Masaya's most famous craft is its cotton **hammocks**, which are perhaps the finest in the world and a tradition that pre-dates the arrival of the Spanish. The density of weave and quality of materials help determine the hammock's quality; stretching the hammock will reveal the density of the weave. You can visit the hammock weavers (normally in very cramped conditions) in their homes; the highest concentration is one block east from the stadium on the *malecón* and one block north of the *viejo hospital*. With a deposit and 48-hours' notice, you can also custom-order a hammock in the workshops. If you have no intention of buying a hammock it is better not to visit the workshops.

Shopping tips

Nicaragua is one of the richest countries in the region for handmade crafts, though many of them, like the wicker furniture, are difficult to take back home. Variety, quality and prices are favourable. Every city and town has its market. Usually the meats, fruits and vegetables are inside the market, while the non-perishable goods are sold around the outside. Some kind of handmade crafts or products of local workmanship can be found in most markets around the country. It may take some digging to find some markets as Nicaragua is not a mainstream tourist destination and the markets are not adapted to the visitor. The major exceptions are the craft market in Masaya, which is dedicated to the talents of the local and national craftsmen, and the central market in Managua, Roberto Huembes, which has a big section dedicated to crafts from all over the country. Crafts sold at hotels tend to be significantly more expensive.

Items to look out for include: cotton hammocks and embroidered handmade clothing from Masaya; earthenware ceramics from San Juan de Oriente, Condega, Somoto, Mozonte, Matagalpa and Jinotega; wooden tableware from Masaya; wooden rocking chairs from Masatepe; wicker furniture from Granada; *jícaro* cups from Rivas; *agave* Panama hats from Camoapa; leather goods from León and Masaya; home-made sweets from Diriomo; *agave* rope decor from Somoto; coconut and seashell jewellery from the Caribbean coast and islands; paintings and sculptures from Managua; balsa wood carvings and primitivist paintings from the Solentiname archipelago.

Shoppers will find visits to artisan workshops interesting and buying direct from the artisan is often rewarding. Prices in the Nicaraguan markets are not marked up in anticipation of bargaining or negotiation. A discount of 5-10% can be obtained if requested, but the prices quoted are what the merchant or artisan hopes to get.

Laguna de Masaya and El Malecón

The best view of the deep blue 27-sq-km Laguna de Masaya and the Masaya volcanic complex is from the *malecón*, or waterfront, often frequented by romantic couples. The lake is 300 m below, sadly polluted and unfit for swimming. Before the pump was installed in the late 19th century, all of the town's water was brought up from the lake in ceramic vases on women's heads: a 24-hour-a-day activity according to British naturalist Thomas Belt who marvelled at the ease with which the Masaya women dropped down into the crater and glided back out with a full load of water. There are more than 200 petroglyphs on the walls of the descent, but no official guides to take you; try the INTUR office or ask around locally.

The festivals of Masaya and the Pueblos de la Meseta are some of the richest, most evocative and staunchly celebrated in Nicaragua.

2-8 February, Virgen de la Candelaria (Diriomo) Festival for the patron saint, brought from Huehuetenango, Guatemala in 1720. Processions run from 21 January to 9 February with 2 February being her main feast day. On 2 February, a pilgrimage leaves from La Iglesia Guadalupe in Granada and arrives in Diriomo at 1000 to join the festivities. Dancing is performed by both children and adults, wearing masks and traditional costume. The dancers lead the procession up to the icon of La Virgen.

16 March, La Virgen de la Asunción (Masaya) Also known as the festival of the cross, commemorating how the icon miraculously diverted lava flows during the 1772 volcanic eruption.

3 April, Jesús del Rescate (Masaya) A procession of ox carts travel from Masaya to San Jorge.

24 April, Tope de las imágenes de San Marcos (San Marcos) This is the famous meeting of the icons of the four main saints of the region: San Sebastián (from Diriamba), Santiago (from Jinotepe), the black Virgen de Montserrat (from La Concepción) and San Marcos himself. They are paraded around in pairs until they all finally meet at El Mojón (on the highway between Diriamba and Jinotepe). It is a huge party with traditional dancing. The next day there is more dancing in the Parque Central and the four saints come out of the church together to tremendous fireworks, confetti and processions.

Week before Palm Sunday, San Lázaro (Masaya) A fun, if highly surreal, celebration in which dogs are dressed up in costumes.

Comunidad Indígena de Monimbó

The famous indigenous barrio of Monimbó is the heart and soul of Masaya. The Council of Elders, a surviving form of native government, still exists here and the beating of drums of deerskin stretched over an avocado trunk still calls people to festival and meetings and, in times of trouble, to war. In 1978, the people of Monimbó rebelled against Somoza's repressive Guardia Nacional, holding the barrio for one week using home-made contact bombs and other revolutionary handicrafts. This and other proud moments in Monimbó's revolutionary past are documented in the flag-draped **Museo Comunitario y Etnográfico La Insurreción de Monimbó** ① *Damas Salesianas 1½ c arriba, orlancabrera@hotmail.com, Mon-Fri 0900-1600, US$0.50.*

The neighbourhood is also famous for its industrious artisan workshops, which export their output all over Central America. They can be toured independently, but it is much easier to enlist a local guide. The highest concentration of workshops is located between the unattractive Iglesia Magdalena and the cemetery.

Mid-May, Santísma Trinidad (Masatepe) This festival for the patron saint lasts over a month from mid-May and includes famous horse parades.

17-29 June, San Pedro (Diría) Festivities include bullfights and violent ritualized fighting with cured wooden palettes.

24 June, San Juan Bautista (San Juan de Oriente) An often wild festival for the patron saint with ritual fighting in the streets between believers and lots of *chichero* music (brass and drum ensembles).

24-26 July, San Santiago (Jinotepe) Festival for the local patron saint.

26 July, Santa Ana (Niquinohomo) Patron saint festival with folkloric dancing and fireworks.

15 August, Día de la Virgen de la Asunción (Masaya) Monimbó festival honouring Mary Magdalene.

17-27 September, San Sebastián (Diriamba) The legendary *Güegüence* is performed by masked dancers in bright costumes accompanied by music played with indigenous and mestizo instruments, which together have come to represent the very identity of Pacific Nicaraguan mestizo culture.

30 September-early December (San Jerónimo, Masaya) 80 days of festivities, making it one of the longest parties in Latin America. Celebrations include processions and dances performed to the driving music of marimbas, such as *El Baile de las Inditas* and *Baile de las Negras* (Sundays throughout October and November), *Baile de los Diablitos* (last Sunday of November) and, most famous for its brutally humorous mocking of Nicaragua's public figures and policies, *El Toro Venado* (last Sunday in October and third Sunday in November).

Last Friday in October, Noche de Agüizotes (Masaya) A festival commemorating bad omens, in which participants dress up like ghouls and monsters.

26 November, Santa Catalina de Alejandría (Catarina) Patron saint festival.

31 December-1 January (San Silvestre, Catarina) The big fiesta in Catarina, with flower-festooned parades.

Fortaleza de Coyotepe

Carretera Masaya Km 28. Daily 0900-1600, US$2. Bring a torch/flashlight, or offer the guide US$2 to show you the cells below. The access road is a steep but short climb from the Carretera a Masaya, parking U$1.

Just outside Masaya city limits is the extinct volcanic cone of Coyotepe (Coyote Hill) and a post-colonial fortress. The fortress was built in 1893 by the Liberal president José Santos Zelaya to defend his control of Masaya and Managua from the Conservatives of Granada. In 1912, it saw action as the Liberals battled the US Marines and lost. Though donated to the Boy Scouts of Masaya during the 1960s, the fortress was used by the second General Somoza as a political prison. There are 43 cells on two floors that can be visited; people have reported hearing the distant echo of screams. The top deck offers a splendid 360-degree view of Masaya, Laguna de Masaya and the Masaya volcanoes, and on to Granada and its Volcán Mombacho.

Tourist information

INTUR
Calle Calvario, Semáforos del Colegio Bautista ½ c arriba delegacionmasaya@ gmail.com. Mon-Fri 0800-1700.
INTUR has a branch office in Masaya. They have maps of the city, flyers and information on events, but are otherwise not very useful.

Where to stay

Quality lodging in Masaya is very limited due to its proximity to Managua and Granada.

$$ Hotel Monimbó
Plaza Pedro Joaquín Chomorro, 1 c arriba, 1½ c norte, T2522-6867, www.hotelmonimbo.com.
The best place in town, situated in the barrio of Monimbó. 7 clean, quiet, comfortable, well-attired rooms with private bath, pleasant patio and garden space with relaxing hammocks. Breakfast included. Recommended.

$$-$ Casa Robleto
Av San Jerónimo, Parque San Jerónimo, 1½ c sur, T2522-2617, www.casarobleto. blogspot.com.
A traditional Nicaraguan guesthouse in an attractive colonial building, ably operated by the hospitable Don Frank and his family. Clean, simple, restful rooms overlook the interior courtyard while the lobby features elegant finishes and antique furniture.

$$-$ Maderas Inn
Bomberos, 2 c sur, T2522-5825, www.hotelmaderasinn.com.
A friendly little place with a pleasant family ambience and a variety of basic, slightly grungy rooms kitted out with private bath, a/c, cable TV. Several other economical options on the same street.

$$-$ Mirador del los Arcángeles
Mercado de Artesanías, 1½ c norte, T2522-3796, sirdi.16@hotmail.com.
A grand old building built at the turn of the 20th century. Rooms are on 2 floors and include cold-water showers and cable TV. Those with a/c cost more (**$$**). Do not leave valuable items unattended in the room. Wi-Fi available.

Restaurants

$$-$ 1900
Palí Central, ½ c sur. Closed Mon.
A well-presented restaurant with huge wooden gates and an outdoor patio with a small performance stage. They serve steaks, seafood, crêpes, sandwiches, coffee and wine. A good-value executive menu (**$**) is available for lunch Tue-Fri.

$$-$ Kaffe Café
East side of the Parque Central, www.restaurantekaffecafe.com.
International grub, including steaks, sandwiches, German sausages, burgers and pastas. Also good for strong coffees, cappuccinos, lattes and frappés. Patio seating inside or outdoors overlooking the park. Live music some evenings.

$ Comidas Criollas
South side of Parque Central.
This large, clean, buffet restaurant serves up healthy portions of Nica fare.

Cafés and bakeries

La Nani

Opposite the southern entrance of the artesanía market, www.lananicafe.com.
A clean, modern coffee shop serving good brews, bread, pastries and typical café fare, including sandwiches.

Festivals

See pages 60-61.

Transport

There are frequent bus services from Managua's Roberto Huembes market and La UCA bus station, as well as Granada's bus terminals. Many buses (including those with final destinations other than Masaya) do not pass through the city centre, but drop you at the traffic lights on the highway, several blocks north of the Parque Central.

Masaya

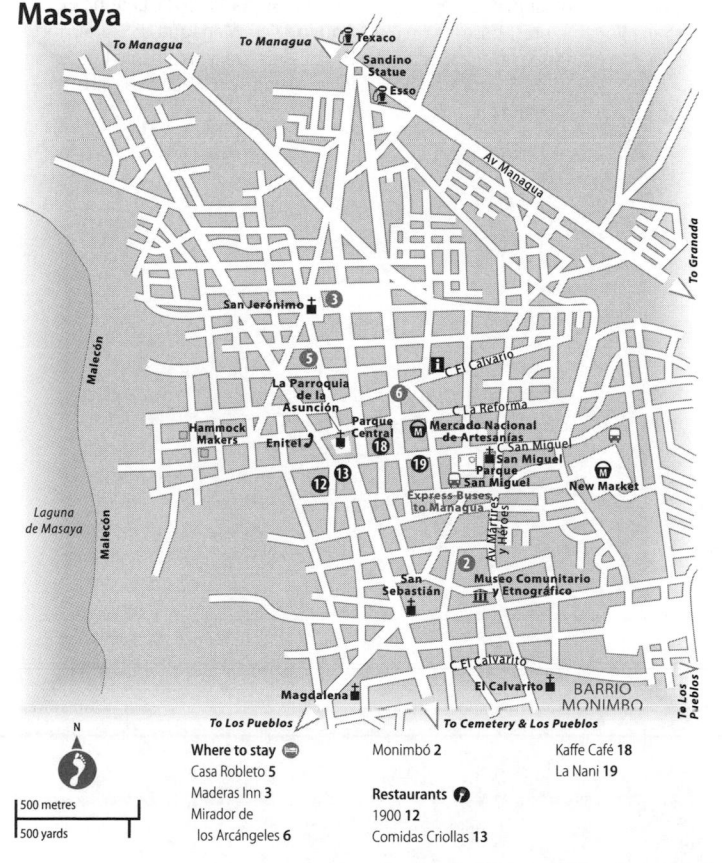

500 metres
500 yards

Where to stay 🛏
Casa Robleto **5**
Maderas Inn **3**
Mirador de
    los Arcángeles **6**

Monimbó **2**

Restaurants 🍴
1900 **12**
Comidas Criollas **13**

Kaffe Café **18**
La Nani **19**

Bus

Most buses depart from the regular market or Mercado Municipal, 4 blocks east of the south side of the artisan market. Express bus to **Managua** (Roberto Huembes), every 20 mins, 0500-1900, US$0.60, 50 mins. To **Jinotepe**, every 20 mins, 0500-1800, US$0.80, 1½ hrs. To **Granada**, every 30 mins, 0600-1800, US$0.50, 45 mins. To **Matagalpa**, 0600, 0700, US$2.75, 4 hrs (schedule subject to change).

From Parque San Miguelito, between the artisan and regular markets on Calle San Miguel, express buses leave for La UCA in **Managua**, every 30 mins, 0530-1900, US$0.60, 40 mins. You can also board any bus on the Carretera a Masaya to **Managua** or towards **Granada**. Note the sign above front windscreen for destination and flag it down. For **Parque Nacional Volcán Masaya** take any Managua bus and ask to step down at park entrance. Buses to **Valle de Apoyo** leave twice daily, 1000, 1530, 45 mins, US$0.70, then walk down the road that drops into the crater.

Taxi

Fares around town are US$0.40 per person anywhere in the city. Approximate taxi fares to: **Granada** US$15, **Laguna de Apoyo**, US$7, **Managua** US$20, **airport** US$25. Horse-drawn carriages (*coches*) are for local transport inside Masaya, US$0.50.

Masaya's intriguing cultural assets are complemented by vivid physical landscapes, including the area around Volcán Masaya, which has been threatening cataclysm for centuries. Hiking trails snake up and around the angry giant, promising unforgettable olfactory encounters and stirring views.

Nearby, the infinitely more sedate Laguna Apoyo is the country's most alluring crater lake, with eternally warm, soothing waters heated by underwater vents. This is a special, peaceful place that is largely unspoiled (although increasingly threatened) by human activities. The surrounding *mesa* of highland villages, known as Los Pueblos Blancos, with their historic churches and spirited festivals, extends all the way from Laguna de Apoyo to the Pacific coast.

Parque Nacional Volcán Masaya
T2528-1444, pvmasaya@ideay.net.ni, 0900-1645, US$4, including entrance to the museum. Any bus that runs between Masaya and Managua can drop you at the park entrance, Km 23, Carretera a Masaya, but the long, hot, uphill walk to the visitor centre, 1.5 km away, make a hired taxi (US$1.50), tour company or private car a valuable asset. Hitching is possible, as are guided hikes, US$0.70-3 per person payable at the museum before you set out.

The heavily smoking Volcán Masaya complex is one of the most unusual volcanoes in the Americas and reported to be one of only four on earth that maintain a constant pool of lava (neither receding nor discharging) in its open crater. It is a place of eerie beauty with its rugged lunar landscapes punctuated by delicate plant life. The main attraction, the smoldering Santiago crater, seems almost peaceful – until one recalls that it is an open vent to the centre of the earth and prone to sudden acts of geological violence.

The complex was called Popogatepe ('burning mountain') by the Chorotega people. In 1529, the Spanish chronicler Oviedo wrote that there were many ceremonies at the base of the mountain, including the supposed sacrifice of young women and boys to appease Chacitutique, the goddess of fire. In the adjacent village of Nindirí, Chief Tenderí told Oviedo about a magical fortune-teller who lived inside the crater: a very ugly old woman, naked, with black teeth, wrinkled skin and tangled hair. Oviedo became convinced that she was the Devil. Around the same time Friar Francisco de Bobadilla hiked to the summit to perform an exorcism and place a large wooden cross above the lava pool to keep the door to Hell (the lava pool) shut.

As it appears today, the Santiago crater, 500 m in circumference and 250 m deep, was created after a violent eruption in 1853. It erupted again in 1858 and fell silent until the 20th century, when it erupted in 1902, 1918, 1921, 1924, 1925, 1947, 1953 and 1965, before collapsing in 1985. In early 2001 the crater's gaseous output came almost to a complete stop and the resulting pressure created a minor eruption. Debris pelted the parking area at the summit (during visiting hours) with hundreds of flaming rocks. Exactly 10 minutes later the crater shot some tubes of lava on to the hillside just east of the parking area, setting it ablaze. Miraculously there were only minor injuries but several vehicles were badly damaged by falling stones. There have been no major explosions since then, but volcanologists noted significant episodes of gas and ash emission, as well as visible incandescence from the crater, in the years 2003 to 2006 and 2008. In 2012, the volcano spat out some hot rocks and began making ominous groaning noises; the park was temporarily closed to visitors, reopening several days later.

During your visit, watch out for any significant change in smoke colour, or any persistent rumbling, which may indicate a pending eruption. Do not spend more than 20 minutes at the crater's edge, especially with children, as the steam and smoke are very toxic. Asthmatics may want to avoid the area altogether (or should at least pack the appropriate inhalers). The park boasts 20 km of trails and the rangers at the visitor centre can tell you which ones are open. **Night tours** provide your best chance to see the red hot lava simmering beneath the earth's surface. They depart daily, 1700, US$10, with a minimum of six people, 2½ hours, book at least one day in advance. The real heroes of the park are the bright green parakeets that nest in the truly toxic environment of the active Santiago crater. They can be spotted late in the afternoon returning to their nests, chattering and soaring happily through the suffocating clouds of hydrochloric acid and sulphur dioxide.

★ Reserva Natural Laguna de Apoyo

Heated by thermal vents, Nicaragua's most beautiful crater lake, Laguna de Apoyo, is clean, clear, comfortably warm, and rich in minerals. Swimming here is a rejuvenating experience, but many come just to gaze at the changing colours of the lake's hypnotic surface. Others choose to hike through the thickly forested surroundings, observing birds and other prolific wildlife.

Created by a massive volcanic explosion some 23,000 years ago, the drop from the crater's edge to the lake is more than 400 m. The lake itself is 6 km in diameter. The maximum depth of the water is yet to be discovered, but it is known to be at least 200 m deep (more than 70 m below sea level), making it the lowest point in Central America. When the Spanish arrived, Laguna de Apoyo was a central point for the Chorotega indigenous tribes, whose capital is thought to have been at Diriá, along the south upper rim of the crater above the lake. The basalt used for many of their ceremonial statues came from inside the crater. Today the reserve's only indigenous remains are petroglyphs submerged on the lower walls of the crater lake which can be seen using diving gear. The crater has seen some increased development in recent years, but at least half of it still consists of thick tropical dry forest.

Access to the inside of the crater is from two cobbled roads, one that starts near Monimbó and the other from the Carretera a Granada at Km 37.5. Both end in a tiny settlement called **Valle de Apoyo** that sits at the crater's north rim. From there, a steep road slices down the northern wall to the lake shore, where you'll find hotels and hostels offering day use of their facilities. It's easiest to go by car, but infrequent buses do run from Masaya (alternatively, take any regular bus between Masaya and Granada, get off at Km 37.5 and walk up the 5-km access road). Hitchhiking is possible though traffic is sparse on weekdays. From Granada, several hotels and tour operators offer private shuttles to Apoyo. **Buena Tours** ⓘ *Calle La Calzada, Granada, T2552-7563, www.buenanicaragua.com*, operates a daily transfer to Hostel Paradiso on the lakeshore, departs 1000 and returns 1600 (US$14 round-trip including use of the facilities). Another option is **Abdalah Tours** ⓘ *Catedral, 1 c al lago, T2552-8672, www.abdalahtours.com, rates include a day pass to the Monkey Hut Hostel*. The other alternative is a taxi from Granada (US$15-20 one-way), Masaya (US$5-7 one-way) or Managua (US$25-30).

Los Pueblos Blancos

Los Pueblos Blancos are politically divided by the provinces of Masaya, Granada and Carazo, but they are really one continuous settlement. This area, like Monimbó and Nindirí, is the land of the Chorotegas, and the local people have a very quiet but firm pride in their pre-Conquest history and culture.

Popular with day trippers from Granada, the attractive hillside village of **Catarina** has a simple church built and an obvious love of potted plants. The town climbs up the extinct cone of Volcán Apoyo until overlooking its deep blue lagoon with a mirador and complex of restaurants. Across the highway from Catarina is the traditional Chorotega village of **San Juan de Oriente**, famous for its elegant ceramic earthenware. At least 80% of the villagers are involved in some aspect of pottery production and sales. To buy direct from the source or to see the artisans at work, you can visit the artisans' co-operative, **Cooperativa Quetzal-Coatl** ⓘ *25 m inside the first entrance to the town, T2558-0337, www.cooperativaquetzalcoatl. wordpress.com, daily 0800-1700.*

Heading south towards the Mombacho Volcano, on the highway between Catarina and San Juan de Oriente, you'll find the historic twin villages of **Diriá** and **Diriomo**. Once the seat of power of the fierce chief Diriangén, who ruled when the Spanish arrived to impose their dominance, Diriá is today one of the sleepiest of the highland *pueblos*, only really coming to life during festivals. Occupying part of the upper rim of Laguna de Apoyo, its mirador is in some ways more spectacular than the complex at Catarina. Neighbouring Diriomo is a farming centre famous for its sorcery and its traditional sweets known as *cajetas*. The most popular of the sweet houses is **La Casa de las Cajetas** ⓘ *Parque Central, opposite the church, T2557-0015, cajeta@datatex.com.ni, tours available, call ahead*. Diriomo's **Iglesia Santuario de Nuestra Señora de Candelaria**, built over the course of over 100 years from 1795 using a mixture of stone and brick, is one of the most visually pleasing structures in Nicaragua.

Best known for its famous son, the nationalist rebel General Augusto C Sandino, **Niquinohomo** is a quiet colonial village founded in 1548 by the Spanish. Tellingly, the name Niquinohomo is Chorotega for 'Valley of the Warriors'. The rebel general's childhood home is today the **public library** ⓘ *Parque Central, opposite the gigantic cross that guards the church, Mon-Fri 0900-1200 and 1400-1800*, and it houses a small display on his life. **Nandasmo** is several kilometres west of

Niquinohomo and borders the south side of Laguna de Masaya. The village itself sees few outsiders and feels neglected. Past its entrance, the highway leads to Masatepe and becomes an endless roadside furniture market. Eight kilometres west of Masatepe, the Pueblos highway enters the coffee-growing department of Carazo and the university town of **San Marcos**. In 2005, the oldest evidence of organized settlement was unearthed here in an archaeological excavation by the National Museum with ceramic and human remains dating from 2500 BC.

South from San Marcos is the highway to the highland town of **Jinotepe**, which has a coffee- and agriculture-based economy and some pretty, older homes. In comparison with many other *pueblos* on the *mesa*, nearby **Diriamba** is a slightly grungy, disorganized place. It was here that the late 17th-century anti-establishment comedy and focal point of Nicaraguan culture, *El Güegüence*, is thought to have originated, and it is performed during the town's patron saint festival for San Sebastián. One of the grandest of the Pueblos churches can be found in front of Diriamba's tired-looking Parque Central.

Listings Around Masaya

Where to stay

Reserva Natural Laguna de Apoyo

$$$-$$ San Simian
South of Norome Resort, T8850-8101, www.sansimian.com.
A peaceful spot with 5 great *cabañas* with Balinese-style outdoor shower or bathtubs – perfect for a soak under the starry sky. Facilities include restaurant, bar, dock, hammocks, kayaks and a catamaran (US$25 per hr). Day use US$5. Yoga, massage, Spanish classes and manicure/pedicure can be arranged. Recommended.

$$-$ Hostel Paradiso
West side of the lake, T8187-4542, www.hostelparadiso.com.
Formerly **Crater's Edge** hostel, this excellent lakeside lodging has comfortable dorms and rooms, full bar and restaurant, direct access to the water, sun loungers, floating dock, Wi-Fi and stunning views. If you don't want to stay overnight, you can use the facilities for US$7 per person per day, US$5 children (excluding transport) from **Buena Tours** on Calle La Calzada in Granada. Advance booking is recommended.

$ Estación Biológica Laguna de Apoyo (FUNDECI-GAIA)
North shore of lake, follow signs for Apoyo Spanish School, T8882-3992, www.gaianicaragua.org.
Friendly, low-key lodging managed by biologist Dr Jeffry McCrary, an expert on the laguna's ecology. Accommodation is in rustic dorms and rooms with tasty home-cooked meals served 3 times daily. Activities include reforestation (volunteers receive discounts), Spanish school, diving, kayaking and birdwatching. The research station also offers biology courses and is a great place to learn about conservation. It's close to the lake and walking trails and is highly recommended.

What to do

Reserva Natural Laguna de Apoyo

Diving

Estación Biológica Laguna de Apoyo (FUNDECI-GAIA), *north shore, T8882-3992, www.gaianicaragua.org.* Visibility is generally good and native species include rainbow bass, freshwater turtles and a few endemic species which you may be asked to record for the purposes of scientific research. A 2-tank dive with the project costs US$60; PADI open water certification around US$305, prior arrangement essential.

Language schools

Apoyo Intensive Spanish School, *inside Estación Ecológica (FUNDECI-GAIA), T8882-3992, www.gaianicaragua.org.* Nicaragua's oldest Spanish school and still one of the best. In the Reserva Natural Laguna de Apoyo, this school offers one-to-one instruction with complete immersion, 1 week US$250, 2 weeks US$470, 3 weeks US$680, 4 weeks US$870; all rates include meals and lodging, native instructors and 3 excursions per week. Excellent tutors.

Los Pueblos Blancos

Language schools

La Mariposa Spanish School, *San Juan de la Concepción, T8669-9455, www.mariposaspanishschool.com.* Well established and highly regarded, La Mariposa offers classes in conversational, environmental and professional Spanish. They have rustic lodgings and offer a range of activities, including day trips to farms and nature reserves.

Transport

Reserva Natural Laguna de Apoyo

Bus

Buses to **Masaya**, 0630, 1130, 1630, 1 hr, US$0.50. To **Granada**, take a Masaya bus, exit on the highway and catch a Granada-bound bus.

Shuttle

Shuttles to **Granada** depart daily from Hostel Paradiso and the Monkey Hut, around 1600, 30 mins, US$6 (return).

Taxi

Taxi to **Granada** costs US$15, to **Masaya** US$5.

Granada
& around

Set against the expansive landscape of Lake Nicaragua and Volcán Mombacho, Granada is Nicaragua's most handsome and romantic city, an endlessly photogenic place that blends wistful colonial grandeur with vibrant local street life. Centuries of attacks by marauding pirates and North American filibusters mean that many of the city's elegant Spanish houses and thronging public squares are reconstructions of earlier structures, but fortunately Granada, a bastion of old money and conservatism, has remained largely faithful to its original design.

Today, despite its numerous reinventions, the city has maintained its colonial good looks and earned its place as a major tourist hub. Weary travellers will delight in its well-developed infrastructure, its reputable hotels and restaurants, and its abundance of helpful tour operators. Others may complain that Granada – Nicaragua's most visited destination – is in danger of losing itself under the swell of international interest. For better or worse, gentrification has transformed the city, but with frenetic local bustle never more than a block away, it seems Granada will always belong to the Granadinos.

charming colonial lakeside city with a volcano backdrop

Despite the repeated ransackings, Granada (altitude 60 m, population, 111,500) has maintained an unmistakable colonial appeal. The architectural style has been described as a mixture of Nicaraguan baroque and neoclassical: a fascinating visual mix of Spanish adobe tile roof structures and Italian-inspired homes with ornate ceiling work and balconies.

Granada's city centre is small and manageable on foot. Parque Central is the best reference point and the cathedral is visible from most of the city. Much of Granada's beauty can be appreciated within an area of five blocks around the centre.

The centre of Granada is generally safe, but it can become very empty after 2100 and some thefts have been reported. Police presence is almost non-existent on weekday nights so take precautions. Avoid walking alone late at night and don't go to the barrios outside the centre. Take care along the waterfront at any time of day and avoid it completely after dark.

Parque Central

The Parque Central is officially called Parque Colón (Columbus Park), though no one uses that name. Its tall trees and benches make it a good place to while away some time and observe local life. On its east side, the Catedral has become a symbol for Granada, last rebuilt and extended after William Walker's flaming departure in November 1856. The original church was erected in 1583 and rebuilt in 1633 and 1751. Reconstruction began again on the cathedral after Walker was shot and buried in 1860, but was held up by lack of funds in 1891. The work in progress was later demolished and restarted to become today's church, finally opened in 1915. It has neoclassic and Gothic touches and its impressive size and towers make it a beautiful backdrop to the city, but the interior is plain.

Calle Real Xalteva

The most attractive of the Granada churches is **Iglesia La Merced**, which can be seen as part of an interesting walk down Calle Real Xalteva. Built between 1751 and 1781 and also damaged by William Walker, La Merced has maintained much of its colonial charm and part of the original façade. You can ascend the bell tower for great views over the city, recommended at dusk (US$1). One block south and two blocks west of La Merced is the **Casa Natal Sor María Romero** ⓘ *Tue-Sat 0800-1200, 1400-1700, free*, a small chapel and humble collection of artefacts and books from the life of María Romero Meneses (born in Granada 1902, died in Las Peñitas, León 1977), who became a Salesian nun at 28 and spent the rest of her life caring for the poor and ill; her beatification was approved in Rome on 14 April 2002 by Pope John Paul II.

Further down the Calle Real Xalteva is the **Plaza de Xalteva**, which has unusual stone lanterns and walls, said to be a tribute to ancient Indian constructions. Granada no longer has an indigenous barrio of any kind, but you can see the remains

Granada

Granada was founded by Captain Francisco Hernández de Córdoba around 21 April 1524. Thanks to the lake and Río San Juan's access to the Atlantic, it flourished as an inter-oceanic port and trading centre, becoming one of the most opulent cities in the New World. It was not long before reports of Granadino wealth began to reach the ears of English pirates occupying the recently acquired possession of Jamaica. Edward Davis and Henry Morgan sailed up the Río San Juan and took the city by surprise on 29 June 1665 at 0200 in the morning. With a group of 40 men they sacked the churches and houses before escaping to Las Isletas. In 1670 another band of pirates led by Gallardillo sacked Granada via the same route.

In 1685, a force of 345 British and French pirates, led by the accomplished French pirate William Dampier, came from the Pacific. The local population were armed but easily overwhelmed. They had, however, taken the precaution of hiding all their valuables on Isla Zapatera. The pirates burned the Iglesia San Francisco and 18 big houses, then retreated to the Pacific with the loss of only three men.

Granada saw even more burning and destruction in the nationalist uprisings for Independence from Spain in 1811-1812 and during persistent post-Independence battles between León and Granada. When León's Liberal Party suffered defeat in 1854 they invited the North American filibuster William Walker to fight the Conservatives, thus initiating the darkest days of Granada's post-colonial history. Walker declared himself president of Nicaragua with the cede in Granada, but after losing his grip on power (which was regional at best) he absconded to Lake Nicaragua, giving orders to burn Granada, which once again went up in flames. For more on William Walker, see box, page 78, and page 221.

of the walls from the colonial period that separated the Spanish and indigenous sectors marked by a small tile plaque. The church on the plaza, **Iglesia Xalteva**, was yet another victim of William Walker. The current version is reminiscent of a New England church – a bit lacking in flair. Continuing further west along the Calle Real Xalteva you'll arrive at the little **Capilla María Auxiliadora** with its interesting façade and the lovely detail work inside. At the end of the street is the 18th-century fort and ammunitions hold, **Fortaleza de la Pólvora** ⓘ *open during daylight hours, US$1-2 donation to the caretaker*. The fort was built in 1749 and used primarily as an ammunitions hold, then as a military base and finally a prison. You can climb up inside the southeastern turret on a flimsy ladder for views down the street.

Calle Atravesada

There are a few sights of interest along the Calle Atravesada. Dating from 1886 and beautifully restored, the **old train station**, at the far northern end of the street, is now a trade school. Several blocks south and opposite Calle Arsenal is **Mi Museo**

ⓘ *T2552-7614, www.mimuseo.org, daily 0900-1700, free.* This museum has an array of well-presented archaeological relics, including many rotund funerary pots that were once 'pregnant' with lovingly prepared human remains. Next door, the **Choco Museo** ⓘ *T2552-4678, www.chocomuseo.com, free,* has branches all over Latin

Granada

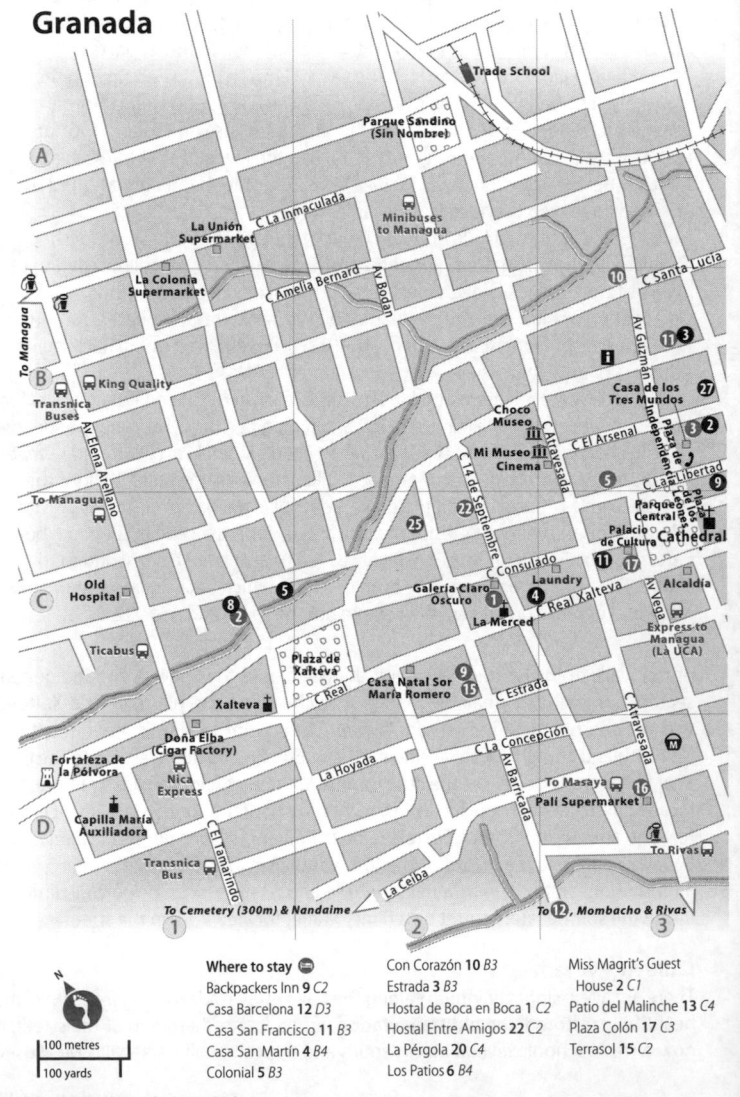

N

100 metres
100 yards

Where to stay 🛏
Backpackers Inn **9** *C2*
Casa Barcelona **12** *D3*
Casa San Francisco **11** *B3*
Casa San Martín **4** *B4*
Colonial **5** *B3*

Con Corazón **10** *B3*
Estrada **3** *B3*
Hostal de Boca en Boca **1** *C2*
Hostal Entre Amigos **22** *C2*
La Pérgola **20** *C4*
Los Patios **6** *B4*

Miss Magrit's Guest
House **2** *C1*
Patio del Malinche **13** *C4*
Plaza Colón **17** *C3*
Terrasol **15** *C2*

America; it can organize tours of a cacao farm and workshops in chocolate making. Past Parque Central on the same street towards the volcano is the bustle and hustle of Granada's **market**. A visit here is a must, if only to compare the noisy, pungent chaos with the relative order of the more well-tended tourist drags.

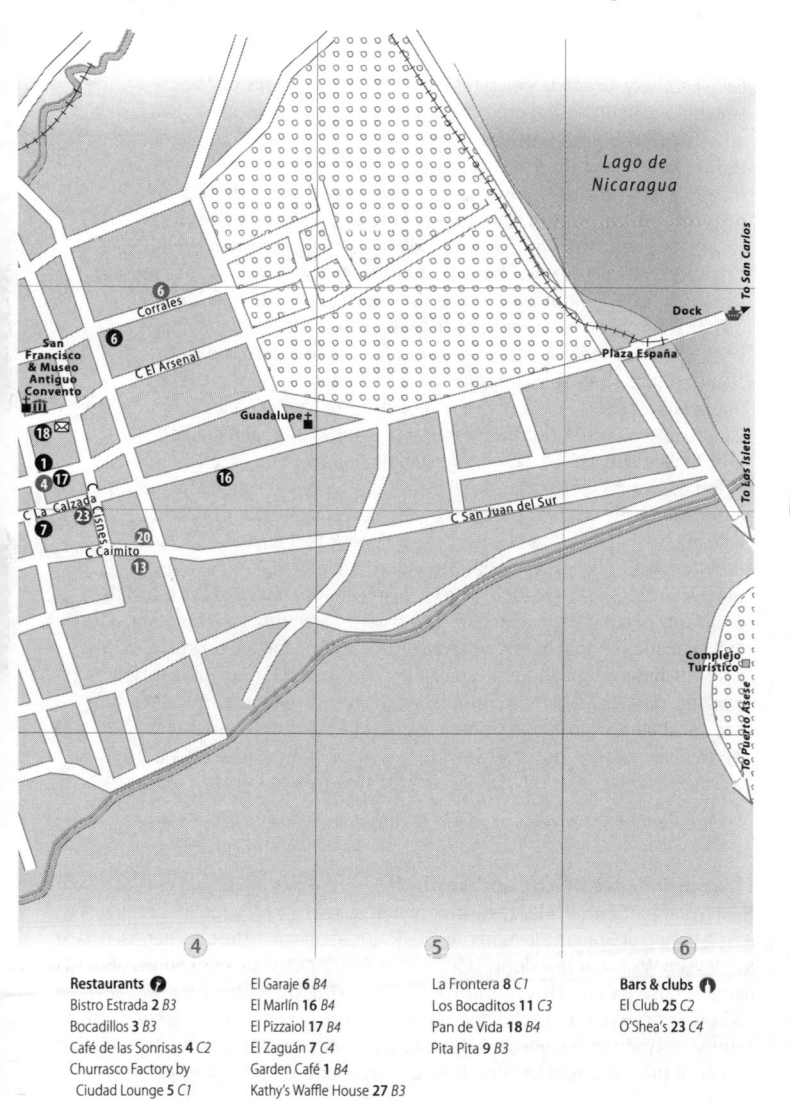

Restaurants

Bistro Estrada **2** *B3*
Bocadillos **3** *B3*
Café de las Sonrisas **4** *C2*
Churrasco Factory by
Ciudad Lounge **5** *C1*

El Garaje **6** *B4*
El Marlín **16** *B4*
El Pizzaiol **17** *B4*
El Zaguán **7** *C4*
Garden Café **1** *B4*
Kathy's Waffle House **27** *B3*

La Frontera **8** *C1*
Los Bocaditos **11** *C3*
Pan de Vida **18** *B4*
Pita Pita **9** *B3*

Bars & clubs

El Club **25** *C2*
O'Shea's **23** *C4*

ON THE ROAD
A time of dreams and roses: Granada's poetry festival

I want to express my anguish in verses that speak of my vanished youth, a time of dreams and roses …

Rubén Darío (1867-1916)

Each February, Granada's elegant colonial courtyards, historic houses, public squares and churches reverberate to the sounds of poetic verse. Since 2005, an annual festival of poetry has been attracting over 100 scribes and thousands of spectators from around the world. Concerts, art exhibits, theatrical performances and impassioned debates accompany the lyrical occasion, but it is recitals from some of the world's finest poets, both Nicaraguan and international, that make it such an important event. Attended with all the vigour of a Catholic Mass, these recitals are a rousing testament to Nicaragua's long-standing infatuation with poetic form.

Granada's poetic roots reach back to the Vanguardia movement of the late 1920s, an alliance of formidable wordsmiths like José Coronel Urtecho, Joaquín Pasos and Pablo Antonio Cuadra, who would meet in the city's public spaces to exchange ideas. Radical and confrontational, the Vanguardia's contributions were important and lasting, and marked a significant departure from Rubén Darío's *modernismo*.

Today, escaping the enduring shadow of this great 'Father of Modernism' is once again the challenge of Nicaragua's newest generation of poets, who are striving to define themselves in a political climate that is largely unsympathetic to creative endeavour. The closure of UCA humanities programmes, the rising cost of books, falling literacy rates and the growing popularity of television mean that they have their work cut out for them. Still, Granada's annual poetry festival, organized and funded privately, is a sign of impending cultural revitalization. The attending crowds of mainly working-class Nicaraguans demonstrate that public enthusiasm for literature has not abated, even if government support has. And the themes of Nicaraguan poetry – poverty, war, identity and nature – are as eternal as words themselves. Conceivably, Nicaragua's love of verse will last forever.

For more information, see www.festival poesianicaragua.com (Spanish only).

Plaza de Independencia and around

Next to Parque Central is Plaza de Independencia, which has a movie-set quality to it. The bishop of Granada lives in the red house, at one time the presidential palace for William Walker. A few doors down is the historic **Casa de Los Leones** (its NGO name is **Casa de Los Tres Mundos**) ⓘ *T2552-4176, www.c3mundos.org, daytime US$0.40; extra admission charged for live concerts on weekend nights,* with its 17th-century Moorish stone door frame that survived all the burning. The building was once the municipal theatre, then a private house where poet-priest Ernesto

Cardenal was born. Now it is a cultural centre particularly renowned for its vibrant art exhibits, music and occasional poetry readings; check their website for details on upcoming events.

One block east from the northeast corner of Plaza de la Independencia is the white **Iglesia San Francisco** (1524), Nicaragua's oldest standing church with original steps. It was burnt down in 1685 by William Dampier, rebuilt, then modified in 1836 before being reduced to flames in 1856 on Walker's departure. It was finally rebuilt in 1868 with a fine restoration of the interior and a controversial decoration of the façade; some complain that it now looks like a birthday cake. Connected to the church is the **Museo Antiguo Convento de San Francisco** ① *T2552-5535, Mon-Fri 0800-1700, Sat-Sun 0900-1600, US$2, US$2.50 extra to photograph*. Originally founded as a convent in 1529, the interior garden is dominated by towering 100-year-old palms, often full of squawking parakeets. In the east wing of the building is one of the country's most interesting pre-Columbian museums, housing large religious sculptures from the island of Zapatera in Lake Nicaragua (see page 87). The sculptures date from AD 800-1200; of particular note are the double standing or seated figures bearing huge animals, or doubles, on their heads and shoulders.

Calle Calzada

East from the Parque Central, the brightly coloured and well-manicured Calle Calzada contains the city's highest concentration of restaurants and foreign tourists. This is the place for people-watching and enjoying a good cold beer. The parade of gringo eateries peters out about halfway towards the lake, where you'll find the **Iglesia Guadalupe**. This church has seen plenty of action, thanks to its location near the water. Walker's forces used it as a final stronghold before escaping to the lake where Walker was keeping well away from the fighting, on a steamship. Originally constructed in 1626, its exterior has a melancholy, rustic charm, although the post-Walker interior lacks character. Beyond the church you'll pass the red cross and a baseball field before arriving at the lake and ferry port. Head south along the shore and you'll reach the fortress-like gates of the **Complejo Turístico**, a large recreation area of restaurants, discos and cafés, popular with the locals, particularly over Christmas, Easter and New Year.

ON THE ROAD
William Walker – the paradox of a villain

It is a name that is a complete mystery to most first-time visitors to Central America. Yet for Nicaraguans, North American William Walker is the epitome of foreign intervention, the model of the evil invader. Had Walker been successful, the history of the isthmus and the United States would be radically different, for it was his plan that Nicaragua should become a new US state to relieve anti-slavery pressure on mid-19th century US plantation owners. History, however, did not favour slave masters; on 12 September 1860, Walker was put against an adobe wall and shot by firing squad in Honduras and seven months later the US Civil War began.

Walker not only brought the bickering states of Central America together against a common enemy, but he was also a fascinating and paradoxical character. Young Billy Walker, the son of a banker from Scotland, spent much of his early childhood taking care of his ill mother, reading Byron and history books. His friends at school were unimpressed and called him 'missy'. He may not have been overly macho, but neither was he slow. By the age of 16 he had earned a graduate degree in Classics from the University of Tennessee. At the age of 19 he received his doctorate in medicine from the University of Pennsylvania and travelled to Europe to pursue advanced medical studies. For a short time he lived in the Latin quarter of Paris. By the age of 22, Walker had become fluent in Spanish, French and Italian and had a good knowledge of Greek and Latin. He had also found time to study US law and pass the bar exam. Walker found work as an editor at *The New Orleans Delta* (where an unknown poet named Walt Whitman worked under him) and his editorials demonstrated a pacifist, anti-slavery and anti-interventionist stance. His newspaper even exposed a plot to take over Cuba and make it a slave state, foiling the project. In New Orleans, Walker had met the love of his life, Ellen Martin, an upper-class girl who was witty, beautiful, mute and deaf. Walker learned sign language and got engaged, but both Ellen and Walker's mother died shortly afterwards from cholera.

Now alone, Walker moved to California during the gold rush and became hardened by the turn of events in his life. Massacres of Native Americans in California perpetrated by gold prospectors and land grabbers were commonplace and, as their defence lawyer, Walker became acquainted with selective law – and with murderers getting off scot-free. Love was gone from his life and Walker was now a proponent of slavery and expansionism. Poorly planned and executed military attempts by Walker at setting up colonies in Northern Mexico and Baja California failed. Yet Walker returned to the US more popular than ever.

In Nicaragua the Liberals of León were unable to defeat the Conservatives of Granada and the Liberal leader looked to the north for help. The job was given to William Walker, setting the stage for the bloody invasion. What the Liberals did not know was Walker's detailed plan to legalize slavery in Nicaragua and annex it to the US. Every year Nicaraguans celebrate his failure.

Tourist information

INTUR
Calle Corrales, Catedral, 2 c norte,
20 vrs abajo, T2552-6858, www.visit
nicaragua.us. Mon-Fri 0800-1700.
Flyers, maps and brochures and, if you're
lucky, English-speaking staff.

Elsewhere, a good source of local
information is the tourist directory
Anda Ya, www.andayanicaragua.com.

Where to stay

$$$ Hotel Colonial
Calle La Libertad, Parque Central,
25 vrs al norte, T2552-7299,
www.hotelcolonialgranada.com.
This centrally located, colonial-
style hotel has a range of pleasant,
comfortable lodgings, including rooms
with 4-poster beds and 10 luxury suites
with a jacuzzi. There are 2 pools, a
conference centre, a tour agency and a
restaurant that serves breakfast only.

$$$ Hotel Estrada
Calle El Arsenal, Iglesia San Francisco,
½ c abajo, T2552-7393,
www.hotelestrada.com.
A tranquil, tastefully restored colonial
house with a charming leafy courtyard
and pleasant, well-lit rooms complete
with 4-poster beds. English, German,
Spanish and French are spoken,
and prices include breakfast and
a welcome drink.

$$$ Los Patios
Calle Corrales 525, T2552-0641,
www.lospatiosgranada.com.
Blending elements of Spanish colonial
and Scandinavian design, Los Patios

is a tranquil boutique lodging
with a penchant for minimalism.
Amenities include a range of calming
and secluded patio spaces, a pool,
hammocks and spa treatments.

$$$ Miss Margrit's Guest House
Iglesia Xalteva, 1½ c al norte, T8983-1398,
www.missmargrits.com.
With a lush tropical courtyard and a
refreshing pool, Miss Margrit's is a very
attractive mid-range option. Rooms are
comfortable and tastefully furnished
in traditional Spanish colonial style.
Recommended.

$$$ Plaza Colón
Frente al Parque Central, T2552-8489,
www.hotelplazacolon.com.
Atmospheric colonial grandeur at
this long-established hotel on the
plaza. Rooms have all the usual luxury
amenities, but those with balconies also
have fantastic views over the square.
There's a pool, restaurant and a small
army of staff to care for your needs.
Recommended.

$$$-$$ Casa San Francisco
Corrales 207, T2552-8235, www.
hotelcasasanfrancisco.com.
Professionally managed and tastefully
decorated, Casa San Francisco is a
well-established Granada favourite.
They have a range of luxury rooms,
suites and mini-apartments complete
with excellent mattresses and cotton
linen. Good restaurant. Recommended.

$$$-$$ Patio del Malinche
Calle El Caimito, de Alcaldía, 2½ c al lago,
T2552-2235, www.patiodelmalinche.com.
This beautiful and tastefully restored
colonial building has clean, comfortable

rooms overlooking an attractive garden and pool. There's a bar and tranquil patio space in which you can have breakfast or simply relax. Tidy and elegant.

$$ Casa San Martín
Calle La Calzada, Catedral, 1 c lago, T2552-6185.

An authentic Granadino guesthouse and beautiful home with 8 clean, cool, spacious rooms. Nice decor and garden terrace. Good service and central location, staff speak English.

$$ Hotel Casa Barcelona
Puente Palmira, 1 c al lago, 1 c sur y 25 vrs al lago, T2552-7438, www.hotelcasabarcelona.com.

Secluded and excellent-value lodging, a 10-min walk from the centre. Simple, clean, comfortable rooms in little *casitas* in the garden. Friendly, helpful owners.

$$ Hotel Con Corazón
Calle Santa Lucía 141, T2552-8852, www.hotelconcorazon.com.

As the name suggests, this 'hotel with heart' strives to be ethical and donates its profits to social causes. Rooms are simple, minimalist and comfortable; all are fitted with a/c, cable TV and fan. There's a pleasant colonial patio, bar, pool and hammocks. Often recommended.

$$ La Pérgola
Calle el Caimito, de la Alcaldía, 3 c al lago, T2552-4221, www.lapergola.com.ni.

Originally a 19th-century colonial home, with comfortable rooms set around a leafy courtyard from where you can see Volcán Mombacho. Hotel services include parking, tours, transfers, Wi-Fi and bar. Clean, tidy and professional. Breakfast included.

$$ Terrasol
Av Barricada, T2552-8825, www.hotelterrasol.net

Rooms are comfortable, modern and adorned with good artwork. Each has cable TV, private bath and a/c (cheaper with fan). Some have balconies with views of the street. The restaurant downstairs has had good reports, thanks to the managers who have a background in the food industry.

$$-$ Backpackers Inn
Esquina Calle Real Xalteva y Av Barricada, 25 m sur, T2552-4609, www.backpackers-inn.com.

A very clean and attractive hostel for independent travellers with small but well-attired rooms and dorms. There's a colonial courtyard, traditional art work, good hammocks, well-tended garden, café, business centre and restaurant. Recommended.

$ Hostal de Boca en Boca
Calle 14 de Septiembre, costado norte de la Iglesia la Merced, T2552-3386, debocaenbocasa@gmail.com.

Downtown hostel offering dorms and private rooms, with or without bath. Amenities include kitchen, bar, hammocks and rooftop terrace. Economical, laid-back and friendly.

$ Hostal Entre Amigos
Calle 14 de Septiembre, de la Iglesia Merced, 2½ c al norte, T2552-3966.

A quiet, friendly, hospitable hostel with simple dorms and rooms, kitchen, common area, DVDs, comfortable beds, Wi-Fi and free salsa classes daily. Laid-back and sociable, but not a party hostel. Helpful owner.

Restaurants

$$$ Bistro Estrada
Calle El Arsenal, www.bistroestrada.com.
The place for a special occasion, the
Bistro Estrada serves high-quality
international cuisine. Starters include
Italian salad and seafood soup. Mains
include sirloin béarnaise, lamb chops
and red snapper. Excellent presentation
and a good wine list.

$$$ Churrasco Factory by
Ciudad Lounge
*Puente Papa Q, 2 c abajo, T2552-6496,
www.ciudadlounge.com. Closed Tue
and Wed.*
A very stylish and well-presented
venue, a cut above the rest.
Recommended for foodies or a
special evening date. Not cheap.

$$$-$$ Bocadillos
*Calle Corrales 207, inside Casa San
Francisco (see Where to stay, above).*
Managed by Shaun and Karina,
Bocadillas serves tasty tapas-style dishes
that draw inspiration from a range of
international sources – try the hoisin
ribs, Venezuelan *arepas* and chicken
tamales. Lovely intimate dining on the
roof terrace, friendly efficient service
and good cocktails.

$$$-$$ El Zaguán
*On road behind cathedral (east side),
T2552-2522. Mon-Fri 1200-1500 and
1800-2200, Sat and Sun 1200-2200.*
Incredible, succulent grilled meats
and steaks, cooked on a wood fire
and served impeccably. Undoubtedly
the best beef cuts in Granada, if not
Nicaragua. Meat-lovers should not miss
this place. Highly recommended.

$$ El Garaje
*Calle Corrales, del Convento de San
Francisco, 2½ c al lago, T8651-7412.
Mon-Fri 1130-1830.*
A wonderful Canadian-owned restaurant
and undoubtedly one of Granada's best
options. The menu changes weekly and
includes tasty specials like chickpea curry,
Italian sausage sandwich, Mediterranean
salad and Szechuan steak wrap. Fresh,
healthy, beautifully presented home-
cooking. Good vegetarian options too.
Highly recommended.

$$ El Marlín
Calle Calzada, Catedral, 2½ c al lago.
Excellent, fresh Peruvian seafood,
including sumptuous shrimps, fillets
and lobster tail. Pleasant interior, good
presentation and service. The place for
an intimate evening meal. Large servings
and friendly owners.

$$ El Pizzaiol
*Calle La Libertad, Parque Central,
1 c al lago.*
An authentic Italian restaurant with a
stylish interior and open-air seating in
the garden. They serve good pastas and
the best stone-baked pizzas in Granada.
Friendly service, take-away available.

$$ Garden Café
*Calle Libertad and Av Cervantes,
Parque Central, 1 c al lago,
www.gardencafegranada.com.*
A very relaxed, breezy and well-
presented café with a lovely leafy
garden and patio space. They do good
breakfasts, sandwiches, wraps, coffees,
muffins, smoothies and cookies. There's
an excellent book collection and Wi-Fi.
Friendly and pleasant. Recommended.

$$ Kathy's Waffle House
*Opposite Iglesia San Francisco.
Open 0730-1400.*

The best breakfasts in Granada. It's always busy here in the morning, especially at weekends. You'll find everything from waffles and pancakes to *huevos rancheros*, all with free coffee refills. Highly recommended.

$$ La Frontera
Iglesia Xalteva, 1½ c al norte.
Closed Mon-Tue.

Casual and unpretentious rock 'n roll joint serving succulent burgers and crinkle-cut fries – try their signature 'Heavy Metal Burger'. Also does Tex-Mex, including nachos and burritos. A bit hidden, but worth hunting down.

$$ Pita Pita
Calle La Libertad.

Falafels, kebabs, shawarma, baklava and other tasty Mediterranean and Middle Eastern fare, all served in the calming environs of a plant-filled courtyard. They also do the best stone-baked pizza in town. Wi-Fi.

$ Café de las Sonrisas
Iglesia Merced, ½ c al lago,
www.tioantonio.org.

An excellent social project run by Tío Antonio and attached to the hammock shop next door, Café de las Sonrisas only employs people who are hearing and speech impaired. They serve unpretentious Nica fare, breakfasts and snacks; menus include illustrations to help with sign language. Recommended.

$ Los Bocaditos
Calle El Comercio. Mon-Sat 0800-2200,
Sun 0800-1600.

A bustling, but clean, locals' joint with buffet from 1100-1500, breakfast and dinner menu.

Cafés and bakeries

Pan de Vida
Calle El Arsenal, Costado Sur del Iglesia
San Francisco. Mon-Wed.

Delicious artisan bread and baked treats cooked in a wood-fired oven. Occasional cook-your-own pizza dinners.

Bars and clubs

The action tends to gravitate towards Calle La Calzada with a kind of thronging carnivalesque atmosphere Fri-Sun evenings. Sit outside to watch the wandering street performers, including mariachis and break dancers, some of them quite good.

El Club
Calle de la Libertad, Parque Central,
T2552-4245.

A modern bar with a European ambience, pumping dance music and a mixture of locals and foreigners. Stylish and a cut above the rest. Most popular Thu-Sat, when parties run late into the night.

O'Shea's
Calle La Calzada, Parque Central,
2 c al lago.

A very popular 'Irish' pub on the Calzada, complete with authentic Nicaraguan staff. They serve Guinness and pub grub, including good fish and chips.

Entertainment

Theatre
La Escuela de Comedia y Mimo,
La Casa de las Botellitas, La Pila de Agua,
Barrio el Mamón, 2 c al lago, T2552-
8310, www.escueladecomedia.org.

A grassroots theatre school that teaches acting, mime, clowning and circus skills to disadvantaged local children.

Check their website for upcoming performances.

Festivals

Feb **Poetry Festival**, a captivating and popular literary festival that draws national and international crowds, check website for dates, www.festivalpoesianicaragua.com.
Mar **Folklore, Artesanía and Food Festival** for 3 days in Mar (check locally for dates).
Aug 1st weekend in August is **El Tope de los Toros** with bulls released and then caught one at a time, much tamer than Pamplona, though occasionally the bulls get away sending everyone running for cover. **Assumption of the Virgin** (14-30).
Dec Celebrations for the **Virgin Mary**, with numerous parades and firecrackers leading up to **Christmas**.

Shopping

Cigars

There is some rolling done in Granada although most of the wrap and filler are brought from Estelí where the best cigars are made outside Cuba (see Estelí, page 184).
Doña Elba Cigars, *Calle Real, Iglesia Xalteva, ½ c abajo, T8893-4227, www. donaelbacigars.com.* A long-established factory where you can learn more about cigar making or just pick up some fresh *puros.*
Mombacho Cigars, *Calle Atravesada, del Parque Sandino, 1 c sur, www.mombacho cigars.com.* A swish Canadian outfit offering rolling demonstrations from their elegant headquarters on the Calzada.

Markets

El Mercado de Granada, *Parque Central, 1 c abajo, then south on Calle Atravesada.* A large green building surrounded by many street stalls. It's dark, dirty and packed and there have been plans to move it for years but for now it remains in its claustrophobic location.
La Colonia, *on the highway to Masaya.* Next door, **La Unión** is also reasonably well-stocked.
Supermercado Palí, *just west of the market.* Dark and dirty, with a selection of low-priced goods.

What to do

Boating and kayaking

NicarAgua Dulce, *Marina Cocibola, Bahía de Asese, T8982-3906, www. nicaraguadulce-ecotourism.com; bookings through Granada Mía on the Parque Central.* An ecologically aware outfit that contributes to local communities. They offer kayak rental by the hour or day to explore the lesser-visited Asese Bay, which can be done with or without a guide, or additional bicycle rental if you wish to explore the peninsula by land. Boat tours of the Isletas are offered, as well as tours to their idyllic private island, Zopango, where you can chill out in a hammock, swim or stroll along the botanical track. Taxi to the marina is supplied when you book a 3-hr tour or more.

Body and soul
Pure Natural Health and Fitness Center, *Calle Corrales, from Convento San Francisco, 1½ c al lago, T8481-3264, www.purenica.com.* A range of well-priced packages and therapies including excellent massage, acupuncture and beauty treatments. Classes include

meditation, yoga, kick-boxing and aerobics. Weights and cross-trainers available in the gym. If you visit, be sure to meet Snoopy, the giant African tortoise!

Butterfly observation
Nicaragua Butterfly Reserve, *3 km west from Granada cemetery, check website for directions, T8863-2943, www. nicaraguabutterflyreserve.wordpress.com. Open 0800-1400, US$5, children US$3.* Private reserve on a 4-ha property, home to 20 species of butterfly endangered by loss of habitat. Tours are self-guided or with a resident butterfly expert.

Canopy tours
Canopy tours can be booked through tour operators in town or directly with the providers. Costs are US$50 per person excluding transport.
Miravalle Canopy Tour, *T8872-2555, www. miravallecanopytour.blogspot.com.* Works with many tour operators in Granada. Costs are lower the larger the group.
Mombacho Canopy Tour, *located on the road up to the Mombacho cloudforest reserve, T8997-5846, www.mombacho.org. Daily 0900-1700 (book at least 24 hrs in advance).* It combines well with a visit to the cloudforest reserve which is on this side of the volcano. Managed by the Cocibolca Foundation.
Mombotour, *Empalme Guanacaste Diriomo, 4 km hacia la Reserva Natural Volcán Mombacho, T8388-2734, www. cafelasflores.com.* Now part of a coffee farm, **Café Las Flores**, with its main office in Managua, but you can also book through their website. Many other options available, including kayaking, hiking on Mombacho, tour of coffee plantation, etc.

Cycling
Cycling is a great way to explore the area, particularly the Península de Asese. Many agencies rent out bikes, but the following are specialists:
Detour, *see Tour operators, below. Good bicycles with shock absorbers, locks, maps, helmets, tips and repair kit at US$2 per hr, US$3 for 2 hrs, US$4 for 3-4 hrs, US$5 for 6 hrs, US$8 for a full 24 hrs.* They also offer excellent and adventurous cycling tours along the old railway lines around Granada, advance booking necessary. Recommended.

Language schools
The following schools are well-established and proven:
APC Spanish School, *Calle Vega, T8866-4581.* Flexible immersion classes in this centrally located language school. There are volunteer opportunities with local NGOs.
Casa Xalteva, *Calle Real Xalteva 103, Iglesia Xalteva, ½ c al norte, T2552-6102, www.casaxalteva.org.* Small Spanish classes for beginners and advanced students, 1 week to several months. Homestays arranged and voluntary work with children. Recommended.
Nicaragua Mía, *Calle Caimito, de Alcaldía, 3½ c al lago, T7779-0209, www.spanishschoolnicaraguamia.com.* All teachers are professional university graduates or university professors, knowledgeable about Nicaraguan culture, history and politics.
One on One, *Calle La Calzada 450, T5749-7785, www.spanish1on1.net.* One on One uses a unique teaching system where each student has 4 different tutors, thus encouraging greater aural comprehension. Instruction is flexible, by the hour or week, with homestay, volunteering and activities available.

Tour operators

Detour, *Dulcería La Miel 75 vrs sur, Calle 14 de Septiembre, Casa 105, T8837-0559, www.detour-nicaragua.com.* Detour works with community co-ops, indigenous and women's organizations to offers a range of very interesting cultural and historical tours in 6 parts of the country, including adventurous trips to the gold mines of Chontales, rural tourism on Isla Ometepe and the Atlantic coast, visits to Rama communities, turtle watching, tours of the rural *llano*, including an overnight stay in a historic house and extensive horse-trekking expeditions. Advance booking necessary.

Oro Travel, *Calle Corrales, Convento San Francisco, ½ c abajo, T2552-4568, www.orotravel.com.* Granada's best tour operator offers quality personalized tours and trips to every part of the country, as well as transfers, package deals and more. Owner Pascal speaks French, English and German. Friendly and helpful. Highly recommended.

Tierra Tour, *Calle la Calzada, Catedral, 2 c lago, T2552-8273, www.tierratour.com.* This well-established Dutch/Nicaraguan agency offers a wide range of affordable services including good-value trips to Las Isletas, night tours of Masaya, cloudforest tours, birding expeditions and shuttles. Helpful and friendly.

UCA Tierra y Agua, *Gasolinera UNO Palmira, 75 vrs abajo, T2552-0238, www.ucatierrayagua.org. Mon, Wed and Fri 0930-1500.* This organization will help you arrange a visit to rural communities around Granada. Very interesting and highly recommended for a perspective on local life and the land.

Volunteering

Several good organizations in Granada are working to improve the lives of local children, including:

La Esperanza Granada, *Calle Corrales, north side of Iglesia San Francisco, T2552-8520, www.la-esperanza-granada.org.* This reputable NGO works with local schools to improve literacy, numeracy and IT skills.

The Girls' Home, *T+44 (0)207 923-2078, www.hogardeninasmadrealbertina.com.* Directed by London-based Rachel Collingwood, a home for orphaned and abused girls, seeking volunteers for a minimum 3-month commitment.

Transport

Boat and ferry

For short expeditions, you can easily find boats by the lakeside *malecón* and in the Complejo Turístico.

At the time of research, the famous long-distance ferry from Granada to Isla Ometepe and San Carlos had been cancelled due to low water levels in the lake. For the latest updates, check locally or consult www.ometepenicaragua.com/ferryboat.php.

Bus

Overland, there are express buses from Managua's UCA terminal (recommended) and slow buses from Roberto Huembes market, as well as services from Masaya and Rivas. Several international bus companies, including **Transnica** and **Ticabus**, stop in Granada on routes north from Costa Rica.

Intercity bus For the border with **Costa Rica** use **Rivas** bus to connect to **Peñas Blancas** service or use international buses; see also Nicaragua–Costa Rica border box, page 256.

Express minibuses to La UCA in **Managua** from a small car park just south of Parque Central on Calle Vega, every 20 mins, 0500-2000, 45 mins, US$1. Another express service departs from a different terminal, shell station, 1 c abajo, 1 c norte, which goes to the sketchy Mercado Oriental, US$1. Either can drop you on the highway exit to **Masaya**, US$0.60, from where it's a 20-min walk or 5-min taxi ride to the centre. Buses to Mercado Roberto Huembes, Managua, US$0.60, also leave from a station near the old hospital in Granada, west of centre, but they're slower and only marginally cheaper.

Leaving from the Shell station, Mercado, 1 c al lago: to **Rivas**, 7 daily, 0540-1510, 1½ hrs, US$1.50, most depart before midday; to Nandaime, every 20 mins, 0500-1800, 20 mins, US0.70; to **Niquinohomo**, every 30 mins, 0550-1800, 45 mins, US$1, use this bus for visits to **Diriá**, **Diriomo**, **San Juan de Oriente**, **Catarina**; to **Jinotepe**, 0550, 0610, 0830, 1110, 1210 and 1710, 1½ hrs, US$0.80, for visits to **Los Pueblos**, including **Masatepe** and **San Marcos**. There's a second terminal nearby, Shell station, 1 c abajo, 1 c norte, serving **Masaya**, every 30 mins, 0500-1800, 40 mins, US$0.50.

International bus To **San José**, Costa Rica, daily, US$29. See individual offices for schedules: **Ticabus**, Av Arellano, from the old hospital, 1½ c al sur, T2552-8535, www.ticabus.com; **Transnica**, Calle El Tamarindo, T2552-6619, www.transnica.com; 2nd branch north on the same street. Also try **Nica Express** or **Central Line**, both on Av Arellano.

Shuttles to Laguna de Apoyo are offered by various hostels and tour operators in Granada, sometimes in conjunction with Apoyo lodgings such as **Hostel Paradiso**, which has visitor facilities (see page 68).

Many companies and tour operators offer shuttle services to other parts of the country, including **Tierra Tours on the Calzada.**

Horse-drawn carriage

Coches are for hire and are used as taxis here, as in Masaya, Rivas and Chinandega. Normal rate for a trip to the market or bus station should be no more than US$1.50. The drivers are also happy to take foreigners around the city and actually make very good and willing guides if you can decipher their Spanish. Rates are normally US$5 for 30 mins, US$10 for 1 hr.

Taxi

Granada taxi drivers are useful for finding places away from the centre, fares to anywhere within the city are US$0.50 per person during the day, US$1 at night. To **Managua** US$25, but check taxi looks strong enough to make the journey. Overcharging is rife.

Granada is not just a pretty face; beyond its disarming aesthetic charms, you'll find scores of enticing outdoor attractions. The expansive waters of Central America's largest freshwater lake, Lake Nicaragua (or Lago Cocibolca, as it's known locally), are home to hundreds of scattered isles and enclaves, many of them occupied by lost-in-time fishing communities.

Volcán Mombacho, looming darkly to the south, is home to Nicaragua's best-managed wildlife reserve, boasting well-tended hiking trails, commanding views, diverse flora and fauna and, for those seeking adrenalin-charged encounters with the arboreal canopy, high-speed zip-lines (see What to do, in Granada section, above).

Las Isletas

Scattered across the surface of Lake Nicaragua, Las Isletas are a chain of 354 islands created by a massive eruption of Mombacho volcano. Birdlife in the archipelago is rich, with plenty of egrets, cormorants, ospreys, magpie jays, kingfishers, Montezuma oropendulas and various species of swallow, flycatcher, parrot and parakeet, as well as the occasional mot-mot. The islands' population consists mainly of humble fishermen and boatmen, though many of the islands are now privately owned by wealthy Nicaraguans who use them for weekend and holiday escapes. The school, cemetery, restaurants and bars are all on different islands and the locals commute by rowing boat or by hitching rides from the tour boats that circulate in the calm waters. The peninsula that juts out between the islands has small docks and restaurants on both sides.

The immediate (north) side of the islands is accessed by the road that runs through the tourist centre of Granada and finishes at the malecón and docks. This is the more popular side and boat rides are cheaper from here (US$20 per boat for two hours). In addition to the many luxurious homes on this part of the islands is the tiny, late 17th-century Spanish fort, **San Pablo**, on the extreme northeast of the chain. Some 3 km from downtown on the southern side of the peninsula lies **Bahía de Asese**, where boats also offer one-hour rides around the islands. Despite the fact that there are fewer canals here you will have a better chance to see normal island life since this southern part of the archipelago is populated by more locals, some of them quite impoverished. Two hours on this side is normally US$40 with both sides charging US$1.50 for parking. A taxi to the docks costs US$4 or less.

Parque Nacional Archipiélago Zapatera

Although the most important relics have been taken to museums, this archipelago of 11 islands remains one of the country's most interesting pre-Columbian sites. Isla Zapatera, the centrepiece and Lake Nicaragua's second largest island, is a very old and extinct volcano that has been eroded over the centuries and is now covered in forest. It has both tropical dry and wet forest ecosystems depending on elevation, which reaches a maximum height of 625 m. It is a beautiful island for hiking, with varied wildlife and an accessible crater lake, close to the northwest shore of the island.

There are conflicting reports on the island's indigenous name, ranging from Xomotename (duck village) to Mazagalpan (the houses with nets). Archaeological evidence dating from 500 BC to AD 1515 has been documented from more than 20 sites on the island, including massive basalt images attributed to the Chorotega people (now housed by the Museo Convento San Francisco in Granada and the Museo Nacional in Managua). The island system is 40 km south of Granada, one hour by *panga* (skiff), more if there are lake swells. Several Granada tour companies offer one-day trips that include lunch, boat and guide, including **Oro Travel** and **Detour**, page 85. **Tours Nicaragua** in Managua, page 51, offers a visit to Zapatera as part of a sophisticated week-long archaeological trip guided by a National Museum archaeologist.

Reserva Natural Volcán Mombacho

T2552-5858, www.mombacho.org, Fri-Sun 0800-1700, US$16, children US$8, including transfer to the reserve from the parking area. If walking (not recommended), entrance is US$3. Tickets are sold at the parking area at the base. It is possible to stay overnight in the research station; cost per person with meals and a night tour is US$40. To get to the reserve, take a bus between Nandaime or Rivas and Granada or Masaya. Get off at the Empalme Guanacaste and walk (or take a taxi) 1 km to the car park. From here you can take a truck to the top of the volcano (great view), 25 mins; they leave from the parking area (Fri-Sun 0800, 1000, 1300, 1500) or try hitching with one of the park rangers.

Mombacho volcano, 10 km outside Granada, is home to one of only two cloudforests found in Nicaragua's Pacific lowlands. Protected as a nature reserve and administered by the non-profit **Cocibolca Foundation**, it is home to many species of butterfly and the famous Mombacho salamander (*Bolitoglossa mombachoensis*), which is found nowhere else in the world. It also has terrific views of extinct craters and, if cloud cover permits, of Granada, Lake Nicaragua and Las Isletas. Most visitors opt for a leisurely one- or two-hour stroll along the **Sendero Cráter**, an easy trail that leads through magnificent cloudforest full of ferns, bromeliads and orchids. An optional guide costs US$7 per group. The **Sendero El Tigrillo** is a short but tough hike to views of the main crater, two hours, guided only, US$12 per group. The **Sendero El Puma** is only 4 km in length but takes around four hours to cover because of the elevation changes. This is the best walk for seeing wildlife, which can be very elusive during the daytime. A guide is obligatory and they charge US$17 per group. English-speaking guides are available for all trails at an additional cost of US$5.

ON THE ROAD
Community tourism around Granada

Granada may well be the country's most conventional tourist destination, but it offers opportunities for some great alternative experiences too. Founded in 1984, **UCA Tierra y Agua** (Union of Agriculture and Fishing Cooperatives 'Earth and Water') is a union of nine co-operatives, one women's association and more than 150 families who supplement their farming-based income with tourism services. This excellent organization arranges tours and homestays in three different communities and your money will directly contribute to their upkeep.

At the base of Mombacho volcano, **La Granadilla** and **Nicaragua Libre** are farming communities offering guided hikes in the cloudforest reserve, horse riding, cycling and tours of the plantations. Your guide will explain the many responsibilities of agricultural life and, if you wish, introduce you to members of the community. At **Agua Agrias** you can hike within an attractive nature reserve and bathe in freshwater streams and lakes. Economical and often delicious meals are available at all three communities.

The best way to learn about Nicaraguan life is to live it. A homestay with a Nicaraguan family, no matter how brief, will afford you a priceless opportunity to observe the daily rhythms of life. And if you roll up your sleeves and muck in, all the better.

For more information and help planning your visit, contact **UCA Tierra y Agua**, Shell Palmira 75 vrs abajo, Monday, Wednesday, Friday 0930-1500, T2552-0238, www.ucatierrayagua.org.

Listings Around Granada

Where to stay

Las Isletas

$$$$ Jicaro Island Ecolodge
On Jicaro island, T2552-6353,
www.jicarolodge.com.
An upscale nature resort with 9 beautifully presented *casitas* and a secluded setting – a fine spot for honeymoons or romantic getaways. Massage and yoga treatments are available, as well as a range of soft adventure tours.

Isla Zapatera

$$$-$$ Santa María
(Managua office)
Frente al Colegio Centroamérica,
Tienda DCO Mediterráneo, T277-5299,
www.islazapatera.com.
This ecolodge is located in the bay of Santa María on Zapatera. They offer 6 pleasant rooms with capacity for 4 people in each, night fishing, bar and deck. Rates are listed for a group of 8, not including transport.

Reserva Natural Volcán Mombacho

$$$ Mombacho Lodge
*Halfway up to the coffee finca
from the park office, T8499-1029,
www.mombacholodge.com.*
Spacious wooden cabins in the jungle
with hot water, verandas and access to
Finca Café Las Flores. Open to visitors,
the restaurant serves fresh international
food. 3 meals for the day, US$30.

$ Treehouse Poste Rojo
*Pozo de Oro, 10 km outside Granada
on the road to Nandaime, T8903-4563,
www.posterojo.com.*
Known affectionately as the **Tree
House Hostel**, it has attractive and
rustic wooden lodgings connected by
Robinson Crusoe walkways. Activities
include volunteering and full-moon
parties. Buzzing and sociable.

Southern
Pacific coast

Empty wave-swept beaches, isolated surf spots and a prime position just off the Panamerican Highway – it's no surprise that Nicaragua's southern Pacific coast is enjoying a special prosperity and burgeoning international interest.

Geographically speaking, this is the youngest part of the country. Backed by swathes of ultra-fertile lowlands, it forms the outer fringe of the tapering isthmus of Rivas, which separates the ocean from the freshwater expanse of Lake Nicaragua. The dry season here is very parched and brown, but during the rest of the year the landscape is flushed green and dotted with flower-festooned gardens. Roadside stalls, shaded by rows of mango trees, offer a bounty of fresh fruit: watermelon, mango, *níspero* and some of the biggest papaya you'll see anywhere.

San Juan del Sur, an hour from the Costa Rican border, has become the region's big tourist mecca. It is one of Central America's big expat towns, but has not entirely lost its small-town fishing village feel with a fleet of little boats anchored off its golden sands. The many kilometres of Pacific shoreline north and south of San Juan's sweeping half-moon bay are prettier, but the real attractions are the olive ridley turtles that have been coming to this stretch of coast for thousands of years.

For the filibuster William Walker, who fought and lost three battles here, Rivas was never a very happy place. Today, as a provincial capital and transport hub, it provides connections south to San Juan del Sur and the Costa Rican border, east to Isla Ometepe, and north to Granada and Managua.

Founded in 1720, the town has a few modest sights but nothing to detain you: the **Templo Parroquial de San Pedro** (1863) on Parque Central has a design reminiscent of the cathedral in León; the neglected **Museo de Antropología e Historia** ① *Escuela International de Agricultura, 1 c arriba, 1½ c norte, T2563-3708, Mon-Fri 0900-1200, 1400-1700, Sat 0900-1200, free,* maintains a dwindling but precious collection of archaeological pieces.

It may seem like an extension of Rivas, but **San Jorge**, where ferries depart to Isla Ometepe, is actually a separate town (see Transport, below). South of Rivas on the Pan-American Highway, at the turning for San Juan del Sur (see page 96), the little windswept village of **La Virgen** has a stunning view of the big lake and Ometepe. It is here that the distance between the waters of Lake Nicaragua and the Pacific Ocean is shortest, only 18 km. South of La Virgen, the Panamerican highway passes the coastal town of **Sapoá** before arriving at **Peñas Blancas** and the Costa Rican border; see also Nicaragua–Costa Rica border box, page 256.

Where to stay

Rivas

$$ Nicarao Inn
*Rivas, northwest corner of Parque
Central, 2 c abajo, T2563-3234.*
The finest hotel in town has 18 tastefully
decorated, comfortable rooms, all with
a/c, cable TV, hot water and Wi-Fi. Services
include laundry, car rental, conference
centre, restaurant and bar. Polite and
professional. Breakfast included.

Transport

Rivas
Bus
The main bus terminal is at the market.
Managua, every 30 mins, 0630-1700,
US$2, 2½ hrs; express buses, US$2.50.
To **Granada**, every 45 mins, 0530-1625,
US$1.50, 1¾ hrs. To **Jinotepe**, every
30 mins, 0540-1710, US$1.50, 1¾ hrs.
To **San Jorge**, every 30 mins, US$0.30,
20 mins. To **San Juan del Sur**, every
30 mins, 0600-1830, US$1, 45 mins.
To destinations south of San Juan del
Sur, including **Playa el Coco**, **La Flor**
and **Ostional**, 3 daily, 1100, 1500, 1630,
US$2.60, 2-3 hrs. To **Peñas Blancas**,
every 30 mins, 0500-1600, US$0.75, 1 hr.

International bus **Ticabus**, de la
UNO, 1½ c norte, T8453-2228, www.
ticabus.com, and **Transnica**, UNO,
1½ c norte, T8898-5195, www.transnica.
com, have buses bound for **Costa Rica**
and **Honduras** stopping at the UNO
station on the highway.

Taxi
From the centre of Rivas to the dock at
San Jorge, US$1 *colectivo* (US$4 private).
To **San Juan del Sur**, US$1.75 *colectivo*
(US$7.50 private). To **Peñas Blancas**,
US$2 *colectivo* (US$8 private). In all cases
beware of overcharging and avoid
'helpful' characters (see Border crossings
box, page 256). *Colectivos* depart from
the corner opposite the bus station.

San Jorge
Boat and ferry
Ferries and boats depart from San Jorge
to the main port of **Moyogalpa** on Isla
Ometepe and to the smaller pier at **San
José del Sur**. The ferries are the larger
and more comfortable option. Services
are subject to random and seasonal
change, but you won't have to wait
more than an hour for a departure.
To **Moyogalpa**, 9 ferries daily, 5 in the
morning, 4 in the afternoon, 0700-1745,
US$3, 6 boats daily, US$1.50-2, 1 hr. To
San José del Sur, 0930, 1400, 1700, ferry
US$3, boat US$2, 1 hr. Reduced services
on Sun. If you have a high-clearance
4WD you may want to take it across on
the ferry (US$20 each way). Arrive at
least 1 hr before the ferry departure to
reserve a spot (if possible call the day
before, T2278-8190, to make an initial
reservation). You will need to fill out
some paperwork and buy a boarding
ticket for each person travelling. Make
sure you reserve your spot as close to the
ferry ramp as possible, but leave room
for trucks and cars coming off the ferry.

a magnet for property developers, US retirees and international surfers

Not long ago this was a special, secret place – a tiny coastal paradise on Nicaragua's Pacific coast. In recent years, however, this little town on a big bay has become very popular. Today, cruise ships anchor in its deeper waters and tourists have arrived in quantity. No more the precious enclave, San Juan del Sur (population 14,621) is a buzzing party town and its transformation into the type

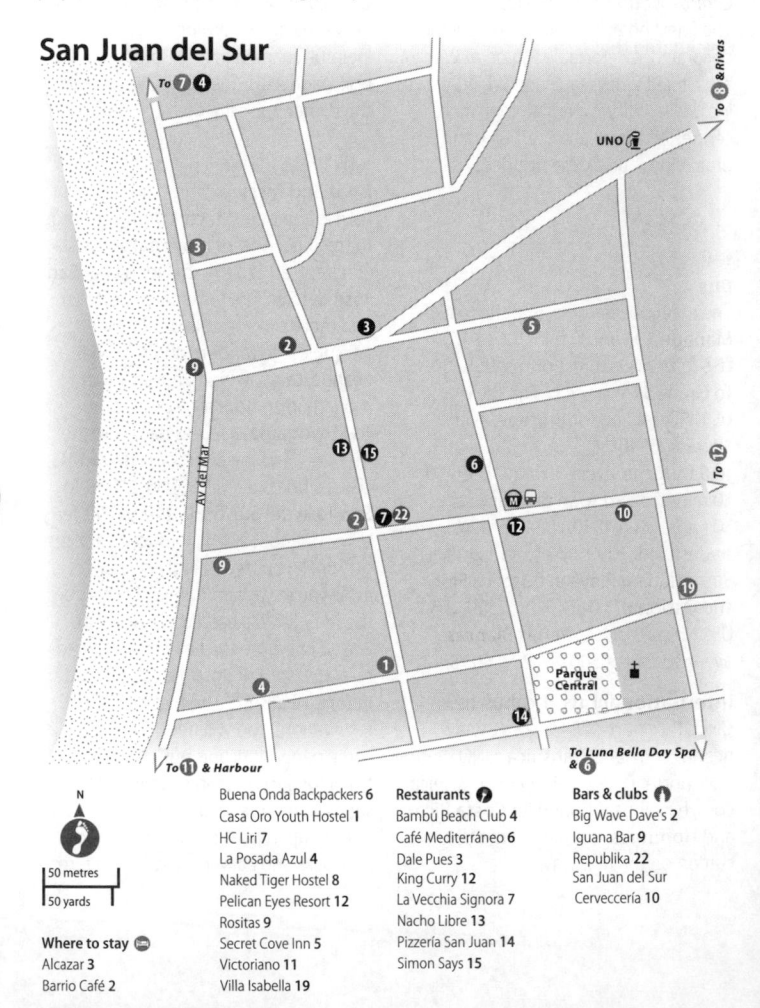

San Juan del Sur

N

50 metres
50 yards

Where to stay
Alcazar **3**
Barrio Café **2**
Buena Onda Backpackers **6**
Casa Oro Youth Hostel **1**
HC Liri **7**
La Posada Azul **4**
Naked Tiger Hostel **8**
Pelican Eyes Resort **12**
Rositas **9**
Secret Cove Inn **5**
Victoriano **11**
Villa Isabella **19**

Restaurants
Bambú Beach Club **4**
Café Mediterráneo **6**
Dale Pues **3**
King Curry **12**
La Vecchia Signora **7**
Nacho Libre **13**
Pizzería San Juan **14**
Simon Says **15**

Bars & clubs
Big Wave Dave's **2**
Iguana Bar **9**
Republika **22**
San Juan del Sur
Cervecería **10**

BACKGROUND
San Juan del Sur

The sleepy fishing village of San Juan del Sur began working as a commercial port in 1827 and in 1830 took the name Puerto Independencia. Its claim to fame came during the California gold rush when thousands of North Americans, anxious to reach California, would travel by boat from the Caribbean up the Río San Juan, across Lake Nicaragua, overland for 18 km from La Virgen, and then by boat again from San Juan to California. It is estimated that some 84,880 passengers passed through the town en route to the Golden State and some 75,000 on their way to New York. As soon as the transcontinental railway in the USA was completed, the trip through Central America was no longer necessary. The final crossing was made on 8 May 1868.

of gringo pleasure resort that is all too common in Costa Rica is nearly complete. Although San Juan del Sur is no longer the place to experience a country off the beaten path, it is fun and convenient, and there are still many empty beaches along local coastline, one of the most beautiful stretches in Central America.

Safety The vast majority of visits to San Juan del Sur are hassle free, but it is essential to check the safety situation of local beaches before heading out – ask a trusted tour agent or hotelier for the latest advice. Under no circumstances walk to Playa Yankee or Playa Remanso, north of San Juan del Sur, as this road is a haunt of thieves. Don't linger on the sand after dark in San Juan del Sur. Lone women should avoid walking on empty and isolated beaches due to the possibility of harassment or worse. If out late drinking, use taxis to get back to your hotel. Do not take valuables to the beach, let alone leave them unattended. Beware rip tides.

Sights
San Juan is a natural bay of light-brown sand, clear waters and 200-m-high cliffs that mark its borders. The sunsets are placed perfectly out over the Pacific, framed by fishing boats bobbing in the water. In 1866, Mark Twain described San Juan as "a few tumble-down frame shanties" and said it was "crowded with horses, mules and ambulances (horse carriages) and half-clad yellow natives"; see also box, page 98.

Today there are plenty of half-clad people, though fewer and fewer are natives, and most are enjoying the sun and sea. What makes San Juan del Sur really different from other Nicaraguan beach towns is the growing expat crowd. For better or worse, the town plays host to scores of rum-soaked gringo bars, thronging party hostels, high-rise condos, boutique hotels and scores of seafood restaurants offering the catch of the day. As ever, intrepid wave-seekers can climb in a boat, escape the crowds and find very good breaks along a coastline that has a year-round offshore breeze. See What to do, below.

ON THE ROAD
Mark Twain – "The Nicaragua route forever!"

Samuel Clemens, better known as Mark Twain, first saw the Pacific coast of Nicaragua on 29 December 1866, after a long boat journey from San Francisco. He described the approach to the bay of San Juan del Sur thus: "…bright green hills never looked so welcome, so enchanting, so altogether lovely, as do these that lie here within a pistol-shot of us."

Travelling on the inter-oceanic steamship line of Cornelius Vanderbilt between the Pacific and the Caribbean, Twain was writing a series of letters to a San Francisco newspaper *Alta California*, letters that were published in book form over 60 years later, in 1940, in a collection called *Travels with Mr Brown*.

He crossed Nicaragua in three days. The first was spent overland in a horse-drawn carriage from San Juan del Sur to the port of La Virgen on Lake Nicaragua. During the only land part of his journey from San Francisco to New York he was amazed at the beauty of the Nicaraguan people and their land. He and his fellow passengers gleefully exclaimed: "the Nicaragua route forever!"

It was at the end of that 3½-hour carriage ride that he first saw the great lake and Island of Ometepe. "They look so isolated from the world and its turmoil – so tranquil, so dreamy, so steeped in slumber and eternal repose." He crossed the lake in a steamship to San Carlos and boarded another that would take him down the Río San Juan to El Castillo, where passengers had to walk past the old fort to change boats beyond the rapids there. "About noon we swept gaily around a bend in the beautiful river, and a stately old adobe castle came into view – a relic of the olden time – of the old buccaneering days of Morgan and his merry men."

Back on the river, Twain enjoyed the beauty that today is the Indio-Maíz Biological Reserve: "All gazed in rapt silent admiration for a long time as the exquisite panorama unfolded itself. The character of the vegetation on the banks had changed from a rank jungle to dense, lofty, majestic forests. There were hills, but the thick drapery of the vines spread upwards, terrace upon terrace, and concealed them like a veil. Now and then a rollicking monkey scampered into view or a bird of splendid plumage floated through the sultry air, or the music of some invisible songster welled up out of the forest depths. The changing vistas of the river ever renewed the intoxicating picture; corners and points folding backward revealed new wonders beyond."

Where to stay

Many hotels in the region of San Juan del Sur double and triple their rates for Semana Santa and around Christmas and New Year.

$$$$ Pelican Eyes Resort
Parroquia, 1½ c arriba, T2563-7000, www.pelicaneyesvillas.com.
Beautiful, peaceful, luxurious houses and hotel suites with private bath, a/c, cable TV, sitting area, great furnishings and views of the bay. The best in town with a plethora of comforts and amenities.

$$$$-$$$ Victoriano
Paseo Marítimo, costado norte Enitel, T2568-2005, www.hotelvictoriano.com.
This gorgeous clapboard mansion is actually a restored English Victorian-era family house. Rooms are simple, stylish and elegant with a/c, cable TV, DVD, Wi-Fi and all the usual amenities. Great restaurant-bar, pool and garden. One of the best in town and a place to be seen.

$$$ Barrio Café Hotel
Mercado, 1 c al mar, T2568-2294, www.barriocafesanjuan.com.
Good, comfortable, modern rooms with 2 queen-sized beds, 32" plasma TVs, a/c and safe deposits. There's Wi-Fi in the café downstairs, which serves highly regarded fusion cuisine. Tours, surfboard rental and transportation available. Breakfast included.

$$$ Hotel Alcazar
Calle el Paseo del Rey, opposite the Eskimo, T2568-2075, www. hotelalcazarnicaragua.com.
Crisp, stylish and contemporary rooms at this boutique hotel on the seafront, each immaculately furnished with tasteful hardwood furniture and their own balcony overlooking the waves. Wi-Fi, pool, cable TV and a/c. Recommended.

$$$ La Posada Azul
BDF, ½ c arriba, T2568-2698, www.laposadaazul.com.
La Posada Azul is a tranquil and intimate lodging with just a handful of comfortable, well-furnished rooms. A beautiful wooden building with lots of history and character. There's a lush garden, self-service bar and a modest pool. A/c, private bath, hot water and Wi-Fi. Full breakfast included. Recommended.

$$$ Villa Isabella
Across from the northeast corner of the church, T2568-2568, www. villaisabellasjds.com.
This lovely, well-decorated wooden house has clean rooms with private bath, a/c, disabled access, ample windows and light. There's a pool, garage parking, Wi-Fi, free calls to USA, video library and breakfast included in the price. English spoken, very helpful. Discounts for groups.

$$ HC Liri Hotel
Suspension bridge,150 vrs northwest, Barrio La Talanguera, T2568-2274, www.hclirihotel.com.
Secluded on the edge of town, this quiet whitewashed hotel with a pool offers simple, comfortable rooms with Primitivist artwork and a/c. Can help arrange surf trips and beach shuttles. Parties on Fri and barbecues at weekends. Ocean views.

$$-$ Rositas
Mercardo, 1½ c al mar, T8326-7733, www.rositashotel.com.

This friendly, family-run cheapie offers 25 private rooms with bath, fan or a/c, and Wi-Fi. Their 'deluxe superior' rooms include a microwave and mini-fridge. Definitely on the basic side, but locally run and hospitable.

$ Buena Onda Backpackers
Barrio Frente Sur, 50 m on the left-hand side past the Casa de Dragón, T8743-2769, www.hostelsanjuandelsur.com.
A bit of a climb to get there, but you'll be rewarded with unrivalled views of the bay at this great backpacker hostel. Private rooms are simple and spartan; amenities include shared kitchen and bar. Superb social areas are comprised of multi-level open-air terraces with very inviting hammocks.

$ Casa Oro Youth Hostel
Hotel Colonial, 20 vrs sur, T2568-2415, www.casaeloro.com.
One of the oldest hostels in town and very popular, with clean, economical dorms (the ones upstairs are better), simple but pleasant private rooms and a plethora of services including Wi-Fi, computer terminals, shuttles, tours and surf lessons. They also have a self-service kitchen, daily surf reports and a breezy bar-terrace that's great for evening drinks. Breakfast served 3 times a week. Youthful, fun and buzzing.

$ Naked Tiger Hostel
Km 138 Carretera San Juan del Sur, T8574-0113, www.nakedtigerhostel.com.
For the boisterous backpacker and savvy millennial, the Naked Tiger is San Juan del Sur's quintessential party hostel. Situated on a hill behind town, this fun, friendly and upbeat lodging offers comfortable dorms and a host of amenities, including pool and shuttle. Book in advance.

$ Secret Cove Inn
Mercado, 2 c sur, ½ c abajo, T8672-3013, www.thesecretcovenicaragua.com.
Intimate and friendly B&B lodging with a handful of clean, comfortable, well-appointed rooms. They offer tours and information, use of kitchen, hammocks, Wi-Fi and a relaxed communal area. Very welcoming and helpful. Nice owners. Recommended.

Restaurants

There are many popular, but overpriced, restaurants lining the beach, where your tourist dollars buy excellent sea views and mediocre food. Only the better ones are included below. For budget dining you can't beat the market.

$$$ Bambú Beach Club
Av Paseo del Rey, 200 m from the bridge, www.bambubeachclub.com.
Conceived and executed by a German-Austrian-Italian trio, the Bambú Beach Club is one of San Juan's finest dining options and often recommended. Mediterranean-inspired seafood with a hint of Nica.

$$ Café Mediterránaeo
In front of the market.
An intimate little Italian restaurant, casual and low-key. Their Italian chef reputedly does the best pasta in town and their menu also includes Mediterranean-style chicken and fish, as well as light snacks, including paninis. Doubles up as a café in the day when you can pick up a good espresso or cappuccino.

$$ King Curry
At the bus stop, opposite the Mercado Municipal.
The perfect antidote to weary taste buds, King Curry serves up feisty and

flavourful Asian cuisine, spicy curries with a Central American twist. Owned by a trained German chef, Marcus, who lived in India. Often packed in the evenings. Recommended.

$$ La Vecchia Signora
Del mercado, 1 c al mar.
Tue-Sun 1730-2200.
Authentic Italian pizzas, oven-cooked to perfection. The best in town, often busy and buzzing.

$$ Nacho Libre
Mercado Municipal, 1 c al oeste,
½ c al norte. Closed Mon.
An awesome array of gourmet beef and veggie burgers, the best in town, all served with tasty home-cut fries. Other options include ceviche and 'Mexican pizza'. Casual and sociable, laid-back ambience. Recommended.

$$ Pizzería San Juan
Southwest corner of Parque Central,
½ c al mar. Tue-Sun 1700-2130.
Often buzzing with expats and visitors, this restaurant serves excellent and authentic Italian pizzas, large enough to satisfy 2 people. Recommended, but perhaps not for a romantic evening meal.

$$-$ Dale Pues
800 m west of Uno gas station.
A self-proclaimed 'tropical dive bar' and 'hangover haven', Dale Pues serves all-day breakfast, burgers, sandwiches and bagels. Fun and funky. Good reports.

Cafés and juice bars

Barrio Café
In Barrio Café I Iotel,
see Where to stay, above.
Popular breakfast spot serving eggs benedict, huevos rancheros, French toast and more. Good coffee, buzzing atmosphere and free Wi-Fi.

Simon Says
Av Vanderbilt, Gato Negro, 60 m sur.
Bohemian little café with good artwork and a host of board games. They serve a variety of nutritious fruit smoothies, wraps, sandwiches, coffee and cooked breakfasts. Chilled ambience. Recommended.

Bars and clubs

Big Wave Dave's
UNO, 200 m al mar, T2568-2203.
Tue-Sun 0830-0000.
Popular with foreigners out to party and hook up with others. Wholesome pub food and a busy, boozy atmosphere.

Iguana Bar
Malecón, next door to Timón.
Also known as **Henry's Iguana**, a very popular hang-out with tourists, often buzzing and a good place to knock back rum and beer. They also do food, including sandwiches, burgers, beer and cheese-drenched nachos. Various happy hours and events, check the website for the latest.

Republika
Mercado, ½ c al mar.
Intimate café-style bar, low-key, with a friendly crowd and occasional live music and barbecue.

San Juan del Sur Cervecería
Av Mercado, www.nicacraftbeer.com.
Closed Tue.
Nicaragua's 1st brewpub, serving its own craft ales in a convivial setting. Live music, brunch and open mic nights. Also known as the Nicaragua Craft Beer Co.

What to do

Fishing

Depending on the season, the waters around San Juan harbour all kinds of game fish, including marlin, jack and dorado. Many hotels and surf shops offer fishing packages.

Language schools

Spanish School House Rosa Silva, *mercado, 50 m al mar, T8682-2938*. 20 hrs of 'dynamic' classes cost US$120, student accommodation or homestay are extra. Activities include swimming, hiking and cooking. All teachers are English-speaking. Teaching by the hour, US$7.
Spanish School San Juan del Sur, *T2568-2432, www.sjdsspanish.com*. Regular morning classes, tutoring with flexible hours.
Spanish Ya, *UNO, 100 vrs norte T8898-5036, www.learnspanishya.com*. One-to-one classes, accommodation, activities and volunteer opportunities. DELE courses and diplomas.

Surfing

The coast north and south of San Juan del Sur is among the best in Central America for surfing, access to the best areas are by boat or long treks in 4WD. Board rental costs US$10 per day; lessons US$30 per hr. The best shop in town is:
Good Times Surf Shop, *Malecón, next to Iguana Bar, T8675-1621, www. goodtimessurfshop.com*. Also known as 'Outer Reef S.A.', This well-established and professional surf shop specializes in quality and customized surfboard rentals, lessons and tours. Tours include day trips as well as multi-day and boat trips to surf hard-to-reach waves. Friendly, helpful and highly recommended. Dave claims he "will never piss on your leg and tell you it's raining". Recommended.

Transport

Buses and shared taxis leave from Rivas bus station. If coming from the Costa Rican border, take any bus towards Rivas and step down at the entrance to the Carretera a San Juan del Sur in La Virgen. If you are visiting outlying beaches you can arrange private transport with local hotels or use one of the converted cattle trucks that shuttle tourists north and south. For the wilder and truly untamed stretches further away from town you will need a decent 4WD (see below) and/or a boat.

Bus

To **Managua** express bus 0500, 0530, 0600, 1730, US$3.50, 2½ hrs, ordinary bus every hour 0500-1530, US$2.50, 3½ hrs. Or take a bus/taxi to Rivas and change here. To **Rivas**, every 30 mins, 0500-1700, US$1, 40 mins. For **La Flor** or **Playa El Coco** use bus to **El Ostional**, 1600, 1700, US$ 0.70, 1½ hrs. Return from El Coco at 0600, 0730 and 1630.

4WD

You can usually find a 4WD pick-up to make trips to outlying beaches or to go surfing. You should plan a day in advance and ask for some help from your hotel. Prices range from US$20-75 depending on the trip and time. You can also hire 4WDs, contact **Alamo Rent a Car**, inside hotel Casa Blanca, T2277-1117, www.alamonicaragua.com.

Shuttles

Several companies run shuttles to the beaches north and south of San Juan del Sur, including **Casa Oro Youth**

Hostel. Several daily departures to **Los Playones**, next to Maderas, and 1 daily departure to **Remanso**, from US$5 return. Note schedules are affected by tides and may not operate in inclement weather.

Taxi
Taxi Colectivo is a very feasible way to get to Rivas and slightly quicker than the bus. They depart from the market, US$1.75 per person, or US$7.50 for the whole taxi, but tourist rates are often double.

There is an access road to beaches north of San Juan del Sur at the entrance to the town. It is possible to travel the entire length of the coast to Chacocente from here, though it is quite a trip as the road does not follow the shoreline but moves inland to Tola (west of Rivas) and then back to the ocean. The surface is changeable from hard-packed dirt to sand, stone and mud; in the rainy season a 4WD or sturdy horse is needed.

Playa Marsella has plenty of signs that mark the exit to the beach. It is a slow-growing destination set on pleasant sands, but not one of the most impressive in the region. North of here, **Los Playones** is playing host to growing crowds of surfers with a scruffy beer shack and hordes of daily shuttle trucks. The waves are good for beginners, but often overcrowded. **Maderas** is the next beach along, where many shuttles claim to take you (they don't, they drop you at the car park at Los Playones). This is a pleasant, tranquil spot, good for swimming and host to some affordable lodgings (book in advance). **Bahía Majagual** is the next bay north, a lovely white-sand beach tucked into a cove.

On the road to Majagual is the private entrance to **Morgan's Rock**, a multi-million dollar private nature reserve and ecolodge, beautiful but costly. Don't even think about dropping by to check it out without first digging deep in your wallet as this is one of the most expensive places to sleep in Nicaragua and, most reports say, worth every peso. While the hotel may not win awards for social consciousness, it is on the progressive edge of conservation and sustainable tourism in ecological terms. If you can afford a few nights here, it is one of the prettiest places on the Central American coast and the cabins are set up high on a bluff wrapped in forest overlooking the ocean and beach.

To the north are yet more pristine beaches, like **Manzanillo** and **El Gigante**, and all have development projects. One that has really got off the ground is **Rancho Santana** ① *www.ranchosantana.com*. This is a massive housing and resort project located on the west side of the earthen highway between Tola and Las Salinas, behind a large ostentatious gate and a grimacing armed guard. Rancho Santana is a very organized and well-developed project for luxury homes built by foreign investors and retirees. The popular surf spot Playa Rosada is included in the complex's claim of five 'private' beaches. California-style hilltop luxury homes have been built here with stunning Pacific views and the 'state within a state' ambience includes a slick clubhouse and a private helipad.

Notable on this coast is the legendary surf spot **Popoyo**. The surf here is very big with a good swell and it still has waves when the rest of the ocean is as calm as a swimming pool. One of the prettiest beaches on the northern Rivas coast is **Playa Conejo**, now taken over by **Hotel Punta Teonoste**. Approximately 10 km north of Popoyo, the diminutive fishing village of **El Astillero** has a few comfortable surf lodges. It is the nearest settlement to Chacocente Wildlife Refuge.

ON THE ROAD
Sea turtles – the miracle of life

Every year between July and February thousands of beautiful olive ridley turtles (*Lepidochelys olivacea*) arrive at La Flor and Chacocente, two wildlife refuges set aside to aid in their age-old battle against predators with wings, pincers, four legs and two.

The sea turtles, measuring up to 80 cm and weighing more than 90 kg, come in waves. Between August and November as many as 20,000 arrive to nest in a four-night period, just one of many arrivals during the nesting season. Each turtle digs a hole with her rear flippers, patiently lays up to 100 eggs, covers them and returns to the water – mission complete. For 45 days the eggs incubate under the tropical Nicaraguan sand. The temperature in the sand will determine the gender of the turtle: temperatures below 29°C will result in males and 30°C and above will be females, though very high temperatures will kill the hatchlings. After incubation in the sand, they hatch all at once and the little turtles run down to the sea. If they survive they will travel as far as the Galapagos Islands.

The huge leatherback turtle (*Dermochelys coriacea*), which can grow up to 2 m and weigh over 300 kg, is less common than the olive ridley and arrives alone to lay her eggs.

Turtle eggs are a traditional food for the Nicaraguans, and although they are not eaten in large quantities, poaching is always a threat. Park rangers and, during peak times, armed soldiers protect the turtles from animal and human threats in both Chacocente and La Flor wildlife refuges. If you have the chance to witness it, don't miss out and get talking to the rangers who have a great passion for their work. Extreme caution must be exercised during nesting season as, even if you see no turtles on the beach, you are most likely to be walking over nests. Limit flash photography to a minimum and never aim a flash camera at turtles coming out of the water.

Camping is the best way to see the turtles in Chacocente or La Flor, but a pre-dawn trip from either San Juan del Sur or Playa El Coco to La Flor, or from Las Salinas to Chacocente is also possible.

Refugio de Vida Silvestre Río Escalante Chacocente

There is a US$5 entrance fee. There is no public transport to the park and a 4WD is necessary during the turtle-laying season from Aug to Nov. There are 2 entrances to the area, one from Santa Teresa south of Jinotepe. Follow that road until the pavement ends and then turn left to the coast. Before you reach the bay of Astillero you will see a turning to the right with a sign for Chacocente. Alternatively, at Km 80 on the Pan-American Highway, on the south side of the bridge over the Río Ochomogo, a rough dirt road runs west to the Pacific Ocean. This is a 40-km journey through small friendly settlements to the same turning for the reserve.

This is one of the four most important sea turtle nesting sites on the entire Pacific seaboard of the American continent. The park is also a critical tropical dry forest reserve and a good place to see giant iguanas and varied birdlife. The beach itself is lovely, with a long open stretch of sand that runs back into the forest, perfect for stringing up a hammock. Camping is permitted – this may well be the most beautiful camping spot along the coast – but no facilities are provided and you will need to come well stocked with water and supplies. The Nicaraguan environmental protection agency MARENA has built attractive cabins for park rangers and scientists and it is possible that they will rent them to visitors in the future. Nesting turtles can also be observed at La Flor wildlife refuge (see page 109).

Where to stay

$$$$ Morgan's Rock Hacienda & Ecolodge
Playa Ocotal, reservations T7833-7600, www.morgansrock.com.
Famous ecolodge with precious wood bungalows and unrivalled views of the ocean and forest. The cabins are built on a high bluff above the beach and are connected to the restaurant and pool by a suspension bridge. The food, included in the price, has received mixed reports; the hotel has rave reviews. Highly recommended if you've got the dosh.

$$$$-$$$ Two Brothers Surf Resort
T8877-7501, Playa Popoyo, www.twobrotherssurf.com.
Stylish whitewashed self-catering *cabañas* and villas set in well-groomed grounds, all different and tastefully attired with hand-carved Indonesian temple doors and arches. The interiors are spacious, comfortable and equipped with cafetière, fridge, microwave, stove, hot water and Wi-Fi. Prices are per villa not per person; surf packages available. Advance reservation essential.

$$$ Buena Vista Surf Club
Playa Maderas, T8863-4180, www.buenavistasurfclub.com.
The Buena Vista boasts several attractive luxury tree houses up on the cliffs, each with private bath, fan and mosquito nets. The communal 'rancho', where guests gather to eat and drink, has superb views of the ocean. Breakfast and dinner included; minimum 2-night stay. Board rental and tours available.

$$$ Hotel Punta Teonoste
Playa Conejo, Las Salinas, reservations in Managua at Hotel Los Robles, T2563-9001, www.puntateonoste.com.
Charming cabins overlooking a lovely beach. The bathroom and shower outside units are in a private open-air area, there's weak water pressure, unusual decor, private decks with hammock and circular bar at beach. All meals included. Avoid windy months from Dec-Mar.

$$$ Hula Kai Hotel
500 m east of Playa Maderas, T8554-7636, www.hulakaihotel.com.
Perched on a cliff overlooking the beach, Hula Kai offers guests a beautifully designed and welcoming space with superb sunset views. For long-term travellers, work exchange is available; 3 months' commitment asked. Great hosts and family dinners.

$$$-$ Hotel Magnific Rock
End of the road to Playa Popoyo, T8237-7417, www.magnificrockpopoyo.com.
A wood and brick built surf and yoga retreat with panoramic views of the ocean and close to some lesser-known breaks. Accommodation includes luxury self-contained apartments and suites (**$$$**) and more modest hostel-style accommodation in shared *cabañas* (**$**).

La Virgen

At the turning from the Pan-American Highway for the highway to San Juan del Sur, this little windswept village has some less-than-clean beaches and a stunning view of the big lake and Ometepe. If you come early in the morning you may see men fishing in the lake while floating in the inner tube of a truck. This curious sight is peculiar to this small village. The fishermen arrive at the beach in the early morning and blow up the big tyre tubes, tie bait to a thick nylon cord and wade out, seated in the tubes, as far as 3 km from the coast. When they get out of the water, often fully clothed, the cord can have 15 or more fish hanging from it.

In the 19th century the lake steamships of Cornelius Vanderbilt stopped here (after a journey from New York via the Río San Juan) to let passengers off for an overland journey by horse-drawn carriage to the bay of San Juan del Sur. The North American novelist Mark Twain came here in 1866, doing the trip from west to east (San Francisco–San Juan del Sur–La Virgen–Lake Nicaragua–San Carlos–Río San Juan–San Juan del Norte–New York). He gazed out at the lake and waxed lyrical about the splendour of Lake Nicaragua and Ometepe from his viewpoint in La Virgen (see box, page 98). The dock used by the steamships is no longer visible and there is some debate among the villagers as to where it actually was.

It is here that the distance between the waters of Lake Nicaragua and the Pacific Ocean is shortest, only 18 km blocking a natural passageway between the Atlantic and Pacific oceans. Incredibly the continental divide lies yet further west, just 3 km from the Pacific; the east face of this low coastal mountain ridge drains all the way to the Caribbean Sea via the lake and Río San Juan. The road is paved to San Juan de Sur and follows to a great extent the path used in the 1800s by carriages and ox carts for the inter-oceanic gold rush route of Vanderbilt. What had previously been a full-day's journey through rough terrain became a trip of just under four hours by the construction of this road in earthen form in 1852 by Vanderbilt's company.

La Virgen to Peñas Blancas

The Pan-American Highway continues south from La Virgen to the coastal town of **Sapoá** on the southernmost shores of Lake Nicaragua and **Peñas Blancas**, the one land crossing between Nicaragua and Costa Rica. The landscape changes dramatically as the rainforest ecosystem of the southern shores of Lake Nicaragua meets the tropical dry forest ecosystem of the Pacific Basin, and the stretch of land is rich pasture crossed by numerous streams. It is possible to follow a 4WD track from Sapoá all the way to the town of **Cárdenas**, 17 km away on the shores of Lake Nicaragua and close to the western border of **Los Guatuzos Wildlife Refuge** (see page 131). From here you could try to hire a private boat to Solentiname, Río Papaturro or San Carlos. For information on crossing the border into **Costa Rica**, see box, page 256.

surf beaches and nesting sea turtles

A paved road runs south from the bridge at the entrance to San Juan del Sur towards El Ostional. There are signs for Playa Remanso, the first and most accessible beach south of San Juan, very popular with surfers. Further on is Playa Hermosa, accessible from a 4-km dirt road roughly 6 km along the Ostional road. After Hermosa, isolated Playa Yankee is also renowned for its waves. Continuing south, the beautifully scenic country road has many elevation changes and ocean vistas. Playa El Coco is a long copper-coloured beach with strong surf most of the year. Beyond El Coco, the road passes El Ostional near the Costa Rican border, a tiny fishing village that's now being sought out by wave hunters.

Refugio de Vida Silvestre La Flor
US$10, US$2.50 student discount, access by 4WD or on foot.

Just past Playa El Coco and 18 km from the highway at San Juan del Sur, La Flor wildlife refuge protects tropical dry forest, mangroves, estuary and 800 m of beachfront. This beautiful sweeping cove with light tan sand is an important site for nesting sea turtles. The best time to come is between August and November. Rangers protect the multitudinous arrivals during high season and are very happy to explain, in Spanish, about the animals' reproductive habits. Sometimes turtles arrive in their thousands (as many as 20,000), usually over a period of four days. Camping can be provided (although there is a limited number of tents) during the season, US$25 per night. Bring a hammock and mosquito netting, as insects are vicious at dusk.

Listings South of San Juan del Sur

Where to stay

$$$$ Orquídea del Sur
Playa Yankee, T8984-2150,
www.orquideadelsur.com.
Secluded beachside oasis with 2 infinity pools and stunning ocean views from its hillside perch. Rooms have private porches, Wi-Fi and dining nooks with views of the starlit sky. Quiet and romantic.

$$$$-$$$ Parque Marítimo El Coco
18 km south of San Juan del Sur, T8999-8069, www.playaelcoco.com.ni.
Apartments and houses right on the sand and close to La Flor Wildlife Refuge. Suits 4-10 people, most have a/c, all have baths, TV and cleaning service included. There's a general store and restaurant in the complex. The beach, backed by forest, can have strong waves. Rates vary according to season, weekday nights are less expensive. Interesting rural excursions are offered.

$$$ La Veranera
Playa El Coco, T8328-6260,
www.laveranera.net.

Located right on the beach, an attractive and intimate little guesthouse built in the style of a traditional Nicaraguan ranch.

Accommodation includes 4 simple, stylish, down-to-earth rooms. Amenities include pool and food on request.

Isla de
Ometepe

Rising dream-like from the waters of Lake Nicaragua, the ethereal isle of Ometepe is composed of two prehistoric volcanoes. Volcán Concepción is the larger of the two, geologically active, temperamental and prone to outbursts of smoke and ash. Now extinct, Volcán Maderas is tranquil and verdant, its fertile slopes cloaked in misty cloudforests.

The ancient Nahuas of Mexico were guided to Ometepe by the gods, so the legend goes, after many years of fruitless wandering. Today, the island's pre-Columbian heritage survives in the form of cryptic petroglyphs and enigmatic statues depicting shamans and animal spirits. Directly descended from those ancient cultures, Ometepe's inhabitants are mostly fisherfolk and farmers and some of Nicaragua's kindest people.

This is a fine place for volunteering or learning about organic farming. The rich volcanic soil means agriculture here has always been organic, but a wave of foreigners are introducing more sophisticated and ecologically aware permaculture techniques. Thus far, tourist development has kept within the style and scale of the island, a UNESCO Biosphere Reserve since 2010, although there are now murmurings of larger, less sympathetic construction projects.

The port of entry for arrivals from San Jorge, this place is an increasingly popular stopover, particularly with those leaving on an early boat or climbing Concepción from the western route. The name translates as the 'place of mosquitoes', but there aren't really any more here than there are elsewhere in the region.

One interesting excursion from Moyogalpa (in the dry season only) is to walk or rent a bicycle to visit **Punta Jesús María**, 4-5 km away, with a good beach and a panoramic view of the island. It is well signposted from the Altagracia road; just before Esquipulas head straight towards the lake.

Moyogalpa to Altagracia
There are two roads from Moyogalpa to Altagracia. The northern route is very rough but also very natural and scenic; it runs through the tiny villages of **La Concepción**, **La Flor** and **San Mateo**. There are commanding views of the

Ometepe

Petroglyphs ⁂

Where to stay 🏠
Albergue Ecológico
  Porvenir **22**
Caballito Mar **4**
Casa del Bosque **14**
Central **5**
Charco Verde Inn **6**
El Zopilote **23**
Finca del Sol **8**

Finca Magdalena **13**
Finca Montania Sagrada **16**
Finca Mystica **18**
Finca Playa Venecia **15**
Finca San Juan de la Isla **17**
Hacienda Mérida **7**
Hospedaje Ortiz **9**
La Vía Verde **21**
Little Morgan's **11**

Puesta del Sol **24**
Totoco Eco-Lodge **12**
Villa Paraíso **3**
Xalli **19**

Climbing the volcanoes

Volcán Concepción There are two main trails leading up to the summit. One of the paths is best accessed from Moyogalpa, where there is lots of accommodation. The other is from Altagracia. Climbing the volcano without a local guide is not advised under any circumstances and can be very dangerous; a climber died here in 2004 after falling into a ravine. Ask your hotel about recommended tour guides; many of the locals know the trail well but that does not make them reliable guides; use extreme caution if contacting a guide not recommened by a tour operator or well-known hotel. The view from Concepción is breathtaking. The cone is very steep near the summit and loose footing and high winds are common. Follow the guide's advice if winds are deemed too strong for the summit. From Moyogalpa the trail begins near the village of La Flor and the north side of the active cone. You should allow eight hours for the climb. Bring plenty of water and breathable, strong and flexible hiking shoes. From Altagracia the hike starts 2 km away and travels through a cinder gully, between forested slopes and a lava flow. The ascent takes five hours, 3½ hours if you are very fit. Take water and sunscreen. Tropical dry and wet forest, heat from the crater and howler monkeys are added attractions.

Volcán Maderas Three trails ascend Maderas. One departs from Hotel La Omaja near Mérida, another from Finca El Porvenir near Santa Cruz, and the last from Finca Magdalena near Balgüe. Presently, the trail from Finca Magdalena is the only one fit enough to follow, but check locally. You should allow five hours up and three hours down, although relatively dry trail conditions could cut down hiking time considerably. Expect to get very muddy in any case. Ropes are necessary if you want to climb down into the Laguna de Maderas after reaching the summit. Swimming in the laguna is not recommended; one tourist got stuck in the mud after jumping in and, rather farcically, had to be pulled out with a rope made of the tour group's trousers. Hiking Maderas can no longer be done without a guide, following the deaths of British and American hikers who apparently either got lost or tried to descend the west face of the volcano and fell. While some hikers still seem reluctant to pay a local guide, it is a cheap life insurance policy and helps the very humble local economy. Guides are also useful in pointing out animals and petroglyphs that outsiders may miss. There is an entrance fee of US$2 to climb Maderas. The trail leads through farms, fences and gets steeper and rockier with elevation. The forest changes with altitude from tropical dry, to tropical wet and finally cloudforest, with howler monkeys accompanying your journey. Guides can be found for this climb in Moyogalpa, Altagracia and Santo Domingo or at Finca Magdalena where the hike begins.

Ceramic evidence shows that the island has been inhabited for at least 3500 years, although some believe this figure could be 12,000 years or more. Little is known about the pre-Conquest cultures. From ceramic analysis carried out by US archaeologist Frederick W Lange (published in 1992), it appears the people of 1500 BC came from South America as part of a northern immigration that continued to Mexico, settling in what is today the town of Los Angeles. In the mid-1990s, a six-year survey revealed 73 pre-Columbian sites with 1700 petroglyph panels, and that is just the tip of the iceberg. One of the most interesting and easily accessible archaeological finds is in the grounds of Albergue Ecológico Porvenir (see Where to stay, page 124), which has a sundial, and what some believe to be an alien being and a representation of the god of death.

volcano with its forests and 1957 lava flow beyond rock-strewn pasture and highland banana plantations, but it is a tough slog by bicycle and impossible by car without 4WD. Most transport uses the southern route to Altagracia, which is completely paved.

The southern road passes the town of **Esquipulas**, where it is rumoured that the great Chief Niqueragua may have been buried, and the village of **Los Angeles**, which has some of the oldest known evidence of ancient settlement. Before the next community, San José del Sur, a turning leads to the **Museo El Ceibo** ① *El Sacremento, T-15, daily 0800-1700, US$8 to view both pre-Columbian and numismatic collections or US$4 each*, which has the best collection of pre-Columbian artefacts on the island along with a fine collection of antique notes and coins, many dating to the beginning of the Republic. Just past San José del Sur is the rough, narrow access road to **Charco Verde**, a big pond with a popular legend of a wicked sorcerer, Chico Largo, who was said to have shape-shifting powers and whose discarnate spirit guards the pond.

Where to stay

Moyogalpa

$$ The Corner House
Main street, 200 m up from the port,
T2569-4177.
A pleasant little guesthouse on the main drag with 4 brick rooms and wooden furniture, views of Concepción, tranquil hammocks and Wi-Fi. Often full and bookings not accepted. Breakfast or takeaway lunch included and a great restaurant downstairs.

$$-$ Hospedaje Soma
Opposite Instituto Smith, up the hill from
the port, left at the church and straight
on for 250 m, a 10-min walk, T2569-4310,
www.hospedajesoma.com.
A tranquil spot offering a mix of dorms ($), private rooms ($ with shared bath, $$ without), and cabins ($$). There's a large leafy garden, hammock space, open porch dining area, barbecue and fire pit. Full breakfast included.

$$-$ The Landing Hotel
Muelle Municipal, 20 vrs arriba,
almost next to the port, T2569-4113,
www.thelandinghotel.com.
A comfortable hostel-hotel with a range of options. For the impoverished there are hammocks and dorms; for the better off there are small private rooms, well-equipped apartments and comfortable *casitas* with open-air kitchen and dining space. Awesome chill-out spaces with breezy views of the lake. Friendly and hospitable.

Moyogalpa to Altagracia

$$ Hotel Charco Verde Inn
Almost next to the lagoon,
San José del Sur, T8887-9302.
Pleasant *cabañas* with private bath, a/c, terrace and doubles with private bath and fan. Services include restaurant, bar, Wi-Fi, tours, kayaks, bicycles, horses and transportation.

$$-$ Finca Playa Venecia
250 m from the main road,
San José del Sur, T2560-1269,
www.hotelfincavenecia.com.
Very chilled, comfortable lodgings and a lovely lakeside garden. They have rooms ($) and *cabañas* ($$) of different sizes, some with lake view and some cheaper ones with fan. There's a good restaurant in the grounds, Wi-Fi, horses, tours, motorcycles, transportation and English-speaking guides. Recommended.

$ Puesta del Sol
Escuela, 1 c al lago y 100 m sur,
La Paloma, 2 km outside Moyogalpa,
T8619-0219, www.puestadelsol.org.
Run by women from 17 campesino families in the community of La Paloma, Puesta del Sol offers very reasonably priced homestay and a host of activities including cycling, kayaking and horse riding. You can also sample and purchase their produce from their community centre, including herbal teas and wine. Authentic Nicaragua. Recommended.

Restaurants

Moyogalpa

Almost all lodges serve meals;
see Where to stay, above.

$$ Los Ranchitos
Muelle Municipal, 2 c arriba, ½ c sur,
T2569-4112.

One of the best in town, with a dirt
floor and thatched roof. They serve
fish, vegetarian pasta, vegetable soup,
chicken in garlic butter, steak, pork and
other hearty meat dishes, all served in
the usual Nica way, with rice, beans,
plantain and salad.

$$ Pizzeria Buon Appetito
Main street, 100 m up from the port.

A well-presented Italian restaurant, the
smartest place in town, great ambience
and reasonable service. The menu of
pizza and pasta is a little pricey and not
consistently good, but the food is filling
and it's a pleasant place to unwind after
a long day hiking volcanoes.

$$-$ The Corner House
Muelle Municipal, 200 vrs arriba,
opposite the petrol station.

A bustling café-restaurant offering
decent coffee and espresso, sandwiches,
creative salads and tasty breakfasts,
like eggs Benedict. All ingredients
are sourced locally. Friendly owners.
Recommended.

$$-$ El Picante
Calle Principal, next the Landing Hostel,
www.picanteometepe.com.

A popular Mexican joint serving
good home-made tortillas and salsa,
veggie quesadillas and more. Friendly
and relaxed.

$ The Chicken Lady
The port, 3 blocks up, 2 blocks to the
right, 2 doors from Yogi's Hostel.

Budget travellers will delight in the
generous and ultra-cheap portions
of chicken and fried yucca at this
informal evening *fritanga*; US$1.50
gets you a plate.

Festivals

Moyogalpa

Jul Dates for some of the festivities vary
according to the solar cycle. The town's
patron saint festival (**Santa Ana**) is a very
lively affair. Processions begin on **23 Jul**
in the barrio La Paloma and continue for
several days. On **25 Jul** there is a lovely
dance with girls dressed in indigenous
costume and on **26 Jul** there's a huge
party with bullfights at a ring north of
the church.

Dec 2nd week of Dec, an impressive
marathon takes endurance runners up
Concepción (25 km), Maderas (50 km) or
both (100 km).

What to do

Moyogalpa
ATVs, biking and motorbiking

Bicycles are now ubiquitous on Isla
Ometepe and are a great way to get
around thanks to the modern paved
road which very nearly circumnavigates
the entire island. Most hotels rent
them and charge US$5-7 per day.
Motorbikes and mopeds are also widely
available, but they have become a
source of controversy. Firstly, there are
no guidelines or regulations governing
their maintenance. Do not assume your
rental is in good working shape or even
covered by insurance. Secondly, there
have been reports of some operators
scamming tourists for preexisiting
damages – if you do choose to rent a
motorbike, examine it thoroughly and
take photos of it before setting off.

Finally, several tourists have been in nasty and expensive accidents. If you've never ridden before, understand that a quick jaunt up and down a football pitch does not qualify you to ride on the roads. If, after all that, you would still like to rent a motorbike or moped, you can expect to pay US$20-35 per day; ATVs rent for US$80 per day. There are many operators; **Dinarte's Rental**, T8366-0588, has been recommended.

Transport

Air

A new airport was opened in **La Paloma** just outside Moyogalpa in 2014. At the time of research, however, flights to and from the island had been suspended. For the latest information, contact **La Costeña**, www.lacostena.com.ni.

Bus

All times are Mon-Sat and subject to change; on Sun there are very few buses. Always confirm times if planning a long journey involving connections. Hitching is possible.

Most of the island is linked by a bus service, otherwise trucks are used. The road is paved almost as far as Balgüe; it remains unpaved and in poor condition towards Mérida.

Moyogalpa
Boat and ferry

Schedules are always subject to change. To **San Jorge**, hourly, 0500-1730, ferry US$3, boat US$2, 1 hr. Reduced service on Sun. See also San Jorge transport, page 95.

Bus

Buses wait for the boats in Moyogalpa and run to **Altagracia** Mon-Sat, every 1-2 hrs, 0530-1830, US$1, 1 hr; Sun, several from 0530-1830. To **San Ramón** Mon-Sat, 0830, 0930, US$1.25, 3 hrs. To **Mérida**, Mon-Sat, 1445, 1630, US$2, 2 hrs; Sun 1245. To **Balgüe**, Mon-Sat, 1030, 1530, US$2, 2 hrs; Sun 1020. For **Charco Verde** and San José del Sur, take any bus to Altagracia and ask the driver where to get out. For **Playa Santo Domingo** or **Santa Cruz**, take any bus bound for Balgüe, San Ramón or Mérida; or go to the Santo Domingo turn-off before Altagracia and get a connection there.

Taxi

Pick-up and van taxis wait for the ferry, along with a handful of spiffy new tuk-tuks. Price is per journey not per person, some have room for 4 passengers, others 2, the rest go in the back, which has a far better view, but is dusty in dry season. To **Altagracia** US$12-15, to **Santo Domingo** US$20-25, to **Mérida** US$30. Try **Transporte Ometepe**, T8695-9905, robertometeour@yahoo.es, or ask a hotel to arrange pickup.

Moyogalpa to Altagracia
Boat and ferry

Boats depart from San José del Sur to **San Jorge**, 0540, 0730, 1330, 1520, ferry US$3, boat US$2, 1 hr. Reduced service on Sun.

ON THE ROAD
Geology, flora and fauna on Isla de Ometepe

Ometepe's two volcanoes rising up out of Lake Nicaragua appear prehistoric and almost other-worldly. The two cones are part of a UN Biosphere Reserve and they are connected by a 5-km-wide lava-flow isthmus. The island is always in the shadow of one of its two Olympian volcanic cones.

The dominant mountain, one of the most symmetrical cones in the world and covered by 2200 ha of protected forest, is **Volcán Concepción** (1610 m high, 36.5 km wide). It is an active volcano that last blew ash in March 2010 and had its most recent major lava flow in 1957. The volcano was inactive for many years before it burst into life in 1883 with a series of eruptions continuing until 1887. Concepción also erupted from 1908 until 1910, with further significant activity in 1921 and 1948 to 1972. Thanks to its hot lava outbursts, one of the cone's indigenous names was *Mestlitepe* (mountain that menstruates). The other well-known name is *Choncotecihuatepe* (brother of the moon); an evening moonrise above the volcano is an unforgettable sight.

Volcán Maderas (1394 m high, 24.5 km maximal diameter) last erupted about 800 years ago and is now believed to be extinct. The mountain is wrapped in thick forest and is home to the only cloudforest in Nicaragua's Pacific Basin other than Volcán Mombacho. The Nicaraguans called the mountain *Coatlán* (land of the sun). The 400 m by 150 m cold, misty crater lake, **Laguna de Maderas**, was only discovered by the non-indigenous population in 1930 and has a lovely waterfall on the western face of the cone. Maderas has 4100 ha of forest set aside and protected in a reserve.

Both cones have monkey populations, with the Maderas residents being almost impossible to miss on a full-day hike on the cone. The forest of Maderas also has a great diversity of butterfly and flower species, as well as a dwarf forest and the island is home to numerous parrots and magpie jays; the latter are almost as common as the pigeons in the squares of European cities. The **Isthmus of Istiam**, the centre of the island's figure-of-eight shape and a fertile lowland finger that connects the two volcanoes' round bases, has several lagoons and creeks that are good for kayaking and birdwatching. Off the northeast side of the isthmus are a couple of islands that also shelter rich birdlife, in addition to the legendary **Charco Verde** on the southern coast of Concepción (see page 116).

calm, unpretentious town, the most important on the island

Altagracia hides its population of around 20,000 well, except at weekends when there is usually dancing and drinking, not to mention the odd fight among the local cowboys. The town predates the arrival of the Spanish and was once home to two tribes who named their villages Aztagalpa (egrets' nest) and Cosonigalpa.

Next to Altagracia's crumbling old church is a **sculpture park** ① *daily 0900-1700, US$1.50*, containing intriguing pre-Columbian statues. They are estimated to date from AD 800 and represent human forms and their alter egos or animal protectors. On the plaza, the **Museo de Ometepe** ① *Tue-Sun 0900-1200, 1400-1600, US$2*, has displays of archaeology and covers local ethnographic and environmental themes (in Spanish only).

Listings Altagracia

Where to stay

$ Hospedaje Ortiz
Del Hotel Central, 1 c arriba, ½ c al sur, follow signs near the entrance to town, T8923-1628, www.hospedajeortiz. blogspot.com.
A very friendly, relaxed hotel managed by the hospitable Don Mario. An amiable family atmosphere. Highly recommended for budget travellers, but bear in mind it's very basic. Noisy neighbourhood dogs, bring earplugs.

$ Hotel Central
Iglesia, 2 c sur, T2569-4426, www. hotelcentralometepe.blogspot.com.
19 rooms and 6 *cabañas*, most with private bath and fan. There's a restaurant and bar, bicycle rental, tours, laundry service, parking and hammocks to rest your weary bones. Dominoes and chess to keep you entertained in the evening.

Festivals

Oct-Nov The town's patron saint, **San Diego de Alcalá**, is celebrated from 28 Oct to 18 Nov with many dances and traditions, particularly the **Baile del Zompopo** (the dance of the leaf-cutter ant), which is famous throughout the country.
Dec The **Purísima** celebrations to the Virgin Mary on 7 Dec are a marathon affair here of singing to a large, heavily decorated image of Santa María on the back of a pick-up truck in what is truly a Fellini-esque setting.

What to do

Archaeology
Professor Hamilton Silva, north side of the Catholic church, or ask at the museum, T8905-3744, is a resident expert on Ometepe's history and archaeology. He speaks a little English and leads interesting good-value tours to the island's petroglyph sites.

Transport

Bus
For **Playa Santo Domingo** use any bus to San Ramón, Mérida or Balgüe.

To **Moyogalpa**, Mon-Sat every 1-2 hrs, 0430-0530, US$1, 1hr; Sun several daily, 0430-1700. To **Balgüe**, Mon-Sat, 8 daily, 0430-1700, US$1, 1 hr; Sun 1040. To **Mérida**, Mon-Sat, 6 daily, 0730-1600, US$1, 2 hrs. To **San Ramón**, Mon-Sat, 1030, 1400, US$1.30, 3 hrs.

Ferry
The port of Altagracia is called San Antonio and is 2 km north of town. However, at the time of research, ferry services between Ometepe, Granada and San Carlos had been suspended, probably permanently. For the latest information, see www.ometepenicaragua.com/ferryboat.php.

Playa Santo Domingo and around *Colour map 3, B5.*
sweeping sandy beach overlooked by Volcán Maderas

Santo Domingo lies on the narrow isthmus between Concepción and Maderas. The coastline of Santo Domingo is one of the prettiest freshwater beaches in Nicaragua and, with the forest-covered Volcán Maderas looming at the beach's end, truly exotic. The warm water, gentle waves and gradual shelf make it a great swimming beach.

It is reached via a paved road which begins near Altagracia's southern exit and after 2 km, passes **El Ojo de Agua** ① *0700-1800, US$3*, where you'll find refreshing man-made swimming pools, a small ranch and some gentle walking trails.

If you wade out from Playa Santo Domingo you'll be able to see the cone of Concepción over the forest; a dual volcano swimming experience. The lake here is reminiscent of a sea (visitors are often surprised to see horses going down to drink from its shores, forgetting that it is fresh water). On this side of the island the trade winds blow nearly all year round and keep the heat and insects at bay. At times the wind is too strong for some visitors. During the early rainy season there can be many gnats if the wind dies. The width of the beach depends on the time of year: at the end of the dry season there's a broad swathe of sand and at the end of the rainy season bathers are pushed up to the edge of the small drop-off that backs the beach. It is not unusual to see a school of freshwater sardines (silversides) bubbling out of the water being chased by a predator. Around the beach there are many magpie jays, parrots, vultures, ospreys and hawks.

Santa Cruz
The diminutive settlement of Santa Cruz lies at the foot of Volcán Maderas, just south of Santo Domingo. The road forks here – one route goes north towards Balgüe, the other heads south to Mérida and San Ramón – making it a good base for exploring both sides of Maderas.

Several hikers have fallen to their deaths trying to reach the summits of Ometepe's volcanoes unguided. Always use professional and qualified guides and beware of local scammers.

ON THE ROAD
Romeo and Ometepetl – a lake story

Centuries ago, there was no Lake Nicaragua or any islands. Instead, there was a lush valley with fruit-bearing trees, full of deer and the songs of beautiful birds. This was a valley of the gods. Tipotani, the supreme god, sent Coapol to watch over the valley and for that it was called the Valle de Coapolca. Coapol was not alone in his duties; other gods such as Hecaltl, Xochipilli, Oxomogo and Cachilweneye helped tend the garden. But despite all the lush trees, green fields and healthy animal life, there was no source of water in the valley. Its lushness was created and maintained by the gods. Several tribes lived around the edge of the Valle de Coapolca and entered the valley often, to use its forests for hunting, to pick its wild fruits and for romance.

One summer afternoon the beautiful Ometepetl from the Nicaraguas tribe met the brave and handsome warrior Nagrando, from the neighbouring Chorotega tribe, and it was love at first sight. The god Xochipilli sent harmonious breezes across the pastures, while other gods offered gentle rain and singing birds. The gods married them for this life and the afterlife. But Ometepetl and Nagrando had to keep their love secret, as their tribes were rivals and war was possible at any moment. (The tribal chiefs had long since passed laws that their sons and daughters could not mix.) One day when they came to the valley to make love, they were seen by some soldiers and Nagrando was sentenced to death for his insolence. The supreme god Tipotani warned the couple of impending danger and the couple was led to a safe hiding place. Still, they knew that the chief's pronouncement was inexorable and they decided they would rather die together than live apart.

After reciting a prayer to the gods, they held each other tightly, kissed an eternal kiss and slit their wrists. Their blood began to fill the valley; the skies went dark and opened in torrential rains. Thunder clapped across the sky and rain filled with meteorites, as shooting stars ran across the heavens. Nagrando, delirious and writhing in pain, rose to his feet, stumbled and fell away from Ometepetl. The valley filled with water. The gods looked on and Nagrando's body came to rest as the island of Zapatera, while Ometepetl became the island of Ometepe, her breasts rising above the waters of the torrential floods. The instigators of the tragedy, those who put politics above love, were drowned in the floodwaters and the punished bodies from each tribe formed the archipelagos of Las Isletas and Solentiname.

Balgüe and around

The road to Balgüe is now paved. The village itself is a little sad in appearance, but the people are warm and friendly. Balgüe is the entrance to the trailhead for the climb to the summit of Maderas (see box, page 115). There are several interesting **organic farms** in the area, including the famous Finca Magdelena, Finca Campestre and Bona Fide farm, where you can study permaculture techniques.

Where to stay

Playa Santo Domingo

$$$ Finca San Juan de la Isla
Playa Santo Domingo, Empalme el Quino, 150 m norte, T8886-0734, www.sanjuandelaisla.com.
This hacienda-style lodge is strikingly situated on the shores of the lake. It offers comfortable rooms and 'rustic-chic' cabins with wood-built fixtures and breezy verandas. Secluded and tranquil.

$$$-$$ Villa Paraíso
Beachfront, T2569-4859, www.villaparaiso.com.ni.
One of Ometepe's longest established and most pleasant lodgings. It has a beautiful, peaceful setting with 25 stone *cabañas* (**$$$**) and 5 rooms (**$$**). Most have a/c, private bath, hot water, cable TV, minibar and internet. Some of the cabins have a patio and lake view. Often fully booked, best to reserve in advance.

$$-$ Xalli
Playa Santo Domingo, T2569-4876, www.xallihotel.com.
An elegantly refurbished beachfront hotel with modern rooms, including 'value' rooms (**$**) for the budget traveller and 'deluxe' rooms (**$$**) with garden views. Service includes restaurant and bar serving locally sourced organic food and drink, Wi-Fi and tours. Sustainably operated and community-orientated. Recommended.

Santa Cruz

$$ Finca del Sol
From the fork in the road, 200 m towards Balgüe, T8361-1754, www.hotelfincadelsol.com.

A lovely natural place with comfortable and ecologically designed *cabañas*. All are equipped with solar power, orthopaedic mattresses, TV, DVD player, shower and compost toilet. They grow their own organic fruit and vegetables and also keep sheep. A maximum of 8 guests are permitted; book in advance. Highly recommended.

$$ La Vía Verde
Between Santa Cruz and Balgüe, T8435-8667, www.viaverde.blinkweb.com.
Set on an organic farm, this Californian-owned B&B has just 2 rooms (maximum 4 guests), both with private verandas overlooking the tree tops. Simple, intimate and comfortable. 2-night minimum stay.

$ Albergue Ecológico Porvenir
T8447-9466, www.porvenirometepe. blogspot.com.
Stunning views at this tranquil lodge at the foot of Maderas. Rooms are clean, simple, comfortable and tidy, with private bath and fan. Scores of petroglyphs are scattered throughout the grounds. Good value. Recommended.

$ El Zopilote
From the fork in the road, 300 m towards Balgüe, T8369-0644, www.ometepezopilote.net.
El Zopilote is a funky organic finca that's popular with backpackers, hippies and eco-warrior types. They offer dorm beds, hammocks and *cabañas*. Tranquil and alternative.

$ Little Morgan's
From the fork in the road, 200 m towards Balgüe, T8714-6475.

Little Morgan's is a fun, popular, youthful place with hospitable Irish management, a pool table and a well-stocked bar. They offer rustic dorms, hammocks and 2 *casitas*, as well as guided tours and kayaks (there's access to a good sheltered bay). Some of the hotel's structures are artfully reminiscent of *Lord of the Rings*.

Balgüe and around

$$$ Totoco Eco-Lodge
Balgüe, sign from the road, 1.5-km steep climb uphill, T8358-7718, www.totoco.com.ni.
Totoco is an ethically oriented and ecologically aware project that includes a permaculture farm, ecolodge and development centre. They have several comfortable custom-designed *cabañas* with solar-powered hot showers. There's a great restaurant with superb views, a lovely pool and they offer a range of excellent tours. Highly recommended.

$$ Casa del Bosque
Del Río Balgüe, 200 m east, 400 m south, www.campestreometepe.com.
Tranquil and natural, Casa del Bosque is set on a 12-ha organic farm. You can enjoy great views of the volcano from the veranda. Same owners as the excellent Café Campestre (see Restaurants, below). They also manage Casa Mono Congo.

$$-$ Finca Magdalena
Balgüe, signs from the road, 1.5-km steep climb uphill, T8498-1683, www.fincamagdalena.com.
Famous co-operative farm run by 26 families, with accommodation in cottages, *cabañas* ($$), doubles ($), singles, dorms and hammocks. Also camping. Stunning views across lake and to Concepción. Friendly, basic and often jammed to the rafters with backpackers.

Good meals served for around US$2-3. You can work in exchange for lodging, 1 month minimum.

Restaurants

Playa Santo Domingo

$$ Natural
Playa Santo Domingo, on the edge of the strip.
Charming little hippy shack on the beach. Serves vegetarian food that's reasonably tasty but not good value. OK.

Santa Cruz

$ Comedor Santa Cruz
From the fork in the road, 50 m towards Balgüe.
Home cooking from the irrepressible Doña Pilar, who serves up the usual hearty Nica meat, fish and chicken fare. Service is achingly slow, so bring a book or a deck of cards.

Balgüe

$$ Café Campestre
www.campestreometepe.com.
Roadside café-restaurant that serves one of the best curries in Nicaragua (hot, spicy and highly recommended). There's tamer fare too, including burritos, burgers, sandwiches and other tasty, well-prepared creations that are sure to please the gringo palate. Juices, coffee and breakfast offered too. Recommended.

What to do

Balgüe
Organic farming
Bona Fide, *www.projectbonafide.com.*
Also known as Michael's farm, Bona Fide offers innovative courses in permaculture as well as volunteer opportunities.

> attractive village with towering palm trees

From the fork at Santa Cruz, the road goes south past small homes and ranches and through the village of Mérida, in an area that was once a farm belonging to the Somoza family. It's possible to hire kayaks from Caballitos Mar (see Where to stay, below) if you wish to explore the nearby Río Istiam, an attractive waterway replete with birds, mammals and caiman.

San Ramón

Further along the eastern shores of Maderas is the affluent town San Ramón. The 'biological station' is the starting point for a hike up the west face of Maderas Volcano to a stunning 40-m cascade, also called **San Ramón**. Sadly the walk has lost some of its charm due to the biological station's bad land management. As well as heavily planting the area with cash crops, they have installed a guard who you will need to pay to pass, US$5. Transport is not as frequent on this side of the island and you may have a long walk if you are not on a tour.

Listings Mérida and around

Where to stay

Mérida

$$ Finca Montania Sagrada
Mérida, T8383-8499, www.
fincamontaniasagrada.com.
A beautiful flower-filled property with many resident animals including horses, dogs, cats and parrots. Accommodation includes rooms with verandas or balconies, compete with rocking chairs and hammocks.

$$-$ Finca Mystica
El Congo, 550 m norte, T8751-9653,
www.fincamystica.com.
Artistically designed round cabins ($$) set on a 10-ha farm. All building materials were locally sourced and the cabins constructed using cob, an organic adobe-like material composed of soil, sand, manure and rice straw. The overall effect is very organic and relaxing. There

is a communal cabin too, for budget travellers ($).

$$-$ Hacienda Mérida
El Puerto Viejo de Somoza, T2560-0496,
www.hmerida.com.
Popular hostel with a beautiful setting by the lake. Lodgings have wheelchair access and include a mixture of dorms and rooms, some with views ($$). There's a children's school on site where you can volunteer, also kayak rental, good-quality mountain bikes, internet and a range of tours available.

$ Caballitos Mar
Follow signs from the road, T8842-6120,
www.caballitosmar.com.
Affordable Mérida alternative that has the best access to the Río Istiam and good kayaks for day or night tours. Fernando, the Spanish owner, is friendly and helpful and cooks up a very decent paella.

What to do

Mérida
Kayaking
Caballitos Mar, *follow signs from the road, T8842-6120, www.caballitosmar.com.*
The best starting point for kayak excursions down the Río Istiam, where you might spot caiman and turtles. Rentals are available for US$5 per hr or US$15 per day. Dawn is the best time for wildlife viewing, pack sunscreen and check lake conditions before setting out. There are also night tours.

Río San Juan
& the
Archipiélago
Solentiname

A natural canal between the Pacific and Atlantic oceans, the Río San Juan has long drawn enterprising factions keen to exploit its commercial and military potential: the British navy, Napoleon III and the US government among them. Fortunately they all failed, and today the river remains one of Central America's great natural attractions: a mini Amazonas where the evening symphony of tropical birds, high-pitched cicadas, ardent tree frogs, and vociferous howler monkeys hints at the multitude of strange creatures inhabiting the darkened rainforests on its banks.

Part of this remote region encompasses the southeastern sector of Lake Nicaragua, including the fabled Solentiname archipelago, a chain of pretty, drowsy islands that were once the site of an intriguing social experiment. In 1965, the poet-priest Ernesto Cardenal came here to preach liberation theology and instruct the locals in artistic methods. His dream was a kind of radical Christian-Communist utopia that combined religion and revolution, spiritual love and community conscience. The result was a school of primitivist art whose vivid output is internationally renowned.

Perched like a ragged vulture between the San Juan river and Lake Nicaragua, San Carlos is a major crossroads, jungle gateway, border crossing (to Costa Rica, south along the Río Frío), as well as the capital of the isolated Río San Juan province. It has a sultry 'last outpost' feel: this is where the last buses arrive from the outside world after a lengthy journey through forests and wetlands.

The locals are philosophical about the future of their town, which stands in contrast to the sublime natural beauty in the surrounding countryside. Los Guatuzos Wildlife Reserve is alive with nature on the southern shores of Lake Nicaragua and the soporific Solentiname archipelago is the place where life finds itself in the lively colours and brush strokes of painted canvases.

Sights
Since the so-called 'discovery' of the Río San Juan by the Spanish Captain Ruy Díaz in 1525, San Carlos has had strategic importance. Its location means controlling

San Carlos

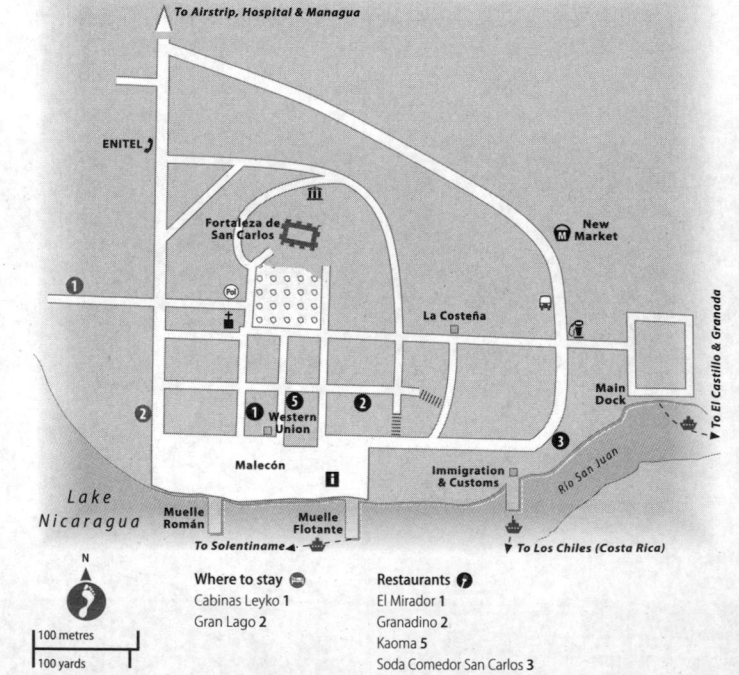

Where to stay 🛏
Cabinas Leyko **1**
Gran Lago **2**

Restaurants 🍴
El Mirador **1**
Granadino **2**
Kaoma **5**
Soda Comedor San Carlos **3**

San Carlos means controlling the water passages from north to south and east to west. The town was first founded in 1526, but it did not officially become a port until 1542. The town (and a fortress that has not survived) were abandoned for an unknown length of time and were re-founded as San Carlos during the 17th century. A new fortress was built but was sacked by pirates in 1670; part of it survives today as a small **museum** ① *0900-1200, 1400-1700, free*, and the town's principal tourist attraction. Today, San Carlos acts as a trading centre and as a staging post for Nicaraguan migrant workers and for a small but growing number of tourists. The city is small and easily navigated on foot. You are advised to bring as much cash as you'll need to the region due to the possible failure of the ATM in San Carlos.

San Carlos to Costa Rica

South of San Carlos, the Río Frio connects Lake Nicaragua and the Río San Juan to Los Chiles in northern Costa Rica. Formalities must be completed in San Carlos before crossing the border; see also Nicaragua–Costa Rica border box, page 256. The river passes through the superb **Refugio de Vida Silvestre Los Guatuzos** (see below) and the east bank is home to a small nature reserve called **Esperanza Verde** (see page 174). The limits of Nicaraguan territory are marked by a little green guard house. Although the river is used mainly as a commuter route, there is some beautiful wildlife and vegetation and it is rare not to see at least one clan of howler monkeys along the banks or even swimming.

As late as the 1870s the indigenous **Guatuzo** people (Maleku) inhabited the river banks of this area (the indigenous name for the river was Ucubriú). The naturalist Thomas Belt recounted battles between the rubber tappers and the Guatuzo people who were fighting to stop the invasion of their land. The Spanish were never able to subjugate the Guatuzo and they gained a reputation for hostility and were left alone for years; the original explorers of the Río Frío are thought to have been attacked and killed by Guatuzo arrows. However, when the India-rubber trade grew and the supply of trees along the Río San Juan was exhausted, the rubbermen were forced to explore the Río Frío. This time they came heavily armed, killing anyone in their path. By 1870, just the sight of a white man's boat along the river sent the indigenous population fleeing into the forest in desperate fear. After that, the end of the culture was quickly accomplished by illegal kidnapping and slave trading with the mines and farms of Chontales. (Today the Guatuzo are known as the Rama and they populate the Rama Cay in Bluefields Bay, see page 196.)

Refugio de Vida Silvestre Los Guatuzos

Nicaraguan biologists consider Los Guatuzos Wildlife Refuge the cradle of life for the lake, because of its importance as a bird-nesting site and its infinite links in the area's complex ecological chain. More than a dozen rivers run through the reserve, the most popular for wildlife viewing being the **Río Papaturro**. The ecosystems are diverse with tropical dry forest, tropical wet forest, rainforest and extensive wetlands. Best of all are the many narrow rivers lined with gallery forest, the ideal setting for viewing wildlife. The vegetation here is stunning with over 315 species of plants, including some primary forest trees over 35 m in height, and 130 species of orchid. The most impressive aspect of the reserve, however, is the density of its birdlife. As well as the many elegant egrets and herons, there are five species of kingfisher, countless jacanas, the pretty purple gallinule, wood storks, the roseate spoonbill, jabiru, osprey, laughing falcon, scarlet-rumped tanagers, trogons, bellbirds and six species of parrot.

Some residents have become involved in the research and protection of the reserve at the **Centro Ecológico de Los Guatuzos** ① *Managua office T2270-3561, www.losguatuzos.com, all visits are guided with options for walking tours, night tours, cacao tours and kayaking*. The ecological centre has over 100 species of orchid on display, a turtle hatchery and a caiman breeding centre. There is also a system of wobbly canopy bridges to allow visitors to observe wildlife from high up in the trees. If you don't suffer from vertigo, this is a wonderful experience allowing you to get right up close to the wildlife. Overnight lodging is available in simple dorms or private rooms (see page 135).

Archipiélago Solentiname

The Solentiname archipelago is a protected national monument and one of the most scenic parts of Lake Nicaragua. It is made up of 36 islands, all very remote, sparsely populated, without roads, telephones, electricity or running water. This is Nicaragua as it was two centuries ago, with only the outboard motorboat as a reminder of the modern world. There is plenty to keep you occupied on the islands, including visits to local artists, boating, swimming and nature walks. The main problem is the lack of public boats; services from San Carlos depart just twice a week (although plans are underway to establish a daily express service). This

BACKGROUND

Archipiélago Solentiname

The islands are the result of ancient volcanic activity, now heavily eroded and partially submerged. Solentiname has been populated since at least AD 500 and is thought to have been populated up until AD 1000, when historians believe it became a ceremonial site. Today the inhabitants are mostly third and fourth generation migrants from Chontales and Isla de Ometepe.

The islanders make a living from subsistence farming and artistic production. In the early 1960s, 12 local farmers were given painting classes at the initiative of the idealistic and much-revered Catholic priest/poet/sculptor Ernesto Cardenal. In addition, the local inhabitants were trained in balsa woodcarving. This small amount of training was passed from family to family; mother to son and father to daughter and soon the entire archipelago was involved in sculpting or painting. The style is *primitivista* and many of the painters have become internationally known and have been invited to study and exhibit as far away as Finland and Japan. The balsa woodcarvings can be found around Central America and the artisans have expanded their themes in recent years. Both the woodwork and oil paintings represent local ecology and legends, with the paintings normally depicting dense tropical landscape and the balsa works recreating individual species of the region.

Ernesto Cardenal ran his church innovatively with participative masses and a call to arms against the oppression of the Somoza government in the 1970s. The islanders, organized by Cardenal and led by local boy Alejandro Guevara, made the first successful rebel attack on a military base at San Carlos in October 1977; one month later Somoza sent helicopters to raze Mancarrón Island. Cardenal, who was defrocked by Pope John Paul II, went on to be the Sandinista Minister of Culture and an international celebrity. The 90-year-old icon still writes poetry, sculpts and visits Solentiname occasionally to stay in his small house on Isla Mancarrón near to his old church, which sadly is no longer in use. Cardenal's glowing memoir of all that was great about the Revolution and his role at the Ministerio de Cultura was published in 2003. The 666-page work, called *Revolución Perdida*, reveals some amazing scenes about his life as the international fundraiser for arms for the Sandinista rebel underground. It also documents in detail his administration of Nicaragua's blossoming culture in the 1980s, the biggest success of the Sandinista years. The book is in Spanish only and available at hotels on the islands and in Managua.

means you will have to hire a boat or use a tour operator to organize your trip or allow plenty of time to find transport when you're out there.

Isla Mancarrón is the biggest island in the chain and has the highest elevation at 250 m. It derives its name from the indigenous word for the coyol palm tree, which is used to make a sweet palm wine. The famous revolutionary/poet/sculptor/Catholic priest/Minister of Culture, Ernesto Cardenal, made his name here by founding a primitivista school of painting, poetry and sculpture, and even decorating the local parish church in naïve art. The church is open and there is a museum just behind the altar (ask permission to visit). It contains the first oil painting ever made on Solentiname, a bird's eye view of the island, and many other curiosities. Mancarrón is good for walking and it is home to many parrots and Montezuma oropendolas. Ask in the village for a guide to show you the way to the mirador, which has super views of the archipelago.

Named for its once-plentiful population of deer, **La Venada** (also known as Isla Donald Guevara) is a long narrow island that is home to many artists, including Rodolfo Arellano who lives on the southwestern side of the island. He and his wife are among the islands' original painters and his family welcome visitors to see and purchase their work. On the north side of the island is a series of semi-submerged caves with some of the best examples of petroglyphs which are attributed to the Guatuzo people. The cave can be visited by boat, though the entrance is dangerous if the lake is rough.

Isla San Fernando, also known as Elvis Chavarría, is also famous for its artisan work and painting. It has some of the prettiest houses in the archipelago and is home to the famous Pineda artist family. On a hill, the **Museo Archipiélago Solentiname** ① *T2583-0095 (in San Carlos), US$2*, has a small pre-Columbian collection, with some interesting explanations of local culture and ecology. It also has a fabulous view of the islands, not to be missed at sunset.

Mancarroncito is a big, wild, mountainous island with primary forest. There is some good hiking in the forest, although the terrain is steep. Ask at your guesthouse for a recommended guide.

On the north side of Mancarrón there is a tiny island with an inlet that holds the wreck of a sunken steamship from the inter-oceanic route. Only the chimney, now covered in tropical vegetation, is still visible above the water. On the far west end of the archipelago, just off the west coast of Mancarroncito, is another bird-nesting site on a little rock pile island, with hundreds of egret and cormorant nests.

Isla de Zapote, which is in front of the Los Guatuzos river of the same name, is home to over 10,000 bird nests, making it perhaps the richest bird-nesting site in Nicaragua. Most of the nests belong to cormorants or white egrets, although there are other egrets, herons, roseate spoonbills, wood storks and two species of ibis among the others.

Between San Fernando and Mancarrón is the small forest-covered island of **El Padre**, named after a priest who once lived there. It is the only island with monkeys (howlers), which were introduced only 25 years ago and are now thriving. With a few circles of the island by boat you should be able to find some of them.

Tourist information

Tourist office
On the waterfront malecón, T2583-0301.
Mon-Fri 0800-1200, 1400-1700.
They have a selection of maps and flyers.
They're helpful, but speak Spanish only.

Where to stay

San Carlos

$$ Gran Lago Hotel
Caruna, 25 vrs al lago, T2583-0075,
www.grandhotelsnicaragua.com.
Has views of the lake and serves fruit
breakfast in the mornings. The rooms
are comfortable, with private bath, a/c,
cable TV, Wi-Fi and 24-hr water. Purified
water and coffee available throughout
the day.

$$-$ Cabinas Leyko
Policía Nacional, 2 c abajo, T2583-0354,
hotecabinasleyko@outlook.com.
One of the better places in town, with
clean, comfortable wooden cabins
overlooking the wetlands, good
mattresses, Wi-Fi, private bath and a/c.
There are some not-so-good rooms too
($), cheaper with fan and shared bath.

Refugio de Vida Silvestre Los Guatuzos

$$ Esperanza Verde
Río Frío, 4 km from San Carlos, T2583-
0127, fundeverde@yahoo.es.
In a beautiful area rich in wildlife, these
280 ha of private reserve inside the Los
Guatuzos Wildlife Refuge have good
nature trails for birdwatching. There are
20 rooms with single beds, fan, shared
bath. Prices include 3 meals per day.

$$ La Esquina del Lago
At the mouth of the Río Frío, T8849-0600,
www.riosanjuan.info.
Surrounded by vegetation and visited
by 61 species of bird, this tranquil and
hospitable fishing lodge on the water
is owned by former newspaper man
Philippe Tisseaux. A range of tours are
available, including birdwatching and
world-class sports fishing. Excellent food,
which uses fresh fish and home-grown
herbs. Free use of kayak and free transport
from San Carlos, a 5-min ride away.

$ Centro Ecológico de Los Guatuzos
Río Papaturro, T2270-3561,
www.losguatuzos.com.
An attractive research station on the
riverfront. Lodging is in wooden rooms
with bunk beds, 1 with private bath.
Meals for guests from US$5, served in a
local house. Guided visits to forest trails,
excursions to others rivers in the reserve.
Night caiman tours by boat. Private boat
to and from San Carlos can be arranged.
All tours in Spanish only, some Managua
tour operators arrange programmes with
an English-speaking guide (see page 51).

Archipiélago Solentiname

$$ Cabañas Paraíso
Isla San Fernando, T2583-9015.
The lack of trees means that the views
are spectacular and the sun hot. Rooms
are very clean, bright and crowded, with
private bath. Feels a bit Miami, but friendly.
Excursions in very fine boats are offered.

$$ Hotel Celentiname or Doña María
Isla San Fernando, T2276-1910, www.
hotelcelentiname.blogspot.com.
This laid-back place is the most traditional
of the hotels here. It has a lovely location

facing another island and a lush garden filled with big trees, hummingbirds, iguanas and, at night, fishing bats. The rustic cabins have private bath and nice decks. Sad dorm rooms are not much cheaper with shared baths. Generated power, all meals included. Friendly owners. Recommended.

$$ Hotel Mancarrón
Isla Mancarrón, up the hill from the cement dock and church, T8852-3380, www.hotelmancarron.com.
Great birdwatching around this hotel that has access to the artisan village. Rooms are airy, screened, equipped with mosquito netting and private bath. The managers are personal and friendly. Prices include 3 great home-cooked meals per day. Recommended.

$ Hospedaje Reynaldo Ucarte
Isla Mancarrón, main village.
4 decent but basic rooms with shared baths. Meals available on request. Friendly, nice area with lots of children and trees.

Restaurants

San Carlos

$$$-$$ Granadino
Opposite Alejandro Granja playing field, T2583-0386. Daily 0900-0200.
Considered the best in town, with a relaxed ambience and pleasant river views. *Camarones en salsa*, steak and hamburgers. Not cheap.

$$-$ Kaoma
Across from Western Union, T2583-0293. Daily from 0900 until the last customer collapses in a pool of rum.
Nautically themed and also decorated with dozens of oropendola nests. There's fresh fish caught by the owner,

good *camarones de río* (freshwater prawns) and dancing when the locals are inspired. Views of the river from the wooden deck and occasionally refreshing breezes. Recommended.

$ El Mirador
Iglesia Católica, 1½ c sur, T2583-0367. Daily 0700-2000.
Superb view from patio of Lake Nicaragua, Solentiname, Río Frío and Río San Juan and the jumbled roofs of the city. Decent chicken, fish and beef dishes starting at US$3 with friendly service. Recommended, though it closes if the *chayules* (mosquitoes) are in town.

$ Soda Comedor San Carlos
Muelle Principal, 100 m sur.
One of many cheap and popular places in the area serving economical Nica food.

Shopping

San Carlos
Stock up on purified water and food for a long journey. The market is a cramped nightmare, but in front of immigration there are stalls to buy goods. High-top rubber boots or wellingtons are standard equipment in these parts, perfect for jungle treks (hiking boots are not recommended) and cost US$5-10.

What to do

San Carlos
Tour operators
San Carlos Sport Fishing, *La Esquina del Lago hotel, at the mouth of the Río Frío, T8849-0600, www.riosanjuan.info.* Operated by Phillipe Tisseaux, who has many years of experience fishing the Río San Juan, where plenty of tarpon, snook and rainbow bass can be caught. He also offers birdwatching, kayaking and cultural tours. Recommended.

Transport

San Carlos
Air
At the time of research (Mar 2019), flights between San Carlos and Managua had been suspended. For the latest updates, contact **La Costeña**, www.lacostena.online.com.ni.

Bus
From San Carlos to **Managua**, 8 daily, US$7, 5-6 hrs; to **Juigalpa**, 4 daily, 1000-1330, US$4, 4 hrs; to **El Rama**, 0900, US$7, 7 hrs.

Motorboat
Small motor boats are called *pangas*; long, narrow ones are *botes* and big broad ones are known as *planos*.

Public Arrive at least 30 mins in advance to ensure a seat on a short ride; allow 1 hr or more for long trips. All schedules are subject to random and/or seasonal changes; check locally before setting out. To **Solentiname**, Tue, Fri, 1300, US$4, 2½ hrs, stopping at islands **La Venada**, **San Fernando**, **Mancarrón**. At the time of research, there was talk of express services starting soon, enquire locally for the latest information. To **Los Guatuzos**, stopping at **Papaturro**, Mon-Wed and Fri-Sat, 0900, 4 hrs, US$3.20; express service at 0945, 2 hrs, US$4.60; returning to San Carlos Sun-Tue and Thu-Fri, 0800, 4 hrs, US$3.20; express service at 0900, US$4.60. To **El Castillo** (and Sábalos), Mon-Sat (express) 0630, 1030, 1630; (slow) 0800, 1200, 1430, 1530; Sun (slow) 1330. Avoid the slow boat if you can, it's a gruelling 6-hr ride. To **San Juan de Nicaragua**, Tue, Thu, Fri 0600, 12-14 hrs, US$14; express services run in the wet season only, Tue 0600, Wed 1000, Fri 0600, and Sun 1000, 6 hrs, US$30. At the time of research, the ferry to **Granada** had been suspended due to low water levels in the lake. For the latest updates, see www.ometepenicaragua.com/ferryboat.php.

Private Motorboats are available for hire; they are expensive but afford freedom to view wildlife. They are also faster, leave when you want and allow you to check out different hotels. Beyond El Castillo downriver there are only 2 boats per week, so private transport is the only other option. Ask at tourism office for recommendations.

Taxi
Taxis wait for arriving flights at the landing strip; if you miss them you will have to walk to town (30 mins). To get to the landing strip, taxis can be found in town between the market and *muelle flotante*. All fares are US$1, exact change is essential. Drivers are helpful.

Archipiélago Solentiname
Boat
Solentiname to **San Carlos**, Tue, Fri 0430, US$4, 2½ hrs. **Los Guatuzos** and **Río Papaturro** to **San Carlos**, Mon, Tue, Thu 0600, US$5, 3½ hrs.

The Río San Juan is Lake Nicaragua's sole outlet to the sea. Three major rivers that originate in Costa Rica and more than 17 smaller tributaries also feed this mighty river, which is up to 350 m wide at points. At San Carlos, enough water enters the river in a 24-hour period in the dry season to supply water to all of Central America for one year – a gigantic resource that Nicaragua has yet to exploit. For the visitor, it is an opportunity to experience the rainforest and to journey from Central America's biggest lake all the way to the thundering surf of Nicaragua's eastern seaboard.

Río Sábalo
Outside the limits of San Carlos, the river is lined with wetlands, providing good opportunities for birdwatching. Deforestation in this section of the river (until El Castillo) is getting increasingly worse, however. The Río Sábalo is an important tributary named after the large fish found in this region, the *sábalo* (tarpon). The town at its mouth, **Boca de Sábalos**, is melancholy, muddy and friendly. There are decent lodges in the area (see Where to stay, below) and the people of Sábalo seem happy to see outsiders. There are some small rapids just past the river's drainage into the Río San Juan. The fishing for *sábalo real* (giant tarpon) is quite good here. They can reach up to 2.5 m and weigh in at 150 kg. Another popular sport fish is *robalo* (snook) and much better to eat than tarpon.

El Castillo
The peaceful village of El Castillo, 60 km from San Carlos, could well be the most attractive riverfront settlement in Nicaragua. Located in front of the El Diablo rapids, El Castillo is a sight to behold: tiny riverfront homes with red tin roofs sit on stilts above the fast-moving river. Behind, on a round grassy green hill, a big, 330-year-old Spanish fort dominates the view of the town. Most people come to see the fort, but the village makes a longer stay worthwhile.

Construction of the 17th-century **Fortaleza de la Inmaculada Concepción** began in 1673 after British pirate Henry Morgan made off down the Río San Juan with £500,000 of loot plundered from the city of Granada. From its hilltop vantage the fort enjoys long views to the east, where it came under attack by the British several times in the 18th century, most notably by Admiral Nelson, who managed to capture it briefly before being forced to abandon by a Central American counter offensive. Inside the fortress you'll find a **library** and **museum** ① *0900-1200, 1400-1700, US$2*; the views alone are worth the price of admission. There is also an educational museum behind the fortress, **Centro de Interpretación de la Naturaleza**, with displays and explanations of local wildlife and vegetation as well as a butterfly farm.

> **Tip...**
> Bring all the cash you need before setting out because there are no banks in El Castillo.

Reserva Biológica Indio Maíz

A few kilometres downstream is the Río Bartola and the beginning of the Reserva Biológica Indio Maíz, Central America and Nicaragua's second largest nature reserve and perhaps its most pristine. A few square kilometres here house more species of bird, tree or insect than the entire European continent. The reserve protects what North American biologists have called "the largest extent of primary rainforest in Central America", its trees reaching up to 50 m in height. Indio-Maíz also has numerous wetland areas and rivers. Covering 3000 sq km of mostly primary rainforest, it's home to more than 600 species of bird, 300 species of reptile and 200 species of mammal including many big cats and howler, white-faced and spider monkeys.

Sleeping is possible in **Refugio Bartola**, a research station and training ground for biologists; it has a labyrinth of well-mapped trails behind the lodge. The hotel guides are very knowledgeable. They will also take you down the Río Bartola in a canoe for great wildlife viewing and birding; see below. Neglect in recent years has made turning up without booking a bit of a gamble, so do book in advance. Camping is possible; ask the park ranger (his house is across the Río Bartola from the **Refugio Bartola** lodge, see page 144).

Río Bartola–Río San Carlos

Travel time about 1 hr.

This is one of the most scenic sections of the river, in particular the area around the rapids of **Machuca** and just upriver from the mouth of Río San Carlos, which originates in Costa Rica. The forest is in good condition on both sides of the river and the trees are

Essential Río San Juan

Finding your feet

A single north-bound highway connects San Carlos with the capital; after years of disrepair it is finally paved, cutting overland journey times to just five hours. At the time of research, flights to San Carlos had been suspended, along with the famous Granada ferry.

Getting around

There are few roads in the sparsely inhabited Río San Juan province. Travel is only possible by boat, with a regular daily service to El Castillo and sparse public boat operations downriver. To really explore, private boat hire is necessary, though expensive.

When to go

Water levels on the river are significantly lower during the dry season, but it can rain heavily at any time of year; pack accordingly and protect your luggage from downpours. High water levels during the wet season, May to November, make transit along the waterways speedier but can also make hiking in the forests unpleasant and challenging; expect hordes of insects and knee-high mud.

Time required

Four to nine days. Travel in the region is time-consuming and/or comparatively expensive.

BACKGROUND
Río San Juan

In 1502 Christopher Columbus explored the Caribbean coast of Nicaragua in search of an inter-oceanic passage. He sailed right past the Río San Juan. The river was populated by the Rama people, the same that can be found today on a small island in the Bay of Bluefields. In the 17th century the biggest Rama settlement was estimated at more than 30,000 in the Boca de Sábalo; at the same time, the capital of Nicaragua had some 40,000 residents. Today the Rama are making a return to the southern forests of Nicaragua, though only in the Río Indio area along the Caribbean coast.

When Francisco Hernández de Córdoba established the cities of Granada and León, he sent Spanish Captain Ruy Díaz in search of the lake's drainage. Díaz explored the entire lake, reaching the mouth of the river in 1525. He was able to navigate the river as far as the first principal northern tributary, Río Sábalo, but was forced to turn back. Córdoba was unfazed and sent a second expedition led by Captain Hernando de Soto (later the first European to navigate the Mississippi river). Soto managed to sail as far as Díaz and was also forced to turn back due to the rapids.

Explorers were busy looking for gold in Nicaragua's northern mountains and the river was ignored until 1539, when a very serious expedition was put together by the Spanish governor of Nicaragua, Rodrigo de Contreras. This brutally difficult journey was undertaken by foot troops, expert sailors and two brave captains, Alonso Calero and Diego Machuca. Having passed the first set of rapids, they encountered more rapids at El Castillo; Machuca divided the expedition and marched deep into the forest looking for the outlet of the river. Calero continued the length of the river and reached its end at the Caribbean Sea on 24 June 1539. This happened to be Saint John the Baptist's saint's day, so they named the river after him. He then sailed north in search of Machuca as far as the outlet of the Río Coco. However, Machuca had left on foot with his troops and returned all the way to Granada without knowledge of what had happened to the Calero party. The newly discovered passage was exactly what the Spanish had been hoping for. It was quickly put into service for the transport of gold, indigo and other goods from their Pacific holdings to Hispañola (Dominican Republic and Haiti today) and then to Spain. The river was part of the inter-oceanic steam ship service of Cornelius Vanderbilt in the mid-1800s and was used by William Walker for his brief rule in Granada. During the Contra conflict, parts of the river were contested by Edén Pastora's southern front troops in attacks against the Sandinista government army.

teeming with parrots. As the vegetation rises out of succulent rainforest, it's easy to see why visitors have been so enchanted over time.

At the mouth of the pristine **Río Sarnoso** is a shipwreck from the 19th-century inter-oceanic steam ship service, though the locals like to claim it is a Spanish galleon wreck. Jaguar can be seen here, one of the most difficult jungle animals to spot thanks to their preference for night hunting and large territories (up to 11 sq km). To enter the Río Sarnoso you will need to receive advance permission from MARENA in Managua (see page 45) and show the letter to the guards east or west of the river.

At the confluence of the **Río San Carlos** there is a checkpoint for the Nicaraguan military and MARENA, where passports must be presented. Across the banks in Costa Rica there is a general store and a basic eatery. Permission can be obtained from the Costa Rican military to make a quick supply or food stop (córdobas are difficult to use on the Costa Rican side, so keep a supply of small note dollars).

There once was a Spanish fortress on the island that lies at the confluence of the San Carlos and San Juan rivers, which predated the structure at El Castillo. The **Fortaleza San Carlos** (not to be confused with the old fort at San Carlos on the lake) was built in 1667 with room for 70 musketeers and a few artillerymen to operate four cannon. Three years later, pirate Lawrence Prince attacked the little wooden fortress with 200 men. Only 37 Spanish soldiers had survived the climate and insects, but nonetheless put up stout resistance, killing six and wounding eight of the pirates and managing to send a boat up to Granada to ask for reinforcements. They never came and the Spaniards had to surrender. Prince sent his fastest canoe double-manned with Miskito oarsmen to overtake the Spanish messenger. He then went on to sack Granada, prompting the construction of the great structure at El Castillo (see page 138).

Río San Carlos–Río Sarapiquí *Travel time about 1 hr.*
Past the Río San Carlos the stunning beauty of the Indio-Maíz reserve on the north bank continues, while the south bank is a mixture of forest and ranch settlements. There are sandbars and beaches most of the year and slow navigation will allow you to spot crocodiles and turtles, as well as monkeys and toucans in the canopy. The muddy, debris-filled **Río Sarapiquí** drains into the Río San Juan at the second river checkpoint for the military and MARENA. The Sarapiquí is in Costa Rica and there is a village where basic boat and motor repairs can be made. This was the scene of several battles between the Edén Pastora-led southern front Contra forces and the Nicaraguan Sandinista military in the 1980s.

Río Sarapiquí–Río Colorado *Travel time about 1 hr.*
Past the drainage of the Sarapiquí, the Río San Juan travels northeast passing some of the river's 300 islands, including the **Isla Nelson**. Petrol is available on the Costa Rican side, which is dotted with sprawling ranches. The Nicaraguan territory (which includes the river and its islands) is pristine rainforest mixed with some secondary growth where land was reclaimed for the biological reserve. At one of the widest parts of the river it branches southeast and northeast. To the southeast is the mighty **Río Colorado** in Costa Rica. To the northeast is the **Río San Juan**. Thanks to sediment build-up in the bay of San Juan since the mid- to late-1800s, the majority of the water now drains out of the Río Colorado to the sea. There is

another checkpoint here. Past the intersection of the two rivers, the Río San Juan becomes narrow and runs almost due north.

Río Colorado–Caribbean Sea *Travel time about 2 hrs.*
This section of the Río San Juan is normally quite good for sighting monkeys, toucans, scarlet macaws and king vultures. As it approaches the sea, the Río San Juan begins to snake wildly. It twists and turns past wetlands and the broad, handsome swamp palms that are common in this area, until it meets the sea at a dark sandbar called simply **La Barra** (the bar). The emerging and submerging sandbar (according to the tides and the force of the San Juan river) has fooled navigators for hundreds of years and has been responsible for many a sailor's death. After hours of dense jungle, the sight of the windswept beach is exhilarating. Here the Caribbean is muddy, filled with sediment from the river and literally teeming with bull sharks that are feeding on the many fish in this rich combination of fresh and salt water. Swimming is only for the suicidal (you could not pay a local to swim here) – strong surf and currents aid the sharks in ripping apart any flesh within its reach.

San Juan de Nicaragua
One of the wettest places on the American continent with more than 5000 mm of rain each year, San Juan de Nicaragua (formerly known as San Juan del Norte) is also one of the most beautiful, with primary rainforest, lagoons, rivers and the desolate surf of the Caribbean Sea. The end-of-the-world feeling is not lost in this little village of winding paths, homes on stilts, and flooded yards.

It is settled by a small population (estimated at 275), though it was once a boom town in the 19th century, when the American industrialist Cornelius Vanderbilt was running his steamship line between New York and San Francisco. Then called Greytown, San Juan de Nicaragua was the pick-up point for the steamship journey to the Pacific via the Río San Juan, Lake Nicaragua to La Virgen and then by mule overland to San Juan del Sur. If in your own boat (chartered), a trip down the **Río Indio** is recommended, with lots of wildlife, virgin forest and Rama (please respect their culture and privacy). A visit to the ruins of old **Greytown** is also interesting, but much of its haunting ambience has been lost with the construction of a new airport in its vicinity.

Edgar 'Rasta' Coulson is the best guide in town, and a good cook too; he waits for new arrivals and owns **Cabinas El Escondite** (see Where to stay, below). There are no banks and the most common currency is Costa Rican colones thanks to the (relatively) easy access to El Limón, Costa Rica. You can pay in córdobas or dollars, but expect change in colones. There is a Nicaraguan customs and immigration at San Juan de Nicaragua, but officially entrance and exit stamps for international travel cannot be obtained here.

Where to stay

Río Sábalo

$$$ Monte Cristo River Resort
2 km downriver from Boca de Sábalos,
T8649-9012, www.montecristoriver
lodge.com.
A well-established ecolodge and resort
set inside its own rambling private
nature reserve. It has comfortable cabins
with private bath, dance floor and **Mark
Twain Bar**. Sometimes loud weekend
parties arrive from El Castillo to use the
dance hall. Rate covers 3 meals and all
activities, including kayaking, fishing and
horses. Recommended.

$$ Hotel Sábalos
On confluence of San Juan and
Sábalo rivers, T8659-0252,
www.hotelsabalos.com.ni.
This simple and friendly wooden hotel
has a good location, with views up and
down the river, great for watching locals
pass in canoes. Wooden rooms have
private bath and fan. The best resting
spot on upper San Juan. Recommended.

$$ Sábalos Lodge
In front of El Toro rapids, just downriver
from Río Sábalo, T8823-5514,
www.sabaloslodge.com.
Funky and attractive mix of huts, cabins,
shacks, some with bath inside, and
hammocks. One nice unit on the river has
a sitting room and deck, all open to the
outside with mosquito netting. Beautiful
grounds but not much forest around.

$ Hotel Grand River Lodge
Between San Carlos and Boca de
Sabalos, 3 km from the community
of Esperanza, T8375-7248,
grandriverlodge@gmail.com.

Simple wooden cabins with private
toilet. They offer a plethora of activities
including horse riding, kayaking,
community tours and hiking. Friendly,
hospitable owners.

El Castillo

$$ Hotel Victoria
El muelle, 400 vrs arriba, at the
end of the end road, T2583-0188.
This friendly and hospitable hotel has
9 wood-panelled rooms with cable
TV, a/c and private bath (**$** with shared
bath). Downstairs there's a pleasant
restaurant overlooking the water and
a nearby stream filled with turtles and
caimans. Tours with accredited guides
include horse-riding and night tours.
The best place in town. Recommended.

$ Albergue El Castillo
Next to fortress above city dock,
T8924-5608.
Comfortable, if simple, wooden rooms
and great views from a shared balcony
overlooking the river. Only 1 room has
a private bath; for extra side ventilation,
the best rooms are Nos 1 and 10, but you
have noisy bats for company in No 10.
Also noisy early morning as the public
boats warm up (0500) motors. Breakfast
and 25 mins of internet included.

$ Hotel Tropical
Calle Principal, del muelle, 130 m sur,
T8699-8883.
A fantastic location overlooking the
river, Hotel Tropical has a smart wooden
balcony for chilling out and a handful of
clean, comfortable rooms with private
bath, some with a/c. The restaurant
downstairs isn't bad either.

$ Nena Lodge
El muelle, 350 vrs arriba, T8821-2135,
www.nenalodge.com.
This hotel has a range of simple budget
rooms equipped with mosquito nets,
soap and towels. Many of them open
onto a communal balcony slung with
hammocks. There is a tour agency on
site, running trips to **Finca Los Cocos**,
Sendero Bartola and **Sendero Aguas
Frescas**, among others.

Río Bartola to the Caribbean

$$$$ Río Indio Lodge
*Between Indio and San Juan rivers, near
San Juan de Nicaragua, T506-2296-0095
(Costa Rica), www.therioindiolodge.com.*
Multi-million dollar lodge, designed for
upscale fishing packages but excellent
for wildlife safaris, birdwatching and
rainforest walks. Named one of the top
10 jungle lodges in the world.

$$$ Basecamp Bartola
*Community of Bartola, on the Río
Bartola, T8433-4664, indio.maiz@
gmail.com.*
A sustainable tourism project organized
and led on a co-operative basis by
the community of Bartola. Lodging
is in tents on wooden platforms with
all-inclusive packets covering transport,
meals and guided tours of the rainforest.
Contact in advance of visit as you will
need guides to locate the camp.

$$ Refugio Bartola
*Confluence of Río San Juan
and Río Bartola, T8873-8586.*
Simple wooden rooms with private
bath, high ceilings and solid beds. Prices
include 3 meals, juice and coffee, bats
in roof and frogs in toilet at no extra
charge. There's a research station on
site, with lots of creepy creatures in jars,

including what could be the world's
largest cockroach. Recommended.

San Juan de Nicaragua

$ Cabinas El Escondite
*Behind the military base north of the pier,
ask for Rasta, T8414-9761.*
Spacious wooden *cabinas* with bunk
beds, private bath and a pleasant
garden. The owner, Rasta, speaks English
and cooks the best Caribbean food in
town (**$$-$**). Great host and relaxed vibe.
Recommended.

$ Hotelito Evo
*Proyecto habitacional, Grupo 'Bed and
Breakfast', Casa 18, west of the pier, ask
around for Enrique's place, T8278-5555.*
This cosy B&B has a relaxed family
atmosphere and 7 simple rooms, most
with private bath. The owner, Enrique,
is friendly and knows the history of the
town. Breakfast included and other
meals available.

Restaurants

El Castillo
Eating is good here; the freshwater
prawns (*camarones de río*) and snook
(*robalo*) are both excellent.

$$$-$$ Bar Cofalito
On the jetty.
Has a great view upstairs overlooking
the river and serves excellent *camarones
de río*, considered by many the best in
town, with fresh fish most evenings.

$$$-$$ Borders Coffee
Next to the dock.
Good but pricey pasta in organic
tomato sauce, vegetarian fare, curries,
shrimps and fresh organic cappuccinos
at this friendly little café. Nice views of
the river and a good place to wait for

your boat. They can also arrange stays at a nearby finca.

$ Vanessa's
El muelle, 1 c arriba.
Great spot by the rapids, with fish and river shrimp. Can be hit and miss; check the catch is fresh before ordering.

Transport

El Castillo
Boat
All schedules are subject to change; confirm times locally.

To **San Carlos**; Mon-Sat (express) 0530, 1130, 1530; (slow) 0530, 1130, 1530; (slow) 0500, 0700, 1400, US$3.75 express, US$2 slow boat, 1½-2½ hrs.
To **San Juan de Nicaragua**, Tue, Thu, Fri 0900, US$12.50, 8-9 hrs. In the west season, express services run Tue and Fri 0800, 5-6 hrs, US$25.

San Juan de Nicaragua
Air
There is an airport on the edge of Greytown, but flights had been suspended at the time of research (Mar 2019). For the latest updates, contact **Costeña**, www.lacostena.com.ni.

Boat
All schedules are subject to change; check times locally.

To **San Carlos**, stopping at **El Castillo**, Thu and Sun 0430, US$12.50 (US$25 express). A service between San Juan de Nicaragua and **Bluefields** usually leaves once a week, but days change and it is very inconsistent. Without careful planning, there is a real risk of getting stranded in the town. The ride, if available, is 3-4 hrs and extremely wet and bumpy. It is not advised for pregnant travellers or those with back problems.

León
& around

León is the artistic and intellectual heart of the country, the spiritual home of Nicaragua's greatest poets, and, since 1979, a hotbed of Sandinista activity. A wealth of satirical murals, bombed-out ruins and bullet-marked buildings are evidence of the city's turbulent revolutionary past, whilst its student population lends it a vibrant nightlife.

After a day exploring León, you can relax in one of its many bars, share a few rounds of Flor de Caña and take in a rousing performance of live folk music.

If the heat and frenetic activity of the downtown area prove too much, the Pacific coastline beyond León is accented by beaches, barrier islands and coastal lagoons. An excursion to the sleepy shores of Poneloya and Las Peñitas, 20 minutes west, is always refreshing and welcome, but the bucolic retreat of Jiquilillo, perched on the remote and less-visited coast of the Coseguina Peninsula, is the place for serious hammock time. Equally, if you're seeking proper adventure, León is the gateway to some immense and extraordinary panoramas. Home to one of the most densely active volcanic chains in the world, the Cordillera Los Maribios, this is a land born of scorched skies and violently shifting geological tempers. Smoking craters, steaming pools, tranquil lakes and stark, rolling, black-sand slopes perfect for high-speed boarding all await exploration.

youthful university town with appealing colonial churches and museums

Though taxis are cheap, the simplest and richest pleasure in León (altitude 109 m, population 155,000) is walking its historic streets, noting the infinite variety of elaborate doors, ceiling work and window ironwork, as well as sneaking peeks inside the grand houses to see their lush interior gardens. Each barrio supports its own unique church and beautiful colonial homes.

The city is laid out in the classic Spanish colonial grid system, based around a central plaza, commonly referred to as Parque Central. The majestic León Cathedral faces west and sits on the park's east side. Roads running east–west are *calles* and those running north–south *avenidas*. Calle Rubén Darío runs directly west from Parque Central, through Sutiava and all the way to the Pacific Ocean.

Cathedral of León
It's possible to climb the cathedral for commanding views of the city and countryside, US$1.

The Cathedral of León, officially the **Basílica de la Asunción**, is the pride of both city and country. This impressive structure – a UNESCO World Heritage Site since 2011 – is the work of 113 years of labour (1747-1860). Legend has it that the plans for the cathedrals of Lima in Peru and León were switched by mistake, but there is no evidence to support that charming excuse for such a big church in such a little country. The design was conceived by Guatemalan architect Diego de Porres and has been described as Central American baroque. Its squat towers and super-thick walls stem from the experience gained from building in the seismically active valley of Ciudad Antigua. Inside, the cathedral houses a very fine **ivory Christ**, the consecrated **Altar of Sacrifices** and the **Choir of Córdoba**. The **tomb of Rubén Darío**, Nicaragua's greatest poet, is guarded by a sorrowing lion.

West of the cathedral
There are several interesting and historic buildings on **Parque Central**, including the **archbishop's house** opposite the south side of the cathedral, and the historic **Seminario de San Ramón**, founded in 1680, which today houses a primary school. Next door, the Gothic **Colegio de Asunción** (primary and secondary school) is often mistaken for a church.

The grand old Palacio Municipal stands on the southwest corner of Parque Central, a 1930s structure that has been decaying since its Somoza-era heyday. Today it houses the pro-Sandinista **Museo de la Revolución** ① *daily 0800-1800, US$3*, where visitors can learn about the 1979 Revolution and hear gripping war stories from former FSLN fighters. Your visit concludes with a trip to the roof for great views over the plaza. One block south of the Palacio Municipal is the beautifully restored **Teatro Municipal José de la Cruz Mena** ① *T8947-7480, Mon-Fri 0800-1230 and 1400-1700, plays and concerts from US$1-15*, built in the 19th century and named after León's greatest classical composer.

León

León served the capital of Nicaragua for 242 years until it was moved to Managua. The present city was founded in 1610 after the abandonment of its cursed original location, known today as León Viejo (see page 162). The site was chosen to be close to the large indigenous settlement of Sutiava and to the Pacific.

In the 1960s and 70s, León became a hotbed for the Frente Sandinista de Liberación Nacional (FSLN) Marxist underground. Fighting against Somoza Debayle (the son of Somoza García) was fierce in León, with much damage suffered by the old city, some of which can still be seen today. After a final brutal battle which lasted from 3 June to 9 July 1979 and was won by the rebels, the FSLN, led by female Comandante Dora María Tellez, succeeded. The city is still strongly Sandinista, with every mayor since 1979 coming from the FSLN party.

Two blocks west of Parque Central is the **Convento y Iglesia San Francisco**. The church was damaged in 1979 during fighting in the Revolution but maintains much of its ancient charm. It was the city's first convent when founded in 1639 and has now been converted into a hotel called **El Convento** (see Where to stay, below). On the corner opposite the church stands the **Museo de Arte Fundación Ortiz-Guardián** ① *T2311-2716, www.fundacionortizgurdian.org, Tue-Fri 0900-1700, Sat 0930-1700, Sun 0900-1600, entrance US$3.50*, a lovely colonial home that doubles as one of the finest art museums in Central America with work from Europe, Latin America and Nicaragua. It is worth a visit to see a classic example of a colonial period home. Across the street, is an annexe holding more modern art. One block west on Calle Central is the **Museo-Archivo Rubén Darío** ① *Calle Central, Iglesia San Francisco, 1 c abajo, T2311-2388, Tue-Sat 0800-1200, 1400-1700, Sun 0800-1200, US$1*, which has an interesting collection of the national hero's personal possessions, photographs, portraits and a library with poetry books in Spanish, English and French. Its other claim to fame is that the great metaphysical poet Alfonso Cortés lost his mind here. See also boxes, pages 153 and 154.

East of the cathedral

On Calle Central, three blocks east of the cathedral, is the **Iglesia El Calvario**. Built in the mid-1700s, it was restored in 2000, the towering Momotombo Volcano in the background supplying a dramatic setting. Two blocks north of the church is the **Museo Entomológico** ① *ENEL, 30 vrs arriba, opposite Western Union, T2311-6586, www.bio-nica.info, daily 0900-1200, 1400-1600, US$0.50*, home to the amazing insect collection of Nicaragua's foremost entomologist, Dr Jean-Michel Maes. **Note** Despite official opening times, the museum is not always open. To arrange a visit, contact jmmaes@bio-nica.info.

North of the cathedral

Two blocks north of Parque Central is the lovely **Iglesia La Merced**, built in the late 1700s. This is León's second most important church and home of the patron saint of León, the Virgen de las Mercedes. In the early 19th century there was a fire in the main altar that holds the image and legend has it that a local black slave rushed into the flames to rescue it. In gratitude for his heroism he was granted

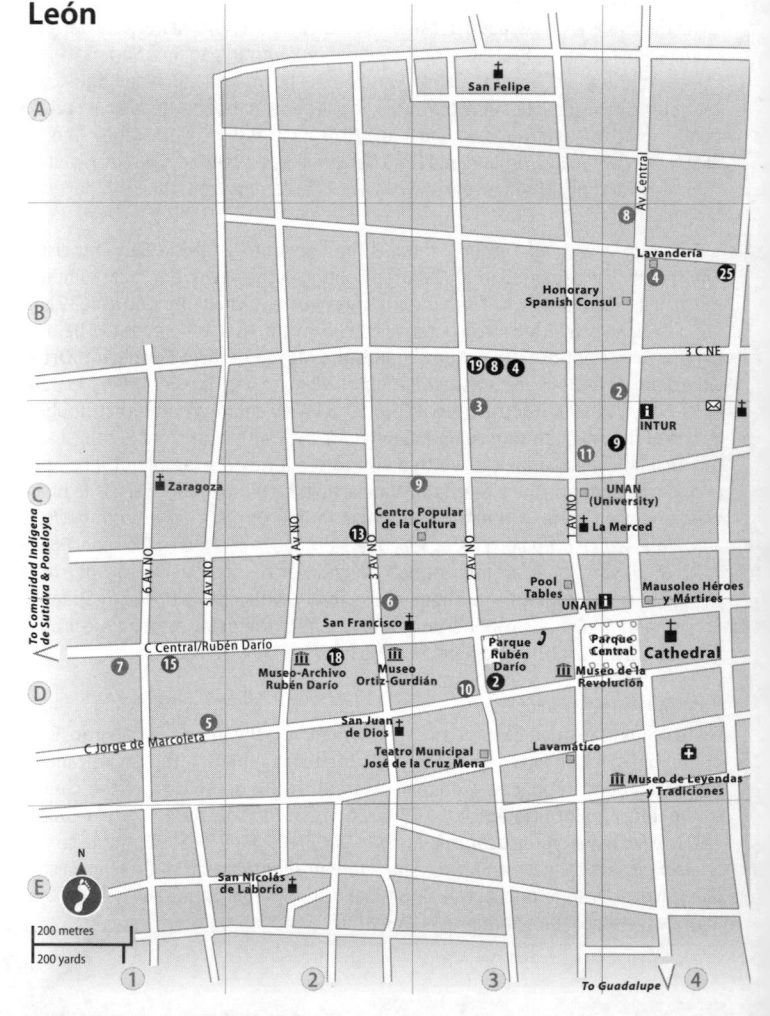

León

his freedom. The interior of the church is arguably the most ornately decorated in Nicaragua.

One and half blocks west of the La Merced, is the **Centro Popular de la Cultura**, which has occasional exhibitions and events (see schedule on bulletin board in front lobby). Three blocks west and one block north, the **Iglesia de Zaragoza** was built from 1884 to 1934 and has two octagonal turrets and an arched doorway with tower above.

To Chinandega & San Jacinto

6 C NE

5 C NE

TSA Tours Travel

San Juan Bautista

Parque San Juan

4 C NE

Mercado San Juan

To Bus Terminal (3 blocks) & Market

La Recolección

2 C NE

Museo Entomológico

La Unión Supermarket
Cinemas

1 C NE

El Calvario

1 C SE

2 C SE

3 C SE

Cimac

4 C SE

Where to stay
Azul 2 B4
Bigfoot Hostel 17 C5
Cacique Adiact 4 B4
Casa de Huéspedes El Nancite 15 C5
El Albergue de León 1 B5
El Convento 6 D2
Flor de Sarta 8 B4
Hostal Calle de los Poetas 7 D1
La Casona Colonial 14 B5
La Perla 11 C3
Lazybones Hostel 3 C3
Poco a Poco Hostel 9 C3
Posada Fuente Castalia 18 A5
Real 19 C5
Tortuga Booluda 5 D1
Via Via 20 C5

Restaurants
Café Nicaragüita 8 B3
Cafetín Don Jacks 6 C5
Carnívoro 9 C4
Comedor Lucía 11 C5
El Bárbaro 2 D3
El Desayunazo 19 B3
El Mississippi 12 D6
La Casa Vieja 13 C2
La Mexicana 4 B3
Libélula 18 D2
Pan y Paz 7 C5
Porky's House 25 B4

Bars & clubs
Gecko's Bar 10 D3
Olla Quemada 15 D1
Via Via 1 C5

Two blocks north of the cathedral's lions on Avenida Central is the **Iglesia La Recolección**, with a beautiful baroque Mexican façade that tells the entire story of the Passion of Christ. Two blocks north and one block east is the simple yet handsome **Iglesia San Juan Bautista**, which sits on the east side of the Parque San Juan, otherwise known as the *parquecito*. Three blocks west and two blocks north, the **Iglesia San Felipe** was built in the late 16th century for the religious services of the city's black and mulatto population.

South of the cathedral

Three blocks south and half a block west of the cathedral is the **Museo de Leyendas y Tradiciones** ⓘ *T2315-4678, www.museoleyendasytradiciones.com, Tue-Sat 0800-1200, 1400-1700, Sun 0800-1200, US$2*. This project of Doña Carmen Toruño is a physical demonstration of some of the many legends that populate the bedtime stories of Nicaraguan children. León is particularly rich in legends and Doña Carmen has handcrafted life-size models of the characters of these popular beliefs to help bring them to life. Most impressive of the displays is the *carreta nahua* (haunted ox cart) a story symbolic of the harsh labour Spanish masters required of their Indian subjects, so much so that the ox cart became a symbol of literally being worked to death.

Three blocks west of the museum, the **Iglesia de San Nicolás de Laborío**, founded in 1618 for the local indigenous population, is the most modest of the León churches, constructed of wood and tiles over adobe walls with a simple façade and altar. The interior is dark, cool and charming, with the feel of a village parish more than a city church. The local *padre* is friendly and willing to chat. If the church is closed you can knock on the little door at the back. The celebration for San Nicolás is 10 September.

Four blocks east of the museum is the **Centro de Iniciativas Medio Ambientales de la Ciudad (CIMAC)** ⓘ *Iglesia de San Sebastián, 4 c arriba, Mon-Fri 0800-1200, 1400-1730, US$1*, an ecological garden with a broad range of local flora on show, including plenty of shady fruit trees, and a gentle interpretive trail that takes no more than 30 minutes to traverse.

Comunidad Indígena de Sutiava

Like Monimbó in Masaya, Sutiava is the one of the last remaining examples of indigenous urban living. The Sutiavans have a fiercely independent culture and a language that survived despite being surrounded by the numerically superior Chorotega culture in pre-Columbian times and later by the Spanish.

Until the 20th century they managed to maintain a significant level of independence, including the indigenous community's land holdings of more than 72,000 acres, west of León proper. The community finally succumbed to pressure from León elites who had been eyeing the communal lands for centuries and Sutiava was annexed to the city in 1902, making it nothing more than a barrio of the colonial city, and opening up communal lands to non-indigenous ownership. It is no surprise that Sutiava was a major player during the planning and recruitment stages of the Sandinista-led Revolution, as the community has

ON THE ROAD
Rubén Darío: the prince of Spanish letters

The great Chilean poet Pablo Neruda called him "one of the most creative poets in the Spanish language" when, together with the immortal Spanish poet Federico García Lorca, he paid tribute to Rubén Darío in Buenos Aires in 1933. In front of more than 100 Argentine writers, Lorca and Neruda delivered the tribute to the poet they called 'then and forever unequalled'.

Darío is without a doubt the most famous Nicaraguan. He is one of the greatest poets in the history of the Spanish language and the country's supreme hero. Born Felix Rubén García Sarmiento in Metapa, Nicaragua in 1867, Rubén Darío was raised in León and had learnt to read by the age of four. By the time he was 10, little Rubén had read *Don Quixote*, The Bible, *1001 Arabian Nights* and the works of Cicero. When he was 11, he studied the Latin classics in depth with Jesuits at the school of La Iglesia de La Recolección. In 1879, at the age of 12, his first verses were published in the León daily newspaper *El Termómetro*. Two years later he was preparing his first book. Later, he became the founder of the Modernist movement in poetry, which crossed the Atlantic and became popular in Spain. His most noted work, *Azul*, revolutionized Spanish literature, establishing a new mode of poetic expression.

As well as being a poet, Darío was a diplomat and a journalist. He wrote for numerous publications in Argentina, the US, Spain and France. In 1916 he returned to the city of León, and, despite several attempts at surgery, died of cirrhosis on the night of 6 February. After a week of tributes he was buried in the Cathedral of León.

Ox that I saw in my childhood, as you steamed
in the burning gold of the Nicaraguan sun,
there on the rich plantation filled with tropical
harmonies; woodland dove, of the woods that sang
with the sound of the wind, of axes, of birds and wild bulls:
I salute you both, because you are both my life.

You, heavy ox, evoke the gentle dawn
that signalled it was time to milk the cow,
when my existence was all white and rose;
and you, sweet mountain dove, cooing and calling,
you signify all that my own springtime, now
so far away, possessed of the Divine Springtime.

'Far Away', Rubén Darío. From *Selected Poems by Rubén Darío*, translated by Lysander Kemp, University of Texas, Austin, 1988.

ON THE ROAD
Alfonso Cortés: the insanity of genius

None of Nicaragua's poets can match the striking simplicity of the metaphysical poet Alfonso Cortés, who spent most of his life in chains, but who, in an impossibly microscopic script, wrote some of the most beautiful poems the Spanish language has ever seen.

Alfonso Cortés was born in León in 1893. He lived in the very same house that had belonged to Rubén Darío and which today is the Museo-Archivo Rubén Darío. It was in this house that Cortés went mad one February night in 1927. He spent the next 42 years in captivity, tormented most of the time but, for the good fortune of Nicaragua, with lucid moments of incredible productivity. Cortés was kept chained to one of the house's colonial window grilles and it was from that vantage point that he composed what poet-priest Ernesto Cardenal called the most beautiful poem in the Spanish language, *La Ventana* (The Window):

A speck of blue has more intensity than all the sky; I feel that there lives, a flower of happy ecstasy, my longing.
A wind of spirits, passes so far, from my window sending a breeze that shatters the flesh of an angelic awakening.

Later, at the age of 34, Alfonso Cortés was committed to a mental institution in Managua, where he was to live out the rest of his life. In these incredibly adverse conditions, Cortés produced a number of great poetic works, most of which were published with the help of his father. When he was not writing he was tied to his bed, with only his guitar, hanging on the wall, for company.

According to Cardenal, the poet spoke slowly while shaking and stuttering, his face changing from thrilled to horrified, then falling totally expressionless. He used to say, "I am less important than Rubén Darío, but I am more profound". Alfonso Cortés died in February 1969, 53 years later than Darío. Today, just a couple of metres separate these two great Nicaraguan poets, both buried in the Cathedral of León.

been involved in numerous antigovernment rebellions since Nicaragua achieved Independence from Spain.

The entrance to the community is marked by the change of Calle Rubén Darío into a two-lane road with a central divider full of plants. Also of note are the neatly presented fruit stands on the street corners and the lack of colonial structures; Sutiava retained its native buildings until long after Spanish rule had ended. The best way to witness the true pride and culture of the barrio is during fiesta time. Celebrations for Holy Week, or *Semana Santa*, in Sutiava showcase spectacular sawdust street paintings made on *Viernes Santo* (Good Friday). However, there are also several sites of interest and Sutiava cuisine is superior to León's, so a visit to eat is also worthwhile. Sutiava's **Iglesia Parroquial de San Juan Bautista de Sutiava**

(1698-1710) is one of the most authentic representations of Nicaraguan baroque and features a representation of the Maribio Sun God on the ceiling; the definitive icon for indigenous pride.

Two blocks north of the San Juan church is the community-run **Museo de la Comunidad Indígena de Sutiava** or **Museo Adiact** ⓘ *T2311-5371, Mon-Fri 0800-1200 and 1400-1700, Sat 0800-1200, donations greatly appreciated*, marked by a fading mural. This is the indigenous community's museum and the only example in Nicaragua of an indigenous people protecting their cultural patrimony in their very own museum. The tiny rooms are crammed full of statues and ceramics from the Maribios culture. The museum is named after the last great leader, Adiac, who was hanged by the Spanish in an old tamarind tree still standing three blocks south and two blocks west of the San Juan church. There is a small *tiangue* or indigenous market with native foods and crafts on the third Sunday in April to celebrate the tree and its importance.

The **Ruinas de la Iglesia de Veracruz** is a sad, crumbling stone relic from the 16th century that was destroyed by an attack from Salvadorian General Malespin in 1844. It is two blocks west from the central plaza of Sutiava and often shut off to visitors by a chain-link fence, though the *comunidad indígena* is doing much to try and make the ruins a cultural focal point. On 7 December, when the Catholic **Purísima** celebration to the Virgin Mary is celebrated, the community mounts an unusual semi-pagan altar to the Virgin in the ruins of the old church complete with torch lighting and a replica of the Sun God. Other interesting celebrations include the festival for the second annual planting of corn between 25 July and 15 August. You'll find another ruined 17th-century church one block north of Sutiava's central plaza, **Iglesia Santiago**, which has a small surviving bell tower.

Three blocks east of the south side of the San Juan Church is the charming **Iglesia Ermita de San Pedro**. Built in 1706 on top of an even older construct, this church is a fine example of primitive baroque design popular in the 17th century. The adobe and red tile roof temple was refurbished in 1986. Santa Lucía is celebrated in Sutiava throughout most of December, with the focal point being the plaza in front of the parish church; Santa Lucía's day is 13 December.

Tourist information

Nicaraguan Institute of Tourism (INTUR)
Pasarela Universitaria 75 vrs al norte, Contiguo a Pizza Roma, T2311-3682.
They have limited information and flyers; staff speak Spanish only.

UNAN
Next to Restaurante El Sesteo, on Parque Central.
A small office run by the tourism students of the university.

Where to stay

There's no shortage of cheap beds in León with new hostels and backpacker hotels springing up all the time; dorms cost US$5-10 per night. If you plan on staying in the city a month or more, many houses rent student rooms at competitive rates (US$100-150 per month).

$$$ Hotel Azul
Catedral, 2½ c norte, T2315-4519, www.hotelazulleon.com.
Hotel Azul is a stylish addition to León's burgeoning hotel scene. Housed in a converted colonial building, it has a small pool and a good restaurant. Rooms are simple and minimalist. Triples are much more spacious than doubles.

$$$ Hotel El Convento
Connected to Iglesia San Francisco, T2311-7053, www.elconventonicaragua.com.
Housed in an old colonial convent, this beautiful, intriguing hotel is decorated with antique art, including an impressive gold-leaf altar and sombre religious

icons. Check their website for weekend deals (**$$**). Recommended.

$$$ Hotel Flor de Sarta
Del Parque San Juan, 2 c abajo, ½ c norte, T2311-1042.
This tastefully renovated colonial house offers large, simple, restful rooms with good showers and a/c. There is also a leafy garden and a pool. Rates include a large buffet breakfast. Good reports.

$$$ La Perla
Iglesia La Merced, 1½ c norte, T2311 3125, www.laperla.zanohotels.com.
This handsome old 19th-century building has been carefully remodelled and now boasts elegant a/c rooms, some with bath tubs, several suites, a bar, restaurant, casino and pool. Spacious and grand.

$$$-$$ Cacique Adiact
Costado noreste de UNAN, 1½ c norte, T2311-0303, www.hotelcaciqueadiact.com.
A Danish/Nicaraguan-owned 'eco-hotel' that uses solar panels and rainwater recycling systems. The building consists of a tastefully restored 2-floor colonial house overlooking a large pool. Lodgings are crisp, clean and comfortable, including 11 apartments (**$$$**) and 6 rooms (**$$**). Recommended.

$$ Hotel Real
Iglesia La Recolección, 150 m arriba, T2311-2606, www.hotelrealdeleon.com.
A pleasant and tranquil guesthouse with a leafy inner courtyard and antique furniture. The rooftop terrace has refreshing breezes and views of the churches. Continental breakfast included. Good reports.

$$ Posada Fuente Castalia
*Iglesia La Recolección, 250 m norte,
T2311-4645.*
A homely guesthouse with traditional
Nicaraguan decor, hospitable family
ambience and a flowery inner courtyard.
Prices include continental breakfast.

$$-$ Casa de Huéspedes El Nancite
*Iglesia El Calvario, 1½ c norte,
T2315-4323.*
Tranquil, tasteful and comfortable.
This orange-themed guesthouse has a
handful of good-value rooms set around
a lush courtyard. Good for couples.
Recommended.

$$-$ La Casona Colonial
*Parque San Juan, ½ c abajo, T2311-3178,
www.casonacolonialguest.com.*
This pleasant colonial house has good-
value, homely rooms with attractive
antique. Management is friendly and
hospitable, and there's a lovely green
garden too. Cheaper with fan (**$**).
Recommended.

$ Bigfoot Hostel
*Banco ProCredit, ½ c sur, T5767-0040,
www.bigfoothostelleon.com.*
Sociable, buzzing and popular with the
whipper-snappers. This hip backpackers'
joint has lots of economical dorm space,
a handful of private rooms, TV, pool table,
bar, lockers and a popular restaurant.
Their *mojitos* are famous and well worth
a taste – happy hour runs 1800-2000.

$ El Albergue de León
*Gasolinera Petronic, ½ c abajo, T8894-
1787, www.hostalelalberguedeleon.com.*
A brightly coloured, laid-back, friendly,
cheerful, helpful and knowledgeable
hostel with a shady plant-filled
courtyard, revolutionary art, ultra-cheap
dorms and basic private rooms. Funky
and alternative. Recommended.

$ Hostal Calle de los Poetas
*Calle Rubén Darío, Museo Darío,
1½ c abajo, T2311-3306, www.
journeynicaragua.org.*
This comfortable, good-value guesthouse
has a relaxed home ambience, 3 spacious
rooms with private and shared bath,
a beautiful garden and friendly hosts.
Often full, so arrive early. Discounts for
longer stays. Recommended.

$ Lazybones Hostel
*Parque de los Poetas, 2½ c norte,
T2311-3472, www.lazyboneshostel
nicaragua.com.*
An efficient, helpful, friendly hostel
with a refreshing pool and extras
including free coffee and tea, Wi-Fi and
DVD rental. Clean dorms and private
rooms; some have private bath, cheaper
without. Check out the mural by one of
Managua's best graffiti artists.

$ Poco a Poco Hostel
*2a Calle norte, del Iglesia Bautista,
½ c arriba, T8720-5334, www.
pocoapocohostel.com.*
This Dutch-owned hostel has been
getting rave reviews. Accommodation
includes small and large dorms, and
1 double room. Amenities include
kitchen, board games, table tennis,
roof terrace and the biggest outdoor
shower in Central America.

$ Tortuga Booluda
*Southwest corner of Parque Central,
3½ c abajo, T2311-4653, www.
tortugabooluda.com.*
A very pleasant, friendly hostel with
clean dorms (**$**), private rooms (**$**) and
an a/c 'suite' with views (**$$**). Wi-Fi,
pancake breakfast, organic coffee,
kitchen, pool table, guitars, book
exchange, tours and Spanish classes
available. Relaxed and recommended.

$ Via Via
Banco ProCredit, ½ c sur, T2311-6142,
www.viavia.world.
Part of a worldwide network of Belgian
cafés, this excellent and professionally
managed hostel offers clean dorm beds
and a range of private rooms, some
with TV. There's a tranquil garden and
popular restaurant-bar. In the manager's
words, "a meeting place for cultures".
Recommended.

Restaurants

$$$ El Bárbaro
Parque de Poetas, ½ c al sur.
Bárbaro is back! In 2014, this iconic León
eatery burned to the ground along with
3 other bar-restaurants in the Zona Rosa,
but it has been rebuilt in a new location,
and it looks even bigger and better than
before. They serve mainly rum and beer
along with local meat and fish dishes.

$$ Carnívoro
Iglesia La Recolección, 1 c abajo,
20 m norte. Closed Mon.
A good steakhouse with a stylish
interior and a diverse menu of Middle
Eastern, North American and even Thai
dishes. Offerings include meat kebabs,
grilled platters, burgers and a few good
vegetarian and seafood options. Their
best and most reliable dishes are the
tender Aberdeen Angus beef steaks.

$$ La Casa Vieja
Hotel El Convento, 1½ c abajo.
Mon-Sat 1600-2300.
Lovely, intimate restaurant-bar with
a rustic feel. Serves reasonably tasty
meat and chicken dishes, beer and
delicious home-made lemonade.
Popular with Nicas.

$$-$ Cafetín Don Jacks
Opposite Clínica Mercedes, de la Unión
grocery store, 1½ c arriba, T2311-1076.
The eccentric Don Jack, a Canadian-born
chef and restaurateur, cooks up a belting
burger and fries. He also does curries,
Caribbean snacks and Tex-Mex grub.
Good value and tasty.

$$-$ Porky's House
Iglesia La Recolección, 2 c norte.
As the name suggests, for lovers of
pork, smoked and grilled. They serve
a variety of chops and steaks, burgers,
sandwiches and tacos, sides of fries and
guacamole, and cold beer.

$ Café Nicaragüita
Iglesia de la Merced, 2 c norte, 90 vrs
abajo. Open for breakfast, lunch, dinner.
Bohemian little eatery serving
economical Nica fare, wraps,
sandwiches, pasta, crêpes and
brochetas. There's a relaxed reading
room and a stock of books.

$ Comedor Lucía
Banco ProCredit, ½ c sur. Mon-Sat.
Reputable *comedor* serving good and
reliable *comida típica* and buffet food,
popular with locals. Dinner is much
simpler and cheaper than lunch.

$ El Desayunazo
Parque de las Poetas, 3 c norte.
Open 0600-1200.
A great breakfast spot where you can
enjoy blueberry pancakes, fruit salad,
waffles and *huevos rancheros*, among
others. Friendly, speedy service.

$ El Mississippi
Southeast corner of the cathedral,
1 c sur, 2½ c arriba.
Also known as **La Cucaracha**, everyone
raves about the bean soup here.
Simple, unpretentious dining at this

locals' haunt. Tasty, energizing and highly recommended.

$ La Mexicana
La Iglesia Merced, 2 c norte, ½ c abajo.
Economical, no-frills Mexican grub, but tasty and completely authentic. The *chilaquiles* and *burritos de res* are the best offerings, particularly after a cold beer or 2. Popular with the locals, greasy and recommended, in spite of the sullen service.

Cafés and bakeries

Libélula
Iglesia San Francisco, 75 vrs abajo.
A very popular coffeehouse with an indoor patio, artistically prepared cappuccinos, cakes, snacks and breakfast. The best coffeeshop in town. Wi-Fi.

Pan y Paz
Northeast corner of the cathedral, 1 c norte, 1½ c arriba, www.panypaz.com.
This excellent French bakery serves what is probably the best bread in Nicaragua. They also offer great-value sandwiches, delicious quiches and scintillating fresh fruit juices. Highly recommended.

Bars and clubs

León has a vibrant nightlife, thanks to its large student population. The action moves between different places throughout the week.

Gecko's Bar
Parque de los Poetas, ½ c sur.
Karaoke and rum, what more could you ask for?

Olla Quemada
Museo Rubén Darío, ½ c abajo.
Popular on Wed nights with live music acts and lots of beer; salsa on Thu. Great place, friendly atmosphere.

Via Via
See Where to stay, ½ c sur.
Good on most nights, but best on Fri when there's live music. Good, warm atmosphere. Popular with foreigners and Nicas and often praised.

Entertainment

Cinema
There is a cinema with 3 screens in the Plaza Nuevo Siglo, next to the La Unión supermarket. It shows mostly US movies with Spanish subtitles, US$2.50.

Festivals

Feb Rubén Darío's birthday celebrations.
Mar/Apr León is famed for the beauty of its religious festivals, particularly **Semana Santa** (Holy Week). Starting on **Domingo de Ramos** (Palm Sun) the cathedral has a procession every day of the week and the Parish church of Sutiava has many events (see page 152), as do all of the other churches of León. (A program of processions and events can be obtained from the Nicaraguan Institute of Tourism, INTUR.)
14 Aug **Gritería Chiquita** (see Gritería, below) was instituted in 1947 to protect León during a violent eruption of the nearby Cerro Negro volcano.
24 Sep Patron saint of León, **La Virgin de las Mercedes**.
7-8 Dec **La Purísima** or **Gritería** (the Virgin Mary's conception of Jesus), like Semana Santa, is celebrated throughout the country, but is best in León, as this is where the tradition began. Altars are built in front of private residences and outside churches during the day.

Shopping

Bookshops
Búho Books, *Hostal Calle de los Poetas, Museo Rubén Darío, 1½ c abajo, T2311-3306, www.journeynicaragua.org. Closed Sun-Mon*. Well-stocked with new and second-hand titles, in English, Spanish, Dutch, German and more.

Crafts and markets
If you're looking for crafts, try the street markets on the north side of the cathedral. Additionally, **Flor de Luna** (Iglesia San Fransisco, 75 vrs abajo, Mon-Sat 0900-1900), stocks Nicaraguan *artesanías*, whilst **Kamañ** (southwest corner of the Parque Central, 20 vrs abajo), sells an assortment of handicrafts, bags and simple jewellery.

Supermarkets
La Unión, *Catedral, 1 c norte, 2 c arriba*. Modern and well stocked.

What to do

Cultural and community tourism
Nicasí Tours, *La Merced, 2 c norte, ½ c abajo, T8999-4754, www.nicasitours. com*. The best cultural and community tours in town. Nicasí offers a diverse range of activities including rooster fights, cooking, cowboy, city and historical tours. Promises unique insights into the Nica way of life. Recommended.

Language schools
León Spanish School, *Casa de Cultura, Iglesia La Merced, 1½ c abajo, T8183-7389, www.leonspanishschool.org*. Flexible weekly or hourly one-on-one tuition with activities, volunteering and homestay options. Pleasant location inside the Casa de Cultura.

Metropolis Academy, *Parque San Juan, 80 vrs abajo, T8932-6686, www. metropolisspanish.com*. A range of programmes from simple hourly tuition to full-time courses with daily activities and family homestay.

Tour operators
Loro Trips, *inside El Albergue de León, Gasolinera Petronic, ½ c abajo www.lorotrips.com*. A socially and ecologically aware tour operator that uses local guides and contributes to local communities. Their tours take in cultural and natural attractions, including trips to the volcanoes, cooking tours, neighbourhood tours and Rubén Darío tours. They also offer personalized tours to destinations further afield and can arrange good volunteer work thanks to their ties with the city.

Tierra Tours, *La Merced, 1½ c norte, T2315-4278, www.tierratour.com*. This Nicaragua travel specialist is Dutch/ Nicaraguan-owned. They offer good information and affordable tours of León, the Maribios volcanoes and Isla Juan Venado reserve. Also domestic flights, multi-day packages and tailor-made trips all over the country, as well as shuttles direct to Granada and other places. Well established and reliable with helpful trilingual staff.

Trekking
Journey Nicaragua, *Calle Rubén Darío, 1½ c abajo, inside Hostal Calle de Los Poetas, T2311-3306, www.journeynicaragua.org*. Kayaking in Juan Venado and Laguna El Tigre, volcano expeditions, poetry tours. Rigo Sampson, the director of Journey Nicaragua, comes from a family of devout hikers and climbers and is Nicaragua's foremost expert on climbing the Los Maribios volcanoes. He also works

closely with educational organizations. Professional and highly recommended. **Quetzaltrekkers**, *Mercantil, ½ c abajo, next to La Mexicana restaurant, T2319-9526, www.leon.quetzaltrekkers.org*. An ethical non-profit organization with proceeds going to street kids. Multi-day hikes to Los Maribios US$20-US$70 including transport, food, water, camping equipment. Quetzaltrekkers is volunteer-led and the team is always looking for new additions. They prefer a 3-month commitment and will train you as a guide. Nice guys and recommended. **Sonati Tours**, *northeast corner of the cathedral, 3 c norte, ½ c abajo, T8591-9601, www.ni.sonati.org*. Affiliated to an environmental education NGO, Sonati offers ecology-focused tours of the volcanoes, forests, mangroves and nature reserves. There is particular emphasis on flora and fauna. Birdwatching in dry forest and mangrove swamps is also offered.

Transport

Bus
The bus terminal is in the far eastern part of town, a long walk (20-30 mins) or short taxi ride from the centre. Small trucks also ferry people between the bus terminal and town for US$0.25.

Note express buses to Estelí and Matagalpa leave only if there are enough passengers; travel on Fri if possible, or simply go to San Isidro for connections. To **Managua**, express bus to La UCA, every 30 mins, 0400-1900, US$2, 1 hr 45 mins. To **Chinandega**, express bus, every 15 mins, 0500-1800, US$1, 1 hr 45 mins. To **Corinto**, every 30 mins, 0500-1800, US$1.25, 2 hrs. To **Chichigalpa**, every 15 mins, 0400-1800, US$0.75, 1 hr. To **Estelí**, express bus, 0520, 1245, 1415,

1530, US$2.50, 3 hrs; or go to San Isidro and change. To **Matagalpa**, express bus, 0420, 0730, 1445, US$2.50, 3 hrs; or go to San Isidro and change. To **San Isidro**, every 30 mins, 0420-1730, US$2.25, 2½ hrs. To **El Sauce**, hourly, 0800-1600, US$2.50, 2½ hrs. To **El Guasaule**, 0500, US$2, 2½ hrs. To **Salinas Grandes**, 0600,1200, US$0.80, 1½ hrs.

Buses and trucks for **Poneloya** and **Las Peñitas** leave from Sutiava market, every hour, 0530-1735, US$0.75, 25 mins. Service can be irregular so check to see when last bus will return. There are more buses on weekends.

Domestic and international shuttles A number of tour operators, including **Tierra Tours**, offer shuttles to the destinations of **Granada** and **Managua** airport. Additionally, some companies now offer comfortable connections to **El Salvador** and **Guatemala**, US$60-80.

International buses Contact individual agencies for schedules and costs; **Ticabus**, San Juan church, 2 c norte, in the Viajes Cumbia travel agency, T2311-6153, www.ticabus.com. **Nica Expresso**, Agencia Benitours, north side of Iglesia San Juan, 25 vrs norte, T2312-4082.

Taxi
Daytime fares are cheap: US$0.75 per person to any destination in the city. They cost US$1 at night. Taxis can also be hired to visit **Poneloya** beach and the fumaroles at **San Jacinto** (see page 163). Rates for longer trips vary greatly, with a trip to **San Jacinto** normally costing US$15-20 plus US$1 for every 15 mins of waiting or a higher flat rate for the taxi to wait as long as you wish. Trips outside must be negotiated in advance.

The Pacific beaches of Las Peñitas and Poneloya lie only 21 km from León down a paved highway; regular buses depart from Sutiava and there is a US$1 entrance fee if you come by car on the weekend. Poneloya is the most popular with Nicas, but Las Peñitas, further on, tends to be a little cleaner and less crowded. The beaches themselves boast wide swathes of sand, warm water and pelicans. Swimming is not recommended however; the currents are deceptively strong and foreigners die here every year assuming that strong swimming skills will keep them out of trouble.

At Km 74 on the Carretera Vieja a León is a scenic dirt track that leads through pleasant pastures to the Nicaraguan Pacific and the long wave-swept beach of Salinas Grandes, known to intrepid surfers. The oil and fishing port of Puerto Sandino, also accessible via a paved road off the Carretera Vieja a León, is gaining popularity too thanks to its world-class breaks; **Miramar Beach**, 6 km south of the town, is reportedly the best. Roughly 17 km south of Sandino on a coast road, the fishing hamlet of El Tránsito has a more remote and rustic setting with a crescent-shaped cove and access to reliable surf.

Reserva Natural Isla Juan Venado
Accessible from Las Peñitas, the Reserva Natural Isla Juan Venado is a 22-km-long island and turtle-nesting site (August to December), home to mangroves, crocodiles, crabs, iguanas and a healthy aquatic birdlife. To explore the canal that runs behind it, you should allow about four hours in a motorboat, US$50-60, or about US$20 for a short trip; touring needs to be timed with high tide. Kayaking is also offered here at the **Hostel Barca de Oro** and local tour operators in León, one of which, **Journey Nicaragua** (see page 160), has a house and sea turtle hatchery in Salinas Grandes and offers a rewarding circuit traversing the entire wildlife refuge, US$25-75 per person depending on group size. Night tours are useful for spotting crocodiles and sea turtles laying eggs, but take plenty of insect repellent.

León Viejo
Daily 0800-1700. US$5, including parking and a Spanish-speaking guide; ask questions first to gauge the depth of the guide's knowledge. The sun is brutally strong here so avoid 1100-1430.

At Km 54 on the Carretera Nueva a Managua is the exit for the 12-km access road to the quiet lakeside village of Puerto Momotombo and the adjoining archaeological site of León Viejo, a UNESCO World Heritage Site and a must for anyone interested in colonial history. At first sight, it consists of nothing more than a few old foundations, but this unfinished excavation site is all that remains of one of the most tragic of Spanish settlements, one which witnessed some of the most brutal acts of the Conquest and was ultimately destroyed by a series of earthquakes and volcanic eruptions between 1580 and 1610.

Los Volcanes Maribios

A scintillating landscape of sulphurous craters, steaming black sand slopes, simmering pools and imminent eruptions, Los Maribios, a rocky 60-km spine made up of 21 volcanoes, five of which are active, are reason enough to visit Nicaragua's northwest provinces. The cones rise from just above sea level to an average height of 1000 m, filling every vista with earthen pyramids. Most have unpaved road access, though some can only be reached on foot or horseback. It is strongly recommended that you climb with a guide from León or use someone from the local communities at the base of each volcano.

Volcán Momotombo At the southern tip of the Maribios range, the symmetrical cone of Volcán Momotombo (1260 m) towers over the shores of Lake Managua, an inspiration to poets over the centuries. The climb to the summit is a long one, normally taking two days, and it is best to go with a León tour operator who can supply a guide and camping gear. The view from the smoking summit is exceptional. However, in December 2015, having been dormant for 11 years, Momotombo erupted. Check its activity status before considering a climb.

Cerro Negro This is a fierce little volcano, the newest in the western hemisphere and the most violent of the Maribios range. In 1850, what was a flat cornfield came to life with 10 days of violent eruption, leaving a hill 70 m high. In the short period since, it has grown to a height of 450 m with persistently violent eruptions shooting magma and ashes up to 8000 m in the air. Fortunately, most of the eruptions have come with ample seismic warning; have a look at www.ineter. gob.ni before climbing. As its name suggests, Cerro Negro is jet-black, made up of black gravel, solidified black lava flows and massive black sand dunes that inspire the local past-time of high-speed volcano boarding; almost any tour operator in León offers this adrenalin-charged thrill, but **Tierra Tour** in Granada (page 85) and **Bigfoot Hostel** in León (page 157) are particularly recommended (hint: sitting on the board is more fun than standing).

Volcán Santa Clara At the base of Volcán Santa Clara, 15 km from the highway between León and Chinandega, is the entrance to the town of **San Jacinto**, marked by a big sign that says 'Los Hervideros de San Jacinto'. The land drops off behind the village to a field of smoking, bubbling and hissing micro-craters; the Maribios range in miniature and the result of the water table leaking onto a magma vein of nearby Volcán Telica (see below). Entrance is US$2 and local children act as guides; choose one and heed instructions as to where it is safe to walk (avoid treading on the crystallized white sulphur and to listen for hissing). Increased caution is required after rains when the ground is prone to collapse.

Volcán Telica Highly active Volcán Telica (1061 m) is part of a 9088-ha tropical dry forest. Its last known eruption was in August 2018 when it exploded and produced a 200-m-high ash plume. There is a long but rewarding hike that starts from just off the highway to Chinandega before the entrance to the village of **Quezalguaque**, following an ox-cart trail up the north shoulder of the cone, around to its east face and then up to the summit. The hike can take three to five hours round trip, or you can continue to San Jacinto. This hike takes six to eight hours and involves three ascents. Local guides are available if you start the climb from San Jacinto or, for the northeast route, use a León tour operator (see page 160).

Volcán San Cristóbal (1745 m) This is another of Los Maribios' very active volcanoes and the highest in Nicaragua. It has had almost constant activity since 1999, with the last recorded eruption in 2012, when 1500 people living in its immediate vicinity were evacuated to safety. One of the most symmetrical and handsome of the Maribios volcano range, San Cristóbal is a difficult climb that should only be attempted with a guide and by hikers who are physically fit. Avoid the windy months (November to March).

Listings Around León

Where to stay

Pacific beaches

$$$-$$ Miramar Surf Camp
Punta Miramar, Puerto Sandino, T2220-9656, www.miramarsurfcamp.com.
Chilled-out surf lodge with 2 large brick-built compounds and 13 simple rooms equipped with a/c. Parking, pool, restaurant, games area and hammocks are among the amenities. Quiet and secluded with great access to local breaks.

$$ Solid Surf Tours and Lodging
El Tránsito, T2350-4781, www.solidsurfadventure.com.
On beachfront with 5 decent a/c rooms and access to some 18 breaks. Seafood and Nica fare, available as part of packages. Beach bonfires, volunteering, surf photograpy and a host of outdoor activities. Bilingual staff.

$$-$ Surfing Turtle Lodge
Isla Los Brasiles, transport from Poneloya, T8640-0644, www.surfingturtlelodge.com.
This solar-powered surfers' lodge is located right on the beach. It has simple wooden cabins (**$$**), double rooms (**$$**) and an economical dorm (**$**). Options include surf lessons, board rental, massage, Spanish lessons, fishing and salsa. Protects the turtles that visit the island.

$ Barca de Oro
Las Peñitas, at the end of the beach facing Isla Juan Venado Wildlife Refuge, www.barcadeoro.com, T2317-0275.
Friendly, funky hotel and day trip hangout with dorm beds and private rooms. Bamboo 'eco-cabañas' sleeping 4 are also available, kitted with solar lighting and water recycling. Services include kayaking, horse riding, body boarding, turtle watching, restaurant and more. The hotel is the departure point for many trips to Isla Juan Venado.

$ The Lazy Turtle
Overlooking the bay, Las Peñitas, T8546-7403, www.thelazyturtle.com.
Canadian-owned guesthouse with a handful of simple, comfortable rooms, all with good mattresses. Their breezy restaurant serves Tex-Mex, burgers,

comfort food and a host of specials depending on what's in season. Friendly and welcoming hosts, the best place in Las Peñitas. Recommended.

$ Rigo's Guest House
Playa las Peñitas, T2317-0211, www.journeynicaragua.org.
Disarmingly tranquil, Rigo's Guest House is located on a quiet stretch of beach a short walk from nearby bars and restaurants. Accommodation includes just 3 simple rooms (2 have private bath) and a dorm. There's also a well-equipped kitchen and, overlooking the waves, a yoga platform with hammocks. Recommended.

Transport

Pacific beaches
Bus
Buses pass through **Mateare**, **Nagarote** and **La Paz Centro** on the Carretera every 15 mins between **León** and **Managua**.

Poneloya and Las Peñitas Buses to León pass hourly, 0530-1730, 20 mins, US$0.60.

Salinas Grandes Buses to **León** daily at 0900 and 1500.

Puerto Sandino Buses to **León** hourly, US$0.75, 30 mins. To **Managua**, hourly, US$1.75, 1 hr.

El Tránsito To **Managua**, 0500, 0600, 0700, US$1, 1½ hrs. To **León**, take a pickup to the Carretera Vieja and catch a passing bus from there, US$1, 30 mins.

León Viejo
Bus
Buses between Puerto Momotombo (León Viejo) and **La Paz Centro** every 1½ hrs, from 0400-1600, US$0.40. Taxi or hired car can be used as roads are good.

Chinandega sits in the middle of the most extensive plain of volcanic soil in Nicaragua, which some believe to be the most fertile valley in all of Central America. The locals are very welcoming and the city has two pretty churches that act as bookends for the downtown area.

South of Chinandega, **Chichigalpa** is a bustling agricultural centre that is best known for its Flor de Caña distillery, which produces what many believe to be the finest rum in the world; tour operators in León can arrange guided visits to its vaults.

Listings Chinandega and around

Where to stay

Chinandega

$$ Los Balcones
Esquina de los Bancos, 50 vrs norte,
www.hotelbalconeschinandega.com.
18 clean, comfortable rooms with cable TV, hot water and a/c. Wi-Fi and breakfast included. Good.

$ Don Mario's
Enitel, 170 vrs norte, T2341-4054.
Great-value rooms and friendly hosts at this homely lodging. Rooms have a/c, private bath and cable TV; cheaper with fan. Chill-out space and tables overlook the plant-filled courtyard and the kitchen is available if you wish. The owners speak excellent English, "anything you want, just ask". Relaxed family atmosphere and highly recommended.

Restaurants

Chinandega

$$ Buenos Aires
Plaza Colonial, 2½ c sur.
A good place for an evening meal. This jaunty, brightly coloured restaurant serves meat, chicken and fish dishes under a thatched *palapa* roof. Specialities include a range of *enchiladas*, beef steaks and breaded shrimp dishes. Not bad.

$$ El Paraíso
Plaza Colonial, 3 c arriba, on the Guasaule highway.
A large outdoor restaurant with a vast *palapa* roof. Serving the usual meat, chicken and fish fare. A favourite of lunchtime businessmen and moneyed Nicaraguans.

$ Las Tejitas
Parque Central, 7 c arriba.
Cheap and cheerful. They serve buffet food, grilled meats and *comida típica*. Very popular and always packed out. A Chinandega institution.

Transport

Chinandega
Bus
Most buses leave from the new market at southeast edge of town. To **Corinto**, buses and microbuses, every 20 mins, 0430-1800, US$0.50, 30 mins. To **Somotillo**, every 3 hrs, 0900-1500, US$2, 2 hrs. To **Guasaule**, every 30 mins,

0400-1700, US$2, 2 hrs. To **Managua**, every 30 mins, 0430-1700, US$2.50, 3 hrs. To **León**, frequent buses 0430-1800, US$1, 1 hr.

Buses for **Potosí**, **El Viejo**, Jiquilillo and **Puerto Morazán** leave from the Santa Ana Mercadito northwest of town. A bus links Terminal, Mercado and Mercadito. To El Viejo, every 20 mins, US$0.60, 10 mins. To **Jiquilillo** and **Reserva Natural Estero Padre Ramos**, 0630, 1000, 1130, 1500, 1630, US$1, ½ hrs. To **Potosí**, 0930 and 1030, US$1.50, 3½ hrs.

El Viejo, 5 km from Chinandega, is a slightly run-down but peaceful place. The 70-cm-tall image in its church of the Immaculate Conception of the Virgin Mary, called La Virgen del Trono, is the patron saint of Nicaragua and one of the most venerated images in all of Central America.

From El Viejo, it is a scenic drive or bumpy bus ride to the Cosigüina Peninsula, which should be done in public bus or 4WD only. If driving, it is essential to buy purified water and fill up with fuel before leaving El Viejo; there are no petrol stations on the peninsula.

There are some long empty beaches on the peninsula's coast. The first section of the highway is paved and passes gigantic ranches. Before the pavement ends, there are two turnings that lead to the desolate beaches of Nicaragua's extreme northwest. The first leads to the sweeping coastline of Aposentillo and the second to Jiquilillo, a quiet, friendly, laid-back community that is now receiving a steady stream of backpackers. Reached by another long, winding dirt and rock path off the highway is the upscale yachters' resort of **Marina Puesta del Sol**, located between Aposentillo and the tiny fishing village of **Los Aserradores**. North of the Playa Aposentillo is the remote coastal estuary reserve of Padre Ramos, named after a priest from El Viejo who drowned here. Access is best from the highway to Jiquilillo, as the ranger station is located at the southern part of the estuary. It is possible to camp here and hire a boat and local guide through the park staff's contacts.

At the northwesternmost point of Nicaragua, **Volcán Cosigüina** has some unique wildlife and 13,168 ha of protected tropical dry forest. The success of the reserve is that it is the last remaining Nicaragua Pacific coast habitat for the **scarlet macaw**. The view from the summit is why most hikers come to Cosigüina: a sweeping panorama that includes the islands in the Gulf of Fonseca and El Salvador to the north, Honduras to the east, and the emerald crater lake 700 m below the summit. Ascents are best arranged with a tour operator in León.

Arriving in Potosí is much like arriving at any remote place. Although it is only 60 km from Chinandega, the rocky road, searing heat and chocolate-brown waters of the prehistoric bay of **Golfo de Fonseca** are other-worldly. From the solitary dock in Potosí, it is only 15 minutes by boat to a commercial shipping port in Honduras and two hours to La Unión in El Salvador (see box, page 257).

Where to stay

$$$$ Marina Puesta del Sol
Los Aserradores, T8880-0019,
www.marinapuestadelsol.com.
Spacious suites overlooking the bay and
marina, all modern with generic decor
and patios. Some have jacuzzi and the
higher-level suites have a great view of
bay and volcanoes.

$$$-$$ Thunderbomb Surf Camp
Playa Santa María del Mar, T8478-0070,
www.thunderbombsurf.com.
A small surf resort and Dutch-
Nicaraguan enterprise with comfortable
lodging (rooms include a/c, TV and
private bath) dorms, Tiki loft, hammocks,
yoga platform and a restaurant. They
can provide transport and offer a range
of all-inclusive packages.

$$$-$ Monty's Surf Camp
Jiquilillo, where Bar Los Gemelos
used to be, 150 m sur, T8272-5654,
www.montysbeachlodge.com.
This rustic surf lodge has a variety of
poolside and oceanfront *cabañas* and
bungalows. Various 'stay and play'
packages available, as well as surf school,
kayaks, volcano tours and horse riding.

$ Rancho Esperanza
Jiquilillo, 200 m behind Disco ONVI, T8680-
0270, www.rancho-esperanza.com.
This friendly and relaxed 'low-impact'
rancho has a good location on the
beach. Various bamboo *cabañas* are
available, as well as dorms, campground
or hammocks for the thrifty. 3 meals a
day cost around US$13. Activities include
surfing, kayaking, hiking and community
tours. Volunteer opportunities are also
available. Good reports.

$ Rancho Tranquilo
Near Pulpería Tina Mata, Los Zorros,
10 mins from Jiquilillo, T8968-2290,
www.ranchotranquilo.wordpress.com.
For people looking to escape the
gringo trail, Rancho Tranquilo is a
relaxed backpacker place with cabins
and ultra-cheap dorms. There are
also hammocks, vegetarian food and
volunteer opportunities. Managed by
Tina, a friendly lady from California.

Northern highlands

RUTA DEL CAFE
GRACIAS ALA GESTION
INTUR ALCALDIA
GRAN DUCADO DE LUXEMBURGO
AÑO 2009
ESC RUBER SANCHEZ DIAZ

Nicaragua's ruggedly beautiful northern mountains and valleys have staged much of the history that has given the country its war-torn international reputation. It was here that indigenous cultures attacked Spanish mining operations in the 16th century and, in the 19th century, fought confiscation of communal lands that were to go to German immigrants for coffee growing. This is where Sandino fought the US Marines' occupation of Nicaragua and where the rebel Sandinistas launched their first attacks against the Somoza administration in the 1960s. Then, in the 1980s, the Contras waged war against the Sandinista Government in these mountains.

Today, most visitors would be hard pressed to see where all this aggression came from, or that it existed at all. Most of the northern ranges and plains are full of sleepy villages with ancient churches, rustic cowboys and smiling children. This is where the soil and the homes blend into a single palette: the red-brown clay earth reflected in the brown adobe walls and red-tile roofs. Nothing is rushed here and many of the region's villages are evidence that time travel is indeed possible, with the 21st century in no danger of showing itself around here anytime soon, at least not until the 20th century arrives.

Set in a broad valley encircled by green mountains, including the handsome Cerro de Apante at 1442 m, Matagalpa (altitude 682 m, population 98,000) is the Nicaraguan capital of coffee production. The town appears quite attractive from a distance, but less so close up: its streets are narrow, noisy and vaguely claustrophobic, and a circular sprawl of scruffy barrios climb the surrounding hills, threatening to one day enclose the city in concrete.

Nonetheless, beyond Matagalpa's rough and ready façade, the town is friendly, laid-back and optimistic about the future. It is an excellent base for exploring the region's arresting mountain scenery, its nature reserves, ecolodges, farming communities and coffee fincas, among the best in the world.

Inexpensive taxis are plentiful around the city, but the downtown area is also easy to walk around and safe. The barrios on the outskirts should be avoided. There are two main streets that run south from the main plaza, Parque Morazán, to the little Parque Darío, where it is a bit more peaceful; of these, Avenida José Benito Escobar is the principal commercial drag.

Sights
Although the main attraction of Matagalpa is the sublime beauty that lies just outside it, the **Catedral de San Pedro de Matagalpa** (1897) on Parque Morazán is worth a visit. There are two other churches that are also pleasant: the late 19th-century **Templo de San José de Laborio** in front of the Parque Darío and the primitive Nicaraguan baroque **Iglesia de Molagüina**, which is the oldest church in Matagalpa, believed to date from 1751.

East of Parque Darío is the **Museo Casa Carlos Fonseca** ⓘ *Parque Darío, 1 c este, T2772-2932, Mon-Fri 0830-1200 and 1400-1700*, a memorial to the principal intellectual and founder of the FSLN, who was shot by the National Guard less than three years before the success of the Revolution. He lived here as a young boy and the museum houses pictures, writings, stories and objects, like the famous glasses, of this national hero. Contributions are welcome for the maintenance of this old house. If closed, ask next door at the tyre repair workshop.

The **Museo del Café** (Coffee Museum) ⓘ *on the main avenue, Parque Morazán, 1½ c sur, T2772-0482, Mon-Fri 0800-1730, Sat 0800-1200*, houses the town's **cultural centre**, offering music and painting classes and displays on the history of local coffee production. Exhibits include photographs and antique objects used in the early days of coffee production in Matagalpa.

Around Matagalpa
Located within the **Reserva Apante** ⓘ *US$1*, a few kilometres southeast of Matagalpa, Cerro Apante offers commanding views of Matagalpa and the surrounding countryside. It takes two hours to reach the summit on the main trail. There is another trail that takes five hours and another still that takes

seven hours, concluding in the village of San Ramón. The two-hour trail can be followed independently, but the others are hard to find and it is recommended that you hire a guide. A guide will be able to lead you to other attractions within the reserve, like streams and waterfalls.

In the west of Matagalpa, the **Mirador El Calvario** ⓘ *US$0.20*, also offers astounding panoramic views, as well as a very modest canopy line, US$4. It is unsafe to walk; take a taxi (US$4).

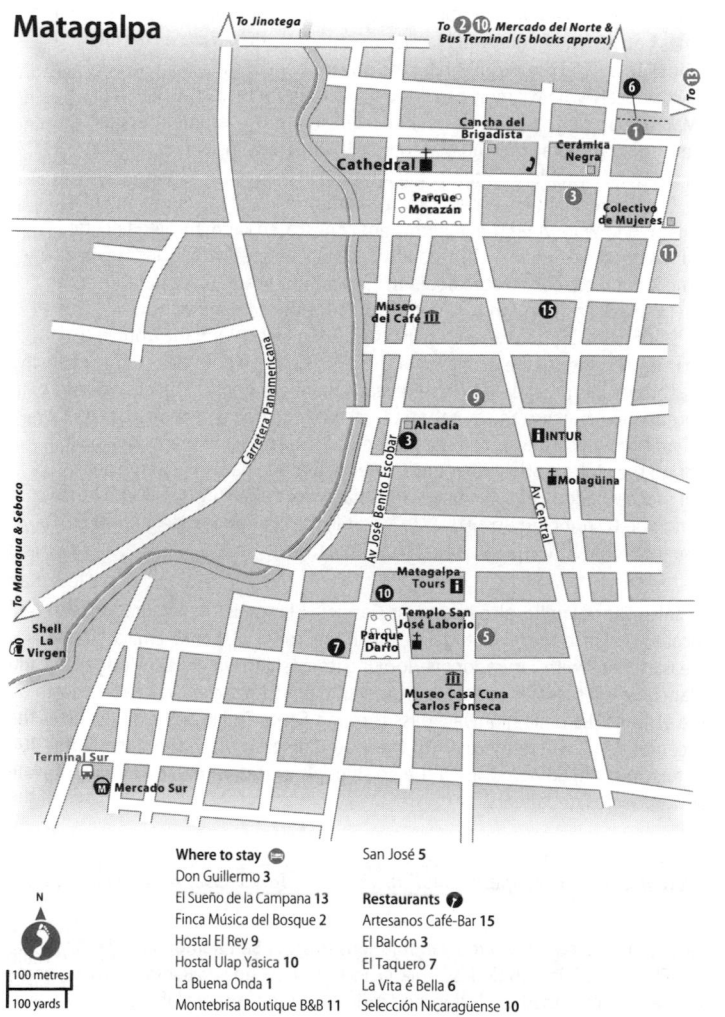

Matagalpa

To Jinotega

To ② ⑩, Mercado del Norte & Bus Terminal (5 blocks approx)

To ⑬

⑥
①
Cancha del Brigadista
Cerámica Negra
Cathedral
Colectivo de Mujeres
③
Parque Morazán
⑪
Museo del Café
⑮
⑨
Alcaldía
③
INTUR
Molagüina
Carretera Panamericana
Av José Benito Escobar
Av Central
To Managua & Sebaco
Matagalpa Tours
⑩
Templo San José Laborio
⑦
Parque Darío
⑤
Shell La Virgen
Museo Casa Cuna Carlos Fonseca
Terminal Sur
Mercado Sur

N

100 metres
100 yards

Where to stay 🛏
Don Guillermo **3**
El Sueño de la Campana **13**
Finca Música del Bosque **2**
Hostal El Rey **9**
Hostal Ulap Yasica **10**
La Buena Onda **1**
Montebrisa Boutique B&B **11**

San José **5**

Restaurants 🍴
Artesanos Café-Bar **15**
El Balcón **3**
El Taquero **7**
La Vita é Bella **6**
Selección Nicaragüense **10**

BACKGROUND
Matagalpa

Matagalpa is the most famous mountain town in Nicaragua. It is in the heart of coffee country, an industry that was started in the 1870s by German and other European immigrants.

In 1881, Matagalpa was the scene of the last significant indigenous rebellion, which was sparked by a combination of factors: forced labour laying telegraph lines between Managua and Matagalpa; attempts to ban *chicha* (fermented corn liquor); and the expulsion by the government of the Jesuits, much loved by the locals, who willingly provided free labour for the construction of Matagalpa's cathedral. The rebellion failed and the government troops' revenge was brutal, moving Matagalpa's indigenous community (which is still quite large) forever to the background in the region's affairs.

The German influence in Matagalpa continued until the beginning of the First World War, when the government confiscated German-owned coffee farms but the Germans returned after the war and re-established themselves. The farms were confiscated again in 1941 when Nicaragua declared war on Germany. Many Germans did not return after the end of that war.

During the Contra War, Matagalpa was often just behind the front line of battle and many of the residents of the city fought on both sides of the conflict.

The city has prospered in recent years, thanks not only to increased coffee production, but also the fact that it boasts a high percentage of high-quality shade-grown coffee and has developed organic growing practices which bring the highest prices. In many respects, Matagalpa is enjoying a phase of much-needed gentrification with smart new coffee houses, youth hostels and hotels springing up all over town. Still, the economic rollercoaster of international coffee prices always carries a threat.

Salto Santa Emilia, also known as Cascada Blanca, is an invigorating waterfall located 15 km outside Matagalpa, near the town of Santa Emilia. There is a pleasant hotel with a mirador overlooking its crashing waters, **Eco-lodge Cascada Blanca**, which serves food to day-trippers. To get the *cascada*, take a bus north on the El Tuma–La Daila highway, pass through Santa Emilia and exit just after the second bridge, where the path to the waterfall leads off to the right. **Note** Due to toxic run-off, do not swim in the crash pools or river during coffee season, late November to late January.

Esperanza Verde
Office in San Ramón, Iglesia Católica, 1½ c este, T8775-5338, www.fincaesperanza verde.com.

East of Matagalpa is the largely indigenous town of **San Ramón** founded by a friar from León, José Ramón de Jesús María, in 1800. Beyond San Ramón is **Yucul**, home to the well-managed ecolodge and private nature reserve of Esperanza Verde, located 3.5 km from the village. This award-winning reserve has a butterfly breeding project, organic shade-grown coffee cultivation, five hiking trails, five waterfalls and great views to the mountains of the region. There are few finer places in Nicaragua for birdwatching and enjoying the nature of the northern mountains. The pine forest shelters a rare species (*Pino spatula sp tecunmumanii*) that reportedly has the finest seeds of its kind on the American continent. There are also howler monkeys, sloths and more than 150 species of bird, plus numerous orchids and medicinal plants. Accommodation is in rustic but comfortable wood and brick built cabins ($$$) with contemplative views of the hills. Buses run to Yucul from Matagalpa's north terminal and there are signs for the reserve from San Ramón.

Selva Negra
Carretera a Jinotega Km 139.5, T8100-9100, www.selvanegra.com.

The highway rises steeply out of Matagalpa giving panoramic views of the city and the surrounding deforestation. About 7 km beyond Matagalpa, the scenery changes dramatically, with pine trees and oaks draped in bromeliads, in a forest that is green year-round.

Selva Negra is a 600-ha coffee hacienda and nature reserve, owned by Eddy and Mausy Kuhl. The property has numerous well-marked hiking trails, great for birdwatching, with more than 200 species documented so far, including trogons, parrots, flycatchers and the elusive but resplendent quetzal. There are some Germanic hotel cabins ($$$$-$) surrounded by forest and flowers; many even have flowers growing out of their roofs. What makes Selva Negra really special, however, are its sustainable farming practices: everything from coffee husks to chicken blood is recycled. Coffee-processing wastewater (a serious pollutant in coffee-growing regions) is run into two-step pressurizing tanks that create methane or 'bio-gas', which is then used on the farm for cooking and other chores. As many as 250 full-time employees work in flower production, with 10 species grown in greenhouses, all vegetables served at the hotel restaurant are grown organically on the farm and meat served at the hotel is also locally raised.

An old Somoza-era tank that was destroyed by the rebels serves as an entrance sign to the hacienda; any bus heading towards Jinotega will drop you off here, from where it is a 1.5-km walk to the hotel; or take a taxi from Matagalpa.

Reserva Natural Cerro Arenal
At Km 145.5 on the Carretera a Jinotega. Matagalpa Tours (see Tour operators, below) operate trips to the reserve.

This is one of the finest cloudforest reserves in Nicaragua that can be accessed by a paved road. The reserve protects **Cerro Picacho** (1650 m) and its surrounding forest which is over 1400 m. There are numerous giant balsa trees, known as *mojagua* (*Heliocarpus appendiculatus*), the favoured nesting sites for the resplendent quetzal, and the forest is also home to giant oak trees, up to 12 m in circumference and 40 m tall, as well as many strangler figs, tree ferns, bromeliads, orchids, mosses, bamboo and even arboreal cacti.

ON THE ROAD

Café Nicaragüense

Large-scale coffee growing in Nicaragua is directly tied to German immigration, promoted by 19th-century Nicaraguan governments that offered 500 *manzanas* (350 ha) of land to any investor who would plant 25,000 coffee trees, bringing migrant planters from Germany, US, England, France and Italy.

The pioneer of Nicaragua coffee planting was Ludwing Elster, originally from Hanover, and his wife Katharine Braun, from Baden Baden who settled in Matagalpa in 1852. In 1875, Wilhelm Jericho arrived and founded the Hacienda Las Lajas, promising to lure 20 more German families to Nicaragua. When the Nicaraguan government started offering the 500 *manzanas* free to inspire production, more than 200 foreign families settled and began growing coffee in Matagalpa and neighbouring Jinotega.

Today Nicaraguan coffee is planted on more than 160,000 *manzanas* by 30,000 different farms with country-leader Jinotega producing around 680,673 100-pound bags of coffee a year, followed by Matagalpa at 624,818 bags. The country's best coffee export customers are the USA, Spain, Belgium and France.

The push for high-quality organic shade coffee has lifted Nicaragua to sixth place in the world in gourmet coffee production, with an annual output of organic coffee three times greater than that of Costa Rica.

The cloudforest has an abundance of the endangered resplendent quetzal (*Pharomachrus mocinno*), considered sacred by the Maya and agreed by all to be one of the most beautiful birds in the world, and the **Sendero Los Quetzales** is one of the best places in Nicaragua to spot it. The path passes plenty of native avocado (*Aguacate canelo*), one of the bird's favourite snacks (the fruit is ripe between March and May). The quetzal shares the forest with 190 documented species, including Amazon parrot, toucans, emerald toucanets, other trogons and numerous colourful hummingbirds, such as the violet sawbrewing hummingbird (*Campylopterus hemileucurus*). The three-wattled bellbird's distinctive song can often be heard, too. There are also 140 documented species of butterfly here, such as the spectacular purple-blue morpho and the almost-invisible, transparent-winged gossamer. Howler monkeys, agoutis and sloths are reasonably common.

Tourist information

INTUR
Banco Ficohsa, 1½ c al sur, T2772-7060.
They have limited, patchy information on local attractions.

Matagalpa tours
North side of Parque Darío, 1 c este, 20 vrs al norte, www.matagalpatours.com.
An excellent source of information, with a thorough knowledge of the city and the surrounding mountains; they speak Dutch and English. See also Tour operators, below.

Where to stay

$$$ Montebrisa Boutique B&B
Parque Morazán, 3 c este, T2772-0354, www.montebrisa.com.
A lovely secluded option with a garden so verdant you wouldn't know you were in downtown Matagalpa. Rooms are spotlessly tidy and well equipped with Wi-Fi, cable TV, security boxes, black-out shades and luxury linens. The best in town.

$$ Don Guillermo
Enitel, 25 vrs oeste, T2772-3182, hostaldonguillermomatagalpa@ gmail.com.
A tastefully attired hotel with 7 big, clean, comfortable, good-value rooms. Each has cable TV, hot water and Wi-Fi. Breakfast is included and there's a night guard on the door. Recommended.

$$ Hotel San José
Behind Iglesia San José, T2772-2544, www.hotelsanjosematagalpa.com.ni.
An immaculately clean and well-kept little hotel, friendly and professional. Rooms are on the small side, but comfortable and equipped with cable TV, fan and hot water. Recommended.

$$-$ Hostal El Rey
Iglesia Molagüina, ½ c al oeste, T2772-3435, www.royalmarinas.com.
Rooms at the Royal Marinas are large, clean and comfortable, equipped with hot water and Wi-Fi, some with cable TV. There's a pleasant front garden and rates include breakfast and free calls to local numbers and the US. A good-value option. Recommended.

$$-$ La Buena Onda
Cancha el Brigadista, 2½ c este, T2772-2135, www.labuenaonda.com.ni.
An excellent friendly, chilled-out hostel with 2 clean, comfortable dorms, each with private bath and large lockers. There are also some spacious private rooms, book exchange, TV room, DVDs, free coffee, laundry service, shared kitchen and more. Knowledgeable and helpful with good connections to **Matagalpa Tours** (page 179). Recommended.

Around Matagalpa

$ El Sueño de la Campana
Contigüo al Instituto de San Ramón, outside Matagalpa in the community of San Ramón, T2772-9730, www.hotellacampanasanramon.com.
This rural farm has a range of single and double rooms and enjoys expansive views of the countryside. Guests can hike or participate in voluntary activities that help the local community.

$ Finca Música del Bosque
20 mins out of Matagalpa (will pick up from the town), T5853-5135, www.fincamusica.com.

A wonderfully tranquil coffee and permaculture farm with simple but cheery rooms, a vegetarian café, citrus trees and plans in the works for a yoga studio and a pizza oven. Great place, lots of birdlife, worth a look. Advance reservation essential, no drop-ins.

$ Hostal Ulap Yasica
Carretera a La Dalia Km 133, 10 mins from the centre, take a taxi, US$1, T2772-6443, www.hostalulapyasica.com.
The grounds are verdant and restful at this low-impact hostel built with wood and solar powered. It has simple dorms and rooms and a restaurant serving light meals. Laundry service, Wi-Fi, common areas and free organic coffee produced on site. Good reports.

Restaurants

$$ Artesanos Café-Bar
Banpro, ½ c este.
This pleasant café-bar has a wooden, rancho-style interior. They do breakfasts, light lunches and hot and cold drinks including *licuados*, iced coffee and excellent cappuccinos. Popular with locals and tourists.

$$ La Vita é Bella
Col Lainez 10, from Buena Onda, ½ c north, then right down an alleyway to an unmarked house, T2772-5476.
An Italian-run restaurant, which has received strong praise from several readers. Pleasant outdoor seating on a patio.

$$-$ El Balcón
Alcadía Municipal, 25 m al sur, www.elbalconmatagalpa.com.
El Balcón serves reasonable to good Nica and international fare, including *pollo a la plancha*, brochetas, steaks, burgers, quesadillas and fish. Served

Mon-Sat, the lunchtime *menú ejecutivo* is very good value and recommended ($). Pleasant interior with the airy upstairs balcony overlooking Matagalpa's main street. A reliable option for breakfast, lunch and dinner.

$ El Taquero
Parque Darío, 1 c al sur, ½ c al oeste. Open 1800-0100.
El Taquero plies a roaring trade in the evening as local families gather to enjoy its mouth-watering flame-grilled meat dishes, including Nica and Mexican staples such as tacos, burritos, *churrasco*, steaks and *enchiladas*. Takeaway available. Recommended.

Cafés

Selección Nicaragüense
Costado Norte Parque Darío.
The best coffee shop in town with excellent hot and cold coffee, including cappuccino, iced coffee and americanos. The interior is contemporary and laid-back, and often buzzing with students in the evening. A small selection of snacks, including cakes, paninis and pies available. Good staff. Wi-Fi.

Bars and clubs

Artesanos Café-Bar
See Restaurants, above.
A popular place that draws a diverse crowd of locals and expats. Cocktails, rum and beer, in addition to coffee. Recommended.

Shopping

Crafts
Artesanías La Alforja Matagalpa,
Cancha el Brigadista, 2½ c al este, inside La Buena Onda Hostel. Mon-Sat 0900-1800.

A broad range of local crafts, including jewellery from San Ramón, hand-woven textiles, black pottery, coffee, chocolate and wood-carvings.

Cerámica Negra, *Parque Darío*. This kiosk, open irregularly, sells black pottery in the northern tradition, a style found only in parts of Chile, Nicaragua and Mexico. There is evidence that this school of ceramics dates back to 1500 BC in this region of Nicaragua. For more information contact Estela Rodríguez, T2772-4812.

Colectivos de Mujeres de Matagalpa, *Banco Uno, 2½ c este, T2772-4462. Mon-Fri 0800-1200, 1400-1730, Sat 0800-1200.* Native fabrics, leather goods, ceramics and an orange and coffee liqueur made by women's cooperatives in El Chile, Molino Norte and Malinche.

Telares Indígenas Nicaragua, *Semáforos Parque Morazán, 1 c al sur, ½ c al este, same building as Matagalpa Tours, T8654-4824.* Fair-trade textiles produced by the indigenous community of El Chile, including purses, backpacks, wallets and carpets, all handmade using organic cotton.

What to do

Coffee tours
The **Coffee Museum**, **INTUR**, **Hostal La Buena Onda** or **Matagalpa Tours** can help you arrange trips to the many coffee fincas in the area. Outside the season, late-Nov to late-Jan, you will not see workers picking in the plantations. **Esperanza Verde** and **Selva Negra** are both interesting coffee fincas (see pages 174 and 175) that can be visited independently. Other options include:
UCA San Ramón, *opposite the Parque Municipal, San Ramón, T2772-5247, www.tourism.ucasanramon.com.*

This organization can arrange a 'hands-on' experience of coffee production, where you meet farming communities and participate in the process.

Language schools
Colibrí Spanish School, *Calle de los Bancos, next to the Biblioteca Central, T8770-3309, www.colibrispanishschool. com, next to Matagalpa Tours.* They offer packages of 15, 20 and 30 hrs one-on-one with options for homestays (meals included) or lodging in an apartment. Courses include all materials and various sociocultural activities including visits to local attractions, social events, cooking and dance classes, films and tours of the city. Costs US$7-10 per hr.

Tour operators
Matagalpa Tours, *north side of Parque Darío, 1 c este, 20 vrs al norte. T2772-0108, www.matagalpatours.com.* This reputable agency explores the north of Nicaragua from a different point of view. Trekking, hiking, birdwatching and rural community tours are among their well-established repertoire, now supplemented by exciting whitewater rafting trips down the Río Tuma (May-Jan, Class II-IV), the first of their kind in the country. Another of their most interesting options involves visiting Mayangna communities and working mines in the remote northeast of the country. Also offers excellent mountain-bike tours, from 2 hrs to several days. Dutch- and English-speaking, helpful and friendly. The best agency in town for all your adventuring needs. Highly recommended.
Northward Nicaragua Tours, *Parque Rubén Darío, 2½ c oeste, T2772-0605.* Founded by Nicaraguan tour guide and outdoors enthusiast Alvaro Rodríguez, who offers a range of custom-made

tours throughout the Nicaraguan countryside. Recommended for hardcore adventurers and adrenalin junkies.

Transport

Bus

Terminal Sur (Cotransur) is near Mercado del Sur and used for all destinations outside the department of Matagalpa.

To **Jinotega**, every 30 mins, 0500-1900, US$1, 1½ hrs (buses are packed on Sun, avoid). To **Managua**, every 30 mins, 0335-1805, US$2.40, 3-4 hrs; express buses (recommended), every hr, 0520-1720, US$2.90, 2½ hrs. To **Estelí**, every 30 mins, 0515-1745, US$1.20, 2-3 hrs. Express bus to **León** (subject to change), 0600, 1500, 1600, US$2.90, 2½ hrs, departs only if there is sufficient demand, otherwise take an Estelí bus to the junction (*empalme*) south of San Isidro and change. Express bus to **Masaya**, 1400, 1530, US$2.90, 4 hrs. Infrequent services run to **Chinandega**.

Terminal Norte, by Mercado del Norte (Guanuca), is for all destinations within the province of Matagalpa including **San Ramón** and **El Tuma**. Taxi between terminals US$0.50.

Taxi

Matagalpa taxis are helpful and cheap. Average fare inside the city is US$0.50. Fare to **Selva Negra** US$4-5 per person.

Jinotega (altitude 1004 m, population 33,000) is the diminutive capital of a sprawling province that has almost no infrastructure to date and remains one of the poorest and least developed parts of the country. Like Matagalpa, it is an important area for the nation's coffee industry and subject to the whim of international coffee prices. Nestled in a valley of green mountains and shaded from the tropical sun, Jinotega's helpful and charming people are its greatest assets. Jinotega is easy to walk around, but avoid walking after 2200 at the weekend.

Sights

Jinotega is not visited by many foreigners, except for those working on international projects. The city has grown rapidly to the east of the centre in recent years, which means that the central park is actually now in the west of town. The area around the main plaza and the very attractive cathedral, **El Templo Parroquial** (1805), is full of broad streets and has a tranquil, small-town feel. The Gothic cathedral has an interior that reflects the local climate, with a lovely clean, cool, whitewashed simplicity. The city's symbol is the cross-topped mountain, **Cerro La Peña Cruz**, to the west of central park. Every 3 May more than 5000 pilgrims walk to the top to take part in a Mass at the summit at 0900. (The hike to the summit takes just over an hour.)

Around Jinotega

The beautiful **Lago de Apanás**, 8 km east of Jinotega, was created by the damming of the Río Tuma in 1964 to form a 54-sq-km shiny blue body of water. To visit the lake take a bus from Jinotega bound for Austurias–Pantasma (hourly 0700-1500, one hour, US$2). You can go out on the lake with one of the members of the fishing co-operative **La Unión del Norte** who charge US$10 per hour for an excursion by motorboat and US$6 per hour by rowing boat. Ask at El Portillo de Apanás.

Protected since 2002, the **Reserva Natural Datanlí-Diablo** ⓘ *www.explore datanli.com*, encompasses a sprawling massif between Matagalpa and Jinotega, concluding at Lago de Apanás in the north. Rising to a height of 1680 m at the challenging peak of El Diablo, the area is punctuated by misty cloudforests and rugged hills, rolling coffee fincas and somnambulant villages. The southern side of the reserve can be accessed by a turning marked 'Fundadora' on the Matagalpa–Jinotega highway; from there, it is 6 km on a dirt road to the **Eco-Albergue La Fundadora** ⓘ *T8855-2573, www.fundadora.org*, which has brick cabins ($), camping space, a simple restaurant and tour guides (if walking, it is just 3 km from the turning of Las Latas to the Eco-Albergue). On the northern side of the reserve, the best facilities can be found at **Finca La Bastilla** ⓘ *T2782-4335, www. bastillaecolodge.com*, which boasts excellent ecologically sound wooden cabins overlooking the landscape ($$-$). Northeast of La Bastilla, a hiking trail connects to the community of **Gobiado**, which has rustic lodging, food and guides. To get to La Bastilla, 20 km northeast of Jinotega, take the road towards Pantasma and look for the second turning on the right after the Jigüina bridge; it is 5 km along a dirt road from here (4WD only). Those using public transport can call ahead for pick-up; or take a taxi from Jinotega, US$20.

Just 25 km northwest from Jinotega is the tiny village of San Rafael, a pleasant, authentic mountain town with a gigantic church and a rich history. **La Iglesia Parroquial** was first built in 1887 and its most famous feature is a mural next to the entrance depicting the temptation of Christ; the devil's face is said to resemble the Sandinista leader Daniel Ortega. The festival for San Rafael usually lasts eight days and takes place around 29 September.

Listings Jinotega

Tourist information

INTUR
Del Parque Otto Casco, 1 c al norte,
T2782-4552, jinotega@intur.gob.ni.
Mon-Fri 0800-1200 and 1400-1600.
One of the country's better tourist offices. The well-informed staff have good information on the town and surrounding areas.

Where to stay

$$$ Hotel Museo La Casa de Los Rizo
West side of Parque Central, T2782-3150,
www.lacasadelosrizo.com.
Atmospheric colonial property on the main plaza, complete with antique furnishings, central patios and brightly painted rooms. Pleasant and memorable, if perhaps on the pricey side.

$$ La Quinta
Parque Central, 7 c norte,
over the bridge, T2782-2522,
becquerfernandez@yahoo.ca.
This Nicaraguan mini-resort has a pleasant setting among the pine trees. There's a range of include Wi-Fi, parking, pool, restaurant, karaoke bar and disco. Recommended.

$ Hotel Sollentuna Hem
Gasolinera Puma, 1 c arriba, 2½ c norte,
T2782-2334, hotelsollentuna@gmail.com.
This clean, safe, family hotel has 16 rooms, all with private bath, cable TV, fan and hot water. The owner, who lived in Sweden for many years, offers a range of beauty treatments, including massage and pedicure. Breakfast and dinner are served, and coffee tours are available. Pleasant and professional.

$ La Biósfera Reserve and Retreat
Km 158 Carretera Matagalpa–Jinotega,
T8698-1439, www.hijuela.com, 3 km
outside Jinotega.
La Biósfera is a socially and ecologically aware lodging committed to green energy, permaculture and 'interpersonal harmony'. Lodging is in spartan rustic cabins and dorms, with opportunities for hiking, star-gazing, alternative therapies and workshops.

Restaurants

$$ La Perrera
Km 158 Carretera Matagalpa–Jinotega,
www.restaurantelaperrera.com.
Oft-praised restaurant 3 km out of town, serving international fare and seafood.

Offerings include steak and chips, *fajitas*, pork chops in barbecue sauce and fried fish fillet.

$$-$ Restaurante El Tico
Across from La Salle athletic field, T782-2530. Daily 0800-2200.
44-year-old establishment in a very modern location, popular with couples, moderately priced dishes, try surf and turf (*mar y tierra*) or *pollo a la plancha*, also cheap dishes and sandwiches. Recommended.

$$-$ Soda Buffet El Tico
Gasolinera Puma, 2½ c sur. Open for breakfast, lunch and dinner.
Reasonable buffet restaurant serving typical Nicaraguan food. Clean, reliable and popular with tourists. Best to get there early when the food is fresh.

Cafés

Flor de Jinotega
Ferretería Blandón Moreno, 1 c abajo, www.soppexcca.org/en.
The best coffee in town, produced by an environmentally aware and progressive cooperative, **Soppexcca**. Highly recommended.

La Casa de Don Colocho
Parque Central, 3 c este, 3 c sur.
The place to imbibe cappuccinos, lattes, espressos and other locally sourced caffeinated fare. Also sweet treats.

What to do

Tour operators
UCA Soppexcca, *Ferretería Blandón Moreno, 1 c abajo, www.soppexcca.org/en.*
This great organization comprises 15 organic coffee cooperatives who offer tours to see how their award-winning beans are cultivated and prepared for export.

Around Jinotega
Canopy tours
Canopy Tour La Brellera, *Carretera San Rafael–Yalí Km 5, T8814-3656, www.canopytourlabrellera.com.* Located just outside San Rafael del Norte, La Brellera is a canopy tour with 1.5 km of zip-lines. Costs per person US$15, open 0800-1800. To get there, take a bus towards Yalí from the Mercado Municipal in Jinotega and ask to get off at La Brellera, US$1; or go to San Rafael del Norte and take a taxi.

Transport

Bus
Most destinations will require a change of bus in Matagalpa. To **Matagalpa**, every 30 mins, 0500-1800, US$1.50, 1½ hrs. Express bus to **Managua**, 11 daily, 0400-1600, US$3.20, 3½ hrs. To **San Rafael del Norte**, departing from the Mercado, 10 daily, 0600-1730 US$1, 1 hr. Taxis in Jinotega are available for local transport, average fare US$.50.

At first glance, Estelí (altitude 844 m, population 107,458) appears to be a jumbled unattractive place, but this is one of the most lively and industrious towns in Nicaragua. It is known nationally as one of the biggest commercial centres in the north and internationally as the cigar capital of Central America and, like Matagalpa and Jinotega, it is set in an area of bucolic villages and verdant countryside. The Sandinistas remain a force to be reckoned with in Estelí and the party colours of black and red can be seen all around town.

The city centre lies to the west of the highway, with the focus of its life and commerce on two avenues that bear south from the Parque Central. Taxis are cheap in the town and walking is safe in the daytime. Exercise caution at night and don't wander around the barrios.

Sights

Estelí was founded in 1711 by Spanish colonists who abruptly left Nueva Segovia, now Ciudad Antigua (see page 191), to escape joint Miskito-British attacks on the old city. Sadly the town was razed in 1978-1979 by Somoza's National Guard, which used aerial bombing and tanks to put down repeated uprisings by the population spurred on by the FSLN. To learn more about the city's revolutionary past, head to the **Galería de Héroes y Mártires** ⓘ *Casa de Cultura, ½ c al norte, T2714-0942, www.galleryofheroesandmartyrs.blogspot.com, Tue-Fri 0900-1630, free*, which has photographic exhibitions and artefacts highlighting the struggle and sacrifice of the city's fallen comrades.

Estelí is known as the capital of **cigars**, with the finest tobacco in Central America grown in the surrounding mountains. Most of the city's factories were founded by exiled Cubans, who brought their seeds and expertise with them in the 1960s. If you would like to see the production process, a handful of local guides and tour operators lead tours to selected manufacturers; see What to do, below.

Around Estelí

The **Reserva Natural Meseta Tisey-Estanzuela** ⓘ *managed by Fundación Fider, Petronic El Carmen, 1½ c abajo, Estelí, T713-3918, fiderest@ibw.com.ni*, is home to rugged mountain scenery quite different from the landscape of Nicaragua's Pacific Basin: there are pine and oak forests, moss-covered granite boulders, rivers and cascades. The biggest attraction is the lovely **Estanzuela waterfall**, accessed by a signed 5 km dirt road just south of Estelí.

North of Estelí, a very poor dirt road runs west to the rural village of **San Juan de Limay**, famous across Nicaragua for the beautiful soapstone (*marmolina*) carvings produced by more than 50 carvers who work in the area. It can take up to two hours to travel the 44 km, but it's worth it for those who like remote villages and crafts.

On the east side of the Pan-American highway, about 25 km north of Estelí, is the sleepy village of **Condega**, another vehemently Sandinista town. Above

Estelí

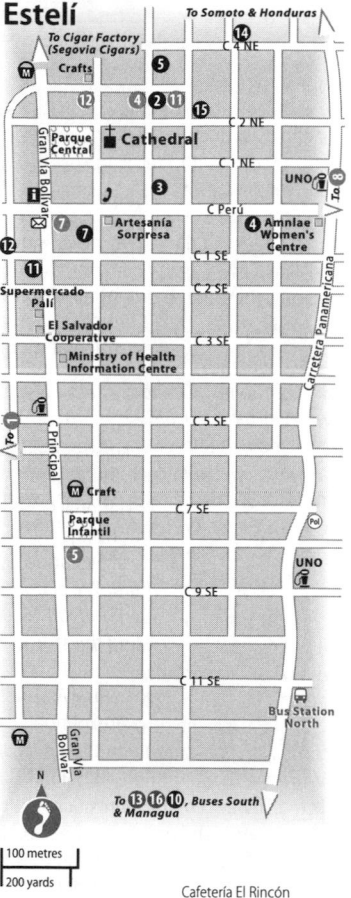

the cemetery there is a park with an old aeroplane from Somoza's National Guard, downed by FSLN rebels in 1979 and now rusting like a dinosaur carcass. The name Condega means 'land of potters' and the local artisans make traditional, red-clay pottery that is both attractive and functional.

Reserva Natural Miraflor

UCA Miraflor, office in Estelí, costado noreste de gasolinera 'UNO Norte', 2 c este, ½ c norte, T2713-2971, www. ucamiraflor.org.

Northeast of Estelí, this reserve is full of diverse wildlife and vegetation and offers opportunities to visit and stay in local communities. The ecosystem changes with altitude from tropical savannah to tropical dry forest, then to pine forest and finally cloudforest at its highest elevations. The legendary quetzal lives here, along with trogons, magpie jays, the turquoise-browed mot-mot, many birds of prey, howler monkeys, mountain lions, ocelots, deer, sloths, river otters, racoons and tree frogs. The reserve also has some gallery forest, ideal for viewing wildlife, a variety of orchids and a 60-m-high waterfall that flows during the rainy season. For unbiased information on lodging and excursions inside the reserve, visit **Treehuggers Tourism** ⓘ *east side of the cathedral, 1 c norte, T8496-7449, www.treehuggers. cafeluzyluna.org.* You are strongly advised to arrange guides and/or accommodation prior to setting out.

Tourist information

INTUR
Southwest corner of the Parque Central,
½ c oeste, 2nd floor of the red building,
T2713-6799.
This office has information on local attractions including nature reserves, cigar factories and Spanish schools.

Treehuggers tourism office
East side of the cathedral, 1 c norte,
T8496-7449, www.treehuggers.
cafeluzyluna.org. Open 0800-2000.
Managed by Luna International Hostel across the street, this place is a great source of English-language information.

Where to stay

$$ Hotel Cuallitlan
Restaurante El Sopón (Km 146.5) 4 c este,
1 c norte, 400 m from the Panamericana,
T2713-2446, www.cuallitlan.blogspot.com.
A secluded and tranquil hideaway with 13 comfortable wooden cabins and a ranch-style restaurant. The grounds encompass a pleasant garden with shady trees, hammocks and patios. Hospitable and helpful. Rustic-chic.

$$ Hotel Los Arcos
Northeast corner of the cathedral,
½ c norte, T2713-3830, www.
hotelosarcosesteli.com.
This brightly painted, professionally managed and comfortable hotel has 32 clean, spacious rooms with private bath, a/c or fan and cable TV. There's also parking, laundry service and Wi-Fi. The attached restaurant, **Vuela Vuela**, is also reputable and profits go to social projects. Breakfast included.

$ Casa Nicarao
Parque Central, 1½ c sur, T2713-2490.
9 clean, basic rooms with fan and private bath, all set around a relaxing, sociable courtyard filled with plants, paintings and sitting space. Friendly with a good atmosphere, but the walls are thin and you'll hear everything going on inside and out. There are cheaper rooms without bath.

$ Casa Vínculos
Almacén Sony, 1½ c abajo, T2713-2044,
www.vinculosesteli.org.
Managed by a non-profit organization, Casa Vínculos has decent rooms, all well priced, spacious, tidy and equipped with Wi-Fi and cable TV. There is a cafeteria on site and families with young kids will love the play areas.

$ Hostal Tomabú
Opposite the Parque Infantil, T2713-3783,
www.hostaltomabu.com.
Friendly, family-run hotel whose name means 'place of the sun'. 15 good, clean rooms with hot water, fan and cable TV, most with Wi-Fi. Bright colours and potted flowers. Lots of connections with tour operators and professional, personal attention. Shared kitchen, lending library and common areas. Recommended.

$ Hotel Puro Estelí
Costado noreste de la Catedral,
1 c norte, 75 vrs este, T2713-6404,
www.hotelpuroesteli.com.
Owned by a major cigar manufacturer, **Drew Estate**, this hotel has a large *humidor* in the lobby where you can stock up on *puros*. Rooms are simple, comfortable and economical, and tastefully adorned with bright artwork. It has the usual amenities. Good value.

$ Luna International Hostel
Catedral, 1 c al norte, 1 c arriba,
T8441-8466, www.cafeluzyluna.org.
This popular hostel is part of an
excellent non-profit social enterprise.
Facilities include 4 dorms, 3 private
rooms, hammock space, an activities
board, tourist information, lockers, hot
water, Wi-Fi, tours, free organic coffee
and drinking water. Volunteer work in
Miraflor can be arranged here; 3 months'
commitment and Spanish speakers
preferred. Discounts for longer stays
and groups. Highly recommended.

Restaurants

$$$ Pullaso's Olé
Autolote del norte, 1 c oeste.
A superb steakhouse and the best
restaurant in town. They serve certified
Angus beef and a range of sumptuous
cuts including sirloin, T-bone, rib eye and
porterhouse steaks. Attentive service, a
good wine list and outdoor seating on
a patio. The place for a special evening
meal. Recommended.

$$$-$$ Cohifer
Catedral, 1 c este, ½ c al sur.
A well-established Nicaraguan
restaurant, considered 'upmarket' for
Estelí and popular with business people
at lunchtime. They serve the usual steak,
chicken, fish and pork dishes, as well
as lighter economical fare. Nothing
extraordinary, but service is good and
the food is generally tasty and reliable.

$$ Tipiscayan
Northeast corner of Parque Central,
2 c norte, 3½ c arriba.
A relaxing space with lots of interesting
artwork and a good balcony upstairs.
They serve a range of meat and chicken
dishes in *jalapeño* and other sauces.

$$-$ Café Luz
Catedral, 1 c al norte, 1 c arriba,
www.cafeluzyluna.org.
This English-owned café is part of a
non-profit enterprise that supports
communities in Miraflor. All salads,
herbs and vegetables are locally
sourced and organic. They serve a
range of wholesome lunches, dinners
and breakfasts, including fruit salads
with home-made yogurt and granola,
pancakes with honey, and *nacatamales*.
Beverages include local coffee and tasty
fresh fruit juices with no added sugar.
Recommended.

$$-$ Cafetería El Rincón Pinareño
Enitel, ½ c sur.
Nicaraguan dishes and home-made
pastries, try *vaca frita* (shredded fried
beef with onions and bell peppers) and
sandwich cubano. Good service and
food, crowded for lunch.

$$-$ Casa Vecchia
Southwest corner of the Parque Central,
2 c sur, 1 c oeste.
A low-key Italian restaurant serving
decent pasta dishes, including lasagne.
Intimate and casual setting.

$$-$ Jerusalem Kebab Grill
Esquina de los Bancos, 50 m norte.
Fresh, healthy and wholesome Arabic
and Israeli cuisine. Options include
falafel, shakshuka, salads and hibiscus
juice. Recommended for vegetarians.
Authentic and tasty.

$ El Quesito
Northeast corner of the Parque Central,
2 c este. Closed Sun.
A little locals' joint with rustic furniture
and the usual hearty Nica fare,
economical and filling. Often full
at breakfast time.

Cafés, bakeries and juice bars

Café Don Luis
Bancentro, 25 vrs al norte.
A buzzing little café on the corner
with tables outside, ideal for people-
watching. They serve paninis, sweet
snacks, coffee, espresso, cappuccino
and excellent cheesecake. Wi-Fi.

La Casita
*Opposite La Barranca, at south entrance
to Estelí on Panamericana, T2713-4917,
casita@sdnnic.org.ni.*
Nicaragua's best home-made yogurt in
tropical fruit flavours. Very cute place with
pleasant outdoor seating underneath
trees on back patio. Recommended.

Bars and clubs

Café Luz
See Restaurants, above.
Most evenings Café Luz sees an
eclectic mix of expats, Nicas,
volunteers and travellers gathering to
drink beer, coffee or rum, or otherwise
engage in relaxed conversation.

Cigarszone
*Carretera Panamericana, southern
entrance to the city.*
Estelí's most modern and popular disco.
Also features live music and boisterous
young things.

Semáforo Rancho Bar
Hospital San Juan de Dios, 400 m sur.
Don your dancing shoes for Estelí's
quintessential night spot. It hosts some
of the best live music in the country,
with nationally and internationally
renowned acts performing regularly.

What to do

Cigar making
Estelí's famous cigar factories can be
toured with independent guides or
agencies. For aficianados, **Drew Estates**
(www.cigarsafari.com, contactable
through Hotel Puro Estelí), offer 'cigar
safari' tours. Also recommended
are **Treehuggers Tours** (see below).
Alternatively, you can contact the
factories directly (a comprehensive list is
available from **INTUR**), although not all
of them offer tours.

Language schools
**CENAC, Centro Nicaragüense de
Aprendizaje y Cultura**, *250 m north
of the UNO gas station, T2713-5437,
www.spanishschoolcenac.com.* 20 hrs
of Spanish classes, living with a family,
full board, trips to countryside, meetings
and seminars, opportunities to work on
community projects, US$200 per week.
Also teaches English to Nicaraguans and
others and welcomes volunteer tutors.
Horizonte Nica, *Cruz Roja, 3 c sur,
T8858-8394, info_spanishhorizonte@
yahoo.com.* Intensive Spanish courses
with a programme of activities and
homestay. They offer excursions
and voluntary work and aim to educate
you about local communities as well as
the language.
Spanish Conversation School, *Costado
del Cine Nancy, ½ c al oeste, T2714-2237,
www.spanishconversation.net.* Full
immersion and non-immersion courses
with options for homestay and activities.
They also offer classes via Skype.

Tour operators
Treehuggers tourism office, *east side of
the cathedral, 1 c norte, T8496-74498405-
8919, www.treehuggers.cafeluzyluna.org.*

In addition to Miraflores excursions, Treehuggers offers tours of Estelí and its murals, cigar factories, Somoto Canyon and beyond. They also run 'extreme hikes' and night hikes to observe nocturnal birds. Good.

Transport

Bus

Estelí is a transport hub with express bus services from Managua, Matagalpa and León. Regular buses connect it with Somoto and Ocotal, both of which connect to the Honduran border; see Nicaragua–Honduras border box, page 255.

Buses enter and leave Estelí via 2 terminals, both on the Pan-American highway. The north terminal deals with northern destinations like Somoto and Ocotal. The south terminal, a short distance away, deals with southern destinations like Managua. A handful of Managua express buses also stop at the Shell station, east of the centre on the Pan-American highway.

North station To **Somoto**, every hour, 0530-1810, US$1.10, 2½ hrs, use this service to connect to El Espino border bus. To **Ocotal**, every hour, 0600-1730, US$1.40, 2 hrs, use this for bus to Las Manos crossing. To **Jinotega**, 5 daily, US$2, 2 hrs. To **El Sauce**, 0900, US$1.25, 3 hrs. To **San Juan de Limay**, 7 daily, US$2, 3 hrs. To **Miraflor**, take a bus heading towards **San Sebastián de Yalí** (not one that goes to Condega first), 3 daily 0600, 1200, 1600, US$2, 1½ hrs. Return bus passes at 0700, 1100 and 1620.

South station Express bus to **León**, 1500, US$2.75, 3 hrs. To **Managua**, every 30 mins, 0330-1800, US$2, 3 hrs; express buses, roughly 30 mins, 0545-1515, US$3, 2 hrs. To **Matagalpa**, every 30 mins, 0520-1650, US$1.40, 2 hrs; express buses, 0805, 1435, US$1.50, 1½ hrs.

Taxi

Taxis are common on the Carretera Panamericana in Estelí, at the bus stations and in the town proper. Fares per person, inside the city centre US$0.50, from the bus stations to centre US$1. Night fares are higher and trips to the dance clubs on the outskirts cost US$2-3. As always, agree on fare before long rides; in town just get in.

Rolling north from Estelí, the Pan-American Highway enters the fragrant pine forests and rugged mountains of Madriz, where everything happens in its own time. West of Somoto, the provincial capital, the international crossing at El Espino provides rapid access to southern Honduras and El Salvador; see also the Nicaragua–Honduras border, page 255. The most direct route to Tegucigalpa, however, is through the neighbouring department of Nueva Segovia, a deeply rural region and early colonial mining centre. Local buses are slow and dusty; for serious exploration of the region's hidden attractions, 4WD is recommended.

Somoto

The sleepy town of Somoto is celebrated for its world-famous sons, the folk musicians Carlos and Luis Enrique Mejía Godoy, and for its superb *rosquillas* (baked corn and cheese biscuits) which are practically a religion. No one seems sure when *rosquillas* became a tradition here, but the oldest residents recall that they were already popular in the 1920s. The most famous baker could be **Betty Espinoza** ① *Enitel, 3 c norte, T2722-2173, Mon-Sat 0500-1000*, who is happy for visitors to watch the process of butter, corn, eggs, milk, sugar and Nicaraguan feta cheese being made into *rosquillas*; her seven employees and big wood-burning ovens crank out 3000 of them per day. For the border crossing to Honduras, see Nicaragua–Honduras border box, page 255.

Somoto Canyon

To get to the canyon, follow the highway about 15 km north of Somoto, where you'll find a signposted dirt track at the bridge over the Tapacalí River; it is a 20-min walk from here. Follow the track 3 km to the end where you will meet guides with a boat who will ferry you to the canyon. Take care on the slippery rocks. A taxi here costs around US$5.

Known locally as Namancambre, Somoto Canyon soars above crystal-clear waters at the source of the great Río Coco, which runs for more than 750 km to the Caribbean Sea. A walk in the 3-km-long canyon is both a contemplative and adventurous experience, requiring careful hiking over slippery rocks that hug the 100-m-high walls. You can swim or tube in the river during dry season, but it can be very dangerous in the rainy season (June to November) and even if not swimming, as the river is prone to flash floods and the currents are very strong. There are various hikes you can undertake in the area lasting anything from three to 12 hours. A cooperative of guides works near the entrance of the canyon, offering its services for around US$25 per day, depending on your requirements, as well as the option of rustic lodging in their community; contact Henri Soriano of Somoto Canyon Tours, Km 229.5 Carretera Panamericana, T5791-9556, www.somotocanyontours.org.

Comunidad Indígena de Totogalpa

Arriving in Totogalpa, a seemingly forgotten town with red-clay streets and lightly crumbling adobe homes, feels like arriving at the very end of the earth. The original settlement dates back more than 1600 years and is located in the community of San José, northeast of the current village, on the banks of the Río Coco. The remains of circular stone houses and ceramics suggest that this was a large settlement AD 400-600.

Ocotal

Named after the ocotl species of pine tree, Ocotal has the dubious distinction of being the first town in the world to be bombed by a fleet of military planes in combat circumstances, courtesy of the US Marines in July 1927. Today, this little city is the financial and trading centre of Nueva Segovia. It has little to offer visitors, but it is a useful base for exploring the region, or to rest before or after the border crossing at Las Manos; see the Nicaragua–Honduras border box, page 255. Its main attraction is **Parque Las Madres**, a lush tropical garden designed by the ex-mayor of Ocotal and tropical plant expert, Don Fausto Sánchez.

Ciudad Antigua

Nestled in a valley of rolling hills, the Ciudad Antigua of today is truly in the middle of nowhere, but that was not always the case. Originally called Nueva Ciudad Segovia, it was founded in 1611 by Spanish colonists who hurriedly abandoned the first Ciudad Segovia settlement (founded between 1541 and 1543 near present day Quilalí) as a result of continued attacks by the indigenous population. In the late 1600s, the city was attacked by pirates and most of the population fled to found Ocotal, or further south to found Estelí. The village has not changed much for the last few centuries, providing an excellent opportunity to step back in time. Its 17th-century **church** features a whitewashed adobe interior with an ornate gold leaf altar bearing a famous image of Jesus or El Señor de los Milagros, said to have been brought to Ciudad Antigua, along with the heavy altar, via a Caribbean port in Honduras by manpower alone.

Where to stay

Somoto

$$ Hotel Colonial
Iglesia, ½ c sur, T2722-2040,
arielbrenes@yahoo.com.
A well-established hotel with an
attractive lobby and exterior, but only
so-so rooms; all have private bath, cable
TV and fan. Popular with businessmen
and NGOs, but not as good as it once
was; ask to see a few rooms (some are
big, others not) and check mattresses
before accepting.

$ Hotel El Rosario
Claro, 1 c este, 2722-2083,
www.hotelelrosario.wordpress.com.
Your best option for value and
hospitality. El Rosario is a basic,
family-run hotel with 13 clean rooms,
all equipped with small flatscreen TVs,
private bath, cold water and fast Wi-Fi;
a/c is US$10 extra.

Ocotal

$$ Hotel Frontera
Behind the Shell station on the
highway to Las Manos, T2732-2668,
hosfrosa@turbonett.com.
The best hotel in town, even if it looks
like a prison compound from outside. It
has an inviting pool, bar, restaurant and
events room.

**$$-$ Casa Huésped 'Llamarada del
Bosque'**
Parque Central, T2732-2643,
llamaradadelbosque@yahoo.com.
Conveniently located, this reasonably
priced hotel has a wide range of rooms,
but those upstairs are more spacious,
modern and comfortable. They also

own the popular restaurant on the
corner of the plaza.

Transport

Somoto
Bus
Buses to **El Espino** and the Honduran
border (see the Nicaragua–Honduras
border box, page 255), every hour, 0515-
1715, US$0.50, 40 mins. To **Estelí**, every
hour, 0520-1700, US$1.25, 2½ hrs; express
buses are Managua-bound, US$1.65,
1½ hrs, they will drop you off at the Shell
station, just east of central Estelí. Express
bus to **Managua**, Mon-Sat, 0345, 0500,
0615, 0730, 1400, 1515, Sun 1400, 1515,
US$4, 3½ hrs. To **Ocotal**, every 45 mins,
0345-1635, US$0.75, 1½ hrs.

Comunidad Indígena de Totogalpa
Bus
Buses pass the village on the highway,
every 15 mins for **Ocotal**, US$0.40, and
Estelí, US$0.80.

Ocotal
Bus
The bus station for Ocotal is on the
highway, 1 km south of the town centre,
15-20 mins' walk from Parque Central.
Buses to **Las Manos/Honduras border**
(see Nicaragua–Honduras border box,
page 255) every 30 mins, 0500-1645,
US$0.80, 45 mins. To **Somoto**, every
45 mins, 0545-1830, US$0.75, 2½ hrs.
Express bus to **Managua**, 10 daily, 0400-
1530, US$4.50, 4 hrs. To **Ciudad Antigua**,
0500, 1200, US$1.25, 1½ hrs. To **Estelí**,
leaves the city market every hour, 0445-
1800, US$1.30, 2½ hrs; express buses are
Managua-bound, 2 hrs, US$1.65, they

will drop you off at the Shell station, just east of central Estelí.

Taxi
Ocotal taxis are cheap, with rides within town costing about US$0.40. A ride to **Las Manos** and the border with Honduras (see the Nicaragua–Honduras border box, page 255) will cost US$7-9.

Ciudad Antigua
Bus
There is 1 bus per day to **Ocotal** at 1400, 1½ hrs, US$1.50.

Caribbean
coast

A world away from its Pacific cousin, Nicaragua's Caribbean coast (or Costa Atlántica) revels in its feisty multicultural heritage. British buccaneers, Jamaican labourers, Chinese immigrants, African-descended Garífunas, indigenous Miskitos, Mayagnas and Ramas have all contributed to the region's exotic flavours. Lilting Creole English, not Spanish, is the traditional lingua franca. The reason why the coast has developed along its own unique trajectory becomes clear if you fly over the region for a bird's eye view: an unrelenting carpet of green tree tops, meandering toffee-coloured rivers and swollen lagoons separate it from the rest of Nicaragua and few roads – or Spanish colonists – have ever penetrated this inhospitable wilderness of rainforest and swamp.

The Corn Islands are the region's principal attraction: two dazzling offshore atolls with white-sand beaches, scintillating coral reefs and turquoise waters. Little Corn is a low-key dive centre, while Big Corn is home to diverse fishing communities and a good place to sample authentic Caribbean life, as long as it lasts. On the mainland, the city of Bluefields, a decaying and shambolic spectre, is ripe with all the sights, sounds and smells of any bustling tropical port. This is the place to drink rum and watch the tropical storms roll in.

the heart and soul of Nicaragua's Caribbean world

Dirty and chaotic but curiously inviting, Bluefields (altitude 20 m, population 48,000) is the capital of the Región Autónoma de la Costa Caribe Sur (South Caribbean Coast Autonomous Region), known by its acronym RACCS. It is located at the mouth of the Río Escondido, which opens into Bluefields Bay in front of the town. The majority of the population is mestizo, with African-Caribbean Creole a close second. The other four ethnic groups of the region are represented and the main attraction of the town is its ethnic diversity and west Caribbean demeanour. The main church is Moravian, the language is Creole English and the music is country and reggae.

Most of Bluefields can be seen on foot, though taxis are recommended at night. All visits to surrounding attractions are by boat. Do not go wandering in the barrios. If desperate for cash **BanPro** in Barrio Central opposite the Moravian church (T2822-2261) has two ATMs. Another ATM can be found at the **LaFise Bancentro** just a block up on the Calle Commercial.

Bluefields is a good jumping-off point to visit Pearl Lagoon and other less explored areas of the wide-open region.

Sights
Lacking any conventional tourist attractions, the appeal of Bluefields lies in getting to know its people; anyone willing to scratch the city's surface will find no shortage of strange stories and colourful characters. A good place to learn about the city's swashbuckling past is the CIDCA-BICU **Historical Museum of the Atlantic Coast** ① *Barrio Punta Fría, Mon-Fri 0900-1700, US$2,* where you'll find an intriguing collection of artefacts including a photo collection showing Bluefields before it was destroyed by Hurricane Joan in 1988. Downstairs there is a very good cultural library. Within Nicaragua, Bluefields is best known for its dancing, best seen during the exuberant annual Maypole (**Palo de Mayo**) celebrations (also known as **Mayo Ya**).

Around Bluefields
El Bluff is a peninsula that separates the sea from the Bay of Bluefields. In happier days it was a busy port, but now a fleet of rusting shrimping boats evidence the town's decline. Its beach is the nearest stretch of sand to Bluefields: long, wide and a little bit dirty, but OK for an afternoon; bring repellent for the sand flies. Boats to El Bluff leave from the southern dock in Bluefields next to the market. The boat costs US$3 and leaves when full, 0730-1730.

In the bay of Bluefields, the tiny island of **Rama Cay** is home to one of the last tribes of the Rama, calm and friendly people who are renowned for their shyness, generosity, and linguistic skills. They are fairly accustomed to visitors but sadly this is the least studied group of all the indigenous peoples in Nicaragua and the most likely to lose its own language. A boat ride to the island,

Bluefields

Bluefields is named after the Dutch pirate Henry Bluefeldt (or Blauvedlt) who hid in the bay's waters in 1610. The native Kukra were hired by Dutch and British pirates to help them with boat repairs and small time trade began with the Europeans. The first permanent European settlers arrived in the late 18th century and the ethnic mix of the area began to change. The 19th century saw a healthy trade in bananas and an influx of African-Caribbeans from Jamaica to work in the plantations. Today, the indigenous and Creole populations have become marginalized with Spanish-speaking settlers from the Pacific dominating the city's economic sphere.

20-30 minutes, costs US$15-50 depending on the number of passengers. Check at the dock next to the market to see if any boats are going; if you hitch a ride, returning could be a problem.

Laguna de Perlas

This oval-shaped coastal lagoon, 80 km north of Bluefields, covers 518 sq km and is fed principally by the jungle-lined Río Kurinwás, but also by the rivers Wawashán, Patch, Orinoco and Ñari. Pearl Lagoon's shores range from pine forests and mangroves to savannah and rainforest.

The village of Laguna de Perlas, in the far southwest of the estuary, is the most developed place in the region and a good place to start your explorations. The local community is predominantly African-Caribbean but there are also plenty of Miskito and mestizo inhabitants. You'll find the best accommodation in the entire region here (see Where to stay, below) and there are boat services to Bluefields three times a day. There are no banks or ATMs in Pearl Lagoon so bring all the cash you need. If you get really stuck there's a **Western Union** office opposite the dock.

Pearl Lagoon is the point of departure for the Pearl Cays, a dazzling white-sand archipelago around 1½ hours away by high-speed *panga*. The cays – composed of numerous small islands – are tranquil and idyllic, but tourism here is uncontrolled and their ownership by wealthy foreigners is fiercely disputed; **Kabu Tours** are recommended as the sustainable option (see What to do, below).

On the north shore of the lagoon, the community of **Orinoco** is home to Nicaragua's largest population of Garífuna people, who are descended from escaped shipwrecked slaves. In a mixture of old African and indigenous influences, many of their dances and culinary customs remain intact. **Hostal Garífuna** has lodging and can organize wildlife tours and cultural presentations, including spectacular drumming. Orinoco has an annual cultural festival from 17-19 November.

Tourist information

INTUR
Opposite the police station, Barrio Punta Fría, T2572-0221, raas@intur.gob.ni. Mon-Fri 0800-1700.
This tourist office has Spanish-speaking staff and very limited information on local attractions. Also see the entertaining *Right Side Guide*, www.rightsideguide.com.

Where to stay

Bluefields
Many hotels in Bluefields are quite basic and grim. Check rooms before accepting.

$$ Hotel Jackani
Barrio Punta Fría, Policía Nacional, 20 m sur, T2572-0440, hoteljackani@gmail.com.
27 clean rooms with private bath, a/c or fan, and cable TV. Services include restaurant with home cooking and à la carte menu, Wi-Fi (US$2 per day) and laundry. Clean and often fully booked, call ahead. Owners helpful.

$$ South Atlantic II
Barrio Central, next to petrol station Levy, T2572-2265.
Upstairs are clean rooms with reasonable mattresses, private bath, cable TV and a/c. Downstairs you'll find the economy quarters ($), which all have a fan and private bath but are also quite damp and dingy. There's a sports bar-restaurant that's good for a beer. Friendly.

$ Hostal Doña Vero
Barrio Central, opposite Mercadito Mas x Menos, T2572-2166.
Clean, well-attended budget lodgings and without doubt the best deal in

town. Rooms on the top floor are large, comfortable and great value. Those downstairs are smaller. Some ultra-cheap quarters have shared bath. Recommended.

Rama Cay
A handful of families offer lodgings to visitors, including that of the Moravian pastor. Enquire at the GTRK office located 2 blocks south of the park in Bluefields.

Laguna de Perlas

$$-$ Casa Blanca
In May 4 sector, T2572-0508, casa_blanca_lp@yahoo.com.
One of the best hotels in town, with a range of clean, light, comfortable rooms; 5 have private bath, 6 have shared bath. The owners, Sven and Miss Dell, are very hospitable and friendly, and offer fishing expeditions, trips to the cays, general information and community tours. They're happy to answer questions by email, and prefer reservations in advance. Restaurant attached and internet available. A good family house, recommended.

$ Hostal Garífuna
In Orinoco, 50 m from the dock, T8648-4985, www.hostalgarifuna.net.
Owned and managed by Kensy Sambola, a respected Garífuna anthropologist, Hostal Garífuna is your one-stop shop for cultural information and tours. Rooms are clean and comfortable with shared bath and there's also a pleasant garden slung with hammocks. Meals are served. Highly recommended.

$ Hotel Slilma
*Enitel tower, 50 vrs sur, 75 vrs arriba
on the left-hand turn, T2572-0523,
rondownleiva@hotmail.com.*
Also known by its Spanish name,
Las Estrellas, Hotel Slilma is a friendly,
helpful lodging, recommended for
budget travellers. They have 20 rooms,
most with shared bath, cable TV and fan,
but a few newer ones also have private
bath and a/c. Various hammocks and
porches for chilling out.

Restaurants

Bluefields

$$$-$$ Chez Marcel
Alcaldía, 1 c sur, ½ c abajo, T2572-2347.
The fading red curtains speak of better
days, but the food is still OK and the
service attentive. As you may be the only
customers, the atmosphere can be a
bit lifeless. Dishes include filet mignon,
shrimp in garlic butter and grilled lobster.

$$ El Flotante
*Barrio Punta Fría, T2572-2988.
Daily 1000-2200.*
Built over the water at the end of the
main street with a great view of the
fishing boats and islets. They serve good
shrimp and lobster, but service is slow.
Dancing at weekends.

$$ Pelican Bay
*Barrio Pointeen, La Punta, at the end of
the road.*
Evenings here are often buzzing with
drinkers and diners. Great breezes from
the balcony, comfortable interior, friendly
service and average food, including
seafood and meat. Not a bad place to
have a few drinks in the evening.

$$ Salmar
*Alcaldía, 1 c sur, ½ c abajo, T2572-2128.
Daily 1600-2400.*
If you're bored of seafood and rice,
this long-running restaurant serves
reasonable (but not fantastic) Tex Mex,
including burritos, as well as the usual
local fare. Attentive service. The best
place in town at last check.

$ Comedor Vera Blanca
Barrio Central, opposite ADEPHCA.
A simple *comedor* offering high-carb
food, including the obligatory chicken
and fish dishes. Often packed with locals
for lunch and dinner.

Laguna de Perlas

$$ Casa Ulrich
Muelle Principal, 300 vrs norte.
Local owner Fred Ulrich was trained as a
chef in Switzerland and you will be hard
pressed to find better food in town. It is
possibly the best restaurant on the coast.
Give them a half-day notice and order the
rundown. The restaurant is upstairs facing
the lagoon. They have good rooms too.

$$ Queen Lobster
*Muelle Principal, 200 vrs norte,
T8662-3393.*
Owned by Nuria Dixon Curtis, this
restaurant ranks highly. This ranch-style
eatery on the water's edge serves good
seafood, including lobster and crab in
red or coconut sauce. Order 'Mr Snapper'
and you'll get a whole pound of fish.
Good views and recommended.

$ Comedor Eva
*Across the street from Green Lodge,
20 m down towards the water.*
All plates including fish, shrimp and
lobster for US$4. And Miss Eva is an
excellent cook.

Bars and clubs

Bluefields

The action starts at **La La**, moves to **Cima** and ends during the early hours at **Four Brothers**.

Cima Club

Banpro, 1 c abajo.

It's hard to miss this centrally located dance hall with 2 floors and a large sign. Popular and often recommended by locals.

Four Brothers

Cotton tree, from Alcaldía, 1 c al mar, 4½ c sur.

The best reggae spot in Nicaragua, a big ranch full of great dancing. Usually open Tue-Sun but Fri and Sat nights can be dancing room only. Admission US$1.

La La Place

Barrio Pointeen.

This wooden construction on the water's edge is popular with the city's Creole population, especially on Fri, Sat and Sun night. They play reggae, country and dancehall through very large speakers.

What to do

Laguna de Perlas
Tour operators

Many restaurants hoteliers are able to arrange guides, tours, or transport; **Casa Blanca** and **Queen Lobster** are highly recommended. For turtle-watching, try: **Kabu Tours**, *WCS office, 75 vrs south of the muelle, T8714-5196.* Kabu is an initiative from the Wildlife Conservation Society that has trained former sea turtle fisherman to be conservationists and guides. They offer day and overnight trips to the cays, turtle-viewing expeditions and snorkelling trips with new equipment (including

a portable toilet). This is the highest-quality tour you will find and the price reflects it, but it all goes to a good conservationist cause. Recommended.

Transport

Bluefields

The new highway from Managua to Bluefields via Nueva Guinea was still under construction at the time of research; check locally for the latest news on its progress. Until the highway opens, overland travellers must take a bus from Managua to El Rama and from there a boat down the Río Escondido. Alternatively, **La Costeña** flies to Bluefields 3 times daily from Managua's domestic terminal, twice daily from the Corn Islands and 3 times a week from Bilwi.

Air

The airport is 3 km south of the city centre, either walk (30 mins) or take a taxi US$0.75 per person. **La Costeña** office, inside the terminal, T2572-2500. All schedules are subject to random and seasonal changes. It's best to get your name on the list several days in advance, if possible, and especially if travelling to Bilwi.

To **Corn Island**, 0725, 1535, ½ hr, US$79 one-way, US$124 return; to **Managua**, 0825, 1210 (Tue, Thu, Sat), 1610, 1 hr, US$97 one way, US$152 return.

Boat

The motorboats (*pangas*) from **El Rama** to Bluefields depart when full, several daily, 0530-1600, US$10, 2 hrs. *Pangas* departing earlier in the day are more reliable, and services on Sun are restricted. The ferry is slightly cheaper and much slower, departing Mon and

Thu around 0800 when the bus has arrived, US$8, 8 hrs.

Note that all schedules (especially Corn Island boats) are subject to change; confirm departure times at the port well in advance of your trip. Pregnant women or those with back problems should think twice before taking long *panga* trips. Use heavy-duty plastic bags to protect your luggage. If the Corn Island ferry is grounded no replacement will be made available.

To **Laguna de Perlas**, 0900, 1200, 1600, US$7.50, 45 mins. To **El Rama**, 0530-1600, several daily, US$10, 2 hrs. To **Orinoco**, Mon, Tue, Sun 0730, US$11, 2 hrs. To **San Juan de Nicaragua**, usually 1 a week, days change, enquire at the port. To **Corn Islands**, US$10-12. *Río Escondido*, Wed, 0900-1200; *Captain D*, Wed, 1200, stopping in El Bluff until 1700; *Island Express*, Fri, leaves directly from El Bluff 0200-0400; *Humberto C*, Fri, leaves directly from El Bluff, 0500; *Genesis*, Sun, leaves directly from El Bluff, 0800. To **El Bluff**, several daily, depart when full from the dock near the market, 0630-1730, US$1.50, 15 mins.

Bus

Buses from El Rama to **Managua** depart roughly every hour, US$8, 9 hrs; express bus (recommended), 0900, US$9.50, 7 hrs. A bus also goes from El Rama to **Pearl Lagoon**, 1600, US$7.50, 3 hrs.

Taxi

Taxi rides anywhere in the city are US$0.50 per person (US$0.75 to the airport or at night).

Laguna de Perlas
Boat

To **Bluefields**, *panga* leaves at 0600, 0700 and 1300. US$7.50, 45 mins, Get to the dock the day before to get your name on the passenger list. Services are restricted on Sun.

Bus

Bus to **El Rama**, 0600, US$7.50, 3 hrs. To **Managua**, it's possible to drive all the way, but the roads are rough. A strong 4WD can get you there in 8 hrs, on a good day.

low-key archipelago home to colourful clapboard houses and idyllic beaches

Seventy kilometres off the mainland of Nicaragua, the Corn Islands (population 6370) are a portrait of Caribbean indolence, with languid palm trees and easy, rum-soaked dilapidation. Divorced from the mainland by 70 km of turquoise sea, many islanders are incurable eccentrics. Few, if any, pay much mind to the world outside, concerning themselves only with the friendships, feuds and often entertaining gossip that is the staple diet of island life.

Big Corn Island

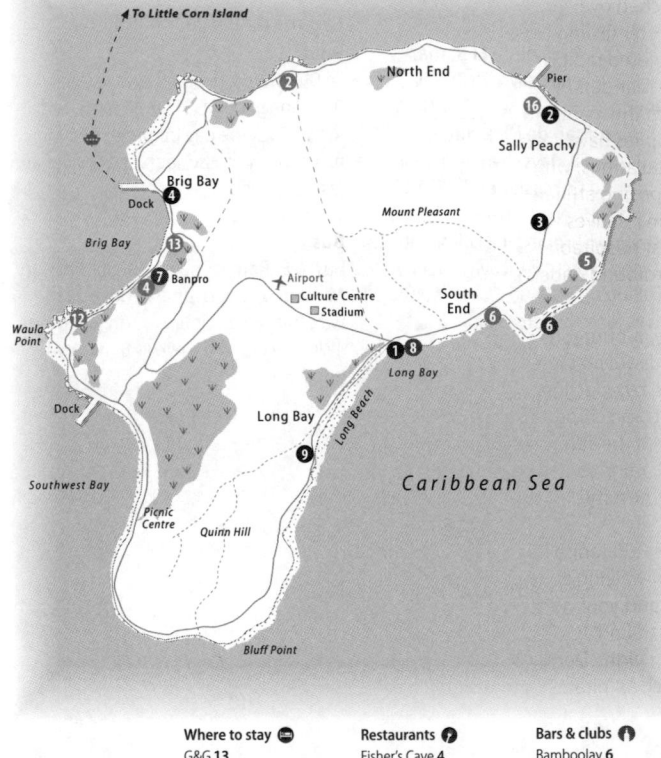

Where to stay 🛏
G&G **13**
Casa Canada **6**
Los Escapados **16**
Paraíso **4**
Princesa de la Isla **12**
Silver Sand **5**
Vientos del Norte **2**

Restaurants 🍴
Fisher's Cave **4**
Island Style **9**
Marlene's Food Place **3**
Seva's Place **2**
Spekito's Place **1**

Bars & clubs 🍸
Bamboolay **6**
Nico's **8**
Xtasis **7**

N

500 metres
500 yards

Corn Islands

During his fourth and final exploratory voyage, Columbus encountered the islands and named them *Islas Limonares*. At the time, they were inhabited by the Kukra people, of which little is known today except for a reported tendency towards cannibalism. During the 18th century the islands became a haven for pirates resting in between pillages. Eventually they were settled by British plantation owners who brought Afro-Caribbeans, mostly Jamaicans, to work the cotton fields. The local economy moved from cotton to coconuts until the devastating winds of Hurricane Joan in 1988, which reached over 200 kph and destroyed most of the palm trees on the island. Lobster fishing took over as the biggest industry, but supplies are being depleted rapidly. Tourism is taking over as the biggest source of income for the islanders. Meanwhile, there has been a migration of Miskito communities from the mainland to the islands to dive for lobster, although dwindling supplies have created unemployment in both native and migrant populations, with some desperate people turning to crime. Yet there is a surprising affluence to both islands thanks to tourism and remittances sent from relatives working abroad. The Corn Island natives remain some of the most hospitable, polite and welcoming people in Nicaragua; a people with a profound understanding of the word 'relaxed'.

Sadly, a burgeoning tourist trade and Colombian 'business interests' mean the islands are no longer the place to experience the authentic Caribbean life of days gone by. Outsiders are steadily infiltrating, bringing tourists, foreign-owned hotels and crime. But like everything else here, the pace of change has been slow. Scratch the surface and you'll discover that many things are as they have always been: rains come and go, mangoes fall, and waves lap the sugar-white beaches in perpetuity.

Safety Paradise has a dark side and you should use common sense at all times. Avoid walking at night on the island anywhere, always use a taxi to get between bars and your hotel. There is now a police force on Little Corn, but they may be hard to find. It's better not to walk alone in the bush, and avoid walking around late at night. Don't go out with locals unless recommended by your hotel; thieves, known as 'pirates', sometimes pose as informal tour guides.

Big Corn
Big Corn does not offer the natural beauty of Little Corn, but it is more lively and those who bore easily or are not interested in snorkelling or diving might prefer the big island. Most of the island's social life, however, is concentrated in the built-up community around Brig Bay. The beaches on the west and southern side of the island are best for swimming. Walking around the island takes about three hours.

Around Waula Point is **Picnic Centre**, a fine beach for swimming and sunbathing. On the sparsely populated southeastern part of the island is the long and tranquil **Long Beach** in Long Bay. With Quinn Hill rising above the western part of the bay it is also very scenic – climb the hill to see an interesting pyramid art sculpture, the **Soul of the World**, www.souloftheworld.com, part of a global installation with counterparts in Botswana, Argentina, New Zealand and other far-off destinations. The most interesting nature is to be found beneath the water, with beautiful reefs and rich marine life. There are also several ancient cannons belonging to a sunken Spanish galleon. Snorkelling is best on the northern coast of Big Corn, just west of **Sally Peachy**.

The eastern side of the island is the most rustic and quieter. Facing the Atlantic, it has good waves for most of the year and plenty of rocks. There is also a lovely community here called **South End**, the most idyllic example of Afro-Caribbean culture on the islands.

There are numerous estuaries and wetlands all around the island, containing a startling amount of fresh water. Birdlife is generally disappointing.

The island celebrates the abolition of slavery with a Crab Soup festival on 27-29 August.

Big Corn has a good landing strip, airport terminal and quite a few decent hotels. 'Bucks' are córdobas in island speak. There is a **Banpro** with a working ATM, Brig Bay; however, it has been known to break down, so bring cash reserves in case of complications. Traveller's cheques are not accepted or changed anywhere, but dollars are widely used. If stuck, you might get a credit card advance at the airport or **Desideri's** café on Little Corn.

Little Corn

Little Corn is more relaxed and less developed than its larger neighbour, although it now suffers from low-level crime and sees huge numbers of visitors in the high season. The locals on the island are keenly aware of the beauty of their home and are learning to adapt to its growing popularity. The small island has some of the

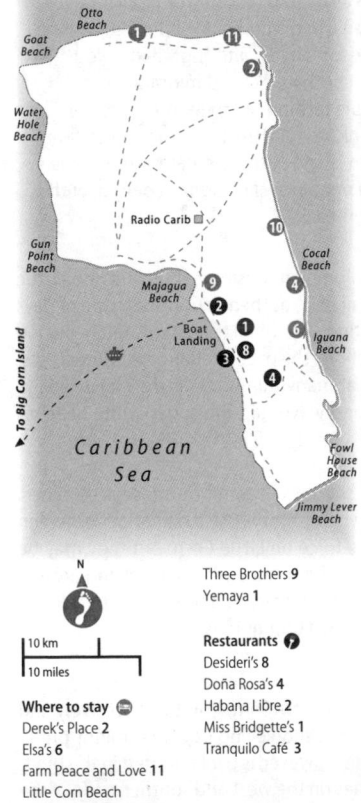

Little Corn Island

Otto Beach
Goat Beach
Water Hole Beach
Radio Carib
Gun Point Beach
Cocal Beach
Majagua Beach
Boat Landing
Iguana Beach
Caribbean Sea
To Big Corn Island
Fowl House Beach
Jimmy Lever Beach

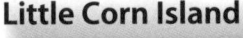

N

10 km
10 miles

Where to stay
Derek's Place **2**
Elsa's **6**
Farm Peace and Love **11**
Little Corn Beach
  and Bungalows **10**
Sunrise Paradise **4**

Three Brothers **9**
Yemaya **1**

Restaurants
Desideri's **8**
Doña Rosa's **4**
Habana Libre **2**
Miss Bridgette's **1**
Tranquilo Café **3**

finest coral reefs in Nicaragua and is a superb place for snorkelling and diving. (*National Geographic Explorer* gave the reefs nine out of 10.)

The island also has good opportunities for walking, with the north end of the island a mixture of scrub forest and grazing land leading down to the brilliant turquoise sea. The prettiest side of the island is also the windward side; visiting during a windy period can be disappointing for snorkellers but helps calm mosquitoes and the heat. The most developed areas are along the western shores of the narrow southern part of the island, separated from the windswept east coast by a large swamp. This is where the boats arrive and there are numerous options for sleeping and eating. The water is calm and good for swimming and there is a good sense of community spirit here.

There are lovely highlands at both ends of the island. The highlands of the southeast have two small but superb beaches; the northern ones also have great beaches and but fewer visitors. East beach is south of an attractive Asian-style lodge called **Derek's Place** (see Where to stay, below), where you will find a spectacular stretch of sand that runs the entire length of the island, broken only by some small rocky points. Near the end of this beach there are good places to eat right on the sand and several lodges. All the beaches have white sand, although it disappears at high tide in places.

Tourist information

There is an official tourist office at the wharf that is closed more often than not. Your best bet is to chat to locals.

Where to stay

Big Corn

$$$ Casa Canada
South End, T8644-0925,
www.casa-canada.com.
Sophisticated, luxurious rooms with ocean views. Each is splendidly equipped with a DVD player, minibar, coffee-maker, leather chairs and mahogany furniture. There's free Wi-Fi for guests and a beautiful infinity pool overlooks the waves. Friendly and hospitable management. Recommended.

$$$-$$ Hotel Paraíso
Brig Bay, T2575-5111,
www.paraisoclub.com.
A professional, friendly hotel, managed by 2 Dutchmen, Mike and Ton, who contribute to local social projects. They have 9 doubles (**$$**) and 5 bungalows (**$$$**). The hotel is next to the beach, and there's good snorkelling at the wreck offshore. Tours, massages and fishing trips can be arranged; ask Mike about seeing the reefs or touring the island in a golf cart. Prices include breakfast at their restaurant. Highly recommended.

$$$-$$ Princesa de la Isla
Waula Point, T8854-2403,
www.laprincesadelaisla.com.
The Princess' setting on a windswept point is eternally romantic. They have 2 bungalows (**$$$**) – often reserved for honeymooners – and a handful

of rooms (**$$**), all with hot water, hammocks and unusual furnishings. The friendly Italian owners also offer good coffee, wine and Italian food (**$$$**) – call 3-4 hrs in advance to get the pasta cooking. Wi-Fi available.

$$ Los Escapados
Little Hill, by the well, Sally Peachy,
www.losescapadosecocabins.com.
This little place is hidden up a steep dirt road and offers 3 'glamping-style' *cabañas* with a great view over the sea. Beds are semi-orthopedic kings that split to singles, and breakfast and Wi-Fi are included.

$$ Vientos del Norte
North End, T2575-5112.
Also known as Ike's place, Vientos del Norte offers a range of well-equipped quarters with fridge, coffee machine, microwave and toaster. Those overlooking the ocean or with a/c cost slightly more. They also have an annex with well-furnished family-sized lodgings and some economy rooms. Friendly, recommended.

$ G&G Hotel/Hostal
Brig Bay, T8824-8237, martinez-
downs69@hotmail.com.
More hotel than *hostal*, G&G offer large rooms with private bathrooms, TV, a/c or fan. There is a pretty good bar/restaurant on site with the constant low drone of reggae music. Wi-Fi is available in both the hotel and restaurant.

$ Silver Sand
Sally Peachy, south of rocky point,
T8948-1436.
Managed by the colourful Ira Gómez, who could well be a character from a *Pirates of the Caribbean* movie. His rustic

fishermen's cabins have seen better days, but their secluded setting near the beach is tranquil and pleasant. Ira can organize fishing trips, and cook up the catch in his bar-restaurant on the beach. Look out for the feisty turkeys and pack insect repellent.

Little Corn

The north end is the greenest, wildest area, but somewhat isolated and difficult to reach at night. The cheapest lodgings are clustered on the south side of the island.

$$$ Derek's Place
At northeastern tip, www. dereksplacelittlecorn.com.
Attractive wooden cabins on stilts, faintly reminiscent of Southeast Asia. All are equipped with renewable energy, mosquito nets, quality mattresses, hammocks, porches, sea views and private bathrooms. The restaurant serves flavourful and interesting food, including fresh fruit juices and various coconut-based dishes, including curries. They also operate the **Little Dive Shack by the Sea**.

$$$ Farm Peace and Love
North end of the island, www.farmpeacelove.com.
Not a hotel, Farm Peace and Love has a cottage and a 'suite', both with fully equipped kitchens and enough space for 3 adults, or 2 adults and 2 children under 10 (sharing a bed). This is the place for people who wish to self-cater and get away from it all. Book your stay well in advance, as they are often full.

$$$ Yemaya
North end of the island, T8272-7362, www.yemayalittlecorn.com.
Treat yourself to spa, massage and yoga in this self-proclaimed eco-hotel and wellness centre. Or just stay in one of the 16 posh *cabañas* overlooking one of the best beaches on the island. In fact, there is no better place to stay anywhere on the Corn Islands.

$$$-$$ Little Corn Beach and Bungalow
On the east beach, T8923-2517, www.littlecornbb.com.
The most popular place on the beach with a mixture of smart bunkhouses ($$), rooms ($$) and bungalows ($$$). All come with fan and sleep up to 4 (US$5 extra for each additional person). The bungalows are particularly comfortable and have good views, wooden floors and decent showers. Restaurant attached.

$$ Sunrise Paradise
On east coast just north of Grace Cool Spot, T8368-6910, www.carlitosplacelittlecorn.com.
Also known as **Carlito's** and managed by the head of the island's informal security service, who is a real gentleman. They offer a range of simple cabins all with fan and electricity. Those with shared bath are cheaper, but the facilities are inadequate for the number of guests sharing. They also have food, beer and hammocks.

$ Elsa's
North along beach from Casa Iguana (see above).
The long-established Elsa's offers simple wooden cabins with sea views and own bath, as well as cheaper lodgings without either. The restaurant serves lobster, fish and vegetarian food for US$6-10 a plate. Snorkels, tours, hammocks and beer available. Hospitable, friendly, safe and relaxed.

$ Three Brothers
20 m south of the triangle, T8658-8736,
www.cornislandhostel.com.
This is the go-to place for most
backpackers. Centrally located, shared
bathrooms and kitchen and 2 of the
friendliest island owners you will meet.
Recommended.

Restaurants

Big Corn

$$$-$$ The Buccaneer
Brig Bay, inside Hotel Paraíso,
see Where to stay, above,
www.restaurantbuccaneer.com.
Open for breakfast, lunch and dinner.
Clean, friendly and presentable restaurant
with a thatched palm roof. They serve
seafood and meat dishes, including lobster,
shrimp, filet mignon and hamburgers.

$$ Fisher's Cave
Brig Bay, by the dock.
This great little seafood restaurant
overlooks the water and fishing boats.
Usually a relaxing spot, although
it's sometimes loud with inebriated
fishermen. Good for a coffee or beer
whilst awaiting the boat to Little Corn.
Check out the pools filled with live fish.

$$-$ Island Style
Long Beach. Open lunch and dinner.
This beach restaurant-bar is earning
a reputation as a cool dining and
drinking spot. Open air, with loud
music and authentic local vibe with
occasional concerts.

$$-$ Marlene's Food Place
South End. Open lunch and dinner.
Friendly, low-key place with outdoor
tables and chairs. A good budget

option for standard Nica fare, they
also serve seafood and have a good
selection of juices.

$$-$ Seva's Place
in Sally Peachy neighborhood.
One of the island's best and longest-
established restaurants. They serve great
seafood, meat and chicken from a fine
location with rooftop seats and ocean
views. Try the lobster *a la plancha.*

$$-$ Spekito's Place
Next door to Nico's Bar, Sally Peachy.
Open lunch and dinner.
The reggae music thumping through the
palm-leaf hut restaurant right over the
water makes their typical seafood dishes
taste even better. The service may leave
something to be desired, but then again
this is the Caribbean.

Little Corn

$$$-$$ Habana Libre
Just north of boat landing.
Really tasty, flavourful dishes including
succulent veal, fish and lobster served
with interesting sauces. There's terraced
seating, good music and amiable staff.
Cuban specialities are available on
request and in advance. Be sure to
try a *mojito*; they're outstanding.

$$ Desideri's
80 m south from the wharf.
A relaxing alternative to the louder
crowd that gather at some of the other
restaurants, you can consider this your
living room away from home. The menu
is international but specializes in Italian
cuisine with lobster thermidor and
lasagne as 2 of their signature dishes.
They also offer a variety of fresh juices,
wines and coffees. Wi-Fi available.

$$ Tranquilo Café
100 m south of the wharf.
Open from 0930.
A range of full meals and light dishes, including smoked ribs, pork bruschetta, ceviche, burgers, chicken fillets, fish tacos, home-made ice cream and cookies. Very popular and quite tasty. Seating is outdoors on a wooden veranda with weekly bonfire parties and cultural presentations. Slow island Wi-Fi available. Gift shop attached.

$$-$ Doña Rosa's
The port, 175 m south, 100 m east, on the path to Casa Iguana.
Reasonably priced for the island, you can get a 3-course meal for US$6 or so, including fish and shrimp dishes. The portions are on the small side though.

$$-$ Miss Bridgette's
The dock, 20 m south, then slightly east, off the path.
A lovely little *comedor* serving wholesome, home-cooked fare. Service is very Caribbean, so be prepared to wait.

Bars and clubs

Big Corn
After dark, always use taxis to get between your hotel and the bars, even if they're close to each other.

Bamboolay
South End. Open 1900-0200.
This is one of the most popular bars on the island. Better for drinking and socializing than dancing, though the dedicated dance room still fills up when the popular songs are on spin. Reggae, dancehall and soul all weekend long.

Nico's
South End. Open 1900-0200.
The action kicks off on Sun, with

wall-to-wall drinking and dancing by the waves. They serve beef soup when you need perking up. Thu features country and western.

Xtasis
Brig Bay. Open 1900-0200.
Same thumping music but a somewhat rougher local crowd. 'Professional' women and the occasional fight are par for the course here.

What to do

Big Corn
Bicycles, golf carts and motorbikes
Corn Island Car Rental, *Southwest Bay, next to Arenas, T8643-9881, also available at Sunrise Hotel, South End.*
A range of **golf carts** available, US$50 for 6 hrs; US$82 for 24 hrs (4 people). **Scooters** US$40 for 6 hrs; US$60 for 24 hrs. **Bicycles** US$15 for 6 hrs; US$25 for 24 hrs.

Fishing
Ira Gómez, *Silver Sand hotel, Sally Peachy, south of rocky point, T8948-1436.* One of those irresistible local characters, Ira is an enthusiastic fishing man.

Little Corn
Diving
Little Corn Island is one of the best and cheapest places in the world to get diving qualifications. Excluding manuals, an Open Water certificate costs US$330; Advanced Open Water US$270. A 1-tank dive costs US$35, 2-tanks US$70.
Dive Little Corn, *boat landing in village, T8823-1154.* There's a strong PADI ethos at this 5-star, Gold Palm centre, with training right up to assistant instructor level. They also offer night dives, single and 2-tank dives, snorkelling tours, and 5- or 10-dive packages; trips leave

several times daily. There's a 10% discount if you stay with **Casa Iguana**; consult their website for more details.

Dolphin Dive, *in the village, south of the dock, T8917-9717, www.dolphindive littlecorn.com.* Dolphin Dive offers PADI instruction to Dive Master level, and a range of customized trips for diving, fishing or snorkelling. Underwater digital camera rental costs US$15 including a CD. Various dive packages are available, including discounts at **Hotel Delfines** next door.

Little Dive Shack By The Sea, *Derek's Place, www.dereksplacelittlecorn.com.* If you are looking for a more personalized and exclusive dive trip, this is it. Groups are capped at 4 people. US$350 for Open Water course taught by a certified PADI instructor all the way down to US$35 1-tank dive or US$70 discovery dive.

Tour operators

Radio Carib, *behind the new Culture Centre, T8232-2661, radiocarib@yahoo. com.* The operators of the local radio station offer **Little Island History Tours** by appointment. It's a great opportunity to learn of the island's pre-Columbian, pirate and natural history.

Transport

Big Corn is 13 sq km and Little Corn is 3.5 sq km. About 11 km of Caribbean Sea separates them. Big Corn has a paved road that does a lap of the island with 1 bus and nearly 100 taxis. Little Corn has no roads; walking or boating are the only ways of getting around.

Air

La Costeña flies from Big Corn Island to **Bluefields**, 0810, 1545, ½ hr, US$79 one-way, US$124 return; and to Managua,

0810, 1545, 1½ hrs, US$122 one-way, US$180 return. Re-confirm seats 1-2 days before travelling or you might be moved to a later flight. **La Costeña** office is at the airport on Big Corn, T2575-5131.

Boat

Inter-island boats Big Corn to Little Corn, daily 1000, 1630, US$6, 30 mins. Little Corn to Big Corn, daily 0630, 1330, US$6, 30 mins. Boats leave from main dock, first come, first served. The open-hull *pangas* with two big outboards run on Sun, Tue, Wed, Fri and Sat, the 100-seat yacht runs on Mon and Thu. If on the *panga*, buy big plastic bags at shop across from dock entrance to keep luggage dry. Sit near the back for a smoother ride, near the front centre, as it's drier, but you can expect to get bounced around quite a bit.

Mainland boats Schedules are always changing, check locally for the latest; 5 boats travel between Corn Islands and **Bluefields**, US$10-12 one-way, including: *Genesis*, Mon, 1800; *Río Escondido*, Thu, 0900; *Captain D*, Sat, 0000; *Island Express*, Sun, 1700; *Humberto C*, Sun, 1700. One service per month Corn Islands to Bilwi, *Captain D*, usually Fri, 1700, US$25.

Bus

A bus circles the paved island road on Big Corn every 30 mins, US$0.50.

Taxi

Taxis charge US$1-2 for trips to and from the airport or any trip after 2000. The usual fare to most destinations is US$0.75. Hourly taxi rates are US$6 per hr, poor value, as there are many taxis and trip fares are cheap.

The Región Autónoma de la Costa Caribe Norte (North Caribbean Coast Autonomous Region), or RACCN, is one of the most isolated and intriguing destinations in Central America, a land steeped in fishing, farming, folklore and magic, accessible only by a treacherous unpaved highway from Managua, or by plane.

Christopher Columbus was the first European to make contact, arriving in the midst of a storm and finding refuge in the bay at the mouth of the Río Coco; he named it Cabo Gracias a Dios (Cape Thank God). In the early 1600s, the British started trading with the coast people and made allies out of the Miskitos, who went on to dominate the region with British help. Various shipwrecks, from pirates to slave ships, brought new cultural influences, as did Moravian missions, international loggers and banana plantations.

Bilwi (Puerto Cabezas) *Colour map 2, B5.*
Principally a large Miskito town, Bilwi, or Puerto Cabezas as it has been known for the last century, is the capital of the RACCN and has a distinct atmosphere from Bluefields. Waspam on the Río Coco is the heart and soul of the Miskito world, but it is here that the Miskito political party Yatama became the first indigenous party to assume control of a provincial capital in the country's modern history. The town itself may not win any beauty contests, but it does have an end-of-the-

Essential North Caribbean Coast Autonomous Region (RACCN)

Finding your feet

La Costena flies to Bilwi two or three times per day from Managua's domestic terminal. Flights from Bluefields were not operating at the time of research. There is a very bad road from Siuna that connects to Managua and it is best traversed during the dry season. It is a gruelling 560-km drive (20-hour bus ride) through some of the most solitary places in Central America.

Getting around

There are few roads in the region and those that exist are mostly unpaved and washed out in the wet season. Single-propeller planes and rugged 4WDs

are necessary to access some areas; otherwise nearly all travel is conducted by boat.

When to go

Rainfall is significantly higher on the Caribbean side than the Pacific. Typically, May to July are the wettest months, but you should expect torrential storms at any time of the year. If you intend to navigate the rivers, late in the dry season is a bad time to visit. Hiking is comparatively poor in the wet season, when conditions are boggy and bug-infested. There's a risk of hurricanes June to November; take particular care travelling in RACCN during that time.

earth feel and a 730-m-long pier that stretches into the Caribbean Sea. A walk along the pier at sunset is highly recommended. The main reasons to visit Bilwi are to experience Nicaragua's only indigenous-run provincial capital and to meet its friendly population.

The town offers an excellent introduction to the Miskito part of the country. There are also significant minorities of Hispanics (referred to as *españoles*) and Afro-Caribbeans (referred to as *ingleses*) here but Spanish is mainly a second language (although most who live in Bilwi speak it well; outside the town many do not as the municipality is 80% indigenous).

For the truly intrepid, the Miskito communities around Bilwi offer some of the most interesting and adventurous community tourism in Central America. The **Asociación de Mujeres Indígenas de la Costa Atlántica (AMICA)** ① *Barrio La Libertad, Bilwi, T2792-2219, asociacionamica@yahoo.es*, can connect you with guides.

Waspam (Wangki) *Colour map 2, A4.*

Waspam is considered the capital of the Río Coco, a transport hub and trading centre for the 116 Miskito communities that line the great waterway. Most travel is by motorized canoes dug out of a single tree (*cayucos*). In the dry season they are punted using long poles. The residents of Waspam and many other communities along the river were seen as allies to the Contra rebels in the 1980s and were evacuated by force as their crops and homes were burned to the ground by government troops. They were allowed to return, but were once again hard hit by Hurricane Mitch in 1998, when the Río Coco's 780 km of water rose to more than 10 m above normal.

From Waspam, you can travel up or down stream, but careful planning and a trustworthy guide are essential; speak to **La Casa de la Rose** (see Where to stay, page 215). The road from Bilwi to Waspam is only open during the dry season. It is a 130-km trip that takes at least three hours by 4WD and six to eight hours by public bus (see Transport, below). This trip will take you through pine forests, red earth plains and several Miskito villages. If you have good maps and experience with wilderness navigation, the dirt tracks between Waspam and Bilwi are great for mountain biking. It's also possible to cross to Leimus in Honduras from Waspam; see the Nicaragua–Honduras box, page 255.

If you don't have the time or inclination to travel far out of Waspam, the traditional village of Kisalaya lies an hour's walk away. Take plenty of water as there is little shade and nowhere to buy drinks. The dirt tracks between Waspam and Bilwi are great for mountain biking; use good maps as it's easy to get lost.

Las Minas mining triangle (Siuna–Rosita–Bonanza) *Colour map 2, B2.*

These three towns are known for their gold and silver mines which are dominated by Canadian mining companies whose employees, along with Evangelist missionaries and US Peace Corps, make up the majority of the foreign population. There is great tourism potential here, but security has always been a big issue. Many locals returned after the war years to face 80% unemployment and subsequently turned to criminal activities. Drug-running, kidnapping and highway robbery were widespread until recently, with most of this lawlessness perpetrated by the

Andrés Casto United Front (FUAC), whose mission was to divert funds and attention into the area. This organization of disenchanted ex-soldiers and mercenaries was effectively broken up by the government in 2001. Still, everyone in this region seems to carry a gun, and land mines may be lurking in the wilderness, despite government assertions to the contrary. Ultimately, any pleasure visits here have to be weighed against potential risks. Tourism is certainly increasing and, despite heavy logging (much of it illegal) and cattle ranching, the area still holds plenty of natural and cultural interest, including more than 50 female medicinal healers, an abundance of pristine forests, wildlife, indigenous communities and old gold mines. With increased security and environmental protection, this area could be one of the great future areas for travel in Nicaragua.

It is possible to go to the Bosawás Reserve without travelling through the mining triangle, but **Siuna** offers the easiest access to the reserve and local guides are widely available here. It is the largest of the three towns and home to lots of interesting wooden architecture faintly reminiscent of the old west. The population is predominately mestizo but there is a Creole minority.

The town of **Bonanza**, 170 km from Bilwi, has seen huge improvements in recent years, thanks in part to the ever-rising value of gold, which is still mined in the surrounding hills. The Alcaldía can help arrange visits to old mines, processing plants and panning streams. Jewellery is widely available throughout town but those buying very large quantities of the yellow stuff may be targeted by bandits. The surrounding countryside is great for hiking and travellers often head to **Cerro Cola Blanca**; guided trips to the summit usually include an overnight stop in the village of **Kukalaya** (bring a blanket, food and water purification tablets). For commanding views over Bonanza, head to a well-known strip-mined hill known as **El Elefante** (taxi US$7 round trip including a one-hour wait).

The rural areas around Bonanza have a significant Mayagna population. Perched on the banks of the Río Waspuk, a major tributary of the Río Coco, the capital of their world is **Musuwas**. All travellers to Musuwas – or anywhere else in the Mayagna territory – must first organize permission with the Casa de Gobierno in Salkiwas, the nearest Mayagna community to Bonanza. For a fee, they will issue you with a 'Carta Aval' granting you right of passage; keep it on your person at all times. They can also advise on routes and guides.

The town of **Rosita** used to be entirely owned by the Rosario Mining Company, but the mines were nationalized in 1979 by the Sandinista government, who moved all the mining operations to Siuna and forcibly evacuated the local inhabitants.

From Rosita you can catch a direct bus to the Miskito town of **Alamikamba**, the main community of the twisting Prinzapolka river. If coming from Siuna, you will have to wait for connections at the highway's turn-off, where you'll find the small village of El Empalme – a good place to stock up on supplies, especially fuel, which is reportedly good quality. Most people come to Alamikamba for the superb sport fishing – the river's waters are teeming with giant, easy-to-snag snook and tarpon.

Río Coco

The source of the Río Coco is in the mountains near Somoto in northwestern Nicaragua. The river passes through Nueva Segovia before heading north to the border with Honduras and then all the way out to the coastal Laguna de Bismuna (about 80 km downriver from Waspam) and finally out to the Caribbean. The river marks the border between Nicaragua and Honduras, but for the Miskitos and Mayagna who live there the divide is hypothetical.

Sadly, much of the river's banks have been deforested as a result of logging and agriculture, and by the brutal currents of Hurricanes Mitch and Felix. The riverbanks and tributaries suffer from a major erosion problem and, during the dry season, the Río Coco now has islands of sandbars, making navigation and communication between communities more difficult.

Reserva de la Biósfera Bosawás *Colour map 1, A6/2, B1.*

This is the largest forest reserve in Central America. The area is not only the most important swathe of rainforest on the isthmus, but also the most important cloudforest, with numerous isolated mountains and rivers. In addition to all the species mentioned in the Indio Maíz Reserve (see page 139), the reserve also has altitude-specific wildlife and vegetation. There are seven mountains above 1200 m, the highest of which is **Cerro Saslaya** at 1650 m. The principal rivers that cross the reserve and feed into the Río Coco are: Río Bocay, Wina, Amaka, Lakus and Waspuk.

Visiting the reserve is still a challenge. The easiest and most organized way to visit is via **Siuna**. Contact the unsigned **Proyecto Bosawás** ① *2 blocks from the airstrip on the road to Rosita, T2794-2036,* for advice, queries and guides. The town's Alcaldía, T8823-7094, may be able to help too. Ecotourism projects are planned but are a long way off, due to the remoteness of the reserve and the instability of the region. However, there is at least one good project, the **Proyecto Ecoturístico Rosa Grande**, supported by Nature Conservancy and the Peace Corps.

The community of **Rosa Grande**, 25 km from Siuna, is near an area of virgin forest with a trail, waterfall on the Río Labú and lots of wildlife including monkeys and big cats. One path leads to a lookout with a view over Cerro Saslaya; a circular path to the northwest goes to the **Rancho Alegre falls**. Guides can be hired for US$7 a day plus food. Excursions for two or more days cost as little as US$13 per person for a guide, food and camping equipment. You may have to pay for a camp guard while hiking. Clarify what is included in the price and be aware of extras that may be added to the bill. Be certain you have enough supplies for your stay. For information contact Don Trinidad at the *comedor* on arrival in Santa Rosa.

There is an alternative way to experience the wilderness of Bosawás. With a great deal of time, patience and a bit of luck, you can see the great forest of Bosawás and explore a large part of the Río Coco in the process. Access is via **Jinotega** in central Nicaragua (see page 181).

Where to stay

Bilwi

$ Casa Museo
Next to Centro de Computación Ansell,
T2792-2225.
Also known as Miss Judy's, this lovely
house has lots of interesting art and
artefacts in the attached museum
and gallery. Rooms are spacious and
comfortable and have private bath, TV
and a/c (cheaper with fan). Friendly and
interesting, with lots of family history.
Restaurant attached, excellent value
and highly recommended.

Waspam

$ La Casa de la Rose
Almost next to the airport, T2792-9112,
cunninghamkain@gmail.com.
This comfortable wooden hotel has
rooms with private bath, hammocks
and screened windows. Tasty home-
cooked meals are available, as well as
internet access. Look out for the red
macaws. Recommended.

Transport

Bilwi
Air
The airport is 3 km north of town, from
where taxis charge US$2 to anywhere

in Bilwi. If flying to Bluefields, try to get
your name on the list several days in
advance. To **Managua**, 0740, 1200, 1540
(Mon, Wed, Fri).
Note Bring your passport as there
are immigration checks by the police
in Bilwi and sometimes in the waiting
lounge in Managua.

Bus
The bus station is a few kilometres
out of town; take a taxi, US$0.50.
To **Managua**, 1100, 1300, US$21,
18-24 hrs. To **Waspam**, 0600, US$6,
6 hrs. All these journeys require a
strong back and stomach.

Las Minas mining triangle
(Siuna-Rosita-Bonanza)
Air
La Costeña flies from Bonanza to
Managua, 1000, 1½ hrs, US$111
one-way, US$174 return; and from
Siuna to Managua, 1000, 1½ hrs,
US$97 one-way, US$142 return.

Waspam
Air
La Costeña flies from Waspam to
Managua, 1340 (Tue and Sat), 1½ hrs,
US$111 one-way, US$174 return.

Background

History

Pre-Columbian history

Nicaragua was at the crossroads between northern and southern pre-Hispanic cultures for thousands of years. The migration from Asia across the Bering Strait is believed to have reached Nicaragua sometime before 18,000 BC. In Museo Las Huellas de Acahualinca in Managua, there are some well-preserved human and animal footprints of what appears to be a family of 10 people leaving the Lake Managua area after a volcanic event in the year 4000 BC. Ceramic evidence of organized settlement in Nicaragua begins around 2500 BC in San Marcos, and by 1500 BC settlements are evident in much of the Pacific area. Nicaragua continued to receive migrations from both north and south until the first arrival of the Spanish explorers in 1523. The best understood culture is that of the **Nicaraguas**, whose final migration to Nicaragua from central Mexico to the shores of Lake Nicaragua occurred just 150-200 years before the arrival of the Spanish. They spoke Náhuat (a rustic version of the Aztec Náhuatl), which became the lingua franca for the indigenous people after the conquest and may have already been widely used for trading in the region before the arrival of the first Europeans.

The Nicaraguas shared the Pacific Basin of Nicaragua with the **Chorotegas** and **Maribios**. The Chorotegas also came from Mexico, though earlier, around AD 800 and were Mangue speakers. The two tribes seemed to have found some common commercial and perhaps religious ground and dominated most of the area west of the lakes. The Maribios, Hokano speakers, and believed to be originally from California and Baja California in Mexico, populated the western slope of what is today the Maribios volcanic range, in northwestern Nicaragua. The Nicaraguas and Chorotegas were a very successful society sitting in the middle of a trade route that stretched from Mexico to Peru.

On the east side of the great lakes of Nicaragua the cultures were of South American origin. The **Chontales** and **Matagalpas** may have used the same language root (Chibcha) as the Caribbean Basin Rama, Mayagna and Miskito (a Mayagna derivative) cultures. In fact it could be that the Mayagna are descendants of the original inhabitants of the Pacific that lost ground to the invading tribes of Chorotegas in the ninth century. The Chontales appear to have been the most developed of the group, though little is known about their culture to date, despite ample and impressive archaeological evidence. Their name means 'barbarian' or 'foreigner' in Náhuatl, and has been applied to many different Mesoamerican groups.

BACKGROUND

The Conquest of Nicaragua: a business trip

The meeting of the Spanish explorer Gil González and the philosophical Chief Niqueragua is a romantic story filled with fate, adventure and tragedy. But a brief glimpse at the cold numbers of the original expedition and the conquest that followed paints a very different picture. According to local historian Patrick Werner, Gil González received authorization for the expedition to make Europe's first business trip to the land of Nicaragua. A company was formed with four shareholders: the Spanish Crown 48%, Andrés Niño 28%, Cristóbal de Haro 15% and Gil González with 9% of the shares. The original investment totalled 8000 gold pesos. They even took an accountant with them, Andrés de Cereceda who later reported the returns on the four-month business trip. The bottom line looked a lot better than your average start-up company: 112,524 gold pesos collected on an 8000-peso investment.

Soon after, it was the turn of Pedrarias Dávila to form a new company, especially for Nicaragua. The chief negotiator for this trip, Captain Francisco Hernández de Córdoba, with an army of 229 soldiers, produced spectacular returns on the investment, recovering 158,000 gold pesos while founding the cities of León and Granada. Within one year of the Conquest, the new franchises of León and Granada had collected a further 392,000 gold pesos. It was all the gold the Indians had ever owned; in less than three years, 700-800 years of accumulated gold had been taken.

The Conquest

Christopher Columbus sailed the Caribbean shores of Nicaragua in 1502 on his fourth and final voyage and took refuge in the far northern part of today's Nicaragua before sailing to Jamaica. The Spanish explorer Gil González Dávila sailed from Panama to the Gulf of Nicoya and then travelled overland to the western shores of Lake Nicaragua to meet the famous Nicaraguas tribe chief, Niqueragua, in April 1523. After converting the Nicaragua elite to Christianity, and taking plenty of gold away with him, González Dávila travelled further north before being chased out of the area by a surprise attack of Chorotega warriors led by legendary chieftain, Diriangén. The Spaniards fled to Panama to regroup. In 1524 a stronger army of 229 men was sent and the local populace was overcome by force. The captain of the expedition, Francisco Hernández de Córdoba, founded the cities of Granada and León (Viejo) on the shores of Lake Nicaragua and Lake Managua respectively. A little is known about the actual battles of the conquest, thanks to a lost letter from Córdoba to the country's first governor describing the events. Nueva Segovia was founded as third city in 1543 to try and capitalize on mineral resources in the northern mountains. The famously cruel Pedrarias Dávila was given the first governor's post in Nicaragua, a position he used as a licence to run a personal empire. His rule set the stage for a tradition of *caudillos* (rulers of personality and favouritism, rather than of constitution and law) that would run and ruin Nicaragua, almost without exception, until the 21st century.

Colonial era

By the middle of the 16th century, the Spanish had realized that Nicaragua was not going to produce the same kind of mineral riches as Mexico and Peru. What Nicaragua did have was a solid population base and this was exploited to its maximum. There are no accurate figures for slave trade in early to mid-16th century Nicaragua as it was not an approved activity and was made officially illegal by the Spanish Crown in 1542. However, it is estimated that somewhere between 200,000 to 500,000 Nicaraguans were exported as slaves to work in Panama and Peru or forced to work in the gold mines near Nueva Segovia. The Consejo de Indias (Indian council) and the Casa de Contratación (legal office) in Seville managed affairs in Spain for Nicaragua. These administrative bodies controlled immigration to the Americas, acted as a court for disputes, and provided nominees for local rulers to the Spanish Crown. On a local level the province of Nicaragua belonged to the Reino de Guatemala (Kingdom of Guatemala) and was administered by a Spanish governor in León. While the *conquistadores* were busy pillaging the New World, there were serious discussions in Spain as to the legality of Spanish action in the Americas. Thanks in part to some tough lobbying by the humanist priest, Fray Bartolomé de Las Casas, laws were passed in 1542 to protect the rights of the Indians, outlawing slavery and granting them (in theory) equal rights. Sadly, enforcement of these laws was nearly impossible due to local resistance, communication obstacles and the sheer distance of the colony from Spain. The estimated indigenous population of the Pacific Basin on the arrival of the Spanish was at least 500,000. Within 40 years the total population was no more than 50,000 people, and by 1610 the indigenous residents of the Pacific slope had been reduced to around 12,000. (It wasn't until the 20th century that the population of Nicaragua returned to match pre-Conquest numbers.)

Due to the exhaustion of the indigenous population and mineral resources, many of the Spanish left Nicaragua looking for greener pastures. The ones who stayed on became involved in agriculture. Cattle were introduced and they took over cacao production, which was already very big, upon their arrival. Indigo was the other principal crop, along with some trade in wood. The beef, leather and indigo were exported to Guatemala, the cacao to El Salvador. The exports were traded for other goods, such as food and clothing, and the local population lived primarily off locally grown corn and beans. There was also a busy commercial route between Granada and the Caribbean colonial states via the Río San Juan and trade between Nicaragua and Peru. Granada became much wealthier thanks to its advantageous position along the international trade routes (although this made it a target for attacks from Dutch, French and British pirates during the 17th century), but administrative and church authority remained in León, creating a rivalry that would explode after Independence from Spain.

Independence from Spain

After 297 years as a colony of Spain, Nicaragua achieved independence. It was not a hard fought independence, but it was one that would release built-up tensions and rivalries into an open and bloody playing field. What followed was the least stable period in the history of the country: a general anarchy that only an outside invader would stop, by uniting Nicaraguans in a common cause, against a common enemy.

The greatest impulse for the demise of Spanish rule came from a new social class created during the colonial period, known locally as *criollos*, the descendants of Spaniards born in Nicaragua. At the beginning of the 19th century they still only represented 5% of the population, but they were the owners of great agricultural empires, wealthy and increasingly powerful, a class only the Spanish Crown could rival. The *criollos* did not openly oppose the colonial system, but rather chipped away at its control, in search of the power that they knew would be theirs without colonial rule.

They continued to organize and institutionalize power until 5 November 1811 when El Salvador moved to replace all the Spaniards in its local government with *criollos*. One week later, in León, the local population rebelled. The people of León took to the streets demanding the creation of a new government, new judges, and abolition of the government monopoly to produce liquor, lower prices for tobacco and an end to taxes on beef, paper and general sales. All the demands were granted. There were also demonstrations in Masaya, Rivas and Granada.

In September 1821 Mexico declared Independence from Spain. A meeting was called in Guatemala City on 15 September 1821. At the meeting were the representatives of the central government in Spain, Spanish representatives from every country in Central America, the heads of the Catholic Church from each province, the archbishop of Guatemala and the local senators of the provinces. Independence from Spain was declared; yet in Nicaragua the wars had just begun.

León versus Granada

In October 1821 the authorities in León declared that Nicaragua would become part of the Mexican Empire, while the Guatemalan office of Central America created a local Central American government office in Granada, increasing sentiments of separatism in Granada. Regardless, Nicaragua remained part of the federation of Mexico and Central America until 1823 when the United Provinces of Central America met and declared themselves free of Mexican domain and any other foreign power. The five members – Guatemala, El Salvador, Honduras, Nicaragua and Costa Rica – were a federation free to administer their own countries and in November 1824 a new constitution for the Central America Federation was decreed. Nicaraguans, however, were already fighting among themselves.

In April 1824 León and Granada had both proclaimed themselves capital of the country. Other cities chose sides with one or the other, while Managua created a third 'government', proclaiming Managua as Nicaragua's capital. The in-fighting continued until, in 1827, civil war erupted. It was not until Guatemala sent another general that peace was achieved and a new chief of state named in 1834. The civilian head of state was Dr José Núñez, but the military chiefs were not pleased and he was soon thrown out. In 1835 José Zepeda was named head of state but still more violence followed. In 1836 Zepeda was thrown in prison and subsequently shot. By this time, the federal government in Guatemala was increasingly impotent and, as the power vacuum of 300 years of colonial rule wreaked havoc upon the isthmus, the state of anarchy in Nicaragua was common across Central America.

On 30 April 1838 the legislative assembly of Nicaragua, in a rare moment of relevance, declared Nicaragua independent of any other power and the Central American Federation collapsed, with the other states also declaring the Federation to be history. A new constitution was written for Nicaragua, but it was one that would have little effect on the constant power struggle.

In 1853 Granada General Fruto Chamorro took over the post of Director of State, with hope of establishing something that resembled peace. Informed of an armed uprising being planned in León, he ordered the capture of the principal perpetrators, but most escaped to Honduras. In 1854 yet another new constitution was written. This one changed the post of Director of State to 'President' which meant that Conservative General Fruto Chamorro was technically no longer in power. However the assembly, going against the constitution they had just approved, named him as president anyway. The Liberal León generals in Honduras had seen enough and decided to attack. Máximo Jérez led the attack against the Conservatives and Chamorro, the León contingent hiring US mercenary Byron Cole to give them a hand against Granada. He signed a contract and returned to the US where he gave the job to the man every single Nicaraguan (but not a single North American) school child has heard of.

William Walker and the Guerra Nacional

On 13 June 1855, North American William Walker and his 55 hired guns set sail for Nicaragua. The group was armed with the latest in firepower and a very well-planned scheme to create a new slave state in Nicaragua. His idea was for a new colony to be settled by North American Anglos (to own the lands and slaves) and blacks (to do all the work). William Walker planned to conquer and colonize not only Nicaragua, but all of Central America, isolating what remained of Mexico, which had just lost one-third of its territory to the US in the Mexican-American War.

In September of the same year, Walker and his little battalion landed in San Juan del Sur, confronted Granada's Conservative Party army in La Virgen and won easily. On 13 October 1855 he travelled north, attacked and took Granada with the local generals escaping to Masaya and later signing a peace pact. As per prior agreement, Patricio Rivas of León's Liberal Party was named President of the Republic and Walker as the head of the military. Rivas, following Walker's wishes, confiscated the steamship line of Vanderbilt, which Walker then used to ship in more arms, ammunitions and mercenary soldiers from the US. Soon he had the best-equipped and most modern fighting force in Central America.

On 6 June 1856, Walker appeared in León, demanding that he be allowed to confiscate the properties of the León elite. President Patricio Rivas and his ministers refused and after numerous meetings and no agreements William Walker left León for Granada. The people with power in León had finally realised what they were up against and contacted generals in El Salvador and Guatemala for help. Soon all of Central America would be united against the army of William Walker.

From 22-24 June 1856 farcical elections were held and William Walker was named President of the Republic. He took office on 12 July with a pompous parade through Granada, while flying his new flag for the country. A series of decrees were proclaimed during that month, including the legalization of slavery, and the immediate confiscation of all properties of all 'enemies of the state'. English was made the official language of business (to ensure that North American colonists would receive all the land confiscated).

The turning point in William Walker's troops' apparent invincibility came at the little ranch north of Tipitapa called San Jacinto. It is a museum today and a mandatory visit for all Nicaraguan primary school children. Walker had never been able to control Matagalpa and a division of the rebel Nicaraguan army was sent south from Matagalpa to try and stop the confiscation of cattle ranches in the area of San Jacinto. The two forces met. The Nicaraguan division used the little house in San Jacinto, with its thick adobe walls, as their fort and it provided great protection. A battle on 5 September was a slight victory for the Nicaraguans, but both sent for reinforcements and on 14 September (the national holiday now celebrated annually), 200 of Walker's troops lost a bloody and difficult battle to 160 Nicaraguan troops. The tide had turned and battles in Masaya, Rivas and Granada would prove victorious for the combined Central American forces. William Walker escaped to a steamship from where he watched the final grisly actions of his troops in Granada, who, completely drunk, proceeded to rape and kill the fleeing natives and then burned the city to the ground. Walker's administrators mounted a mock procession in Granada, burying a coffin in Central Park with a sign above it that said, "Here was Granada".

Walker would later return to Nicaragua, before just escaping with his life. He then tried his luck in Honduras where he was taken prisoner by Captain Salmon of the British navy and handed over to the Honduran authorities. He was tried, put against a wall and shot by the Honduran armed forces on 12 September 1860.

General José Santos Zelaya

For the next 30-plus years, the wealthy families of Granada would control the government (now based in Managua), thanks partly to a law stating that, to have the right to vote, you must have 100 pesos, and in order to be a presidential candidate, over 4000 pesos. But, in 1893, the Conservative president was overthrown by a movement led by Liberal Party General José Santos Zelaya.

General Zelaya did much to modernize Nicaragua. A new constitution was written in 1893 and put into effect the following year. The separation of church and state was instituted, with ideas of equality and liberty for all, respect for private property, civil marriage, divorce, mandatory schooling for all, the death penalty abolished and debtors' prison banned and freedom of expression guaranteed. Construction was rampant, with new roads, docks, postal offices, shipping routes and electricity installed in Managua and Chinandega. A whole raft of new laws were passed to facilitate business, proper police and military codes, and a Supreme Court was created. The Caribbean coast was finally officially incorporated into the country in 1894. Despite all of this, however, Zelaya did not endear himself to the US. With the canal project close at hand in either Panama or Nicaragua, Zelaya insisted that no single country would be permitted to finance a canal project in Nicaragua and, what's more, only Nicaragua could have sovereignty over a canal inside its country. The project went to Panama. In 1909 as Zelaya was flirting with Japan to build a rival canal, he was pushed out of power with the help of the US Marines.

US Marines – Augusto C Sandino

In 1909 there was an uprising in Bluefields against Zelaya. Led by General Juan Estrada, with the support of the Granada Conservative Party, two American mercenaries were caught and executed during the battles. The US Marines entered in May 1910 to secure power for Estrada who took control of the east coast in what they termed a 'neutral zone'. General Estrada marched into Managua to install himself as the new president of Nicaragua. Stuck with debts from European creditors, Juan Estrada was forced to borrow from the North American banks. He then gave the US control over collection of duties, as a guarantee for those loans. The Nicaraguan National Bank and a new monetary unit called the *córdoba* were established in 1912. The Granada aristocrats were not happy with General Estrada and a new round of fighting between León Liberals and Granada Conservatives erupted.

On 4 August the US Marines entered Managua to secure order and establish their choice, Adolfo Díaz, as president of the country. Two years later, under occupation of the Marines, Nicaragua signed the Chamorro-Bryan Treaty, with Nicaragua conceding perpetual rights of any Nicaraguan canal project to the US, in exchange for US\$3 million, which went to pay US banks for outstanding debts. There was no intention to build a canal in Nicaragua; the deal was rather to keep Nicaragua from building a competing one.

In 1917, with Emiliano Chamorro in control of the presidency, more problems followed. Díaz, still fighting to regain the presidency, called for more Marines to be sent from the US. Over 2000 troops arrived and Díaz was put back into the presidency, but nothing could be done to bring together the various factions.

In what were then considered to be fair elections (albeit under occupation) in 1924, moderate Conservative Carlos Solórzano was elected to the presidency with Liberal Party physician Dr Juan Sacasa his vice president. In 1925 the Marines withdrew from Nicaragua. Two and a half months later a revolt broke out led by hard-line Conservative Emiliano Chamorro. Solórzano fled with Sacasa to Honduras. Chamorro purged Congress and was declared President in 1926. The Liberals rebelled, but the US Marines returned to prop up the president.

In May 1927, the US State Department agreed a plan with the Nicaraguan authorities to organize a non-political army, disarm both the Liberal and Conservative armies and hold new elections. The new army would be called the Guardia Nacional. Most parties agreed to the solution, with the exception of General Augusto Sandino, who had been fighting under the command of Liberal General José María Moncada. Sandino returned to the northern mountains determined to fight against the government of Adolfo Díaz, whom he panned as a US puppet president, and the occupation of the Marines, something the nationalist Sandino found unacceptable.

In 1928, José María Moncada won the elections under supervision of the US government. Despite the fact that a Liberal was now president, Sandino refused to lay down his arms as long as Nicaragua was under occupation. Fighting side by side with the Marines, to exterminate Augusto Sandino's rebel army, was the newly created Guardia Nacional. The Marines thought they would defeat General Sandino's rebel forces quickly, in particular because of their vastly superior artillery and advantage of air power. However, the charismatic general had widespread support in the north and was not defeated. He relentlessly attacked US Marine positions with what some say was the first use of modern guerrilla warfare. Finally, with elections approaching in 1933, and with the National Guard under the command of General Anastasio Somoza García, the US announced that the Marines would pull out when the new president took power. Juan Bautista Sacasa was elected, and the day he took power, 1 January 1933, the last regiment of Marines left Nicaragua by boat from Corinto. Twenty-four years of intervention had ended.

The Somoza family

With the US Marines gone, General Augusto Sandino went to the presidential palace (today the Parque Loma de Tiscapa) and signed a peace and disarmament treaty with President Sacasa. The treaty stipulated that the rebel army would gradually turn over their weapons and receive amnesty, with ample job opportunities for ex-rebel fighters. One year later, on 21 February 1934, when Sandino returned to the presidential palace for dinner with President Sacasa, the commander of the Guardia Nacional, Anastasio Somoza García plotted the abduction and death of Sandino, which was carried out while Somoza was enjoying a concert. After Sandino left the dinner party he was stopped at a road block, sent to a rural part of Managua, shot and buried. With the death of Sandino the Liberal Party was divided into two camps, one that supported Somoza and the other President Sacasa. Somoza attacked the fort above León in May 1936 and the Guardia Nacional demanded Sacasa's resignation. A month later Sacasa resigned and new elections were won by Somoza García. Yet again, a leader of Nicaragua's military took state office. Various 'presidents' were elected from 1937 to 1979, but there was never any doubt who was running the show. Anastasio Somoza García and later his son Anastasio Somoza Debayle maintained effective power as the head of the National Guard.

Nicaragua enjoyed a period of relative stability and economic growth. The relationship between the US and Nicaragua had never been better, with close co-operation, including the use of Nicaragua as a training and launching ground for the Bay of Pigs invasion in Cuba. Somoza used the Guardia Nacional to keep the populace at bay and the technique of *pactos* (political pacts) to keep Conservative political opponents in on some of the Somoza family's ever-increasing riches and power. During the Second World War, Nicaragua entered on the side of the US and Somoza García used the war to confiscate as much property from German nationals as possible (including what is today Montelimar Beach Resort). This formed a basis for building a business empire that used state money to grow.

After accepting the Liberal Party nomination for the election of 1956, Somoza García was shot and killed by a young León poet named Rigoberto López Pérez. Despite his death, the family dynasty continued with Somoza García's sons, Luis and Anastasio. Together they lasted 42 years in power, one of the longest dictatorships in Latin American history.

Sandinista National Liberation Front

The first attack of the FSLN was along the Río Coco in 1963 in which Tomás Borge and ageing Sandino fighter Santos López participated; they were routed. More than 200 civilians died in January 1967 when the National Guard broke up a 60,000-person opposition rally in Managua by firing into the crowd. The FSLN rebels regrouped and carried out a number of urban bank robberies and minor rural attacks, but later that year they were attacked at Pancasán, Matagalpa, and many founding members of the party were killed. In the same year one of the bank robbers, Daniel Ortega, was thrown in jail and Tomás Borge escaped to Cuba, leaving the FSLN almost completely disbanded or in exile. Founder Carlos Fonseca was jailed in Costa Rica in 1969 and Somoza made one of many public blunders by broadcasting the National Guard attack of an FSLN safe house. As the house was being shelled into ruins, rebel Julio Buitrago defended it alone, against tanks, troops and helicopters, inspiring the Nicaraguan public. An aeroplane hijacking achieved the release of Carlos Fonseca and Humberto Ortega from a Costa Rican jail in 1970 and the next year rebels regrouped in the northern mountains, including flamboyant rebel Edén Pastora.

In 1972 a massive earthquake destroyed Managua, killing 5000-15,000 people and leaving some 200,000 homeless. The millions of dollars of aid and reconstruction money were funnelled through Somoza's companies or went straight into his bank accounts and the Nicaraguan elite started to lose patience with the final Somoza dictator.

Somoza was elected to yet another term as president in September 1974, but on December of the same year, an FSLN commando unit led by Germán Pomares raided a Managua party of Somoza politicians, gaining sweeping concessions from the government including six million dollars in cash, a rise in the national minimum wage, the release of 14 prisoners including Daniel Ortega, and the broadcast of a 12,000-word FSLN communiqué.

The FSLN was at a crossroads in 1975, with the three principal Sandinista ideological factions at odds on how to win the war against Somoza. FSLN General Secretary Carlos Fonseca returned from five years of exile in Cuba to try and unify the forces. The most pragmatic of the three factions, led by the Ortega brothers Daniel and Humberto, proposed a strategy of combining select assassinations and the creation of broad alliances with non-Marxist groups and a whole range of ideologies. Too conveniently for some, party founder and devout Marxist Carlos Fonseca, who was in the mountains of Matagalpa expecting a reunion of the leaders of the three bickering factions, was ambushed and killed by the National Guard on 8 November 1976, one week before the three-faction summit. Early the following year the Ortega faction came out with a highly detailed 60-page plan on how to defeat Somoza; they also quickly solidified their domination of FSLN leadership, an iron grip that Daniel Ortega has held until today.

During the Somoza family reign, control of the military was critical, but so was the weakness of the Conservative Party (today almost defunct), which was continually bought out by the Somozas whenever they made too much noise. The exception was *La Prensa* newspaper publisher Pedro Joaquín Chamorro. A man who could not be purchased and who was the most vocal opposition to Somoza rule in Nicaragua, PJ Chamorro was the Conservative Party's great hope, a natural to take over leadership of the country if the Liberal dictator could be disposed of. On 10 January 1978 Pedro Joaquín Chamorro was riddled with bullets in Managua on his way to the office, a murder attributed to the National Guard. The country erupted. Over the following days rioters set fire to Somoza businesses, 30,000 people attended the funeral and the entire country went on strike. The National Guard attacked many of the public gatherings in Managua; the FSLN went into action with Edén Pastora leading an attack on Rivas barracks; and Germán Pomares led attacks in Nueva Segovia in early February. The Catholic Church published a letter in *La Prensa* approving of armed resistance and one week later the indigenous community of Monimbó was tear-gassed by the National Guard at a Mass for Pedro Joaquín Chamorro and took over their town in a spontaneous rebellion that surprised even the FSLN. Somoza, after one week of defiance by citizens armed with hunting rifles and machetes, had to use tanks and planes to retake Monimbó, killing more than 200. The indigenous community of Sutiava also rebelled, as did the largely indigenous city of Diriamba in the same month. Monimbó rioted again in March 1978, and between April and August there were many rebellions and skirmishes, but the insurrection was beginning once again to stall, until the most famous act of the Revolution brought it back to life: the attack by FSLN commandos on Nicaragua's parliament in session that lasted from 22-24 August. The rebels held the congressmen hostage, along with more than 1000 state employees in the National Palace, until demands were met. The strike, led by Edén Pastora and female Comandante Dora María Tellez, won the release of 58 prisoners and US$500,000 in cash and a plane ride for the prisoners (including Tomás Borge) and commandos to Panama.

In September 1978, the FSLN launched their most ambitious series of attacks ever, winning National Guard posts in east Managua, Masaya, León, Chinandega and Estelí, though the National Guard with air and tank support took back each city one by one causing hundreds of deaths. The National Guard was overrun again in Monimbó one week later and fighting broke out along the border with Costa Rica, while in Diriamba more than 4000 died in uprisings. The public and the rebels, sometimes together, sometimes working apart, continued harassing the National Guard for the next eight months, as international pressure was stepped up on Somoza. He in turn accused Venezuela, Panama, Cuba and Costa Rica of supporting the FSLN (which they were). From February to May 1979, rebels attacked Nicaraguan cities at will.

In June the attacks became more prolonged, the forces of the FSLN swelling with new recruits as the general public became part of the rebellion and doing even more fighting than the FSLN. There was total insurrection around the Pacific, central and northern regions, with Edén Pastora forces occupying Somoza's elite troops in a frontal battle in southern Rivas. On 20 June American news reporter Bill Stewart from ABC was put on the ground and executed by the National Guard in front of his own cameraman who captured the scene, which was broadcasted across the USA.

By the end of June, Masaya, Diriamba, eastern Managua, Chontales and other rural areas were liberated by the FSLN and under their control. By 6 July, Jinotepe, San Marcos, Masatepe and Sébaco had fallen, cutting off supply routes for the National Guard north and south. León was finally liberated on 9 July; four days later Somoza flew to Guatemala looking for military aid which was denied. At 0100 on 17 July Somoza finally resigned and his National Guard disintegrated, some escaping out of San Juan del Sur on commandeered shrimp boats, while others fled to Miami, Honduras and Guatemala.

At the huge cost of more than 50,000 Nicaraguan lives, Somoza Debayle and the Guardia National were finally defeated. Nicaragua was in ruins, but free. A huge party was held in front of the Old Cathedral and National Palace on 20 July. Somoza escaped to Miami and later to Paraguay, where he was killed by an Argentine hit squad on 17 September 1980.

Sandinista Government and the Contra War

A national reconstruction committee assumed power of Nicaragua on 20 July 1979. It was made up of five members: FSLN leader Daniel Ortega, novelist Sergio Ramírez, physics professor Dr Moisés Hassan, widow of the slain *La Prensa* publisher Violeta Barrios de Chamorro and businessman Alfonso Robelo. It looked to be a well-balanced group, but what the public did not know at the time was that Ramírez and Hassan were both sworn secret members of the FSLN, giving them three to two control of the ruling board. Within a year both Doña Violeta and Alfonso Robelo would resign.

The committee abolished the old constitution and confiscated all property belonging to Somoza and his 'allies'. A new legislative body was organized to write a new constitution. Several key bodies were created by the Sandinistas that helped them to consolidate power quickly, like the Comités de Defensa Sandinista (CDS) that were organized in the *barrios* of Managua and the countryside to be the 'eyes and ears of the Revolution'. Much of the Nicaraguan public who fought had believed that the Revolution was about getting rid of Somoza (and not much beyond that) while many also hoped to establish a democratic system based on the Costa Rican model. However, the Sandinistas' aim was to change society as a whole, installing a semi-Marxist system and, in theory, reversing over four centuries of social injustice.

The peace in Nicaragua was short lived. Thanks to the pre-victory death of legendary non-Marxist FSLN rebel leader Germán Pomares in Jinotega in May 1979 – by what was at first said to be a National Guard sniper, then revised as a 'stray bullet' – the first anti-Sandinista rebel units formed in Nueva Segovia. Four days after the first anniversary of the victory over Somoza, a group of ex-Sandinista

The Contra War

Then US President Ronald Reagan labelled the Contras the 'Freedom Fighters', and on one occasion even sported a T-shirt that read, 'I'm a Contra too'. His administration lobbied to maintain and increase military aid to the Nicaraguan Contras fighting the Sandinista Revolution during the 1980s. The first bands of Contras were organized shortly after the Sandinistas took power in 1979. The leaders were mainly ex-officials and soldiers loyal to the overthrown general Anastasio Somoza Debayle. Thanks to the United States, the Contras grew quickly and became the largest guerrilla army in Latin America. When they demobilized in May 1990, they had 15,000 troops.

The Contras divided Nicaragua in two: war zones and zones that were not at war. They also divided United States public opinion between those who supported President Reagan's policy and those who opposed it. The US House of Representatives and the Senate were likewise divided. The Contras are also associated with one of the biggest political scandals in the US after Watergate. The so-called 'Iran-Contra Affair' broke at the end of 1986, when a C-123 supply plane with a US flight crew was shot down over Nicaraguan territory. The scandal that followed caused some US government officials to resign, including Lieutenant Colonel Oliver North. The intellectual authors of the affair remained unscathed.

The most famous Contra leader was former Guardia Nacional Colonel Enrique Bermúdez, known in the war as 'Commander 3-80'. In February 1991, Bermúdez was shot dead in the parking lot of Managua's Intercontinental Hotel. The 'strange circumstances' surrounding his death were never clarified, and the killers were never apprehended. After agreeing to disarm in 1990, the majority of the Contra troops returned to a normal civilian life. However, most of them never received the land, credit, work implements, etc they had been promised. The Contras live on today as the Partido Resistencia Nicaragüense (Nicaraguan Resistance Party), which has been ineffective due to internal disputes and divisions.

rebels attacked Sandinista Government troops, overrunning the local military base in Quilalí. The Contra War had begun. By August 1980, ex-National Guard members were also forming groups in Honduras and, thanks to organization by CIA, at first directed via Argentine generals, and then with direct control from ex-Guard members, the movement began to formalize rebel groups. The first planned CIA attack was carried out in March 1982 with bombs planted to destroy key bridges in the north. Although the original Contras and the majority of the Contra fighters had nothing to do with the National Guard, the Resistencia Nicaragüense (better known as the Contras – short for counter-revolutionary in Spanish) was to be commanded in Honduras by former Guard members and funded by the US government under Ronald Reagan. The war waged by the Contras was one of harassment and guerrilla warfare like Sandino had used against the US Marines. But, unlike Sandino, the Contra bands attacked freely 'soft (civilian) targets' and country infrastructure as part of their strategy. A southern front against the Sandinista administration was opened up by ex-FSLN hero Edén Pastora who was disillusioned with the new Sandinista government and the meaningless roles he was given to play in it. By introducing mandatory military service the Sandinista army swelled to over 120,000 to fight the combined Contra forces of an estimated 10,000-20,000 soldiers. The national monetary reserves were increasingly taxed, with more than half the national budget going on military spending, and a US economic embargo that sent inflation spinning out of control, annihilating the already beleaguered economy that was finally killed by the collapse of partner states in the Soviet bloc. Massive migration to avoid the war zones changed the face of Nicaragua, with exiles choosing departmental capitals, Managua or Costa Rica, while those who could afford it fled to Miami. Indigenous groups suffered greatly during this period with the Mayagna in the heart of the Contra War and the Miskitos being forced to live in internment camps while their village homes and crops were razed by government troops. The Miskitos formed their own rebel Contra groups who attacked from the Caribbean side and the Río Coco.

The Sandinistas are credited with numerous important socio-political achievements including the **Literacy Crusade**, a fresh sense of nationalism, giant cultural advances and improved infrastructure. Yet the Contra War, US economic embargo, a thoroughly disastrous agriculture reform program, human rights abuses and dictatorial style of running the government would spell their doom. Progress in education and culture was undeniably impressive during the Sandinista years, especially considering the circumstances, but the cost was too high for the majority of the Nicaraguan people. Personal freedoms were the same or worse (especially regarding freedom of speech and press) as they had been in the time of Somoza's rule, and fatigue from the death and poverty caused by the Contra War was extreme. Hundreds of studies have been written on what happened in the 1980s in Nicaragua and defenders of the FSLN rule point out that they never had a chance to rule in peace. Their detractors, on the other hand, highlight that democracy was never on the agenda for the party.

A peace agreement was reached in Sapoá, Rivas and elections were held in 1990. Daniel Ortega (40.8%) lost to Violeta Chamorro (55.2%). After losing the elections the Sandinistas bravely handed over power to Doña Violeta. Then they proceeded frantically to divide and distribute state-held assets (which included hundreds of confiscated properties and businesses) among leading party members in the two months between the election loss and handing over power, in what has since been known simply as *la piñata*.

After an entire century of limited personal freedoms and military-backed governments, most Nicaraguans considered the election of Doña Violeta as the beginning of true democracy in Nicaragua. She was forced to compromise on many issues and at times the country looked set to collapse back into war, but Nicaragua's first woman president spent the next six years trying to repair the damage and unite the country. The Nicaraguan military was de-politicized, put under civilian rule and reduced from over 120,000 to fewer than 18,000. Uprisings were common with small groups taking up arms or demonstrations meant to destabilize the government. But by the time Doña Violeta handed over the presidency in 1997, Nicaragua was fully at peace and beginning to recover economically.

In 1996 Liberal Party candidate Arnoldo Alemán won 51% of the vote against the 37.7% garnered by Daniel Ortega, with the rest split among 21 different presidential candidates. However, behind closed doors, a politically expedient pact between the Liberals and the Sandinistas compromised and politicized government institutions and created much controversy. Sandinista objectors to the pact were tossed out of the party. Meanwhile, Alemán made great strides in increasing economic growth and foreign investment and improved education and road infrastructure. He also managed to steal more than US$100 million of state funds and left office with an approval rating of less than 25%.

In 2001, the electorate once again voted for the Liberals, or more precisely against Ortega, electing Liberal Party candidate Enrique Bolaños in a record turnout of 96% of registered voters. Bolaños promised to attack the corruption of his party leader Arnoldo Alemán and he did exactly that. At great political cost to Nicaragua's executive branch, Bolaños had Alemán tried, convicted and sentenced to 20 years in prison on corruption charges. But the Liberal congressmen, all purchased by Alemán, refused to abandon their leader and insisted on amnesty for Alemán, who continued to rule the Liberal party from his luxury ranch and enjoyed full movement about the country. Despite the great victory against state thievery, Bolaños' administration has been largely ineffectual; the war against corruption left him without support in the Nicaraguan Congress. Furthermore, Alemán and Ortega entered into a new pact that promised freedom for Alemán after Liberal parliamentary members voted the Sandinistas into power at all levels of non-Federal government, from Parliament to the Supreme Court.

Ortega returns

Following elections in 2006, Daniel Ortega returned after winning 38% of the vote. Despite ample promises of help from new allies such as Venezuela and Iran, change to Nicaragua's daily reality was initially slow, with the rising cost of living outpacing mandated salary adjustments. Ortega was widely criticized for employing the same neo-liberal policies of the last 17 years. *The Economist* called it 'Ortega's Crab Walk': tough revolutionary, anti-imperialist rhetoric combined with a textbook IMF economic policy. Ortega amended the Nicaraguan constitution to allow a president to hold office for two consecutive terms in 2009. Making no secret of his ambitions for perpetual re-election, he ran as the Sandinista candidate in 2011 and won a landslide victory against a poorly organized and divided Liberal opposition. In 2013, Congress approved legislation that allowed Ortega to run for a third successive term, and on 6 November 2016, he was re-elected with 72.1% of the vote. His supporters claimed that Nicaragua's robust economic performance and its relatively low crime levels compared to El Salvador, Guatemala and Honduras had won the day for the FLSN.

According to the Supreme Electoral Council, voter turnout had been 66%. However, the opposition coalition Broad Front for Democracy (FAD) estimated that more than two-thirds of voters had stayed home. In fact, five months prior to election day, the Nicaraguan Supreme Court had intervened in favour of the ruling FSLN by stripping the opposition of its leadership. First, the court deposed the leader of the Independent Liberal Party (PLI), Eduardo Montealegre, and replaced him with Pedro Reyes Vallejos, ostensibly an Ortega puppet. Then, when 16 PLI deputies protested, the Supreme Electoral Council expelled them from the National Assembly and ordered Reyes to replace them.

The party was left without any effective means of contesting the election, but it ran anyway, winning just 4.51% of the vote. Meanwhile, international electoral observers were not permitted to scrutinize the election – a decision the Carter Center described as "an attack on the international community" – but a delegation from the Organization of American States did meet with state officials on 5-7 November.

A new dictatorship?

On 18 April 2018, protestors in several cities staged demonstrations against proposed social security reforms which included higher taxes on payrolls and a 5% cut in pension payments. The police responded with live ammunition, causing the protests to escalate. At least 26 people died in the ensuing violence, including a journalist, Angel Gahona, who was shot in Bluefields while broadcasting live on Facebook. Ortega quickly moved to suppress news of the protests by suspending transmissions of four TV channels, but on 22 April he backed down and cancelled his reforms. Then, on 14 April, he released 200 protesters who had been detained by the police.

Ortega's problems might have ended there, but the incident proved to be an overture to more serious unrest. With demonstrators now demanding Ortega and his vice president, Rosario Murillo step down, protests intensified. The State responded with crack-downs and repression, leading to months of discord that ultimately tore apart the country. By August, Ortega has reasserted his authority over Nicaragua, but at great social and political cost. To date, international human rights groups have accused the Ortega regime of arbitrary detention, torture and extrajudicial killings, as well as the suppression of freedom of expression. In October 2018, the Interamerican Commission on Human Right (IACHR) found that 325 people had died in the clashes, including 21 police officers and 24 children and adolescents. Ortega, now the face of resurgent *caudillismo*, has transformed into the kind of strongman he spent his youth fighting against.

Culture

People

With a population of 5.5 million, population density is low: 43 people per sq km, compared with El Salvador's 322. Nine out of 10 Nicaraguans live and work in the lowlands between the Pacific and the western shores of Lake Nicaragua, the southwestern shore of Lake Managua, and the southwestern sides of the row of volcanoes. In latter years settlers have taken to coffee-growing and cattle-rearing in the highlands at Matagalpa and Jinotega. Elsewhere, the highlands, save for an occasional mining camp, are very thinly settled.

The origin of the Nicaraguan, as with much of the Americas' population, is typically diverse. The pre-conquest cultures of the central and western sections of the countries mixed with small waves of European immigration, beginning in the 16th century and continuing today. The eastern section of Nicaragua remained in relative isolation for the first several centuries and fairly well defined indigenous ethnic cultures are still present in the communities of Miskito, Rama and Mayagna as well as Afro-Caribbeans from Jamaica (Creole) and San Vincent (Garífuna) Islands.

Ultimately, however, the Hispanic mestizo culture of the western two-thirds of the country dominate the ethnic profile of the Nicaraguan. Recent surveys indicate a country 96% mestizo, with 3% indigenous and 1% Afro-Caribbean. Among the peoples classified as mestizo are many of close to pure indigenous roots who have lost their distinguishing language, but retained many cultural traits of pre-Columbian times. There is also a very small, nearly pure European sector that has traditionally controlled the country's economic and land assets. Massive movements of population during the troubled years of the 1980s has also blurred these once well-defined lines, although you can still see some definite ethnic tendencies in each province of the country.

Religion

By 1585, the majority of the local population had been converted to Christianity. Surveys suggest that now only 59% of the population is Roman Catholic. Evangelical groups have made great strides in recent years in attracting worshippers, and Baptist, Methodist, Church of Christ, Assembly of God, Seventh Day Adventists, Jehovah's Witness, Mormon and other churches now account for 29% of the population, with the remainder claiming no church affiliation. Religion and spirituality in general are very important parts of Nicaraguan life. The combined forces of the Evangelist churches have their own political party in Camino Cristiano (who joined in alliance with the Liberal party for the elections in 2001) and won the third largest tally of votes in the 1996 campaign. The Catholic Church has no official political wing, but plays heavily on the political scene.

Dance

During the early years of Spanish colonization, dance as a discipline did not have a defined style. Indigenous dances were considered heretical due to the ceremonial nature of some of them (although many were danced for pure pleasure) and therefore discouraged or banned. The dances considered folkloric or traditional in Nicaragua today are a mixture of African, indigenous and European dances and cultures. In the colonial period, celebrations of religious festivities saw the performance by the upper-class Spanish of European dances that were in fashion back home. The manner of dancing and behaviour of the upper class was observed by the native, African and mestizo populations and then mixed with each culture's respective dances.

The terms *el son* or *los sones* are used to define the dances that first appeared in the 1700s, such as the **Jarabe**, **Jaranas** and **Huapangos**. These dances are the local adaptations of the Fandango and Spanish tap dance. In Nicaragua the dances or *sones Jarabe Chichón* and *Jarabe Repicado* are still performed today in the festivals of Masaya and its *pueblos*. Many traditional dances have a love message; a good example is the flirtatious **Dance of the Indian Girls** (*Baile de las Inditas*) or the entertaining physical satire on relationships known as the **Dance of the Old Man and Lady** (*El Baile del Viejo y la Vieja*).

Other well-known dances are the **Dance of the Black Girls** (*Danza de las Negritas*), another dance performed by men in drag, and a spectacular and colourful traditional dance **The Little Demons** (*Los Diablitos*). This is a native mock-up of an Iberian masquerade ball, danced in the streets and with performer's costumes consisting of every possible character from Mr Death to a tiger, or a giant parrot or the Devil. One of the most traditional dances from Masaya is **El Torovenado**, which follows the rhythm of *marimbas* and *chicheros*. The participants are all male and dress in costumes representing both male and female politicians and members of the upper class. Their handmade masks and costumes are created to satirize important events happening in the country or behaviour of the moneyed class. The Torovenado is a street performance-protest against social injustice and government corruption. Another of the many traditional Nicaraguan dances is the **Dance of the Hungarians** (*Danza de la Húngaras*), which developed from early 20th-century immigration of eastern European gypsies to Nicaragua.

Masaya is far from unique in its local dances, for Nicaraguan regional dance is rich and impressive across the board. The most famous of all, **El Güegüence** has disputed origins – it is either from the highland village of Diriamba or from Masaya. The small, but historic village of Nindirí is home to many dances like **The Black Chinese** (*Los Chinegros*), **El Ensartado** and **Las Canas**. León is the origin of the spectacular joke on the early colonizers called **El Baile de La Gigantona y el Enano Cabezón**, in which a 3-m-tall blond women spins and dances in circles around an old dwarf with a big bald head. León is also home to **Los Mantudos** and **El Baile del Toro**. Managua has **La Danza de la Vaca** and Boaco has the **Dance of the Moors and the Christians** (*Los Moros y Cristianos*). Very peculiar inside

Nicaragua is the dance only performed on the Island of Ometepe in the village of Altagracia called the **Dance of the Leaf-Cutter Ants** (*El Baile de Los Zompopos*).

In the northern cities of Matagalpa and Jinotega, the coffee immigrants from Germany and other parts of northern Europe in the late 19th century had violin and guitar-driven polkas, *jamaquellos* and *mazurkas*.

The Caribbean coast is home to some little-known Garífuna dances that are now being performed in Managua and some native Miskito dances that have also been recognized and performed by dance troupes on the Pacific side. The favourite of both coasts for its raw energy may be the **Palo de Mayo** (maypole) dances, a hybrid of English maypole traditions and Afro-Caribbean rain and fertility dances.

Aside from the tradition of dancing in festivals, the dances of Nicaragua have been brought to the stage and are performed regularly by numerous groups and professional companies in Managua and Masaya with less frequent performances all over Nicaragua. Masaya often has dance groups performing on Thursday nights at the artisans' market and the **Centro Cultural Managua** and **Teatro Rubén Darío** also have regular shows.

Literature

Early Nicaraguan poetry and narrative, influenced from the beginning by the chronicles of the West Indies, uses a straightforward descriptive style to depict the life of the indigenous people and the Spanish conquest through colourful narratives. This type of **native literature** was the most prevalent during the pre-Hispanic era. One of the original works was *Canto al sol de los Nicaraguas*, dedicated to the principal cultures to inhabit this remote region, the Nicaraguas and Chorotegas. The writing of the indigenous peoples, generally pictographs, is largely anonymous. While the native languages would later become mixed with Spanish, a series of primitive dialects were conserved, so that later it was possible to recover and compile different works, including **Sumu poetry**, **Miskito songs**, **Sutiavan poems**, **Carib music** and **native myths** from different regions of Nicaragua. These were songs related to the Spanish conquest or religion – a product of the colonization process – sayings, riddles, ballads and children's games that would later reappear in different narratives and poetic forms. The first book attributed to Nicaraguan-born Spanish descendants was *Relaciones verdaderas de la deducción de los indios infieles, de la provincia de Teguzgalpa* (True Revelations about the Pagan Indians from the Province of Teguzgalpa) by Francisco Fernández Espino, which appeared in 1674. The work was little known. In 1876, according to literary critic Ricardo Llopesa, the first literary group La Montaña, was founded in Granada. Two years later the first anthology titled *Lira Nicaragüense* was published.

Rubén Darío

The Father of Modernism Rubén Darío (1867-1916) overshadowed everyone with his proposals for innovation in the Spanish language through the Modernist movement, which he himself founded. The Modernist school advocated aestheticism, the search for sensory and even sensual values, and the artistic effects of colour, sound, voice and synthesis. His first verses were published in 1879. In 1881 he edited his first complete work, *Poesías y artículos en prosa*, which was published after his death, and *Epítolas y poemas* in 1888. That same year, *Azul*, one of the fundamental works for understanding Modernism, was published. In 1896, he published *Los Raros y Prosas Profanas*, in Buenos Aires. In 1901 a second edition of this work was published. Upon returning to Valparaíso, Chile, he published *Abrojos* (1887) and his novel *Emelina*. Other Darío narratives include *El Fardo, Invernal, El Rey Burgués* and *La Ninfa*. Darío's works had a significant impact on the Spanish language, especially his literary production, personal letters and stories. In 1916, after many years of absence, Darío returned to the city of León, where he died on 6 February. See also box, page 153.

The Vanguard

A significant group of poets were followers of Darío, but with very individual styles. These included Father **Azarias H Pallais** (1884-1959), **Alfonso Cortés** (1893-1969; see page 154) and **Salomón de la Selva** (1893-1959). These world-class poets were known for their innovation and experimentation. Literature, and especially poetry, has always been attractive to Nicaraguan youth. For that reason the Vanguard movement was born. Founded by **Luis Alberto Cabrales** (1901-1974) and **José Coronel Urtecho** (1906-1994) this movement exerted an important renovating influence on Nicaraguan literature. Coronel Urtecho's work *Oda a Rubén Darío* (1927) contains the essence of the new style and marks the transition from the Darío school of Modernism to the Vanguard movement. **Pablo Antonio Cuadra** (1912-2002), the movement's principal author, wrote a declaration reaffirming the national identity, which was later incorporated into his first book *Poemas Nicaragüenses* (1934). His literary production was truly prolific and included *Libro de horas* (1964), *El Jaguar y la Luna* (1959). He wrote about the life of the mammal in *Cantos de Cifar* and *Al mar dulce* (1926); his excellent treatise against dictatorships in *Siete arboles contra el atardecer* (1982) and *Poemas para un calendario* (1988). Cuadra's work has been translated into several languages. For more than a decade he was the general director of the *La Prensa* daily newspaper. Cuadra, together with Coronel Urtecho, Luis Cabrales and **Joaquín Pasos** (1914-1947) author of the dramatic poem *Canto de Guerra de las Cosas*, summarized their programme and released the *Anti-Academia de la Lengua* declaration. Another member of the Vanguard was **Manolo Cuadra** (1907-1957) who became known for his poems, *Perfil* and *La palabra que no te dije*, published in *Tres Amores* (1955).

The 1940s

The main themes of the generation of the 1940s were love and freedom, reflected in the poetry of **Francisco Pérez Estrada** (1917-1982), **Enrique Fernández Morales** (1918-1982), and **Julio Ycaza Tigerino** (1919-2001). However, this period is especially known for the emergence of two great poets. **Ernesto Mejía Sánchez** (1923-1985) cultivated a style marked by brevity and precision in his most important works *Ensalmos y conjuros* (1947) and *La carne contigua*

(1948). **Carlos Martínez Rivas** (1924-1999) used a modern rhythm, making his ideas felt through quick turns of phrase and ruptures of his own language. *El paraíso recobrado* (1948) was a revelation and the publication of *Insurrección solitaria* (1953) even more so. He published a series of poems titled *Allegro irato*, in 1989, which continued a very experimental line.

Expressionist poetry

The poetry of **Ernesto Cardenal**, born 20 January 1925, reflects spoken language and contains simple expressions. He is the founder of the expressionist poetry current, which opposed the subjectivity of lyrical poetry. Through his poetry he attacked the Somoza family dictatorship for over four decades. Also a priest, he founded the Christian community of Solentiname on a group of islands in Lake Nicaragua. His extensive work has been translated into several languages. *La ciudad deshabitada* (1946), *Hora 0* (1960), *Oración por Marylin Monroe y otras poemas* (1966), are poems reflecting religious, historical and Christian themes as well as the topic of social commitment.

The 1950s and 1960s

In the 1950s, **Guillermo Rothschuh Tablada** (1926) and **Fernando Silva** (1927-2016) stand out. Rothschuh wrote *Poemas Chontaleños* (1960), while Silva follows the traditional-regional approach, reflecting the spoken language of the rural areas. His work *Barro de Sangre* represents a vernacular renewal in the authenticity of its theme and language. In the 1960s, the left-leaning **Grupo Ventana** (Window Group) emerged led by students at the Autonomous National University of León, including **Fernando Gordillo** (1940-1967), who left only a scattered poetic work, and **Sergio Ramírez Mercado** (1942). Other poets of this generation include **Octavio Robleto** (1935-2009) and **Francisco Valle** (1942), a surrealist and a writer of prose. **Beltrán Morales** (1945-1986) is the most outstanding poet of this generation for his synthesis and irony, reflected in *Agua Regia* (1972). Other groups emerging in this period were the **La Generación Traicionada** (The Betrayed Generations) and **Grupo M**, both from Managua, **Grupo U** from Boaco, and **Los Bandeleros** (The Bandoliers) from Granada. **Mario Cajina-Vega**, a poet and thoughtful but comic narrator, published *Breve Tribu* in 1962. **Julio Valle-Castillo**, poet, narrator and critic, published one of his first books *Materia Jubilosa* in 1953. Along with **Jorge Eduardo Arellano** (1946), Julio Valle is one of Nicaragua's most respected researchers.

The 1970s

In the 1970s, the modern short story was born in Nicaragua with **Lisandro Chávez Alfaro**'s *Los Monos de San Telmo* (1963), known for its innovative technique and themes. Chronicles from poor Managua neighbourhoods are found in *Se Alquilan Cuartos* (1975), by Juan Aburto (1918-1988). **Sergio Ramírez Mercado** is one of the best internationally known writers to have ever come out of Nicaragua. The ex-vice president of Nicaragua under Daniel Ortega has published novels and books of short stories including *De Tropeles y Tropelias* (1972) and *Charles*

Atlas también muere (1976). In 1998 he won the International Prize for Fiction of the Alfagura publishing house of Spain who also published his later works. He is considered among the finest novelists in Latin America today.

Poetic revelations

The revelation of the 1970s was **Gioconda Belli**. Her first book *Sobre La Grama* (1974) is a sensual work of poems that broke ground with its frank femininity. *De La Costilla De Eva* (1987) speaks of free love at the service of revolutionary transformation. Her novels, *La mujer habitada*, *Memorias de amor y de guerra* and *El país bajo mi piel*, among others, have been published in more than 20 languages. Along with Belli, other writers emerging in this period included **Vidaluz Meneses, Daisy Zamora, Ana Ilce Gómez, Rosario Murillo**, and **Christian Santos**.

Exteriorism

In the 1980s, a new literary phenomenon called Exteriorism became popular. Founded by **Ernesto Cardenal**, who at the time was the Sandinista government's Minister of Culture, this movement advocated political poetry, and promoted what he called "objective poetry: using fragments of narrative, anecdotes, and employing proper nouns with imprecise details and exact statistics." This style was taught in widespread poetry workshops where members of the army, the recently literate farming population and other sectors of the country were encouraged to write. The use of a unified style was later criticized and with the end of the Sandinista government the poetry workshops disappeared.

Modern trends

From the 1990s onwards, a more intimate poetry emerged. The traditional literary topics are prevalent: death, existentialism and love, along with new themes including homosexuality, women's rights and the environment. New writers have emerged: poets like **Blanca Castellón, Erick Aguirre, Pedro Xavier Solís, Juan Sobalvarro, Isolda Hurtado, Marta Leonor González** and **Ariel Montoya**. There are also new literary groups and magazines such as *400 Elefantes*, *Decenio* and *Cultura de Paz*.

Music

Music is a very integral part of Nicaraguan life with everything from traditional festivals to political rallies using music as its driving backbone. Rock, pop, folk, regional, romantic and protest music are all a part of the national offering.

Marimba

The marimba is the most traditional among these varieties of rhythms. The instrument is known as Nicaragua's 'national piano' and although its origin has never been well defined, most believe it has its roots in Africa. In musical terms it is a complex instrument: shaped in the form of a triangle and comprising 22 wood keys. The marimba player uses two sticks with rubber heads called *bolillos*. The instrument has very clear and sonorous tonalities. In the past the marimba was used to play folk pieces and typical music of the countryside, but today it has been diversified, *marimberos* performing anything from salsa to *merengue* and *cumbia*. The country's best *marimberos* are from the indigenous barrio of Masaya, Monimbó, which has a generations-long tradition of marimba playing.

Classical music

Classical music was the music of *criollos* in Nicaragua and the original European-influenced music of the country. The classical symphony music of the Nicaraguan artists in the 19th century was played by orchestras in León. Key names like **Juan Bautista Prado**, **Manuel Ibarra**, **Alfonso Zelaya**, **Salvador Martínez**, **Santos Cermeño**, **Alfonso Solórzano** and **Lizandro Ramírez** dominated the classical music scene of Nicaragua that survives today, although original compositions have diminished greatly since the end of the 1800s. The greatest of all Nicaraguan classical composers was the León artist **José de la Cruz Mena**, who received international recognition before dying of leprosy (see León, page 148). The poet **Salomón Ibarra Mayorga** wrote the Nicaraguan national anthem. The short piece was written on 16 December 1910 and performed by the greatest musicians of the time, the masters **Abraham Delgadillo Rivas** and **Carlos Alberto Ramírez Velásquez**.

Folk music

Folk music also has its roots in Masaya, with many artists known as *orejeros* (those who learn to play by ear). Nicaraguan rhythms such as *Mamá Ramona* come from the city. The *orejeros* are famous for their deft guitar playing. One of the most important creators of the Nicaraguan song is **Víctor M Leiva** who wrote the song *El Caballo Cimarrón* (The Untamed Horse) in 1948, the first Nicaraguan song recorded in the country. During his more than 50 years of performing and composing he painted portraits of the Nicaraguan's daily life, landscape and labour. Some of his most famous compositions include *Santo Domingo de Guzmán*, *Tata Chombo*, *Coffee Season*, *El Toro Huaco* and *La Chapandonga*. He received a Gold Palm award in United States, as the second greatest folkloric composer in Latin America. Another important folk singer songwriter is **Camilo Zapata** (1917-2009), known as 'The Master of Regionalism'. He wrote his first song *Caballito Chontaleno* (Little Horse from Chontales) at the age of 14. His songs are nourished by culture and Nicaraguan critics have crowned him as the face and heart of Nicaraguan regionalism. In 1948 Zapata came to national fame with songs like *El Nandaimeno*, *El Ganado Colorado* (The Pink Cattle), *El Solar de Monimbó* (The Backyard of Monimbó), *Flor de Mi Colina* (Flower from my Hill), *Minga Rosa Pineda*, *El Arriero* (The Muleteer) and some other romantic ones such as *Facing the sun*, *Cariño*. El Maestro Zapata continued to compose and perform into his eighties.

Chicheros
Chicheros are an integral part of any festival or traditional party. The Chichero band consists of six to eight amateur musicians who play snare drums, bass drum, cymbal, trumpet, flute, clarinet and trombone. Their music ranges from energetic dance tunes to solemn funeral marches.

La Misa Campesina
With marimbas, guitars, *atabales* (drums), violins and mazurcas and Nicaraguan rhythm, a new style in popular religious music was born with *La Misa Campesina* or the Peasant Mass. The Mass is composed of 10 songs, written by legendary folk singer Carlos Mejía Godoy and recorded in the 1980s by the Popular Sound Workshop. It was composed in Solentiname, where Ernesto Cardenal was preaching, and was later extended to all the 'peoples' churches and even to Spain. The Catholic Church in Nicaragua prohibited the work on orders from Pope John Paul II. The lack of acceptance by the church did little to diminish the worldwide acceptance of the music. *La Misa Campesina* has been translated into numerous languages and is even sung by Anglicans, Mormons and Baptists in the United States. Among the most loved are the *Welcome Song*, *The Creed*, *The Meditation song*, *Kirye*, *Saint* and *Communion*. The music has also been chosen as one of the hundred hymns of the Mennonite Church in the United States.

Protest music
Protest music had its glory days during the years leading up to the Revolution. This music of pop and folkloric rhythms brought to fame such bands as Engel Ortega, Norma Elena Gadea and Eduardo Araica, the Pancasan Band, Duo Guardabarranco formed by Katia and Salvador Cardenal, Keyla Rodríguez and Luis Enrique Mejía Godoy.

Palo de Mayo
Palo de Mayo is a collection of native music from the Caribbean coast of Nicaragua. The music is characterized by its vibrant rhythm. The songs that are a joy hymn for the Afro-Caribbean Nicaraguans include *Tululu Pass Under*, *Oh Nancy, Oh*, *Simón Canta Simón*, *Mayaya Oh*. To perform the Caribbean rhythms, local musicians incorporate instruments such as cow and donkey jawbones, combs and pots, as well as more common instruments like drums and guitars.

Land &
environment

Geography

Nicaragua can be divided into three principal sections. The **Caribbean lowlands**, which include pine savannahs in the north and, further south, the largest remaining expanse of rainforest on the Central American isthmus, are crossed by numerous rivers that drain the central mountain range to the emerald sea. The **central and northern mountains and plains** are geologically the oldest in the country, with many long-extinct volcanoes. The mountains are low, ranging from 500 m in the far south of the zone to 2000 m as they reach the border with Honduras in the north. This is a mineral-rich area that has been prospected for centuries. The diversity of the ecosystem is immense, with rainforest giving way to tropical dry forest in the south, and cloudforest to pines in the north.

The third division is the **Pacific Basin**, which is marked by numerous crater lakes, the two great lakes of Managua and Nicaragua and the lumpy spine of volcanoes, the Cordillera Los Maribios, that run from the extreme northwest at Volcán Cosigüina to the dual volcano island of Ometepe in Lake Nicaragua. The area is a mixture of tropical dry forest and savannah with two cloudforests on Volcán Mombacho and Volcán Maderas, and a pine forest on the Volcán Casita.

Lakes and rivers

In the Pacific Basin plain are 15 crater lakes and the two largest expanses of water in Central America. The capital, Managua, lies on the shores of **Lake Managua** (also known as *Xolotlán*), which is 52 km long, 15-25 km wide, and sits 39 m above sea level. Its maximum depth is only 30 m and it has a surface area of 1025 sq km. The Peninsula of Chiltepe juts out into Lake Managua and holds two crater lakes, Xiloá and Apoyeque. Managua also houses four small crater lakes. Lake Managua drains to Lake Nicaragua via the Río Tipitapa just east of the capital. The mighty **Lake Nicaragua**, often called by one of its pre-Conquest names, *Cocibolca*, is 160 km long, 65 km at its widest, and 32 m above the level of the sea. This massive sheet of water averages 20 m in depth with a maximum depth of 60 m. Lake Nicaragua covers a total of 8264 sq km. Just 18 km separates the big lake from the Pacific Ocean on the southern part of its western shores. But Lake Nicaragua drains 190 km to the Caribbean Sea via the **Río San Juan**, the second longest river in Central America behind the 680-km Río Coco in Nicaragua's north. In total there are 96 principal rivers, most lying east of the great lakes.

Volcanoes

Nicaragua is one of the most geologically active countries in the world. It lies at the intersection of the Coco and Caribe continental plates. Subduction of the Coco plate underneath the Caribe plate is at a rate of 8-9 cm per year, the fastest rate of plate collision in the hemisphere. The newest of the countries in the Americas in geological terms (8-9 million years old), its constant subterranean movement results in over 300 low level tremors per day in the region, with the majority occurring on the Pacific shelf. Another result of the land in upheaval is a line of more than 40 beautiful volcanoes, six of which have been active within the last 100 years. The volcanoes run 300 km from north to south along a fault line that is full of magma 10 km below the topsoil.

The northernmost is **Volcán Cosigüina** (800 m), overlooking the Golfo de Fonseca, with a lake in its crater. Its final eruption was in 1835, in what is believed to have been the most violent in recorded history in the Americas, with ash being thrown as far as Mexico and the ground shaking as far south as Colombia. To the southeast continues the Maribios volcanic chain, with the now-extinct **Volcán Chonco** (1105 m) and the country's highest, the cone of **Volcán San Cristóbal** (1745 m). San Cristóbal began erupting again in 1971 after a long period of inactivity following the highly explosive years of 1684-1885. Since 1999 it has been throwing up a lot of ash; its last activity was in 2006.

Just south rises the extinct cone of **Volcán Casita**, which is notable for its pine forest, the southernmost of its kind in the American continent's northern hemisphere. One side of Casita collapsed during the torrential rains of Hurricane Mitch in 1998, burying numerous villages in the municipality of Posoltega and killing more than 2000 people. Further south, just before León, is the very active **Volcán Telica** (1061 m) with eruptions occurring often in the 1990s and the last one in 2013. It was recorded erupting in 1529, 1685 and between 1965 and 1968 with more activity in 1971. It seems to erupt in unison with San Cristóbal. Next to the bald, eroding summit of Telica are the dormant cones of little **Volcán Santa Clara** (or **Volcán San Jacinto**) and **Volcán Rota** or **Volcán Orata** (836 m), which is believed to be the oldest in the chain.

Just south of León is one of the youngest volcanoes on the planet, **Cerro Negro**; born in 1850, it has risen from just above sea level to 450 m in this short period. Major eruptions have occurred 12 times since 1867, including three times since 1990. This is the most dangerous of the volcanoes with violent eruptions and lava flows, and the eruption in August 1999 opened new craters at its southern base.

Volcán Pilas is formed of various craters, the highest of which rises 1001 m and contains one active crater known as *El Hoyo*, which last erupted from 1952 to 1955, though it is still smoking. Other extinct cones lie between Pilas and the majestic **Volcán Momotombo** (1300 m), which overlooks the shores of Lake Managua. Momotombo's eruptions in the late 1500s convinced the residents of León Viejo to leave. It erupted with force in 1764, regularly erupted from 1858 to 1866, and had a significant eruption in 1905 with a large lava flow to its east side. Today a geothermal plant on the base of its west side utilizes its considerable fumarolic energy on a daily basis. In December 2015, Momotombo erupted again, having been dormant for 110 years. The chain ends with little extinct **Volcán Momotombito**, which forms an island in Lake Managua. Managua's volcanoes are all extinct and six contain crater lakes.

The **Dirianes** volcanic chain begins just north of Masaya with the complex of **Volcán Masaya**, including the smoking, lava-filled **Santiago** crater as well as four extinct craters and a lagoon. Masaya is the only volcano on the American continent, and one of four in the world, with a constant pool of lava. During its very active recent history there have been noteworthy eruptions in 1670, 1772, 1858-1859, 1902-1905, 1924, 1946, 1965 and 1970-1972. It fell dormant for two decades before coming alive again with up to 400 tonnes per day of sulphur output from 1995 until today. It had a small, but nasty little eruption on 23 April 2001, with more expected.

South between Masaya and Granada is the extinct **Apoyo**, which died very violently 20,000 years ago, leaving the deep blue Laguna de Apoyo, 6 km in diameter. Along the shores of Lake Nicaragua and shadowing Granada is dormant and mildly fumarolic **Volcán Mombacho** (1345 m), wrapped in cloudforest. Mombacho had a major structural collapse in 1570 that wiped out a Chorotega village at its base. Fall-out and lava flows from a prehistoric eruption (around 6000 BC) of the Mombacho cone created Las Isletas in Lake Nicaragua.

The volcanoes of Lake Nicaragua include the extinct and heavily eroded cone that forms the **Isla de Zapatera** (600 m), a national park and a very important pre-Columbian site. The last two volcanoes in the Nicaraguan chain of fire make up the stunning Isla de Ometepe. The symmetrical and active cone of **Volcán Concepción** (1610 m) became very active in 1883-1887, 1908-1910, 1921 and 1948; the last major lava flow was in 1957 and has had ash emissions as recently as 2007. The cloudforest covering **Volcán Maderas** (1394 m), believed to be extinct, holds a lake in its misty summit.

In reality there are many, many more volcanoes; some are so heavily eroded that they merge with the landscape, but Nicaragua, in essence, is one string of volcanoes from west to east varying in age from eight million to 160 years.

Flora and fauna

Like all neotropical countries, Nicaragua is blessed with rich biodiversity and, thanks to its relatively low population, economic underdevelopment and many nature reserves, much of the country's native wildlife and vegetation have been preserved. Some species endangered in neighbouring countries are prevalent here, like the **howler monkey**, which enjoys many habitats and a population of thousands. Nonetheless, Nicaragua has not been immune to the world crisis of deforestation, most of which has occurred to clear land for farming, along with limited logging. Forest coverage has been reduced from 7,000,000 ha in 1950 to under 4,000,000 ha in the 21st century. Compounding the problem is the dominant use of wood for energy, with kindling wood (*leña*) still the main fuel for cooking. *Leña* represents 57% of the national consumption of energy, while petroleum is only at 30%. The development of responsible tourism in Nicaragua's outstanding natural areas provides hope for economic viability and nature conservation.

Principal ecosystems

The Pacific Basin is dominated by **savannah** and **tropical dry forest**. There are several significant **mangrove forests** and major areas of **wetlands** in diverse parts of the country. The biggest expanse of **cloudforest** in Central America is present on Pacific volcanoes and northern mountain ranges, especially within the Bosawás reserve. **Pine forests** run along the northern territories all the way to the Caribbean with the central-northern mountains home to extensive, but dwindling numbers. Transitional **tropical wet forests** are present on the east side of the great lakes and Lake Nicaragua's southern coast. The most extensive growth of **primary rainforest** on the isthmus dominates the Río San Juan's Indio-Maíz reserve and much of the northeastern and Caribbean lowlands. **Plant species** are, of course, diverse with 350 species of tree, part of some 12,000 species of flora that have been classified so far, with at least another 5000 yet to be documented. Those classified include more than 600 species of orchid alone. **Animal species** are equally impressive, most of all the insect life, with an estimated 250,000 species, although only about 10,000 of those have been documented to date. Mammals include some 251 species along with 234 different variations of reptile and amphibian. Bird diversity is particularly impressive with the ever-growing list of species currently totalling 714.

National parks and reserves

The Ministro de Medio Ambiente y Recursos Naturales (Ministry of Environment and Natural Resources) better known as **MARENA** ① *Km 12.5, Carretera Norte, Managua, T233-1278, www.marena.gob.ni,* is responsible for the administration of Nicaragua's 83 protected areas, which cover more than 18% of its land. The organization is gravely underfunded and understaffed, but tries hard to overcome these shortcomings to preserve Nicaragua's spectacular natural resources. The ministry is open to tourism, but has yet to utilize visitors as a means of financing preservation. The exceptions are the well-organized parks where the non-profit Cocibolca Foundation has joined forces with MARENA to offer a viable ecological experience for foreign and national visitors. If you have some grasp of Spanish you will find the *guardabosques* (park guards) to be very friendly and helpful in any natural reserve. It is important to realize that the MARENA park guards are serious about their responsibility, despite being considerably underpaid. They will ask for proof of permission for entrance into some areas and should be treated with respect and appreciation for the critical role they play in the preservation of reserves and parks. Check with MARENA before setting out to visit one of the lesser-known reserves. Parks and reserves that charge admission (see individual destinations) are prepared and welcome visitors, but many areas, like the remote reaches of the Indio-Maíz Biological Reserve, cannot be entered without prior consent from MARENA.

Volcanic parks and reserves

Along with the flagship Parque Nacional Volcán Masaya, many of Nicaragua's volcanoes have forests set aside as a reserve. Ancient volcanoes in the central and eastern regions all have forest reserves on them, critical for the local climate and water tables. In many parts of the country they are covered in rain and cloudforest and there are more than 28 such reserves set aside as protected areas, including the following Pacific Basin volcanoes: **Momotombo**, **El Hoyo**, **San Cristóbal**, **Casita**, **Telica**, **Rota**, **Concepción**, **Maderas**, **Cosigüina** and **Mombacho**. Volcanic crater lakes and their forests are also set aside as protected areas, such as **Laguna de Apoyo**, **Laguna de Asososca**, **Laguna de Nejapa**, **Laguna de Tiscapa** and the two crater lakes of Península de Chiltepe, **Laguna Apoyeque** and **Laguna Xiloá**.

Turtle nesting sites and mangroves

Some of the most rewarding of all parks to visit are the wildlife refuges set aside for the arrival of egg-laying sea turtles. Along the central Pacific coast is **Chacocente** and its tropical dry forest reserve. More accessible is the beach at **La Flor**, south of San Juan del Sur. **Isla Juan Venado** is also a place to see turtles, not in the quantity of the other reserves, but with the added attraction of accessible mangroves and their wildlife. The Pearl Cays are a major nesting site for hawksbill turtles, but they are not set up for tourism (see box, page 246).

BACKGROUND
Save the turtles

Nicaragua's Caribbean coast is home to declining populations of endangered green, loggerhead, leatherback and critically endangered hawksbill turtles. Consumption of green turtle meat is permitted by law for the coast's indigenous and Afro-descendant peoples, whose traditions include the hunting of turtles for sustenance. Unfortunately, the capture and consumption of green turtles now exceeds 11,000 per year and the commercial trade in turtle meat – although a viable and potentially sustainable local economy – may soon face collapse through over-fishing. Uncontrolled development around the Pearl Cays has also harmed the numbers of nesting hawksbills, as has the trade in turtle shell jewellery and eggs. Please consider your role as a visitor to the region and adhere to the following advice:

· Please don't eat turtles and don't provide a market for commercial turtle fishing. Many locals may expound the delicious virtues of *carne de tortuga*, but laws permitting turtle consumption were not designed with tourists in mind.
· Please don't buy jewellery made from turtle shell, no matter how beautiful – it belongs on the turtle's back.
· Please avoid eating turtle eggs. Nicaraguans have long attributed aphrodisiac qualities to turtle eggs which they often eat raw or in seafood stews. However, the chances of survival for hatchling turtles are slim enough as it is.
· Please think carefully before setting out to the Pearl Cays – they may be among the most stunning offshore islands in Central America, but uncontrolled tourism here has seriously harmed local turtle populations.
· Please donate generously to turtle conservation projects, especially the Wildlife Conservation Society, www.wcs.org, who have a research station in Pearl Lagoon and are trying to develop ecologically aware tourism programmes for the Pearl Cays.

Cloudforest reserves
Given the the great challenges of visiting the hard-to-reach protected cloudforests of the Bosawás Reserve, the best place to enjoy the wildlife of the cloudforest is on the **Volcán Mombacho**, just outside Granada, and **Volcán Maderas** on Ometepe Island. In Matagalpa, the **Selva Negra Reserve** is also easy to access, as is the **Arenal Reserve** on the border of Jinotega and Matagalpa, and **El Jaguar** in Jinotega; another good option is the **Miraflor Reserve** in Estelí.

Rainforest reserves
With the two biggest rainforest reserves in Central America, Nicaragua is the place for the rainforest enthusiast who does not need luxury lodging. The best, for its access and reliable lodging, is **Indio-Maíz**. **Bosawás** is the biggest area of forest on the isthmus, accessible from the northern highlands or Caribbean side

of the country. Travel safety is an issue in the region and, although it is improving, this vast wilderness is generally the preserve of hardened adventure travellers. If you are planning to visit Bosawás, always check with MARENA in Managua to see which entrance to the park is most advisable. They can put you in contact with guides too, as well as supply maps.

Wetland reserves
Nothing can match the natural splendour of the wetlands in **Los Guatuzos**, which one US environmental writer called "one of the most beautiful places on earth". This wildlife refuge has only basic and rustic lodging, but it is well worth the effort to see its fauna.

National monument parks
Archipiélago Solentiname is great for culture lovers as well as birders. Solentiname's 36 islands are teeming with birdlife and are home to a very interesting community of rural artists. The fortress at **El Castillo** is an important historic landmark set on a beautiful hill above the majestic Río San Juan.

Books
& films

Anthropology

Field, LW *The Grimace of Macho Ratón* (Duke University, 1999). A cultural anthropological look at Nicaragua's national play, *El Güegüence*, and how it relates to Nicaraguan identity, in particular its effect on definitions of indigenous and mestizo in Pacific Nicaragua. This curious wandering work also focuses on Nicaragua's ceramic artisans as a model for understanding Nicaraguan social-behavioural traits, and on occasion slips into being a travel diary.

Gould, JL *To Die in this Way, Nicaraguan Indians and the Myth of Mestizaje 1880-1965* (Duke University Press, 1998). A fascinating, though academic, study of the tragic trajectory of Nicaragua's Pacific and central indigenous communities and the resulting effect on the definitions of the country's ethnic make-up. A very important work for anthropology and also for the history of Nicaragua and its injustice to its most vulnerable citizens. Despite the breadth and quality of the research, readers are still left wondering about the 'myth of *mestizaje*', and how should we define 'indigenous' in today's Nicaragua?

Lange, FW *Archaeology of Pacific Nicaragua* (University of New Mexico, 1992). Dr Lange is an expert on Nicaraguan archaeology. Though not meant as an introduction for the lay

person, this book is very interesting in its descriptions and observations about Nicaraguan archaeology in the extraordinarily ceramic-rich Pacific region.

Fiction

Belli, G *The Inhabited Women* (translated by Kathleen March, Warner Books, 1994). One of Nicaragua's most famous writer/poets, her work is famously sensual and this story is no exception. A yuppie turns revolutionary after being inspired by a native spirits tale. The hero joins an underground rebel group for a story based partially upon historic events. It works well, at least until its action-film ending, and is an enjoyable read, with some beautiful and magical prose.

Ramírez, S *To Bury Our Fathers* (translated by Nick Caistor, Readers International, 1993). Nicaragua's finest living author (see page 237) recounts life in the Somoza García period of Nicaragua, from the viewpoint of exiled rebels in Guatemala. Sergio Ramírez paints a detailed picture of the Nicaraguan character and humour.

Narratives and travelogues

Beals, C *Banana Gold* (JB Lippincott Company, 1932). A true jewel. Although half of the book gripes about the life of a journalist travelling through southern

Mexico and Central America, the half that deals with Beals' harrowing trip on horseback from Tegucigalpa to Sébaco during the war between Sandino and the US Marines is fascinating, humorous, tragic and beautiful. Beals' poetic prose further adds to the thrill as we ride along on his unrelenting quest to meet with August C Sandino and interview him. At once both a brilliant travel and political history work.

Cabezas, O *Fire from the Mountain* (translated by Kathleen Weaver, Crown Publishers, 1985). This first-hand account of a revolutionary rebel in the making, and later in action, was dictated into a tape recorder and reads like a long, tragic and often hilarious confession. This very honest book is a must for those who wish to get the feel of this time in Nicaraguan history and the irreverent Nicaraguan humour.

Rushdie, S *The Jaguar Smile* (Penguin Books, 1988). A detailed and entertaining account of Rushdie's visit to Nicaragua during the volatile Sandinista years.

Twain, M *Travels with Mr Brown* (Alfred A Knopf, 1940). Although his observations on Nicaragua make up only a small part of this book, Twain's irrepressible humour and use of language make this memoir an enjoyable read. Twain describes in detail the Nicaraguan inter-oceanic steamship route from San Francisco to New York, using the Río San Juan and Lake Nicaragua as a crossing from ocean to sea, which was so popular with gold-rushers at that time.

Walker, W *The War in Nicaragua* (University of Arizona Press, 1985). A reproduction of the 1860 original by the walking evil empire himself, General William Walker, who tried to annex Nicaragua to the USA in 1856.

Walker wrote the book in the USA while planning his final attack on Central America.

Nature

Belt, T *The Naturalist in Nicaragua* (University of Chicago, 1985). Reprint of a 1874 classic. Very enlightening in its observations of insect life and acute observations of 19th-century Nicaragua. Described by Charles Darwin as "the best of all natural history journals which have ever been published", this book by a mining engineer also sheds light on the mentality of a naturalist 130 years ago. Alongside brilliant and sensitive analytical observation, Belt freely admits beating his pet monkey and shooting dozens of birds and laments not bagging a giant jaguar he encounters in the forest.

Poetry

Darío, R *Selected Poems* (translated by Lysander Kemp, prologue by Octavio Paz, University of Texas, 1988). This attractive collection of some of Darío's best-known poems has the original Spanish and English translations on facing pages.

Gullette, DG, *!Gaspar! A Spanish Poet/Priest in the Nicaraguan Revolution* (Bilingual Press, 1993). A sentimental but balanced look at the Spanish Jesuit rebel-priest, Gaspar García Laviana, who died in action during the Revolution, a great hero among the poor of Nicaragua's southern Pacific coast during the 1970s. This volume includes poems about the plight of the Nicaraguan *campesino* in the original Spanish with English translations, as well as a biographical sketch and some humorous accounts of early botched battles.

Political history

Brody, R *Contra Terror in Nicaragua* (South End Press, 1985). Written at the height of the Contra War to demonstrate to the US Congress what was happening to the Nicaraguan public during the conflict, this is a graphic condemnation of the methods used by the Contra rebels during the war, often horrifying and tragic. A strong message directed at Ronald Reagan's many fans who must consider the full ramifications of his statement that the Contras were "the moral equivalent of our founding fathers".

Brown, TC *The Real Contra War* (University of Oklahoma Press, 2001). Written by a former 'Senior Liaison to the Contras for the US State Department' one would expect an apology for the Contras and that is exactly what one gets. However, the book grinds its axe with great elegance and brings to light some very little-known aspects of the grass-roots origins of the Contra rebellion. Well researched and a valuable counterweight to the numerous books batting on the other side of the fence.

Dickey, C *With the Contras* (Simon and Schuster, 1985). This is a mixture of journalism and sensationalist reporting, with the theme of the Contra insurgency and the US government's role in the war. Despite being too colourful for its own prose at times, the book manages to highlight many key characters in the conflict and exposes the difficulty of defining good and bad guys in real life war dramas. When Dickey enters the battlefield his self-satisfied irreverence cools off and he starts reporting. A valuable first-hand account.

Hodges, DC *Intellectual Foundations of the Nicaraguan Revolution* (University of Texas, 1986). An in-depth study of Nicaragua's 20th-century political players and the lead up to the Revolution of 1978-1979. A very good account of the nationalist hero Augusto Sandino. Written with a rare combination of balance and eloquence, this book is a must for those who wish to understand 20th-century Nicaraguan politics.

Kinzer, S *Blood of Brothers, Life and War in Nicaragua* (Doubleday, 1991). A landmark book on the Revolution and its aftermath. Kinzer spent many years in Nicaragua working for the *Boston Globe* and *New York Times* and aside from occasional fits of arrogance has produced one of the most interesting and informative books ever written by a foreigner about Nicaragua.

Mulligan, J *The Nicaraguan Church and the Revolution* (Sheep and Ward, 1991). Mulligan's book deals with liberation theology and its direct effect on the Nicaraguan Revolution and the local Catholic Church.

Pezzullo, L and R *At the Fall of Somoza* (University of Pittsburgh Press, 1993). Written by the last US Ambassador to Somoza's Nicaragua with the help of his son, this is a riveting book that is much more balanced and sympathetic to the Revolution than most would expect. Great writing on heroism during the rebellion and the head games of the US government and Somoza.

Zimmermann, M *Sandinista, Carlos Fonseca and the Nicaraguan Revolution* (Duke University Press, 2000). A very detailed biography of the founder of the FSLN who died before the final victory. A well-researched and interesting work.

Films

Cox, Alex *Walker* (USA, 1987). This counter-culture take on filibuster William Walker was shot in Nicaragua during the Contra War, mostly in Granada. Belonging to the creative sub-genre of 'acid western', it features a soundtrack by Joe Strummer and was so politically contentious at the time it earned director Alex Cox a lifetime place on the Hollywood blacklist.

Herzog, Werner *Ballad of the Little Soldier* (West Germany, 1984). In this arresting 45-min documentary, Herzog turned his attentions on Nicaragua's Miskito coast, focusing on child soldiers who had been enlisted by the Contras to fight against the Sandinistas. The film was described by the *New York Times* as "a lament about the idiotic state of the world and a praise of the human spirit."

Loach, Ken *Carla's Song* (Scotland, 1996). With big points for originality, this film ends up playing like a Sandinista party film. The film – a love story between a Glaswegian bus driver and a Nicaraguan immigrant – shows some great elements of Nicaraguan life in the 1980s.

Meiselas, Roberts and Guzetti *Pictures from a Revolution – A Memoir of the Nicaraguan Conflict* (USA, 1991). In 1978, the 30-year-old Susan Meiselas was an inexperienced documentary photographer who had never covered a major political story. Just after joining the most prestigious photo agency in the world, **Magnum**, she read about the assassination of the *La Prensa* editor Pedro Joaquín Chamorro and soon found herself in Managua with no knowledge of Spanish and doubts about what she was even to photograph there. When she returned from shooting the Nicaraguan Revolution, she had became a world-famous, award-winning war photographer. In this film she returns 10 years later to Nicaragua to find out what happened to her photo subjects.

Spottiswoode, Roger *Under Fire* (USA, 1983). Hollywood does the Nicaraguan Revolution. This film starring Nick Nolte and Gene Hackman is a hearty attempt at historical drama, with a lot of factual events being massaged to keep the necessary love story plot thumping along. Some details like authentic Nicaraguan beer and village street signs are made all the more impressive by the sad fact that not one scene was actually shot in Nicaragua. The murder by Somoza's army of a US journalist is factual, if twisted, and gives the movie a surprise element.

Practicalities

Getting there

Air

Managua is home to the country's only working international airport, Aeropuerto Internacional Agusto C Sandino. It handles direct flights from a limited range of carriers in the USA, Central and South America. Travellers outside those areas will usually have to transit in the US, but it is sometimes cheaper to fly into Costa Rica and catch a connecting bus from there. The city of Liberia is an hour and a half from the border with Nicaragua and is served by Delta, American and United Airlines among others.

Note all travellers to the US (including those in transit) who are eligible for a visa waiver must submit to the Electronic System for Travel Authorization (ESTA); see page 271.

Buying a ticket

Good deals are often hard to come by. Generally speaking local carriers **Avianca** and **Copa** are less expensive from the USA, Central and South America than US and European carriers, although code sharing means you can often combine the two from Europe.

TRAVEL TIP
Packing for Nicaragua

Travelling light is recommended. Your specific list will depend largely on what kind of travelling you plan to do. Cotton clothes are versatile and suitable for most situations. A hat, sun lotion and sunglasses will protect you from the instant grilling that the Nicaragua sun could cause. A light sweater or very light jacket is useful for those heading into the highlands or rainforest. English-language books are very rare in Nicaragua, so bring reading material with you. Contact-lens wearers and people with special medical needs must bring all prescription medicines and lens-cleaning products. If you intend to hike in the volcanoes you will need very sturdy, hard-soled trekking shoes, which should also ideally be lightweight and very breathable. A lightweight pack filled with energy bars and a flask is useful. Take mosquito netting if travelling on the cheap or to the jungle or Caribbean coastal regions. Wellington boots, worn by the locals in the countryside, will allow you to tackle any rainforest trail, and can be acquired at local markets. Insect repellent is a must in these areas. Rain poncho, zip-lock bags and heavy-duty bin liners/trash bags (for backpacks) are highly recommended for rainforest travel. A fairly powerful torch is useful all over Nicaragua's countryside as electric power is either irregular or non-existent. A penknife and a roll of duct tape are the traveller's indispensable, all-purpose items. For maps, see page 262.

Border cooperation

In June 2006, Guatemala, El Salvador, Honduras, and Nicaragua entered into a 'Central America-4 (CA-4) Border Control Agreement'. Under the terms of the agreement, citizens of the four countries may travel freely across land borders from one of the countries to any of the others without completing entry and exit formalities at immigration checkpoints. US citizens and other eligible foreign nationals, who legally enter any of the four countries, may similarly travel among the four without obtaining additional visas or tourist entry permits for the other three countries. Immigration officials at the first port of entry determine the length of stay, up to a maximum period of 90 days.

Flights from the UK There are no direct flights from the UK to Managua. British Airways uses Miami as a hub to connect with Central American carriers. Delta Airlines, United Airlines and American Airlines also fly from London to Managua via the US. Prices start at US$650.

Flights from the rest of Europe There are no direct flights to Managua from Europe and travellers are required to transit through the US or Central America. European carriers include Amsterdam-based KLM and the Spanish airline Iberia. Prices start at around US$600.

Flights from North America Several US carriers now fly directly to Managua, Nicaragua from a handful of US cities, including Delta Airlines from Atlanta and Los Angeles, United Airlines from Houston, Avianca from Miami, American Airlines from Miami, Dallas and Fort Worth, Spirit Airlines from Fort Lauderdale and Houston, and Air Transat from Montreal and Toronto.

Flights from Australia and New Zealand The most efficient route to Nicaragua from Australia, at a cost of around US$1800, is direct from Sydney with Qantas to Los Angeles, then to Houston with United Airlines for a direct flight from Houston to Managua or a TACA flight to Managua via El Salvador. From Auckland with the same connections and routes the fare comes to about US$1600.

Flights from Central America and Mexico Avianca flies to Managua from all countries in Central America several times daily, as does the Panamanian carrier COPA, with superior in-flight service to Managua from Guatemala and Panama. Additionally, Aerocaribbean flies from Havana, Cuba and Aeroméxico from Mexico City. There are no budget airlines in Central America and both Avianca and Copa represent poor value.

BORDER CROSSINGS

Honduras–Nicaragua

Guasaule

There are good roads at this crossing, the preferred route of international buses. If driving, it might be worth hiring a 'helper' to steer you through the formalities. There is a bank by Nicaraguan immigration and lots of money-changers (beware children trying to distract you while you make the transaction). Both Honduran and Nicaraguan immigration are open 0800–1600. On the Nicaraguan side, there are buses to Chinandega and León every 30 minutes, one to two hours, along with a few direct services to Managua. In Honduras, there are regular buses to Choluteca, 45 minutes.

Las Manos–Ocotal

This is recommended as the best route if travelling between the capital cities of Managua and Tegucigalpa. If driving, *tramitadores* will help you through the paperwork (for a US$5 tip). Both Honduran and Nicaraguan immigration are open 0800–1600. Exchange rates are better on the Nicaraguan side. Buses to run Ocotal in Nicaragua every 30 minutes, from there you can connect to Estelí or Managua. In Honduras, there are direct connections to Tegucigalpa.

El Espino–Somoto

Border formalities are reportedly very tedious at this crossing. There are places to eat, but no hotels at the border itself. In Nicaragua, buses run from the border to Somoto every 30 minutes; taxis also run, but beware of overcharging. There are roughly six daily buses to Managua, 3½ hours. In Honduras, taxis and minibuses shuttle passengers from the border to Choluteca.

Leimus–Waspam

This is a hardcore crossing in the heart of the Mosquitia and not for fainthearted. You are strongly advised to seek up-to-date advice from immigration officials before attempting the crossing as it may be impossible to travel between border posts on the same day, requiring additional paperwork. There are no banks or ATMs in the region so bring all the cash you need. Shop owners in Waspam may change currency. In Honduras, obtain your stamps in Puerto Lempira. There is no known immigration office in Waspam, the nearest may be in Bilwi (Puerto Cabezas), a gruelling six hours away on rough dirt roads, which may be impassable in wet season. In Honduras, Leimus has road connections with Puerto Lempira.

Airport information

Managua's **Aeropuerto Internacional Agusto C Sandino** ⓘ *www.eaai.com.ni*, is a small but modern international airport with a range of amenities including parking, restaurants, souvenirs shops, car rental agencies, a tourist information booth and ATMs. The airport is situated on the Carretera Norte about 20 minutes

BORDER CROSSINGS

Nicaragua–Costa Rica

Entry requirements for Costa Rica include proof of funds (US$300) and an onward ticket.

Peñas Blancas

This is the only Nicaragua–Costa Rica road crossing. It's hectic on the Nicaragua side with lots of helpers and hustlers who may try to sell you forms and paperwork; no purchase is necessary, however, as these are free at the immigration window. There's a branch of BCR in the customs building and no shortage of money changers, but beware being short changed. Immigration on both sides is open Monday-Saturday 0600-2200, Sunday 0600-2000. International buses are subject to customs searches. On the Nicaraguan side, there is a municipality tax, US$1 plus exit tax US$2 or entrance tax, US$12. On the Costa Rican side, the exit tax is US$7, payable at a machine with passport and credit card only. If your passport in not readable, pay at the BCR. Onwards to Costa Rica, several daily express buses depart from behind the immigration terminal, five to six hours; also to Liberia, every 30-60 minutes, 1½ hours. To Nicaragua there are buses to Rivas every 30 minutes, where you can catch connections to Granada, Managua, or Isla Ometepe. For San Juan del Sur, exit at La Virgen. Direct buses also run from Peñas Blancas to Managua, every 30 minutes, 3½ hours.

Los Chiles–San Carlos

This crossing was opened in 2015 thanks to a new Japanese-built bridge over the Río San Juan. It has rendered the classic river crossing redundant. The bridge starts in Santa Fe, approximately 28 km from San Carlos on paved highways; regular buses from San Carlos. On the other side, you'll find the Nicaraguan immigration office at the border in Las Tablillas, 0800-1600. Entrance tax to Nicaragua, US$12 plus US$2 aduana fee. Exit tax for Costa Rica is US$7. There is an ATM near the immigration office. Onwards to Costa Rica, buses run to La Quesada with many onward services to La Fortuna. Onwards to Nicaragua, from San Carlos you can travel east up the Río San Juan or north towards Managua.

from the city centre and you are strongly advised to use officially licensed taxis working the grounds. The domestic terminal is located next to the main terminal in a separate building. See also page 51.

BORDER CROSSINGS

El Salvador–Nicaragua

La Unión–Potosí

It is possible to travel between El Salvador and Nicaragua by crossing the Gulf of Fonseca between La Unión and Potosí. Depending on demand, tour operators offer the trip two to three times a week. The journey takes four hours including two hours for formalities, US$65 one-way, with onward connections to León, San Salvador and Suchitoto. Try Ruta del Golfo, www.rutadelgolfo.com, T2315-4099. Note the route is much more expensive than going overland, but not necessarily faster. You may get a cheaper deal by gathering a group and negotiating with local boatmen (US$60-100), but check the vessel is seaworthy and includes life jackets. Salvadorean immigration is located in La Unión next to the post office, Avenida General Cabañas and Calle 7a Poniente, T2604-4375, 0600-2200. Onward transport in Nicaragua includes onward buses to Chinandega, three hours, but tour operators can include shuttles with your passage. In El Salvador, there is a bus to San Salvador every 30 minutes. There are also regular buses to the beaches and San Miguel.

Road

Bus

International buses are a cheap and efficient way to travel between Nicaragua and other Central American countries. Buses are available to and from Honduras, El Salvador, Guatemala, Costa Rica and Panama. When leaving Managua you will need to check in one hour in advance with your passport and ticket. International bus lines include **Ticabus** ⓘ *Antiguo Cine Dorado, 2 c arriba, T2298-5500, www.ticabus.com*, which travels to Mexico, Honduras, El Salvador, Guatemala, Costa Rica and Panama; **Transnica**, ⓘ *Rotonda Metrocentro, 300 m norte, 25 m este, T8287-1188, www.transnica.com*, with services to Honduras and Costa Rica; **Transporte del Sol** ⓘ *Antiguo Cine Dorado, 2 c arriba, T2222-4420, www.transportedelsol.com*, with services to El Salvador, Guatemala and Costa Rica; and **Platinum** ⓘ *end of Calle 27 de Mayo, opposite Plaza Inter, T2222-3065, www.platinumcentroamerica.com*, with services to Honduras, El Salvador and Guatemala. The buses all have air conditioning, toilet and reclining seats; most have TV screens and offer snacks. Additionally, some tour operators offer international shuttles (combi vans) between Nicaragua and neighbouring countries. In Costa Rica, one option is Fortuna-based **Agua Trails** ⓘ *5 km east of Fortuna, next to ice factory QR, T506-2479-8667, www.aguatrails.com*, which offers transfers from Costa Rica to Managua, Granada, San Juan del Sur and San Carlos.

Car and motorcycle

There are three main land crossings into Nicaragua from Honduras, plus one more remote route; see box, page 255.

The only road crossing that connects Nicaragua to Costa Rica and unites Central America via road is at **Peñas Blancas** (see box, page 256), 144 km south of Managua.

Sea and river

It is possible to enter Nicaragua at **Potosí** by boat from El Salvador; see box, page 257.

Getting around

A decent road system covers the west of Nicaragua and the country's small size makes car or bus travel practical and fairly simple. Buses run between all Pacific and central cities and villages on a daily basis and fares are very cheap. A 4WD is needed to get off the beaten path in all parts of the country. Boat and plane are the only options for long-distance travel on the Caribbean coast and in the rainforest areas of the north and south where roads are generally horrible to non-existent.

Air

La Costeña ① *T2298-5360, www.lacostena.com.ni*, operates services to Bluefields, Corn Island, Bilwi (also known as Puerto Cabezas), Bonanza, Siuna and Waspam. (see Managua Transport, page 51, and other relevant chapters for details). At the time of research, flights to Isla Ometepe, Rosita, San Juan del Nicaragua (also known as San Juan de Norte) and San Carlos had been suspended, but may resume in the future with enough demand; contact La Costeña for the latest news. No seat assignments are given and flights are often fully booked or overbooked – always allow for possible delays of up to 48 hours. Early arrival at the airport is essential and La Costeña now requires you to check in two hours prior to departure. Note that domestic return flights should always be reconfirmed immediately on arrival at a destination in order to be assured a seat on your chosen date. The stowed luggage maximum is 13.6 kg on most flights. Domestic departure tax is US$2.

Road

The road network has been greatly extended and improved in recent years. The Pan-American Highway from Honduras to Costa Rica is paved the whole way (384 km), as is the shorter international road to the Honduran frontier via Chinandega. The road between Managua and Rama (for boat access to Bluefields) is paved, but not in good condition. A high proportion of Nicaragua's roads are unpaved with lots of mud bogs in the wet season and dusty washboard and stone-filled paths in the dry season. Be flexible with your schedules.

Bus

Local buses are the cheapest in Central America and often the most crowded. This is how most Nicaraguans get around and schedules are pretty reliable except on Sundays. It is best to arrive early for all long-distance buses, especially if it is an express or an infrequent service. On routes that leave every hour or half-hour you only need to check the destination above the front window of the bus and grab a seat. You can flag down most buses that are not marked 'Express'. Fares are collected as you board city buses and en route on intercity buses. For some express buses, you need to purchase your ticket in advance at the terminal or from the driver; some buses have reserved seating. Baggage loaded on to the roof or in the luggage compartment may be charged for, usually at half the passenger rate or a flat fee of US$0.50.

Most Nicaraguan buses are 'retired' US school buses and have very limited legroom. Sitting behind the driver may alleviate this problem for tall passengers and is a good idea if you plan to get off before the final destination.

Buses often fill up to the roof and can be very hot and bumpy, but they are a great way to meet and get to know the Nicaraguan people. Most major destinations have an express minibus service, which makes fewer stops and travels faster; for longer journeys a minibus could mean cutting travel times in half.

Car
Petrol stations are very rare in the countryside; it's best to fill up the tank (unleaded, premium grade fuel and diesel are available everywhere) if going into the interior. There are 24-hour petrol stations in the major cities, elsewhere they close at 1800. 4WD drive for travel within the Pacific Basin is not necessary, although it does give you dramatically more flexibility across the country and is standard equipment in mountain and jungle territory.

It is obligatory to wear a seatbelt. You may be stopped on a routine check and the law states that all cars must carry an emergency triangle reflector and fire extinguisher. Note that in Nicaragua you must hold your lane for 30 m before and after a signal. If you are involved in a car accident where someone is injured, you may be held for up to two days, guilty or not, while blame is assessed. Hiring a driver covers this potentially disastrous liability. Be careful when driving at night, few roads are lit and there are many people, animals and holes in the road. See also Police and the law, page 269.

Car hire While not everyone has the time or inclination to travel with their own car, the freedom that goes with renting for a few days is well worth considering, especially if you can get a group of three or four together to share the cost. The main international car hire companies operate in Nicaragua, but tend to be expensive. Most agents have an office at the international airport and offices in other parts of Managua. Hotels and tourist agencies will tell you where to find cheaper rates, but you will need to check that you have such basics as a spare wheel, toolkit, functioning lights, etc. If you plan to do a lot of driving and will have time at the end to dispose of it, investigate the possibility of buying a secondhand car locally; since hiring is so expensive it may work out cheaper and will probably do you just as well.

Renting a vehicle costs around US$25-40 a day for a basic car, rising to US$60-100 for a 4WD. Weekly discount rates are significant and if you want to cover a lot of sites quickly it can be worthwhile. A minimum deposit of US$500 is required in addition to an international driver's licence or a licence from your country of origin.

Insurance is US$10-25 depending on cover. Before signing up check the insurance and what it covers and also ask about mileage allowance.

Cycle

Unless you are planning a journey almost exclusively on paved roads – when a high-quality touring bike would probably suffice – a mountain bike is strongly recommended. If you hire one, look for a good-quality, rugged bike with low gear ratios for difficult terrain, wide tyres with plenty of tread for good road-holding, cantilever brakes and a low centre of gravity for improved stability. Imported bike parts are impossible to find in Nicaragua so buy everything you need before you leave home. Most towns have a bicycle shop of some description, but it is best to do your own repairs and adjustments whenever possible. Take care to avoid dehydration by drinking regularly. In hot, dry areas with limited water supplies, be sure to carry an ample supply on the bike. Because of traffic it is usually more rewarding to keep to the smaller roads or to paths. Watch for oncoming, overtaking vehicles, protruding or unstable loads on trucks. Make yourself conspicuous by wearing bright clothing and a helmet.

Hitchhiking

Hitchhiking is a common way to travel in the countryside, less so in the cities and on regular bus routes. Men will find it significantly more difficult to get a ride if they do not have a female companion. Pick-up trucks are the best bet, you should offer to help pay for fuel. Picking up hitchhikers is a great way to make friends, but not advisable if there is more than one man, unaccompanied by at least one woman. In the deep countryside it is considered quite rude not to offer a ride if you have room, particularly for women with babies. Note there are always risks associated with hitchhiking and it is not recommended for lone women.

Shuttles

On some fixed routes, shuttle buses (combis) are the de facto 'express' option. They are safer, quicker and more comfortable than chicken buses and worth the extra córdobas. Numerous tour operators also offer daily 'tourist' shuttles between Managua, Granada, Masaya, San Jorge (Isla Ometepe), León and San Juan del Sur. These services pick you up from your hotel and are the safest and easiest way to get around the country, but they are not cheap. One option is **Nica Shuttle**, www.nicashuttle.com.

Truck

In many rural areas and some cities, flat-bed trucks – usually covered with a tarpaulin and often with bench seating – are used for getting to places inaccessible by bus or to fill in routes where no buses are available. The trucks charge a fixed fare and, apart from eating a bowlful of dust in the dry season or getting soaked in the wet, they can be a great way to see the country. Communication with the driver can be difficult, so make sure you know more or less where you are going; other passengers will be able to tell you where to jump off. Banging the roof of the driver's cabin is often necessary to tell the driver he has arrived at your destination.

Sea and river

In a country with two oceans, two great lakes and numerous lagoons, estuaries and rivers, a boat is never far away and is often the only means of travel. The main Pacific ports are Corinto, San Juan del Sur and Puerto Sandino. The two main Atlantic ports are Bilwi and Bluefields. Public river boats are often slow but private boats can be hired at some expense if you are short on time, travelling in a large group, wish to view wildlife or want to make stops along the way. There are regular services between the two Corn Islands and a big boat runs from Bluefields to Big Corn three or four times a week. Apart from the Bluefields route and regular high-speed *panga* services to Pearl Lagoon, boat travel along the Pacific and Caribbean coasts is usually difficult.

Maps

Since road signage is weak, it is important to have a map and some basic Spanish to get even a little way off the main highway. Unfortunately, detailed road maps are yet to be adopted in Nicaragua and internationally produced maps are often poor quality, but they are improving. **National Geographic Adventure**, **Reise Know-How** and **International Travel Maps** have all produced worthy efforts – look for them in book stores before leaving home. Detailed maps (1:50,000) can also be bought at the government geological survey office, **INETER** ① *across from the Nicaraguan Immigration main office in Managua, T2249-3590*, useful if you are planning to escape the beaten track and/or go trekking.

Essentials A-Z

Accident and emergency

Police: 118. **Fire**: 115. **Ambulance**: 128.
In case of emergency, contact the
relevant emergency service and your
embassy (see page 264) and make sure
that you obtain police/medical reports
in order to file insurance claims.

Children

Nicaragua is not a difficult country
to travel in with children and the
Nicaraguan people, renowned for
their kindness and openness, are
even friendlier if you have kids in tow.
However, the lack of sophisticated
medical services in rural Nicaragua
can make travelling with babies less
attractive. Travel outside Managua, León
and Granada is not recommended for
people with children under 2. Children
over the age of 5 will find much of
interest, not least Nicaraguan children
of their own age. Many of the luxuries
taken for granted at home (eg snacks)
will be unavailable, so warn your children
in advance. Hotels do not charge for
children under 2 and offer a discount
rate for 2-11 year olds; those aged 12
and above are charged as adults.

Very small children sitting on their
parent's lap should travel free on public
buses and boats. On internal flights
children under the age of 2 pay 10%
the normal fare; 2-11 year olds pay 50%
and anyone aged 12 or older pays the
adult fares.

The website **www.babygoes2.com**
has useful advice about travelling
with children.

Customs and duty free

Duty free import of 200 cigarettes or
500 g of tobacco, 3 litres of alcoholic
drinks and 1 large bottle (or 3 small
bottles) of perfume is permitted. Avoid
buying products made from snakeskin,
crocodile skin, black coral, turtle shell
or other protected species on sale in
some Nicaraguan markets; apart from
the fact that they may be derived from
endangered species, there may be
laws in your home country outlawing
their import. Note that taking pre-
Columbian or early colonial pieces out
of Nicaragua is illegal and could result
in 2 years in prison.

Disabled travellers

Nicaragua is not an ideal place for
disabled travellers. The country has
very little in the way of conveniences
for disabled people, despite the fact
that many Nicaraguans were left
permanently disabled by the war years
of the late 1970s and 1980s. Outside
of Managua Nicaraguans are warm,
helpful people and sympathetic to
disabilities. Emotional solidarity may
not compensate, however, for lack
of wheelchair ramps, user-friendly
bathrooms and hotel rooms designed
for the disabled. There are elevators in
the international airport and hotels such
as the **Holiday Inn** and **Crowne Plaza**;
the **Hotel Seminole Plaza** has special
rooms for the disabled on its 1st floor
at a slightly higher cost. Nicaraguan
public buses are not designed for
wheelchair users, but most long-haul

bus attendants will be helpful with travellers who need extra help – if you arrive early. The local airline **La Costeña** has small Cessna aircraft that use a drop-down door ladder, but they are also very helpful with passengers in need of assistance. If using a tour operator it would be wise to book a private tour to assure proper flexibility. For wildlife viewing the Solentiname and Río San Juan areas are ideal as there is a great deal of nature to be seen by boat throughout the region, though private transportation on the river and lake is essential.

Dress

Most Nicaraguans make an effort to dress well whatever their economic means. In particularly rural or conservative areas, a very scruffy or dirty appearance may raise an eyebrow or two. Women should be aware that topless bathing is unacceptable and that short skirts tend to elicit a great deal of attention from men. Male travellers shouldn't expose their chests anywhere but on the beach. Everyone must dress respectfully when entering rural churches.

Drugs

Recreational drugs of any kind are illegal in Nicaragua and society puts marijuana in the same category as heroin – and prosecutes accordingly. If you find yourself in any trouble with the law, drug-related or otherwise, contact your embassy or consulate in Managua right away. They may or may not be sympathetic to your plight, but they should at least be able to put you in touch with a lawyer.

Electricity

Voltage is 110 volts AC, 60 cycles, and US-style plugs are used throughout the country.

Embassies and consulates

For a list of Nicaraguan embassies abroad, see http://embassygoabroad.com.

Health

See your GP or travel clinic at least 6 weeks before departure for general advice on travel risks and vaccinations. Try a specialist travel clinic if your own GP is unfamiliar with health conditions in Nicaragua. Make sure you have sufficient medical travel insurance, get a dental check, know your own blood group and if you suffer a long-term condition such as diabetes or epilepsy, obtain a Medic Alert bracelet/necklace (www.medicalert.co.uk). If you wear glasses, take a copy of your prescription.

Vaccinations

No vaccinations are specifically required to enter Nicaragua, however, most doctors will recommend immunization against tetanus, diptheria, hepatitis A, hepatitis B, typhoid and, in some cases, rabies. In addition, yellow fever vaccination is required if entering from an infected area (ie parts of South America). The final decision, however, should be based on a consultation with your GP or travel clinic. In all cases you should confirm your primary courses and boosters are up to date.

Health risks

The major health risks posed are those caused by insect disease carriers such as mosquitoes and sandflies, especially during the wet season and east of the great lakes and Nicaragua's Caribbean coast. The key parasitic and viral diseases are **malaria**, **Chagas disease** (South American tyrpanosomiasis) and dengue fever. **Dengue fever** is increasingly present, including in Managua; it is particularly hard to protect against as the mosquitoes can bite throughout the day as well as at night (unlike those that carry malaria and Chagas disease). Cases of the **Zika virus**, similarly spread, have also been reported in Nicaragua. Try to wear clothes that cover arms and legs and also use effective mosquito repellent. Mosquito nets dipped in permethrin provide a good physical and chemical barrier at night.

Some form of **diarrhoea** or intestinal upset is almost inevitable, the standard advice is to be careful with drinking water and ice; if you have any doubts about the water then boil it or filter and treat it. In a restaurant buy bottled water or ask where the water has come from. Tap water is not recommended for drinking outside Managua, León and Granada. Food can also pose a problem, be wary of salads if you don't know whether they have been washed or not. Intestinal parasites are relatively common in rural areas with symptoms including profuse diarrhoea and/or vomiting. For a proper diagnosis, submit stool samples to a local laboratory for up to 5 consecutive days – if the results are positive, consult a doctor for immediate antibiotic treatment.

There is a constant threat of **tuberculosis** (TB) and although the BCG vaccine is available, it is still not guaranteed protection. It is best to avoid unpasteurized dairy products and try not to let people cough and splutter all over you.

Further information

www.btha.org British Travel Health Association.

www.cdc.gov US government site that gives excellent advice on travel health and details of disease outbreaks.

www.fco.gov.uk British Foreign and Commonwealth Office travel site has useful information on each country, people, climate and a list of UK embassies/consulates.

www.fitfortravel.scot.nhs.uk A-Z of vaccine/health advice for each country.

Insurance

Always take out travel insurance before you set off and read the small print carefully. Check that the policy covers the activities you intend or may end up doing. Also check exactly what your medical cover includes (eg ambulance, helicopter rescue or emergency flights back home). Also check the payment protocol. You may have to cough up first before the insurance company reimburses you. To be safe, it is always best to dig out all the receipts for expensive personal effects like jewellery or cameras. Take photos of these items and note down all serial numbers.

Internet

Since most Nicaraguans can't afford computers there is no shortage of internet cafés offering full computer services. Many internet cafés also offer low-rate international telephone services and internet calls (Skype) through their hook-ups. Almost all lodgings now offer Wi-Fi, but connections are not always reliable and signals may only reach communal areas.

TRAVEL TIP

Nicañol: Nicaraguan Spanish

You've done your Spanish course and you're ready to chat up the Nicaraguan people. But wait, what's that? ¿Cómo, perdón? Err…¿Qué dice?

It seems all that hard work in class has yet to pay off. Nicaraguans (Nicas) are famous for their creativity and humour and this carries over to their use of the Spanish language, nothing is sacred. In fact the Nicaraguans are credited with hundreds of words unique to their inventive, heavily indigenous-influenced version of Spanish. Here are some essentials for a head start, ¡dale pues! (go for it!):

Nica-speak	Meaning		
chele	white person	jaño/a	boyfriend/girlfriend
chapín	barefoot	palmado	broke, penniless
charula	worthless thing	pinche	stingy
chiringo	old clothes	tapudo	big-mouth
cipote	little boy	tuanis	cool
fachento	arrogant	turcazo	hard punch

Language

Spanish is spoken widely throughout Nicaragua and, while you will be able to get by without knowledge of Spanish, you will probably become frustrated and feel helpless in many situations. A pocket dictionary and phrase book together with some initial study or a beginner's Spanish course before you leave are strongly recommended. If you have the time, book 1-2 weeks of classes at the beginning of your travels. Granada has a reputation for language classes and the better-known centres normally include a wide range of cultural activities and supporting options for homestays. A less well-known centre is likely to have fewer English speakers around. For details, see Language schools in the What to do sections of individual towns and cities.

Understanding Nicaraguan Spanish can be difficult for many non-fluent speakers (see box, above). However, people are usually helpful and happy to repeat themselves. English will generally only be spoken in the more upmarket hotels in Managua, Granada and León, as well as at tour operators and car rental agencies. On the Caribbean coast Spanish, Creole English, Mayagna, Rama and Miskito are all spoken. See also page 275.

LGBT travellers

There are very small gay scenes in Managua, Granada, San Juan del Sur and León, but it is important to bear in mind that many rural areas remain decidedly macho and quite conservative in outlook. Whilst you do not need to conceal your sexuality, be aware that public displays of gay affection may not always be received warmly. By the same token, some gay travellers have reported almost constant amorous attentions from heterosexual men. The best advice is to relax, proceed carefully and play it by ear. For more general information, try the **International Gay and Lesbian Travel Association**, www.iglta.org.

Media

Newspapers and magazines

The country's oldest and most influential daily is **La Prensa**, www.laprensa.com.ni, centre-right in leaning; though normally anti-Sandinista they are willing to criticize all politicians. The other major daily is centre-left **El Nuevo Diario**, www.elnuevo diario.com.ni, which, despite a tendency to be sensationalist and focus on crime news, does have some very good provincial coverage. **El 19**, www.el19digital.com is a left-leaning daily news source available only in digital format. There are numerous weekly papers which are generally hard to find outside Managua or are only available on-line. They include **Confidencial**, www.confidencial.com.ni, an investigative news magazine edited by Carlos Fernando Chamorro, son of the assassinated La Prensa director.

Radio

Since the volatile days leading up to the success of the Revolution, when the mobile station Radio Sandino kept the rebels and population up to date on the fighting and where to attack next, radio has been an essential means of transmitting the latest in events to Nicaraguans. **Radio Sandino** (AM 740) has long since been above-ground and can be found just north of the Mirador Tiscapa restaurant in Managua, though the populist voice of the FSLN, **Radio La Nueva Radio Ya** (AM 600), is the number-one rated. The polar opposite to the Sandinista radio stations has always been **Radio Corporación** (AM 540),

Nicaragua's oldest station, which holds the Liberal Party line.

Television

Visitors are quite often amazed at the penetration of television in Nicaragua. The most out-of-the-way, humble of homes are wired-up and tuned in nightly to the collective passion of after-dark viewing, the *telenovela* (or soap). The most influential station is **Canal 2** which has good nightly news broadcasts (1830 and 2200 weekdays). The Sandinista **Canal 4** has news broadcasts weekdays at 1830 and **Canal 8** has the most bloody of the sensationalist newscasts that are sweeping Nicaragua television at 1800 nightly.

Money

US$=C$33; £1=C$42.5; E1=C$36.8 (Apr 2019)
For up-to-the-minute exchange rates visit www.xe.com.

Currency

The unit of currency is the **córdoba** (C$), divided into 100 centavos. Notes are used for 10, 20, 50, 100 and 500 córdobas and coins for 1 and 5 córdobas and 5, 10, 25 and 50 centavos. 100 córdoba notes can be a problem to change for small purchases, buses and taxis, so use them at supermarkets as well as in restaurants and hotels and hang on to the smaller notes for other purchases. Nicaraguans often use the generic term 'pesos' to describe the córdoba. 'Cinco reales' means 50 centavos. On the Caribbean coast 'bucks' means córdobas.

Exchange

For money exchange, it is not possible to change currencies other than US dollars and euros (**BanCentro** only) and identification is required. It's usually quicker and easier to change money with 'coyotes' on the street, but calculate what you expect to receive before handing over any cash and carefully count what they give you before walking away. You can pay for almost anything in US dollars as well, but the exchange rate will be unfavourable, change will be given in córdobas and anything larger than a US$5 note may trigger a change crisis. Also, only notes in mint condition will be accepted. Avoid 500 córdoba notes as no-one will have change for one.

Credit cards, debit card and ATMs

Traveller's cheques (TCs) are a nuisance in Nicaragua, with only 2 banks and 1 *casa de cambio* willing to cash them. **VISA**, **MasterCard** and **American Express** are widely accepted with VISA being the most prevalent. ATM machines are increasingly common, easily found in Managua and other major cities. Debit cards using the Cirrus and MasterCard credit systems work with the 'Red Total' or 'Credomatic' which can be found in shopping malls, **Banco de América Central** (**BAC**) and **Uno** and **Puma** station stores. However, it would be unwise to rely too heavily on debit/credit cards; if there are communication problems with the outside world, which is not uncommon, Nicaraguan ATMs will not approve the transaction and you will have to try again later. For this reason, never allow your cash to run out, especially when travelling between places. Take all the cash you need (and some more) when visiting the Atlantic departments and Río San Juan region, which have limited or no ATM facilities.

Currency cards

If you don't want to carry lots of cash, prepaid currency cards allow you to preload money from your bank account, fixed at the day's exchange rate. They look like a credit or debit card and are issued by specialist money-changing companies, such as **Travelex** and **Caxton FX**, as well as the **Post Office**. You can top up and check your balance by phone, online and sometimes by text.

Cost of living and travelling

Most visitors to Nicaragua are surprised to find prices higher than expected and the country is no longer the great bargain it once was. The cost of public transport, however, ranges from reasonable to very cheap. A normal taxi fare is US$1-2 with buses costing less than US$1 in almost all domestic cases. The cost of local flights is rising with oil prices, starting at around US$120 for a round-trip from Managua. Car rental is comparable with other countries around the world. Food can be cheap depending on the quality: dishes from street vendors cost from US$1-3; moderate restaurants have marginally more healthy fare that ranges from US$3-6; and quality restaurants charge US$6-12 per dish. Fresh fruit from the markets remains abundant and cheap. As a rule, hotels in Nicaragua are not great value and those in Managua tend to be overpriced; anything under US$30 in the capital usually means very poor quality. Outside Managua, hotels are more reasonable and you can find some very good deals in all price brackets.

Opening hours

Banks Mon-Fri 0830-1200 and 1400-1600, Sat 0830-1200/1300. **Churches** Usually open daily during the daytime but be respectful when entering during services if you only want to look around. **Government offices** Officially open Mon-Fri 0800-1700, but many close at lunchtime.

Police and the law

You may well be asked for identification at any time, and if you cannot produce it you will be jailed. In the event of a vehicle accident in which anyone is injured, all drivers involved are automatically detained until blame has been established (see page 260). It's best to carry an international driver's license to avoid losing your normal one. Never offer a bribe unless you are fully conversant with the customs of the country. Do not assume that an official who accepts a bribe is prepared to do anything else that is illegal. If an official suggests that a bribe must be paid before you can proceed on your way, be patient (assuming you have the time) and they may relent. Note that Nicaraguan police pride themselves on being the least corrupt in Latin America, and as such, they generally do not ask for bribes.

Post

Correos de Nicaragua, www.correos. gob.ni, is very slow but reliable. The average time for a letter to the USA is 18 days while European letters normally take 7-10 days. The cost of mailing normal-sized letters is: US$0.80 to Europe, US$0.55 to North America and just over US$1 to Australia and Asia. Parcels should be left open to be inspected and sealed at the post office. Courier services from Nicaragua, available from companies like DHL and UPS, are expensive.

Safety

Crime is not a major issue for visitors to Nicaragua as long as sensible precautions are taken. Money belts and leg pouches are useful, but keep small amounts of cash in your pocket. Spreading money and credit cards around different parts of your body and bags is a good idea.

Don't try to mount Managua's overflowing buses with luggage or rucksacks. Pickpocketing and bag slashing occur in Managua in crowded places, and on buses throughout the country. Once settled in a hotel, the best way to get around town is by bus or taxi during the daytime and by taxi at night. **Note** Managua taxis are now a risk in themselves and you should take extreme care when using them. Avoid dark areas and places that are not full of people. Do not wander the streets of Managua after dark. Most other town centres are safe to stroll until about 2300, but common sense rules apply. Bus stops are notorious hotspots for pickpockets.

Outside Managua Nicaragua is pretty safe, but there are theives in Granada and Estelí and pickpockets throughout the country. Public buses in the north central and northeastern extremes of Nicaragua are subject to hold-ups by thieves. Most beaches are no go at night, and some should be approached cautiously in the day; seek local advice before setting out. Most country bars should be avoided on Sun when fights often break out. See specific chapters for relevant warnings. Rape is not a common threat for travellers in Nicaragua, although normal precautions should be taken. See also Women travellers, page 272.

In hotels hide valuables away in cases or in safe deposit boxes. Budget travellers should bring locks for doors and luggage. If something goes missing ask the hotel manager to investigate and then ask them to call the police if nothing can be resolved.

Student travellers

If you are in full-time education you will be entitled to an **International Student Identity Card (ISIC)**, www. isic.org, which is distributed by student travel offices and travel agencies in 77 countries. The ISIC gives you discounted prices on all forms of public transport and access to a variety of other concessions and services.

Tax

There is an arrival tax of US$10 payable at immigration when you enter Nicaragua by air and a departure tax of US$42 payable at the airline check-in counter when you leave (although it's often included in the price of your ticket). All hotels, restaurants and shops charge 15% IVA (VAT).

Telephone

The Nicaraguan telephone company, **ENITEL**, is now owned by the behemoth international phone network, Claro. They have offices in all cities and most towns and theirs is often the only telephone in a small village. Calls can be placed to local or international destinations with pre-payment for an allotted amount of time. To make a reverse-charge (collect) call to any country in the world you will need to name the country in Spanish and say 'una llamada por cobrar'. The average rate for direct calls to Europe or the USA is about US$3 for the 1st min and then US$1 per min thereafter; collect calls cost more. **US operators**: dial 171 for Sprint, 174 for AT&T and 166 for MCI. **European operators**: for Belgium dial 172; Canada 168; Germany 169; The Netherlands 177; Spain 162; and the UK 175. Public phones accept phonecards, which are available for purchase in petrol station convenience stores.

Phone numbers in Nicaragua have 8 digits; landlines are preceded by the digit 2, mobiles by 8. To make international calls from Nicaragua, dial 00 and then the country code. To call into Nicaragua, dial your international access then 505 and the number, minus the 1st zero.

Claro sells pre-pay mobile phones at affordable prices, as does their competitor, **Movistar**, although their network is not as comprehensive. When you need to top up credit, you can buy a *recarga* from *pulperías* or wherever you see a sign. Some networks, eg **O2**, provide an app so you can use the time on your contract in your home country if you access the app via Wi-Fi.

Internet calls (eg via **Skype**, **Whatsapp** and **Viber**) are also possible if you have access to Wi-Fi.

Time

The official time is 6 hrs behind GMT (7 hrs during daylight saving). Note that a European or North American sense of punctuality does not exist in Nicaragua.

Tipping

The 10% service charge often included in restaurant bills in tourist hubs is not mandatory, although most people choose to pay it. This charge usually goes to the owners, so if you want to tip a waiter or waitress it's best to give it to them directly. For porters at the airport or in an upmarket hotel the normal tip is US$0.50 per bag. Taxi drivers do not expect tips unless hired out on an hourly or daily basis. About US$0.20 is usual for people who offer to look after your car (usually unnecessary, but a way to make a living). The going rate for local guides at national parks is US$5 or more, while kids in the market who help you with translations expect about US$3-5. A tip of anything lower than 5 córdobas will likely be considered an insult.

Tourist information

Useful websites

www.nicanet.org The latest activist issues.

www.nicaragua.com General English language website that gives a good overview of the country.

www.vianica.com A very handy website that has good travel information including bus schedules and descriptions of popular attractions.

www.visitanicaragua.com The government tourist board is a good place to start.

Tour operators

Many tour operators specializing in Latin American travel will arrange trips to Nicaragua if requested, although sadly few of them know the country well. Recommended tour operators are listed

below. For tour operators in Managua, see page 51.

UK

Exodus Travels, T020-8675-5550, www.exodus.co.uk.
Geodyssey, T020-7281 7788, www.geodyssey.co.uk.
Journey Latin America, T020-3773 5966, www.journeylatinamerica.co.uk.
Pura Aventura, T01273-676712, www.pura-aventura.com.
Steppes Travel, T01285-880980, www.steppestravel.co.uk.

Rest of Europe

Nuove Esperienze, Italy, T06-3972 5999, www.nuove-esperienze.it.
Rese Konsulterna, Sweden, T031-758-3100, www.resek.se.
Sawadee Reizen, Netherlands, T020-420 2220, www.sawadee.nl.
Tropical Tours, Greece, T210-324 9504, tropical@ath.forthnet.gr.

North America

Big Five Tours & Expeditions, T800-244 3483, www.bigfive.com.
Global Exchange, T415-255 7296, www.globalexchange.org. An interesting, socially aware organization involved with human rights, which runs 'Reality Tours' to Nicaragua, such as the Fair Trade Coffee And Sustainability Tour.
Latin American Escapes, T1-800-510-5999, www.latinamericanescapes.com.

Visas and immigration

If you are thinking of travelling from your own country via the USA, or of visiting the USA after Nicaragua, you are strongly advised to get your visa and find out about any other requirements from a US consulate in your own country before travelling. If you are eligible for a visa waiver, you are required to register in advance with the **Electronic System for Travel Authorization** (ESTA), www esta cbp dhs gov/esta. You will need to do this before setting out.

Visitors to Nicaragua must have a passport with a minimum validity of 6 months. In rare cases you may be asked to show proof of an onward ticket or some cash. Most visitors, including those from the UK, USA and EU countries, do not require visas and will simply pay the tourist card fee – US$10 at the airport and US$12 plus US$1 Alcaldía fee at land and river immigration checkpoints. Tourist cards are usually valid for 90 days and under the 2006 Central America Border Control Agreement (CA-4) permit the carrier to travel between Nicaragua, Guatemala, Honduras and El Salvador without additional paperwork; see box, page 254. You are still required to pass border formalities and obtain appropriate entrance and exit stamps, however. For a list of countries whose citizens require a visa, see www. nicaragua.com/visas. Visa application at the border is not recommended as approval can be very slow.

If you need an extension of your tourist card beyond the standard 90 days you receive upon entering the country, you will have to visit the **Dirección de Migración y Extranjería**, costado oeste de la DGI Sajonia, Edif Silvio Mayorga, Managua, T2222-7538 ext 3, www.migob.gob.ni/migracion, Mon-Sat 0800-1700. However, it is highly recommended that you use the much faster and conveniently located Migración office in the Metrocentro shopping centre (Mon-Sat 1000-1800, Sun 1000-1300). Take your passport,

preferably in the early morning, and ask for an extension form; the current rate for a 30-day extension is US$23. The whole procedure should not take more than 1-2 hrs, unless queues are unusually long. Note that citizens of Colombia, Cuba, Ecuador, Bangladesh, China and India may have difficulties acquiring an extension. If you overstay your visa or tourist card you will be charged US$2 per day, payable upon exit.

Weights and measures

The metric system is the official one in Nicaragua but in practice a mixture of metric, imperial and old Spanish measurements (including the *vara*, which is equivalent to about 1 m and the *manzana* which is 7000 sq m) is used. Petrol in gallons, speed in kph, fabric in yards, height in centimetres and metres, weight in pounds and temperature in Celsius.

Women travellers

A lone female walking down the street is a sight to behold for Nicaraguan men: horns will sound, words of romance (and in Managua some less than romantic phrases) will be proffered and in general you may well feel as if you are on stage. Attitudes to foreign women are generally more reserved, although this is changing rapidly. Touching a woman, Nicaraguan or foreign, is not socially acceptable and is normally greeted with a hearty slap or a swift kick. The best advice is to dress for the amount of attention you desire; it is not necessary to travel clothed as a nun, but any suggestive clothing will bring double its weight in suggestions. In Managua it is dangerous to walk alone at night for either gender; there is more risk of robbery than rape, but it should be avoided. 2 women walking together are less likely to be targeted by thieves. For more advice, see www.journeywoman.com.

Working in Nicaragua

Finding paid work in Nicaragua is a monumental challenge for Nicaraguans and even more so for visitors who hope to get by in the country by working for a short period. It is a good idea to research your own country's aid programmes to Nicaragua and to make contact well in advance of arrival. The sister-city programmes that most countries have with Nicaragua are good examples. Finding English teaching work may be possible although rents are high and survival on a teaching salary will be difficult. It is best to go through an organization that will help with any legal documentation and accommodation. There are numerous opportunities for volunteer work. The following list is a selection of organizations, although it is by no means exhaustive:

El Porvenir, www.elporvenir.org, is an off-shoot of **Habitat for Humanity** and deals with water, reforestation and sanitation projects.

Habitat for Humanity, www.habitat.org, is involved with housing projects in the northern highlands.

The Miraflor Foundation, cafeluzyluna.org, need volunteers to work in a variety of roles for their numerous social projects. Spanish speakers and a 6-month commitment is preferred.

The Nicaragua Solidarity Campaign, www.nicaraguasc.org.uk, can arrange volunteer work within rural communities.

Quetzaltrekkers, www.quetzaltrekkers.com, need volunteers to get involved with their hikes around León.

Witness for Peace, www.witnessforpeace.org, is dedicated to peace, economic justice and social development.

Footnotes

Basic Spanish for travellers

Learning Spanish is a useful part of the preparation for a trip to Latin America and no volumes of dictionaries, phrase books or word lists will provide the same enjoyment as being able to communicate directly with the people of the country you are visiting. It is a good idea to make an effort to grasp the basics before you go. As you travel you will pick up more of the language and the more you know, the more you will benefit from your stay.

Spanish words and phrases

Greetings, courtesies

hello	*hola*	I speak Spanish	*hablo español*
good morning	*buenos días*	I don't speak Spanish	*no hablo español*
good afternoon/ evening/night	*buenas tardes/ noches*	do you speak English? I don't understand	*¿habla inglés? no entiendo/ no comprendo*
goodbye	*adiós/chao*		
pleased to meet you	*mucho gusto*	please speak slowly	*hable despacio por favor*
see you later	*hasta luego*		
how are you?	*¿cómo está? ¿cómo estás?*	I am very sorry	*lo siento mucho/ disculpe*
I'm fine, thanks	*estoy muy bien, gracias*	what do you want?	*¿qué quiere? ¿qué quieres?*
I'm called...	*me llamo...*	I want	*quiero*
what is your name?	*¿cómo se llama? ¿cómo te llamas?*	I don't want it leave me alone	*no lo quiero déjeme en paz/ no me moleste*
yes/no	*sí/no*		
please	*por favor*	good/bad	*bueno/malo*
thank you (very much)	*(muchas) gracias*		

Questions and requests

Have you got a room for two people?
  ¿Tiene una habitación para dos personas?
I'd like to make a long-distance phone call
  Quisiera hacer una llamada de larga distancia
How do I get to_? *¿cómo llego a_?*
How much does it cost?
  ¿cuánto cuesta?/¿cuánto es?
Is service included?
  ¿está incluido el servicio?

Is tax included?
  ¿están incluidos los impuestos?
When does the bus leave (arrive)?
  ¿a qué hora sale (llega) el autobús?
Where is the nearest petrol station?
  ¿dónde está la gasolinera más cercana?
When? *¿cuándo?*
Where is_? *¿dónde está_?*
Where can I buy tickets?
  ¿dónde puedo comprar boletos?
Why? *¿por qué?*

Basics

bank	el banco	market	el mercado
bathroom/toilet	el baño	note/coin	el billete/
bill	la factura/		la moneda
	la cuenta	police (policeman)	la policía
cash	el efectivo		(el policía)
cheap	barato/a	post office	el correo
credit card	la tarjeta de crédito	public telephone	el teléfono público
exchange house	la casa de cambio	supermarket	el supermercado
exchange rate	el tipo de cambio	ticket office	la taquilla
expensive	caro/a		

Getting around

aeroplane	el avión	insurance	el seguro
airport	el aeropuerto	to insure yourself	asegurarse contra
arrival/departure	la llegada/salida	against	
avenue	la avenida	luggage	el equipaje
block	la cuadra	motorway, freeway	el autopista/
border	la frontera		la carretera
bus station	la terminal de	north	norte
	autobuses/	south	sur
	camiones	west	oeste (occidente)
bus	el bus/el autobús/	east	este (oriente)
	el camión	oil	el aceite
collective/fixed-	el colectivo	to park	estacionarse
route taxi		passport	el pasaporte
corner	la esquina	petrol/gasoline	la gasolina
customs	la aduana	puncture	la ponchadura
first/second class	primera/segunda	street	la calle
	clase	that way	por allí/por allá
left/right	izquierda/derecha	this way	por aquí/por acá
ticket	el boleto	tyre	la llanta
empty/full	vacío/lleno	unleaded	sin plomo
highway, main road	la carretera	to walk	caminar/andar
immigration	la inmigración		

Accommodation

air conditioning	*el aire acondicionado*	power cut	*el apagón/corte*
		restaurant	*el restaurante*
all-inclusive	*todo incluido*	room/bedroom	*el cuarto/ la habitación*
bathroom, private	*el baño privado*		
bed, double/single	*la cama matrimonial/ sencilla*	sheets	*las sábanas*
		shower	*la ducha/regadera*
		soap	*el jabón*
blankets	*las cobijas/mantas*	toilet	*el sanitario/ excusado*
to clean	*limpiar*		
dining room	*el comedor*	toilet paper	*el papel higiénico*
guesthouse	*la casa de huéspedes*	towels, clean/dirty	*las toallas limpias/ sucias*
hotel	*el hotel*	water, hot/cold	*el agua caliente/ fría*
noisy	*ruidoso*		
pillows	*las almohadas*		

Health

aspirin	*la aspirina*	diarrhoea	*la diarrea*
blood	*la sangre*	doctor	*el médico*
chemist	*la farmacia*	fever/sweat	*la fiebre/el sudor*
condoms	*los condones*	pain	*el dolor*
contact lenses	*los lentes de contacto*	head	*la cabeza*
		period/ sanitary towels	*la regla/las toallas femeninas*
contraceptive pill	*la píldora anti- conceptiva*	stomach	*el estómago*

Months, days and time

January	*enero*	Thursday	*jueves*
February	*febrero*	Friday	*viernes*
March	*marzo*	Saturday	*sábado*
April	*abril*	Sunday	*domingo*
May	*mayo*		
June	*junio*	at one o'clock	*a la una*
July	*julio*	at half past two	*a las dos y media*
August	*agosto*	at a quarter to three	*a las tres menos quince*
September	*septiembre*		
October	*octubre*	it's one o'clock	*es la una*
November	*noviembre*	it's seven o'clock	*son las siete*
December	*diciembre*	it's six twenty	*son las seis y veinte*
		in ten minutes	*en diez minutos*
Monday	*lunes*	five hours	*cinco horas*
Tuesday	*martes*	does it take long?	*¿tarda mucho?*
Wednesday	*miércoles*		

Numbers

one	*uno/una*	sixteen	*dieciséis*
two	*dos*	seventeen	*diecisiete*
three	*tres*	eighteen	*dieciocho*
four	*cuatro*	nineteen	*diecinueve*
five	*cinco*	twenty	*veinte*
six	*seis*	twenty-one	*veintiuno*
seven	*siete*	thirty	*treinta*
eight	*ocho*	forty	*cuarenta*
nine	*nueve*	fifty	*cincuenta*
ten	*diez*	sixty	*sesenta*
eleven	*once*	seventy	*setenta*
twelve	*doce*	eighty	*ochenta*
thirteen	*trece*	ninety	*noventa*
fourteen	*catorce*	hundred	*cien/ciento*
fifteen	*quince*	thousand	*mil*

Index

Entries in bold refer to maps

FOOTPRINT

Features

Notes

Notes

Notes

Credits

Footprint credits
Publisher: John Sadler
Project editor: Felicity Laughton
Production and layout: Emma Bryers
Maps and colour section: Gail Armstrong

Photography credits
Front cover: Roberto Destarac Photo/
Shutterstock.com
Back cover top: Dirk Ercken/
Shutterstock.com
Back cover bottom: James Wagstaff/
Shutterstock.com
Inside front cover: A. Blanke/Shutter
stock.com, Riderfoot/Shutterstock.com,
Ted PAGEL/Shutterstock.com,
Simon Dannhauer/Shutterstock.com

Colour section
Page 1: SL-Photography/Shutterstock.com.
Pages 2-3: Sam Strickler/Shutterstock.com.
Page 4: Marc Venema/Shutterstock.com.
Page 5: PixieMe/Shutterstock.com, Adriana
Margarita Larios Arellano/Shutterstock.com,
GUIZIOU Franck/Superstock.com.
Page Page 7: Riderfoot/Shutterstock.com,
Daniel Lauziere/Shutterstock.com.
Page 8: Milosz Maslanka/Shutterstock.com.

Duotones
Page 30: Ppictures/shutterstock.com.
Page 56: alfotokunst/shutterstock.com.
Page 70: SotoGrant/Shutterstock.com.
Page 92: LMspencer/Shutterstock.com.
Pages 112 and 130: Simon Dannhauer/
shutterstock.com.
Page 148: steve100/shutterstock.com.
Page 174: gaborbasch/Shutterstock.com.

Printed in India

Print and production managed by
Jellyfish Solutions

Publishing information
Footprint Nicaragua
7th edition
© Compass Maps Ltd
August 2019

ISBN: 978 1 911082 65 1

CIP DATA: A catalogue record for this
book is available from the British Library

® Footprint Handbooks and the
Footprint mark are a registered
trademark of Compass Maps Ltd

Published by Footprint
45 Chalcroft Road
London SW13 5RE, UK
footprinttravelguides.com

Distributed in the USA by
National Book Network, Inc.

Every effort has been made to ensure
that the facts in this guidebook are
accurate. However, travellers should still
obtain advice from consulates, airlines,
etc about travel and visa requirements
before travelling. The authors and
publishers cannot accept responsibility
for any loss, injury or inconvenience
however caused.

Map symbols

- □ Capital city
- ○ Other city, town
- International border
- Regional border
- ⊖ Customs
- Contours (approx)
- ▲ Mountain, volcano
- Mountain pass
- Escarpment
- Glacier
- Salt flat
- Rocks
- Seasonal marshland
- Beach, sandbank
- Waterfall
- Reef
- National highway
- Paved road
- Unpaved or ripio (gravel) road
- Track
- Footpath
- Railway
- Railway with station
- ✈ Airport
- Bus station
- Ⓜ Metro station
- Cable car
- Funicular
- Ferry
- Pedestrianized street
- Tunnel
- One way-street
- Steps
- Bridge
- Fortified wall
- Park, garden, stadium
- Where to stay
- Restaurants
- Bars & clubs

- Building
- Sight
- Cathedral, church
- Chinese temple
- Hindu temple
- Meru
- Mosque
- Stupa
- Synagogue
- Tourist office
- Museum
- Post office
- Police
- Bank
- Internet
- Telephone
- Market
- Medical services
- Parking
- Petrol
- Golf
- Archaeological site
- National park, wildlife reserve
- Viewing point
- Campsite
- Refuge, lodge
- Castle, fort
- Diving
- Deciduous, coniferous, palm trees
- Mangrove
- Hide
- Vineyard, winery
- Distillery
- Shipwreck
- Historic battlefield
- Related map

Map 1

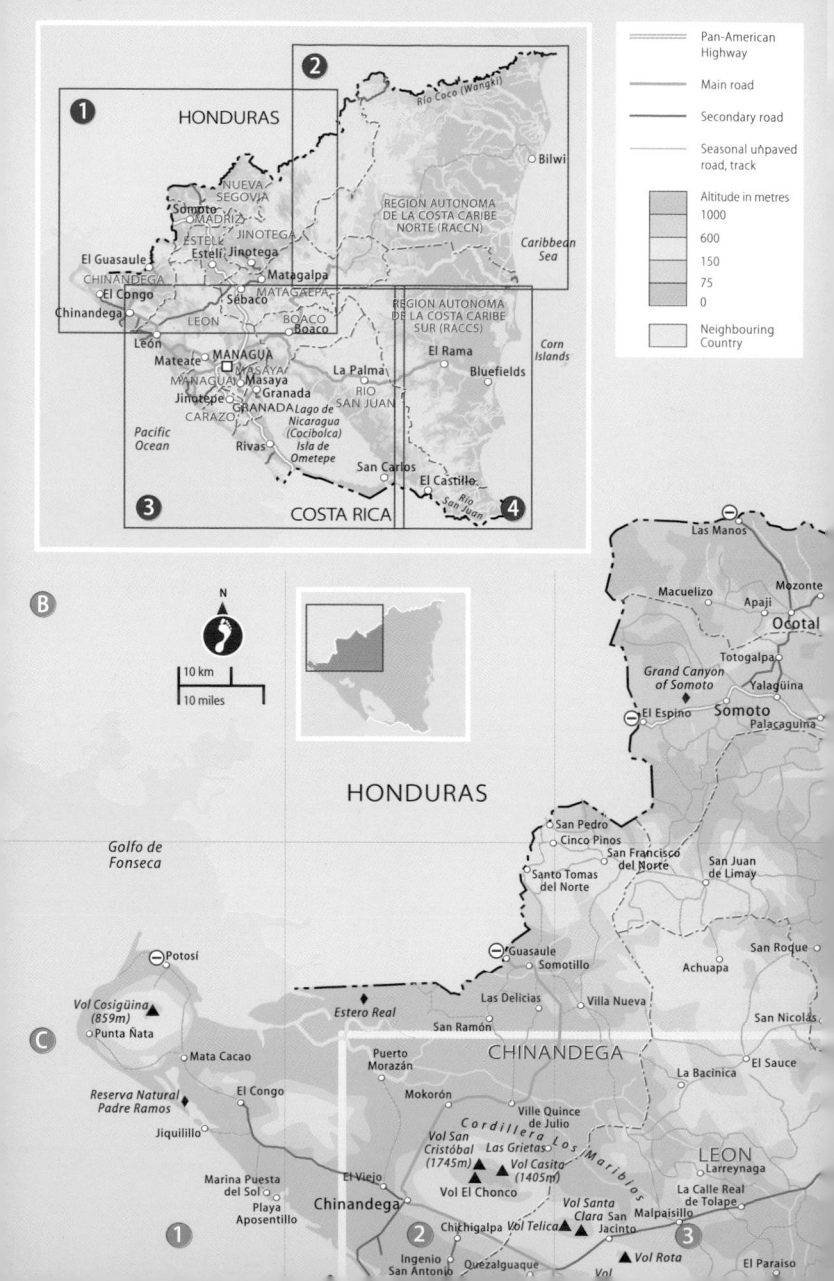

≡≡≡≡	Pan-American Highway
———	Main road
———	Secondary road
———	Seasonal unpaved road, track

Altitude in metres
1000
600
150
75
0

Neighbouring Country

Map 1 inset labels:

HONDURAS

Río Coco (Wangki)

NUEVA SEGOVIA
Somoto
MADRIZ
ESTELÍ
JINOTEGA
El Guasaule
Estelí Jinotega
CHINANDEGA
El Congo
Chinandega
León
MATAGALPA
Matagalpa
Sébaco
BOACO
Boaco
REGIÓN AUTÓNOMA DE LA COSTA CARIBE NORTE (RACCN)
Caribbean Sea
Bilwi

REGIÓN AUTÓNOMA DE LA COSTA CARIBE SUR (RACCS)
Corn Islands

Mateate
MANAGUA
MANAGUA MASAYA Masaya
Jinotepe Granada
CARAZO GRANADA
Lago de Nicaragua (Cocibolca)
Isla de Ometepe
Rivas
La Palma
RÍO SAN JUAN
El Rama
Bluefields
El Castillo
San Carlos
Río San Juan
COSTA RICA
LEÓN
Pacific Ocean

Main map labels:

Las Manos
Macuelizo Mozonte
Apají Ocotal
Totogalpa Yalaguina
Grand Canyon of Somoto Somoto
El Espino Palacaguina

HONDURAS

Golfo de Fonseca

Potosí
Vol Cosigüina (859m)
Punta Ñata
Mata Cacao
Reserva Natural Padre Ramos
El Congo
Jiquilillo
Marina Puesta del Sol
Playa Aposentillo

San Pedro
Cinco Pinos
Santo Tomas del Norte
San Francisco del Norte
San Juan de Limay
San Roque
Guasaule
Somotillo
Las Delicias Villa Nueva
San Ramón
Achuapa
San Nicolás

Estero Real
Puerto Morazán
Mokorón
CHINANDEGA
Ville Quince de Julio
Vol San Cristóbal (1745m) Las Grietas
Vol Casita (1405m)
Vol El Chonco
Cordillera Los Maribios
La Bacínica
El Sauce
LEÓN
Larreynaga
La Calle Real de Tolape

El Viejo
Chinandega
Chichigalpa Vol Telica
Vol Santa Clara San Jacinto
Malpaisillo
El Paraiso
Ingenio San Antonio
Quezalguaque
Vol Rota

Raiti

A

Bosawás
Biosphere
Reserve ♦

Río Bocay

Tolecacinte

Jalapa

2 →

NUEVA SEGOVIA

Wamblán

Valle
Congjas

Wambuca
El Plantel

JINOTEGA

Murra

Santa Clara

Río Coco

San Fernando

Susucayan

Plan de Grama

El Ocote

B

Ciudad
Antigua

Wiwilí

Rosa

San José
de Bocay

El Naranja

MADRIZ

Río Coco

Puerto Viejo

Valle Ducali

El Cuá

Condega

Piedra Larga

*Reserva
Natural
Miraflor* ♦

San Rafael
del Norte

*El Jaguar
Cloud Forest
Reserve* ♦

*Lago de
Apanás*

La Dalia

Río Tuma

Estelí

Reserva Natural Arenal

Río Tuma

*Reserva Natural
Meseta Tisey Estanzuela*
*El Salto de
Estanzuelo* ♦

Jinotega

El Tuma

Las Lajitas

Disparate
de Potter

*Selva Negra
Cloud Forest
Reserve* ♦

*Esperanza
Verde/Yucul* ♦

MATAGALPA

La Trinidad

San Isidro

Monte Grande

Santa Elsa

Río Blanco

3

Matagalpa

La Rosa

La Garita

Pancasán

Cordillera Dariense

Güilique

C

El Ch

San Ramón

Chagüitillo

El Caracal

San Pablo

Río Grande Sébaco

Santa Rosa
del Peñón

Matiguás

Río Matagalpa

Bocana de
Paiwas

La Cruz de
la India

Ciudad Darío

Terrabona

Muy Muy

El Trapichito

Veracruz

Pineda

Río Grande de Matagalpa

▲ *Santa María
(1210m)*

Tierra Azul

Valle El
Orégano

Esquipulas

Río de Janeiro

Santa Fe

4

*Laguna
Moyuá*

El Cacao

San José
de las Remates

5

El Portón

6

San
Francisco
Libre

Puertas
Viejas

El Guanacaste

El Paraíso

BOACO

Map 2

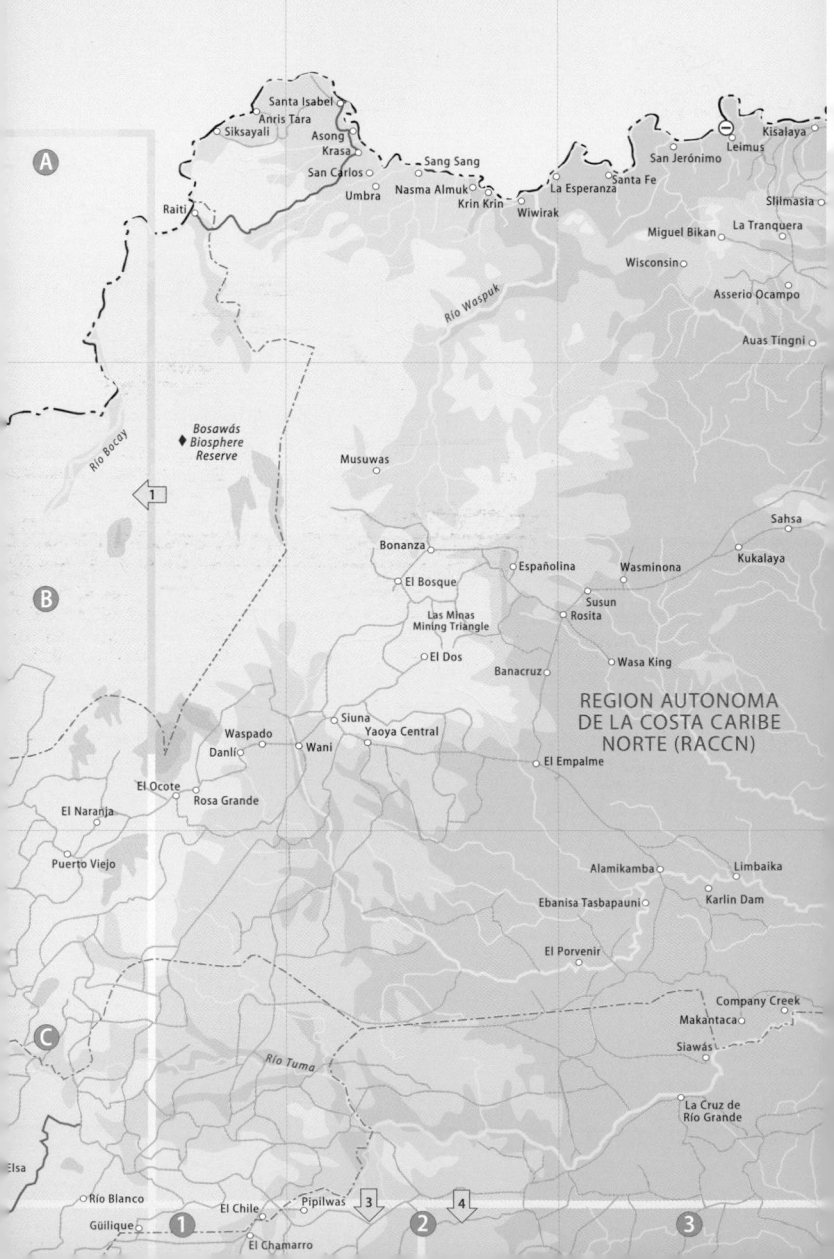

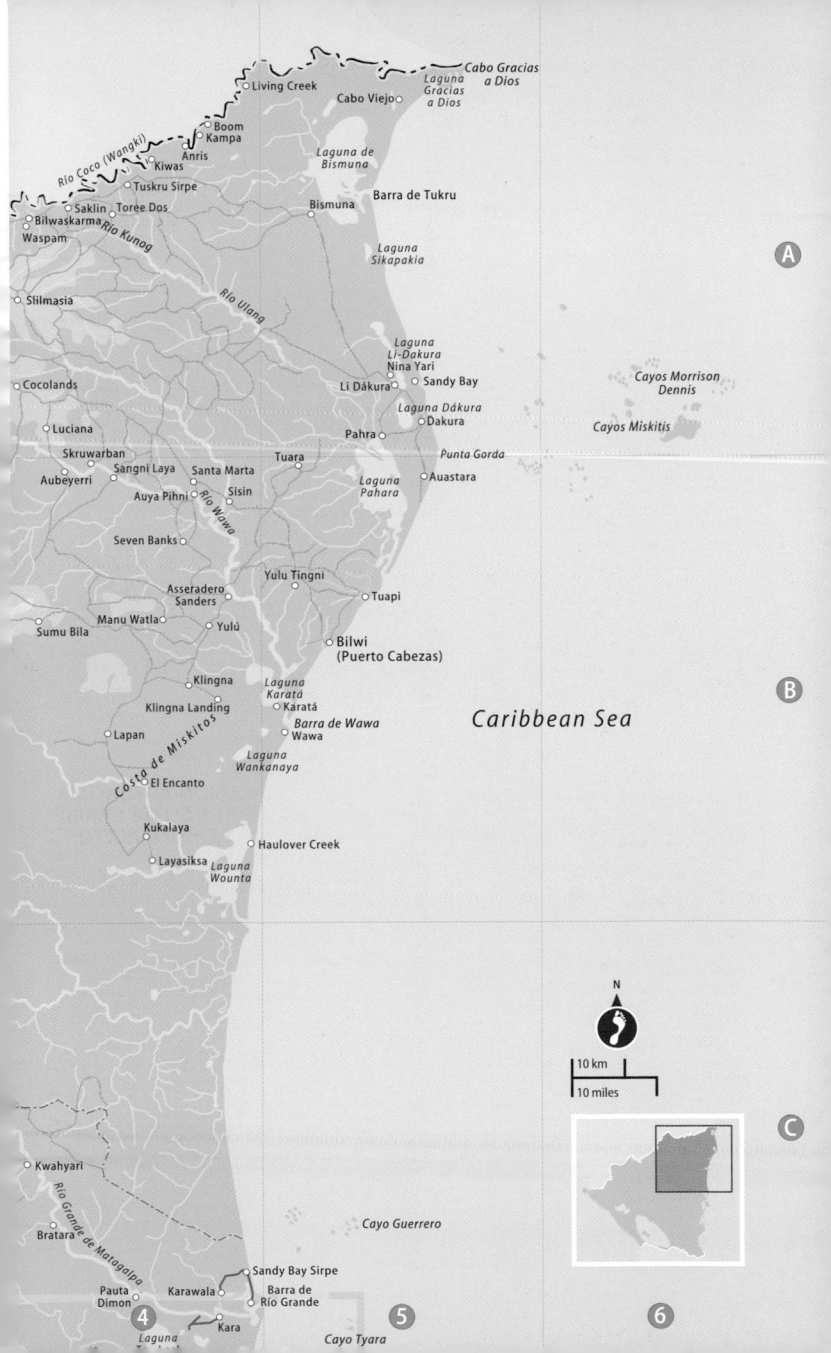

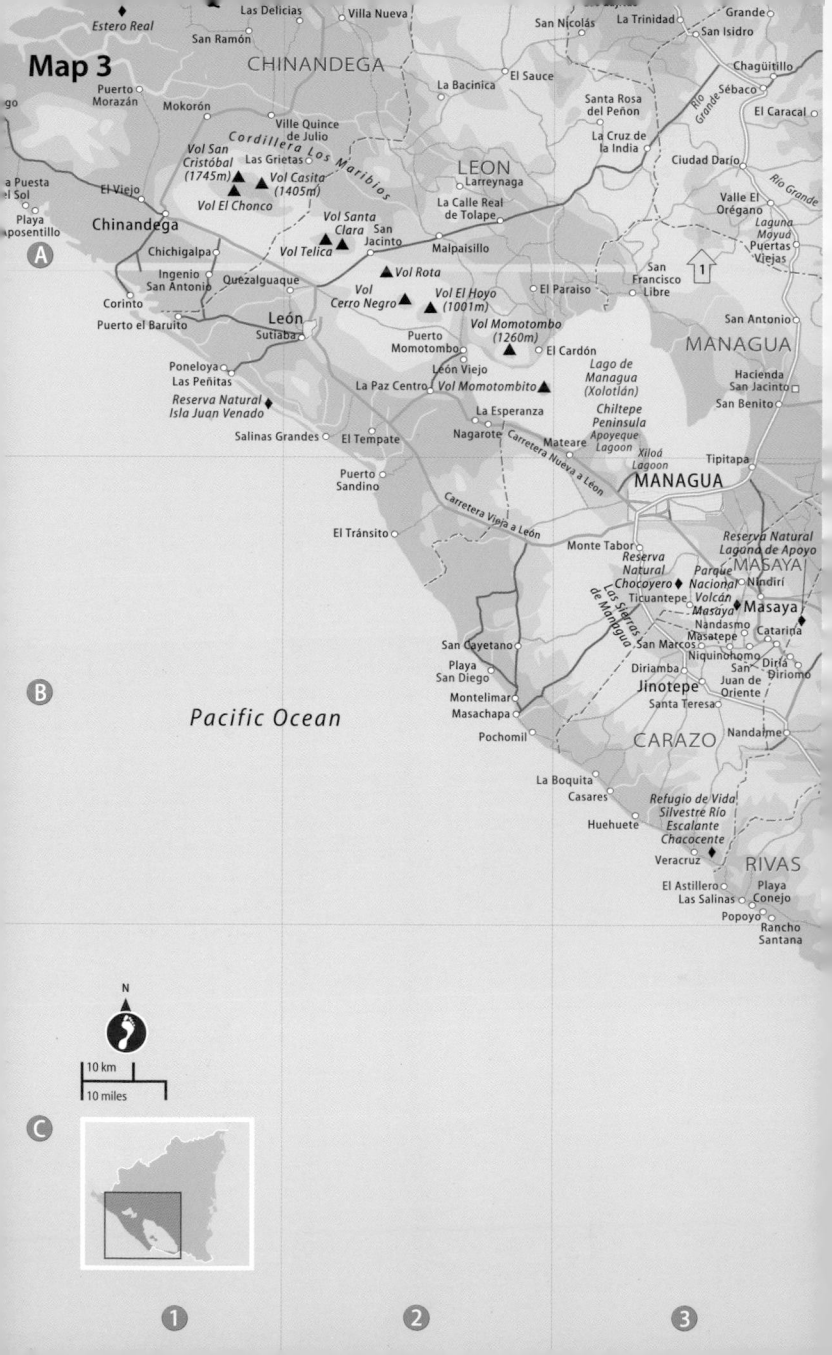

Map 4

Sandy Bay Sirpe
Pauta Dimon
Karawala
Barra de
Río Grande
Kara
Cayo Tyara

Tortuguero
Río Kurinwás
Laguna
Top Lock

Cayo King
Pequeño

Tasbapauni

REGION AUTONOMA
DE LA COSTA CARIBE
SUR (RACCS)

Marshall
Point
Wawasang
Orinoco
Punta
Set Net

La Fe
Pearl
Lagoon/
Laguna de
Perlas
Cayos de
Perlas

Brown Bank
Set Net

Kakabila

Río Siquia

Pearl Lagoon

Corn Islands
(70km east of
Tierra Dorada)

Little Corn

La Esperanza
El Recreo
Laguna
Grande
Tierra Dorada

El Rama
Laguna
Grande

El Banco
Río Escondido
Big Corn

Cara de Mono
Sisi

Muelle de
los Bueyes
Krisimbila
San Antonio
Laguna
Smokey
Lane

La Batea
El Bluff

El Cacao
amate
Bluefields

a Río
na
El Coral
Caribbean
Sea

Bay of
Bluefields
Rama Cay

El Almendro

Nuevo Guinea
Verdún
La Esperanza
Yolaina

La Letra
El Serrano

El Almacén
La Fonseca

RIO SAN JUAN
Río Punta Gorda
Punta Gorda

N

10 km

Los Chiles
Río Maíz
10 miles

el Galán
Bahía
Punta Gorda

La Azucena
Río Sábalo
Buena
Vista
Río Santa
Cruz

Carlos
San Francisco
La Esperanza
Las Colinas

rea
Boca de Sábalos
El Castillo
Río Bartola

Los Chiles
Bartola

San Juan
del Nicaragua
La Barra
Bahía de San Juan

Río Indio
Greytown

COSTA RICA
Reserva Biológica
Indio-Maíz

San Carlos
Río San
Carlos
Río
Sarapiquí
Sarapiquí
RíoColorado